W9-BBN-998

FORDHAM UNIVERSITY
LIBRARY
NEW YORK, N.Y.

THE MISSION OF
VINCENT BENEDETTI
TO BERLIN 1864–1870

FORDHAM UNIVERSITY
LIBRARY
NEW YORK, N. Y.

THE MISSION OF VINCENT BENEDETTI TO BERLIN 1864-1870

FORDHAM
UNIVERSITY
LIBRARIES

WITHDRAWN
FROM
COLLECTION

by

WILLARD ALLEN FLETCHER

FORDHAM UNIVERSITY
LIBRARY
NEW YORK, N. Y.

THE HAGUE / MARTINUS NIJHOFF / 1965

DC
300
.B4F5
op.2

Copyright *1965 by Martinus Nijhoff, The Hague, Netherlands*
All rights reserved, including the right to translate or to
reproduce this book or parts thereof in any form

FORDHAM UNIVERSITY
LIBRARY
NEW YORK, N.Y.

PRINTED IN THE NETHERLANDS

TO JEAN, IAN, COLIN, HILARY AND BRIAN

7047 OCT 14 '66

PREFACE

The historical significance of the period 1864–1870, epitomized by the establishment of Prussian hegemony in Germany, has been perpetuated in numerous studies. The diplomatic history of these decisive years has proven especially fascinating, for the fundamental changes in Germany's political frame had a momentous influence upon the course of European history. The war of 1866 destroyed the last vestiges of Austrian supremacy in Germany and inaugurated a reorganization under Prussian domination. The international repercussions of this transformation in the heart of Europe are fully reflected in the diplomacy of the period, in view of the disruptive effect upon the existing power equilibrium. The manner in which Napoleon III and his government reacted to the events was of crucial portent for the future of his empire. An inquiry into Ambassador Benedetti's mission to Berlin contributes materially to an understanding of imperial diplomacy, primarily as related to Prussia, in this critical period.

The present study was suggested by Dr. Lynn M. Case and began to take shape in his seminars on European diplomatic history. Benedetti's constant association with French diplomacy between 1864 and 1870 seemed to warrant a detailed and critical examination of his mission. Despite the advent of the telegraph diplomatic representatives continued to form an important part of the diplomatic apparatus and Benedetti was no exception. Past studies based exclusively on his career are very few. Frensdorff's *Preussische Jahrbücher* article appeared shortly after the outbreak of the war in 1870. The superficial and biased treatment of the subject and the totally inadequate documentation place his account outside the rank of scholarly inquiries. Luise Schoeps' *Graf Vincent Benedetti*, which appeared in 1915, had been written as a doctoral dissertation sponsored by Richard Fester. This work is of only limited value today, since the author was unable to draw upon the vast documentary collections in the European diplomatic archives. The beginning publication of the French diplomatic correspondence permitted her to consult but the first few volumes of this primary source material, hence making a definitive study of Benedetti's mission impossible. An attempt by Charles Saurel to write a detailed study of Benedetti was cut short by the author's death after he had completed a monograph entitled *Juillet 1870. Le drame de la dépêche d'Ems*. Benedetti's own accounts, in *Ma mission en Prusse*, *Essais diplomatiques*, and in the *Revue de Paris* of 15 September 1895, are highly subjective and inaccurate versions. Evaluations of the ambassador's record are often quite incidental in form, based upon an isolated diplomatic event rather than upon the entire career. It is thus not surprising that Benedetti is mainly remembered in connection with the Ems episode, cast in the role of a bungling diplomat. That his historical reputation should rest upon such a brief moment is a deplorable fact.

As one in a series of inquiries directed by Dr. Case into European diplomatic history of the second half of the nineteenth century, this study is sharply focussed upon Benedetti's activities. No attempt has been made to present a detailed history of diplomacy between 1864 and 1870, although the wider historical background needs to be borne in mind. Benedetti's mission falls into three distinct phases. The first of these, from his appointment to Sadowa, was characterized by a rather favorable disposition of France *vis-à-vis* Prussian ambitions in Germany. The second phase, extending to the London conference, was marked by repeated French efforts to redress the balance of power between Prussia and France and by the gradual disenchantment which followed the frustration of these efforts. The final phase, ending with the outbreak of war in 1870, witnessed the fatal progress from an uneasy *modus vivendi* to a clash of arms which obliterated the empire of Louis Napoleon. Benedetti's words and actions reflect the changing moods of imperial diplomacy toward Prussia, and a study of his performance between 1864 and 1870 makes it possible to view his role in proper perspective. Use has been made of a wide variety of manuscript and printed sources. The author has relied principally on the diplomatic archives of the Second Empire, but supplemented by appropriate files in Prussian, Austrian, Dutch, Belgian, British, Luxemburg and other archives. A vast literature in the form of printed source collections, memoirs, biographies, monographs and articles eased the task of ferreting out details about Benedetti's activities. The author profited from the labors of many historians, but he wishes to cite in particular among recent contributors Bonnin, Dittrich, Case, Steefel, Pflanze and Halperin.

The author wishes to express his deep appreciation and sincere thanks to all those who have helped him in his task. He is especially grateful to his teacher and mentor, Dr. Lynn M. Case, whose untiring help, constructive criticism and valuable aid cannot be adequately acknowledged in words. Many thanks are due the Graduate Council of the University of Pennsylvania which made possible the research in archives and libraries abroad. Two grants from the Council on Research and Creative Work of the University of Colorado made possible the acquisition of microfilms and the preparation of the manuscript for publication. Among those who contributed of their time and effort, the author wishes to thank the staff of the University of Pennsylvania Library. He is especially indebted to the late Mr. Hans Burckhardt. Acknowledgment is made of the unfailing courtesy and help of the staffs of the *Bibliothèque nationale* and the *Archives du ministère des affaires étrangères* in Paris, the British Museum and Public Record Office in London, the *Rijksarchief* in The Hague, the *Archives du ministère des affaires étrangères* in Brussels, the *Bibliothèque nationale* and the *Archives de l'état* in Luxemburg, the *Haus- Hof- und Staats-Archiv* in Vienna, and Norlin Library of the University of Colorado. The author is most appreciative to Dr. C. Vincent Confer and Dr. Daniel H. Thomas for the timely loan of their manuscript guides to the French and Belgian foreign office archives. The kind interest of Count Benedetti of Paris and the friendly help of Dr. and Mrs. Clarence King of London, Professor and Mrs. Alphonse Nies of Luxemburg, Mrs. Robert Buchholtz of Luxemburg, Mr. Guste Scharlé of Buenos Aires and Mr. Willy Metzler of Luxemburg are gratefully remembered. The author is deeply grateful to Dr. Howard L. Scamehorn and Mrs. Phyllis Groves for their ready and untiring help in the final preparation of the manuscript. To Mrs. Virginia Grieder who typed the manuscript under unusual circumstances go very warm thanks. To his wife, whose encouragement and devoted help made this work all the more worthwhile, the author owes a lasting debt of gratitude.

Luxembourg-Ville, 1964   WILLARD ALLEN FLETCHER

CONTENTS

LIST OF ABBREVIATIONS

AD	*Archives diplomatiques.*
AHR	*American Historical Review.*
APP	GERMANY. HISTORISCHE REICHSKOMMISSION. *Die auswärtige Politik Preussens.*
BAE CP	BELGIUM. MINISTÈRE DES AFFAIRES ÉTRANGÈRES. ARCHIVES. Série générale. Correspondance politique.
BGW	BISMARCK-SCHÖNHAUSEN, OTTO, FÜRST VON. *Die gesammelten Werke.*
FAE CC	FRANCE. MINISTÈRE DES AFFAIRES ÉTRANGÈRES. ARCHIVES. Correspondance consulaire.
FAE CP	FRANCE. MINISTÈRE DES AFFAIRES ÉTRANGÈRES. ARCHIVES. Correspondance politique.
FAE MD	FRANCE. MINISTÈRE DES AFFAIRES ÉTRANGÈRES. ARCHIVES. Mémoires et documents.
FAE PR/A	FRANCE. MINISTÈRE DES AFFAIRES ÉTRANGÈRES. ARCHIVES. Papiers de Cerçay. Fonds: Rouher/Allemagne.
FbpG	*Forschungen zur brandenburgischen und preussischen Geschichte.*
HHStA	AUSTRIA. HAUS- HOF- UND STAATS-ARCHIV. Politisches Archiv.
HVj	*Historische Vierteljahrschrift.*
HZ	*Historische Zeitschrift.*
LAE H	LUXEMBURG. ARCHIVES DE L'ÉTAT. Régime constitutionnel.

LAE L   LUXEMBURG. ARCHIVES DE L'ÉTAT.
            Secrétariat du Roi Grand-Duc à La Haye.
MMP   BENEDETTI, VINCENT. *Ma mission en Prusse.*
ODG   FRANCE. MINISTÈRE DES AFFAIRES ÉTRANGÈRES.
            Les origines diplomatiques de la guerre de 1870–71.
PJ   *Preussische Jahrbücher.*
PRO FO   GREAT BRITAIN. PUBLIC RECORD OFFICE. FOREIGN
            OFFICE. ARCHIVES.
            Foreign Office Correspondence.
QDPO   *Quellen zur deutschen Politik Österreichs.*
RBZ   THE NETHERLANDS. RIJKSARCHIEF. MINISTERIE VAN
            BUITENLANDSE ZAKEN. ARCHIEF.
            Correspondentie.
RH   *Revue historique.*
RHM   *Revue d'histoire moderne.*
RHMC   *Revue d'histoire moderne et contemporaine.*

CHAPTER I

THE MAN AND HIS MISSION

On 5 October 1864 Emperor Napoleon III appointed Vincent Benedetti as his ambassador extraordinary and minister plenipotentiary
to the king of Prussia.[1] For the distinguished veteran it meant a return
to the diplomatic corps from which he had resigned in 1862, after
twenty-two years of service to his country. Benedetti was born in
Bastia, on the island of Corsica, on 29 April 1817, the son of François
Benedetti, the presiding judge of the court of criminal jurisdiction in
Bastia. After completion of his secondary education, young Benedetti
had left for metropolitan France to pursue legal studies, as his father
and grandfather had done before him. In the family tradition he had
matriculated at the University of Marseilles and completed his studies
with success, obtaining his license in law.[2]

In preference to a legal career in his native Corsica, Benedetti had
decided to enter the diplomatic service. Thus, at the age of twenty-
three, he had begun his career as secretary of the French mission in
Egypt. By 1845 he had risen to the rank of consul and carried on
those duties in Cairo until 1848.[3] During his tour of duty there, Benedetti had married the adopted daughter of the Danish consul general
in Alexandria, Mariethe d'Anastasie. A young woman of Greek origin,
she became known as one of the most beautiful women of the Second
Empire.[4] In 1848 Benedetti had been posted to Palermo where he had
remained for three years. His stay in Sicily evidently had had definite
effects on the diplomat, since he was to become such an ardent and

---

[1] *Moniteur universel*, 5 October 1864; *Journal des débats*, 8, 9 October 1864; A. FRANGULIS
(ed.), *Dictionnaire diplomatique* (Paris, 1933–1937), V, 84.
[2] Statement obtained in personal interview of Count Benedetti, grandson of the diplomat,
Paris, 13 April 1955.
[3] FRANGULIS, V, 84.
[4] Statement by Count Benedetti, personal interview, Paris, 13 April 1955; L. THOUVENEL,
Pages de l'histoire du Second Empire (Paris, 1903), p. 413, ft. 2; E. FRENSDORFF, "Graf Benedetti," *PJ*, XXVI, Heft 2 (1870), pp. 193–194.

lasting supporter of Italian national aspirations. One can presume that he had come in contact with Italian patriots and that he had been influenced by their idealistic devotion to the unification cause. This first contact with the Italian problem had ended in 1851, when Benedetti was transferred to Constantinople. By the time the Crimean war pitted France and her allies against the Russian empire, he had risen to the rank of *chargé d'affaires*.

Benedetti had not remained in the Near East until the end of the war; in 1855 he had assumed the important function of head of the *direction politique* at the *Quai d'Orsay*. The appointment must be considered as a mark of distinction in view of the diplomat's early age. He had remained at this post for six years, and during the Paris congress had exercised the duties of principal secretary.[1] Although his work had centered primarily around the drafting of the treaty protocols, he had definitely contributed to the successful effort to place the Italian question before the congress.[2] He had earned himself the gratitude of Cavour and, therefore, it is not surprising that in 1860 he had been sent on a special mission to Italy to complete the negotiation of the Treaty of Turin on 24 March 1860, by which Nice and Savoy were ceded to France.[3]

The selection of Benedetti as the first French envoy to the Italian kingdom in 1861 had not been unexpected. His knowledge of Italian affairs and his friendship with Italian political leaders were influential factors in his appointment. Of even greater significance, in regard to the appointment and his later career, was his association with the Italian faction in political circles of the Second Empire. This group, which included among others Prince Napoleon, Princess Mathilda, Eugène Rouher, Edouard Thouvenel, Marquis Charles de La Valette, Madame Hortense Cornu, Jacques Bixio and others, was unequivocably opposed to the European political system based upon the Vienna settlement of 1815, and thoroughly in sympathy with Italian nationalist aspirations. It was hostile to the reactionary camp with which it associated the Austrian and Papal governments.[4]

Benedetti's career, once he had risen high in the imperial diplomatic

---

[1] FRANGULIS, V, 84.

[2] J. M. THOMPSON, *Louis Napoleon and the Second Empire* (Oxford, 1954), pp. 173–174.

[3] P. DE LA GORCE, *Histoire du Second Empire* (Paris, 1894–1905), III, 209–212.

[4] R. SCHNERB, *Rouher et le Second Empire* (Paris, 1949), pp. 127–128. Benedetti's appointment to Turin, coupled with that of La Valette to Rome, caused Mérimée to write: "These two good Catholics... are the proper ones to persuade our Holy Father that his kingdom is no longer of this world" (Mérimée to Panizzi, Paris, 3 September 1861, P. MÉRIMÉE, *Lettres à M. Panizzi 1850–1870*, ed. L. Fagan [Paris, 1881], I, 222).

apparatus, had become of course increasingly subject to purely political considerations. Thus, when the emperor's bid for the support of the clericals in the elections of 1863 necessitated a change in the imperial cabinet, Thouvenel, one of the "italianissimes," had been promptly eliminated. His dismissal had entailed also the recall of both Benedetti and La Valette, the respective ministers in Turin and Rome.[1] Thouvenel had been replaced by Édouard Drouyn de Lhuys, whose appointment effectively closed the diplomatic service to Benedetti. The new foreign minister was a spokesman for the traditionalist faction in French diplomacy which favored collaboration with Austria and which opposed changes in the existing equilibrium in Germany and in Europe. Upon leaving Turin in the fall of 1862, Benedetti had revealed his personal feelings toward the new foreign minister when he had declared that only after the dismissal of Drouyn de Lhuys would he return to active service.[2]

Despite his declared intention, Benedetti did return long before the resignation of the foreign minister. The prolonged inactivity to which he had been condemned since October 1862 must have been intolerable to the former envoy. The gatherings at Princess Mathilda's Paris home, and at Saint Gratien during the summer, where he frequently met Count Ottaviano Vimercati, Prince Gabrieli, Marquis Primoli, La Valette, and others and discussed with them international affairs, must have stimulated his desire to return to active political life.[3] His correspondence with Thouvenel, who had become president of the administrative council of the *Compagnie de l'Est*, also had kept him in touch with public affairs.[4] Moreover, Thouvenel's close friendship with Rouher placed the former in an excellent position to further Benedetti's hopes. He apparently aspired to a seat in the senate but Thouvenel had advised him to be patient and to forego the ambition "... to be buried alive in the Luxemburg catacomb."[5] He had reminded Benedetti that Drouyn de Lhuys would not head the foreign ministry forever and that his successor would undoubtedly offer him a high post in the diplomatic service. He had assured his friend that Rouher, the "vice-emperor" of the Second Empire, would find suita-

---

[1] SCHNERB, pp. 128–129.
[2] "That is to say, as long as the Italian question is not taken up" (Solvyns to Rogier, Paris, 12 October 1864, BAE CP, Italie/2 [1863–1865], no. 109).
[3] Bamberg to foreign office, Paris, 11 October 1864, *APP* (Oldenburg i.O., 1932–39), V, 440.
[4] THOUVENEL, pp. 407–408.
[5] Thouvenel to Benedetti [Paris?,] 28 April 1864, *ibid.*, pp. 410–411.

ble public office for him in which he could await a change at the *Quai d'Orsay*.[1]

Benedetti did not have to mark time in a temporary post, for in October 1864 he was offered the appointment of imperial ambassador to the king of Prussia.[2] The Berlin mission had always been one of the major posts of the French diplomatic service, and Benedetti accepted without delay. His selection, the work of Rouher, did come as a surprise to many, in view of the fact that Benedetti and Drouyn de Lhuys were representatives of two conflicting schools of thought in French foreign policy. Benedetti's appointment most likely was presented to the foreign minister as a *fait accompli*.[3] To many observers the return of Benedetti implied a defeat for Drouyn de Lhuys and the policy he represented; indeed, his resignation from office was expected to be announced momentarily.[4] This expectation did not materialize, and it seems that Benedetti's appointment was simply part of a deliberate design to increase the flexibility of French foreign policy. Since the end of the Danish war the emperor had become concerned about the possibility that the Holy Alliance might be resurrected against France. He apparently thought it advisable therefore to have an ambassador in Berlin who was not a traditionalist and who, by inference, could be considered sympathetic to the designs which Bismarck was thought to contemplate against the old order in Germany. The imperial government would seek, through Benedetti, to further a *rapprochement* with Prussia and draw her away from Austria, while, through the retention of Drouyn de Lhuys, it would keep open the way for collaboration with Austria. It was hoped that a flexible policy, if shrewdly manipulated, would ward off the danger of a coalition against France and permit the imperial government to play off Prussia against Austria.[5] Clearly, such a course held a promise of success, but every advantage of this double-edged policy could be

---

[1] *Ibid.*

[2] The French legation in Berlin was elevated to embassy status on 7 October 1864.

[3] Solvyns to Rogier, Turin, 12 October 1864, BAE CP, Italie/2 [1863–1865], no 109.

[4] L. SCHOEPS, *Graf Vincent Benedetti*, "Historische Studien," VII (Halle, 1915), p. 25.

[5] See Benedetti to Drouyn de Lhuys, [Berlin,] 30 April 1865, *ODG* (Paris, 1910–1934), VI, 192; P. DE LA GORCE, *Études d'histoire contemporaine: La Prusse avant Sadowa* (n.d.), pp. 106–107. Cf. P. MATTER, *Bismarck et son temps*, "Bibliothèque d'histoire contemporaine" (Paris, 1908), II, 229; F. VALSECCHI, "Considerazioni sulla politica europea di Napoleone III," *Rivista storica italiana*, LXII (1950), pp. 31 ff.; A. PINGAUD, "La politique extérieure du Second Empire," *RH*, CLVI (1927), pp. 41–68; P. BERNSTEIN, "The Rhine Policy of Napoleon III: A New Interpretation," *The Lock Haven Bulletin*, Series 1, Number 4 (1962), pp. 47–67; H. GEUSS, *Bismarck und Napoleon III. Ein Beitrag zur Geschichte der preussisch-französischen Beziehungen 1851–1871* (Cologne, 1959), pp. 112–116.

lost if rivalry, rather than coordination, marked its implementation. Distrust between minister and ambassador could produce a fatal weakness, open to intrigues and damaging exploitation. In time of crisis and delicate negotiations a high degree of confidence and harmonious collaboration between minister and envoy would be an absolute prerequisite.

Recorded impressions about Benedetti's appointment are few, but they do indicate that the emperor's motives were plain to political observers. Dr. Felix Bamberg, the Prussian consul in Paris, established a direct connection between the appointment and the emperor's intention to woo Prussia. He was convinced that Drouyn de Lhuys had been forced to accept Benedetti and thought that even the foreign minister had to agree that the choice was a good one.[1] Baron Eugène Beyens, Belgian envoy in Paris, summed up the general reaction in the French capital by the statement that Benedetti's appointment had been well received in Berlin and that it would contribute to an improvement in Franco-Prussian relations. Although he knew the ambassador as a man of decided opinions on diplomatic affairs, Beyens did feel that he could effectively further the emperor's designs in Berlin.[2] From Berlin the Belgian minister, Baron Jean-Baptiste Nothomb, wrote that Benedetti was regarded as a personal agent of the emperor, "who can and will say everything." [3] Thus, the diplomatic world had no illusions about the selection of Benedetti and it remained to be seen how successful he would be at the "most arduous and dangerous post in Europe." [4]

Benedetti had qualifications which gave promise of a successful mission. He possessed both the professional and social experience of the career diplomat and the quick and analytical mind of the trained negotiator. As director of the political section of the foreign ministry and as minister to Turin, he had become thoroughly acquainted with the objectives, problems and implementations of French foreign policy. His sympathies for the Italian cause, and corresponding enmity toward Austria and the old order it symbolized, made him a felicitous choice. A decided handicap was his inability to use the German language. To be sure, French was still the language of diplomacy, but Benedetti's effectiveness as an observer and negotiator could not but

---

[1] Bamberg to foreign office, Paris, 11 October 1864, *APP*, V, 440.
[2] Beyens to Rogier, Paris, 10 October 1864, BAE CP, France/23, no. 207.
[3] Nothomb to Rogier, Berlin, 17 December 1864, *ibid.*, Prusse/22, no. 242.
[4] N. BEYENS, *Le Second Empire vu par un diplomate belge (Baron Eugène Beyens)* (Bruges, 9216), II, 151-152.

suffer from this shortcoming. Although severe criticism was to mark the close of his career as ambassador to Prussia, there was no reason, at the time of his appointment, to question his ability to promote the interests of France in Prussia.

As the envoy of a ruler whose policies were not easily predictable Benedetti's task was not to be an easy one: the ever-present possibility that his views were no longer in favor at the Tuileries was hardly likely to augment his self-assurance. Even in possession of the emperor's confidence he still faced many problems in his new post. For instance, court ceremonial permitted only occasional contact with King William and practice and tradition would restrict Benedetti to Bismarck in the conduct of affairs. Although the king was the final authority on all matters, Benedetti could not hope to call on him whenever he would wish to do so. He could not expect to discover and exploit differences in views between sovereign and minister-president, as could the Prussian ambassador in Paris, Count Robert von der Goltz, who had relatively easy access to the emperor.

Information about Benedetti's own reaction to his appointment is unfortunately lacking and one can only presume its general tenor. In the light of his correspondence with Thouvenel it would appear that he had hesitated to seek a diplomatic post. Indeed, only after his hopes for a senate seat had been defeated, in consequence of more formidable claims by others, did he wish to return to the diplomatic service. The offer of the Berlin post was of course a flattering one and, considering that Drouyn de Lhuys was still foreign minister, Benedetti could indeed think of himself as the emperor's personal agent in the Prussian capital. The prospect of isolating Austria by seeking a *rapprochement* with Prussia must have appealed to him, since he saw in it the possibility of freeing France, and Italy as well,[1] from the shackles of the Vienna treaties. He remained about seven weeks in France, presumably for briefing purposes, before leaving for his post. Benedetti arrived in Berlin on 22 November, and that very evening he was received by the Prussian minister-president, Otto von Bismarck-Schönhausen, to whom he remitted a copy of his letter of accreditation with a request for a royal audience.[2] Next day he formally entered upon his new duties by assuming the direction of the imperial embassy in Berlin.

---

[1] "In consequence [of Benedetti's expressed views] his elevation is a very encouraging sign for the Italian cause" (Solvyns to Rogier, Turin, 12 October 1864, BAE CP, Italie/2, no. 109).

[2] Benedetti to Drouyn de Lhuys, Berlin, 23 November 1864, FAE CP, Prusse/350, no. 106.

CHAPTER II

FROM VIENNA TO GASTEIN

Benedetti's first political discussion with Bismarck took place on 22 November 1864, and had as its theme the future of the duchies of Schleswig-Holstein. The treaty signed at Vienna on 30 October [1] had ended the state of war between the Germanic powers, Austria and Prussia, and the Danish kingdom.[2] The last obstacle concerning the treatment of the two national groups in Schleswig had ostensibly been removed, and the negotiations had been brought to a close.[3] When Benedetti assumed his duties in Berlin, many issues arising out of the peace settlement had yet to be resolved. Already a controversy had arisen over the refusal of Saxony and Hanover to withdraw their troops from the duchies on the ground that certain matters touching upon the competency of the Germanic Confederation had not yet been cleared. Bismarck told Benedetti that he was determined to obtain the withdrawal of those troops and to organize a provisional government in the duchies. The topic was again taken up next day, when Bismarck visited the ambassador at his temporary residence at the Hotel Royal.[4] The Prussian minister appeared annoyed by the reluctance of the Austrian government to agree to forceful measures to assure the withdrawal of the Confederation forces, but he foresaw no real trouble in eventually obtaining his demands. He hinted at the possibility of an agreement on a ruler for the duchies, provided certain accords would be con-

---

[1] For the text of the treaty see *ODG*, IV, 368–376.

[2] For the diplomatic history of the conflict, see L. STEEFEL, *The Schleswig-Holstein Question*, "Harvard Historical Studies," XXXII (Cambridge, 1932), pp. 44–250.

[3] Dotézac to Drouyn de Lhuys, Copenhagen, 31 October 1864, FAE CP, Danemark/248, no. 212. The Danish government had rejected the clause guaranteeing equality of treatment on the grounds that it might permit the German powers to intervene in internal Danish affairs. The issue gained new significance in connection with Article V of the Prague Treaty which became the springboard for subsequent French efforts on behalf of North Schleswig.

[4] Benedetti to Drouyn de Lhuys, Berling, 23 November 1864, *ibid.*, Prusse/ 350, no. 107; H. KOHL, *Fürst Bismarck: Regesten zu einer wissenschaftlichen Biographie des ersten deutschen Reichskanzlers* (Leipzig, 1891), I, 245.

cluded between such a ruler and the Prussian government. No indication of the character of such arrangements was made. While no
inference of a territorial gain could be attributed to his remarks,
Bismarck was of course credited with such a design, if not with the
ultimate annexation of the duchies by Prussia.[1] During an interview
following Benedetti's audience with King William of 27 November, as
well as during a conference next day, Bismarck further elaborated
upon Austro-Prussian views on the issue.[2] Recurrent references to
Austria's rights under the Treaty of Vienna made it obvious that
Bismarck did not for the time being desire a break with his former co-
belligerent. On the contrary, he hoped to continue co-operation with
Austria to the exclusion of the other members of the Confederation.
Benedetti wondered whether Bismarck had resigned himself to accept
Duke Frederick of Augustenburg and to forego territorial acquisitions.
He viewed Austria's opposition to annexation as the most constant
factor checking Prussia's acquisition policy and wondered if Austria
might have shown herself more accomodating if, in the past summer,
Prussia had guaranteed Austria's Venetian possessions. He thought it
premature to speculate whether Bismarck was prepared to break with
Austria in order to annex the duchies.[3]

While listening to Bismarck, the ambassador did not comment upon
the position of his own government. It was fully understood in Berlin
that the imperial government supported an annexation of the duchies
by Prussia.[4] The record of Franco-Prussian diplomatic relations, dating
back to 1863, bears ample testimony to this fact.[5] Napoleon III,
anxious to destroy the old political order based on the Vienna treaties,
hoped to achieve this end with Prussian support. By actively furthering
Prussian expansionist aspirations, he could hope to split the Germanic
Confederation, isolate Austria, earn the gratitude of Prussia and finally
achieve the territorial ambitions of France in the Rhineland.

The unsettled future of Schleswig-Holstein continued to hold Be-

---

[1] Benedetti to Drouyn de Lhuys, Berlin, 25 November 1864, FAE CP, Prusse/350, no. 108.
[2] KOHL, I, 245.
[3] Benedetti to Drouyn de Lhuys, Berlin, 28 November 1864, FAE CP, Prusse/350 no.
110. For background information on Austro-Prussian efforts toward a common policy, see
W. LIPGENS, "Bismarcks Österreich-Politik vor 1866," *Die Welt als Geschichte*, X (1950),
pp. 240–262; HEINRICH RITTER VON SRBIK, "*Die Schönbrunner Konferenzen vom August
1864*," *HZ*, CLIII, Heft 1 (1935–1936), pp. 43–88.
[4] Goltz to Bismarck, Paris, 25 November 1864, *APP*, V, 511–512. Although supporting
the idea of annexation, it was expected that Napoleon, in conformity with his support of the
principle of national self-determination, would demand a plebiscite in North Schleswig.
[5] GEUSS, pp. 77–112; O. PFLANZE, *Bismarck and the Development of Germany*, Vol. I,
The Period of Unification, 1851–1871 (Princeton, 1963), pp. 233–253.

nedetti's attention. On 1 December Austria and Prussia proposed that the diet should declare the federal execution ended and invite Saxony and Hanover to withdraw their troops. Benedetti predicted acceptance of this proposal and also thought that a diet decision concerning the various dynastic claims would be rejected by Prussia. To safeguard his own interests, Bismarck would insist on a prior agreement with Austria should the approbation of the diet to a settlement be sought. Rather than try and determine at present the character and results of the negotiation yet to come, Benedetti pointed out that the first contest, a preliminary one, would decide whether Austria and Prussia alone would control the future of the duchies or whether the issue would be submitted to the diet.[1] He felt certain that Prussia would not retire from Schleswig-Holstein without having gained decided advantages. Should annexation plans be shelved, then Prussia would undoubtedly seek other compensation, particularly concessions for naval installations in the Kiel area.[2] As predicted by Benedetti the diet adopted the Austro-Prussian proposal on 5 December and the governments of Saxony and Hanover ordered their troops to withdraw from the duchies. While acknowledging the ambassador's accurate forecast, Drouyn de Lhuys cautioned: "While awaiting the final solution, the consequences of which we shall have to examine from the point of view of general intentions, we watch the events which are occurring in Germany with a sentiment of reserve which does not change our friendly disposition." [3] The situation regarding the duchies was still far from a definite solution, and Benedetti speculated that Austria could take advantage of the general hostility to Prussia in the diet, barely overcome during the vote of 5 December, should she decide to join the opposition. Or, should Austria consent to Prussian annexation of the duchies, she could quite conceivably demand compensation

---

[1] On 14 November, Prussia tried to obtain Austrian concurrence in a joint demand that Hanover and Saxony withdraw their troops and officials. The Austrian government then tried to persuade Bismarck that the two powers present the peace treaty with Denmark to the diet, along with a proposal that the troops of the Confederation be withdrawn after sovereignty had been granted to the duke of Augustenburg. It was finally agreed to consult the diet and to drop the Austrian effort on behalf of Augustenburg (*BGW*, V, 4 ff., 18–19, 29 ff.; *QDPO* [Oldenburg i.O., 1934–1938], IV, 429 ff.).

[2] Benedetti to Drouyn de Lhuys, Berlin, 4 December 1864, FAE CP, Prusse/350, no. 111. For background information on Bismarck's plans relative to the duchies, see A. O. MEYER, "Die Zielsetzung in Bismarcks schleswig-holsteinischer Politik von 1855 bis 1864," *Zeitschrift der Gesellschaft für Schleswig-Holsteinische Geschichte*, LIII (1923), pp. 112 ff.

[3] Drouyn de Lhuys to Benedetti, Paris, 9 December 1864, FAE CP, Prusse/350, no. 67. "Drouyn de Lhuys... said to me, 'We assist now as impassive spectators at the discussion of Germany, without interfering in anything'" (Goltz to Bismarck, Paris, 9 December 1864, *APP*, V, 551–552).

for such acquiescence. A third possibility not overlooked by Benedetti was that Austria might not demand any compensation, for reasons which she could not publicly avow. Such a sacrifice, for the sake of an *entente* existing perhaps already between Prussia, Russia and Austria, seemed not improbable to some observers of the diet proceedings. The fact that Benedetti referred to this possibility indicates that he did not discount the possibility of a new Holy Alliance.[1]

Before returning to Paris for the Christmas holidays,[2] Ambassador Benedetti gained further information about Bismarck's impending plans. The minister-president related to him the content of a communication which he was about to address to the Austrian government: a proposal that Austria support Prussia's contention that the diet had no legal right to dispose of the future of Schleswig-Holstein. Prussia and Austria might delegate their rights to the diet, but the latter could not assume them short of such a delegation. For the moment, Bismarck noted, Prussia had no plans to abdicate her rights. He insinuated that the best solution would be the annexation of the duchies by Prussia. However, he did not expect Austria's ready concurrence with such a step and planned first to encourage negotiations with Austria toward a temporary solution of the question.[3] Benedetti listened with care to Bismarck's ideas regarding future developments and then raised the question of a possible retrocession of North Schleswig to Denmark, a matter which the emperor and Drouyn de Lhuys had already touched upon in talks with Goltz.[4] He asked specifically if the Prussian government planned to take the initiative for such an act during the coming negotiations with Austria. Bismarck replied that the king had been disposed to give him such authority, out of deference to the wishes of the French emperor. He added, however, that during the last few days the attitude of the king had undergone a slight change in the face of criticism regarding a division of Schleswig; he feared that Prussia's enemies might conceivably turn German public opinion against her if such a division were to take place. The losses and sacrifices of the war, particularly at Düppel, were apparently still too fresh in the public mind to allow a retrocession of territory. Bismarck indicated that he

---

[1] Benedetti to Drouyn de Lhuys, Berlin, 10 December 1864, FAE CP, Prusse/350, no. 112. It was thought that such an *entente* might have been concluded during the Carlsbad and Kissingen meetings of June 1864. Benedetti's concern was not entirely ill-placed, in light of the Rechberg draft considered but discarded at Schönbrunn in August 1864.

[2] Same to same, Berlin, 14 December 1864, FAE CP, Prusse/350, no. 114.

[3] *Ibid.*, no. 113bis.

[4] Goltz to Bismarck, Paris, 9 December 1864, *APP*, V, 551–552.

himself would support the return of North Schleswig to Denmark, should the emperor insist upon it. Speaking of a retrocession of North Schleswig, Bismarck implied that a slight divergence in view might exist between him and the monarch. He could take advantage of Benedetti's inability to verify the king's views directly and use this unique situation to screen reversals in his own views by depicting them as being those of the sovereign. Or else he could hide his unwillingness to carry out an earlier-professed promise by citing the king's opposition to it. Benedetti was aware of a possible reservation on the part of Bismarck himself.[1] It is doubtful, however, that he considered it portentous; as yet he had little occasion to become acquainted with the subtlety of Bismarck's machinations.

Benedetti's consultations with Drouyn de Lhuys in Paris during Christmas holidays [2] would indicate that he still believed that no immediate annexation of the duchies would occur, and that Prussia had not offered Austria a guaranty for her Venetian territories. Evidently Bismarck had reassured Benedetti on these points before his departure for Paris.[3] During Benedetti's absence from Berlin, the embassy was under the direction of Count de Rayneval, the *chargé d'affaires*,[4] through whose reports Benedetti learned that the duke of Augustenburg was reportedly willing to bargain with Bismarck for the title of hereditary governor,[5] although the Prussian government had instructed the Prussian crown syndics to examine possible succession rights the house of Brandenburg might possess through the marriage, in the sixteenth century, of Elizabeth of Denmark and the margrave of Brandenburg.[6] Benedetti returned in time for the opening of the parliamentary session on Saturday, 14 January 1865, at which time William touched upon the duchies in vague terms, without giving an indication of the future course of the Prussian government.[7] Bene-

---

[1] Benedetti to Drouyn de Lhuys, Berlin, 14 December 1864, FAE CP, Prusse/350, no. 113bis.

[2] Commenting on Benedetti's activities in Berlin, Baron Nothomb, the Belgian envoy, felt that the ambassador would have one constant worry, namely, the conclusion of an Austro-Prussian alliance (Nothomb to Rogier, Berlin, 17 December 1864, BAE CP, Prusse/22, no. 242; same to same, Berlin, 24 December 1864, *ibid.*, no. 249).

[3] "On his return from Biarritz, Mr. Bismarck stopped for several days in Paris and was received twice by the emperor. His Majesty asked him three times over whether the king of Prussia and he, his prime minister, or whether the king alone, or even if he alone, had given Austria a guarantee for Venetia. Mr. Bismarck answered *no*" (same to same, Berlin, 22 December 1864, *ibid.*, no 243).

[4] Benedetti to Drouyn de Lhuys, Berlin, 13 January 1865, FAE CP, Prusse/ 351, no. 6.

[5] Rayneval to Drouyn de Lhuys, Berlin, 20 December 1864, *ibid.*, 350, no. 115.

[6] Same to same, Berlin, 29 December 1864, *ibid.*, no. 117.

[7] Benedetti to Drouyn de Lhuys, Berlin, 14 January 1865, *ibid.*, 351, no. 9.

detti could do little more than bide his time and he told Nothomb:

The moment has not yet arrived for us to declare ourselves. Before my departure for Paris Bismarck told me that he does not think of annexation. Goltz, every time the occasion offers itself, speaks the same language; that must suffice for us, at least for the present. We have another security motive, namely the presence of the Austrians in the duchies; it is evident to us that the Austrian government will not deliver these areas to Prussia; if Austrian co-occupation ends, it will be through conditions acceptable to Austria. We wait! The question is in Vienna. Right now a French chargé d'affaires would suffice in Berlin.[1]

Benedetti did not hide the fact that the imperial government was thus far satisfied with the attitude of the Prussian government; like France, so Prussia seemed anxious to destroy the old political order established by the Congress of Vienna.[2]

Benedetti must have been pleased to learn that relations between the two German powers has worsened over the publication in the Vienna press of two notes, dealing with Schleswig-Holstein, which Bismarck had addressed to the Austrian government in December. These notes, calling for Austrian support against the anticipated interference of the diet, gave rise to numerous conjectures bearing on a possible territorial readjustment between the two powers. The ambassador found it difficult to believe that Austria might have been offered territorial compensation for a Prussian annexation of the duchies; he had considered it unlikely that negotiations had reached the stage where such an offer could be made by Prussia. According to his own impressions, the Prussian government had at present no desire to hasten developments. Likewise, remarks by members of the Austrian legation to Benedetti indicated that the Austrian government was not particularly anxious to bring about a solution now. All evidence pointed to a stalemate and the ambassador acknowledged his inability to predict which of the two powers would accept the sacrifice necessary for a solution.[3] He told Baron Adriaan Zuylen van Nijevelt, the Dutch envoy in Berlin, that Austria could, if she chose to be reasonable, dictate the law to Prussia and thus regain all her influences with the secondary states in Germany.[4]

---

[1] Nothomb to Rogier, Berlin, 19 January 1865, BAE CP, Prusse/23, no. 5.

[2] *Ibid.* Benedetti's conversations probably took place at a reception for the ambassador by Crown Prince Frederick on 18 January (FRIEDRICH III., *Tagebücher von 1848–1866*, ed. H. O. Meisner [Leipzig, 1929], p. 383).

[3] Benedetti to Drouyn de Lhuys, Berlin, 18 January 1865, FAE CP, Prusse/351, no. 11. The Saxon minister in Berlin held a similiar view and suspected Bismarck was only biding his time until Austria was at war with Italy and France to force approval of annexation at the price of Prussian neutrality (Werner to Mensdorff, Dresden, 21 January 1865, *QDPO* IV, 534).

[4] In his conversation with the Dutch envoy, Benedetti added the interesting comment

Benedetti was able to confirm his observation, relative to the publication of the Prussian notes in the Vienna press, when he obtained from an unidentified source a copy of Count Alexander von Mensdorff-Pouilly's reply of 21 December. He found the tone of the Austrian note quite severe and thought the possibility of a solution most unlikely. From Bismarck he learned that the Prussian government was disappointed and displeased with the reception Austria had accorded to the Prussian proposal. Bismarck expected to continue the course thus far pursued and to reject any proposal or interference calculated to harm the interests of Prussia. His attitude made it obvious to Benedetti that Prussia would not agree to compensate Austria with Prussian territory for the sake of an undisputed possession of the duchies. A hint by the Austrian envoy in Berlin, Count Aloys Károlyi de Nagy-Károlyi, that Austria might accept compensation in Silesia had not even led to the exploration of such a solution.[1] The visit of Prince Frederick Charles to Vienna also failed to bring the two governments closer to an agreement.[2] The mission of keeping Prussia and Austria apart appeared to be anything but a challenge to a career diplomat.

Repeated talks with Bismarck and other diplomats, as well as communications from the foreign ministry in Paris, permitted Benedetti to draw upon a wealth of materials in his effort to penetrate deeply into the thorny Schleswig-Holstein issue, and after a certain amount of study and reflection he presented his considerations to the foreign minister. Benedetti noted the desire of the Prussian government ultimately to annex the duchies. Bismarck had hoped to achieve this end with Austrian support but had failed. He then had presented claims of the Prussian royal house to the duchies and, while their examination was pending, had launched a propaganda campaign in case the duchies were to be consulted, a development he would welcome. The

that if the wishes of the population were to be consulted north of Germany the same ought to be effected north of France. It would seem that Benedetti, on his own initiative, was hinting about the possibility of a Franco-Dutch agreement for the partition of Belgium (Zuylen to Cremers, Berlin, 21 January 1865, RBZ, Pruisen/1865, no. 718).

[1] Benedetti to Drouyn de Lhuys, Berlin, 23 January 1865, FAE CP, Prusse/351, no. 13. After succeeding Rechberg, Count Mensdorff had offered Prussia a proposal to resolve the future of the duchies. His plan called for either the creation of a new principality under Augustenburg rule or the annexation of the duchies by Prussia, with suitable compensation for Austria in Silesia and in the Hohenzollern possessions in Württemberg (PFLANZE, p.254).

[2] Benedetti to Drouyn de Lhuys, Berlin, 23 January 1865, FAE CP, Prusse/351, no. 14. "I send you... the copy of a dispatch of the duke of Gramont which confirms the information gathered through your attention. You will see that the prince seems to have avoided every political subject in his conversations, and that his sojourn in Vienna appears to have been only a simple courtesy visit" (Drouyn de Lhuys to Benedetti, Paris, 30 January 1865, ibid., no. 12).

Austrian government had not been responsive to Bismarck's various suggestions and preferred to let the diet decide the entire issue. Benedetti was convinced that neither power was deliberately seeking an open break; their differences had arisen from a divergence in ultimate aims. Prussia hoped for territorial expansion and greater power, while Austria was anxious to maintain the existing power ratio. The ambassador refrained from making predictions of the outcome of the struggle but called the minister's attention to his impression that Bismarck had convinced King William of the eventual success of his plans. The fact that Bismarck could hold the Prussian *Landtag* so well in check was added cause for Benedetti's opinion. The consequences for Austria of a Prussian expansion were also touched upon by the ambassador. He advanced the opinion that such an event would end Austrian pre-eminence in Germany, and thus one could expect the Austrian government to try to prevent it. He did not deny the possibility that Austria might be able to strengthen her leadership in Germany, provided she knew how to profit from the distrust of the secondary states toward Prussia. A second Olmütz was not altogether impossible, but Benedetti did not think that Austria had the vigorous and imaginative statesmen for the accomplishment of such a task. He thought the final solution still distant but warned that Bismarck's tenacity, coupled with the traditional tendencies of the Hohenzollern and the national aspirations of the Prussian people, made for a powerful combination in the pursuit of a common goal. Benedetti had discussed the entire issue with his colleagues, Lord Francis Napier and Count Paul d'Oubril, who maintained the reserve he did and shared his views on the situation. Benedetti's observations, scattered through some of his earlier dispatches, were thus drawn together in an attempt at a comprehensive picture of the major problem in Germany. He confined his remarks to the issue and its consequences to Germany and did not endeavor, at this time, to lift the matter onto the international plane, a fact which does not detract from the validity of his comments.[1]

Benedetti was of course aware of the possibility that Bismarck might forego outright annexation of the duchies. He felt certain that the minister-president would, if necessary, agree to such a course provided that certain demands be met: cession of the Kiel port to Prussia,

---

[1] Benedetti to Drouyn de Lhuys, Berlin, 14 February 1865, *ibid.*, no. 22. For the attitude of Russia and Britain see W. Mosse, *The European Powers and the German Question, 1848–1871* (Cambridge, 1958), pp. 146 ff.; R. Stadelmann, "Das Jahr 1865 und das Problem von Bismarcks deutscher Politik," *HZ*, Beiheft 29 (1933), pp. 6, 17.

cession of a second port, concession in regard to a two-ocean canal, induction of Schleswig-Holstein sailors into the Prussian navy, organization of the military forces of the duchies on the basis of and according to the regulations of the Prussian army, and entry of the duchies into the *Zollverein*. Benedetti of course considered these demands nothing other than a disguised annexation.[1] Those stipulations were cited by Bismarck when he described to Benedetti the relationship between Prussia and an eventual government of the duchies. The extent of the Prussian demands made it seem unlikely that Austria would acquiesce. The ambassador hinted that Prussia would have to assume large obligations *vis-à-vis* Austria if such severe conditions were to be accepted. However, Bismarck insisted that his demands were rather limited in scope and he added that he had deliberately asked for "little" in order to escape obligations toward Austria. He told Benedetti that an Austro-Prussian *rapprochement* could only be occasioned by French hostility toward Prussia in respect to the duchies question, or by the hostility of the secondary German states. Benedetti denied the likelihood of the first possibility and assured the minister-president of the friendly disposition of the French government. These assurances were motivated, at least in part, by a desire to prevent a Prussian *rapprochement* with Austria.[2]

The last major step in the Austro-Prussian settlement attempts during February 1865 was the presentation of these Prussian demands to Vienna. Benedetti wondered if the conciliatory attitude of the Austrian ambassador might foreshadow a change in the attitude of the Austrian government. Ever since his return from Vienna, Károlyi had seized opportunities to minimize the differences between the two powers. Benedetti avidly watched for any sign which might reveal an alliance between the two powers or a Prussian guarantee of Venetia. His personal partiality for the Italian cause lent impetus to his official acumen whenever irredentism came into question.[3] Although Bismarck's latest note, of 23 February, had initiated a further step in the Austro-Prussian negotiations, the attitude of the French government still remained unchanged. To be sure, the conditions under which Bismarck visualized the relations with a new Schleswig-Holstein government, while still unclear, were not likely to take the French

---

[1] Benedetti to Drouyn de Lhuys, Berlin, 15 February 1865, FAE CP, Prusse/351, no. 27. Cf. same to same, Berlin, 24 March 1865, *ibid.*, no. 40.

[2] Bismarck to Goltz, Berlin, 17 February 1865, *APP*, V, 676–678. Benedetti makes no allusion to this part of Bismarck's conversation (*ODG*, V, 407, ft. 1); GEUSS, pp. 117–118.

[3] Benedetti to Drouyn de Lhuys, Berlin, 23 February 1865, FAE CP, Prusse/351, no. 29.

government by surprise. While recognizing the existence of alliances between Prussia and certain secondary states within the federal system, no relationship such as Bismarck contemplated with the duchies had ever been established. The dependence of Schleswig-Holstein upon Prussia would reduce the duchies to a vassal, shorn of every vestige of sovereignty. Although distrustful of Bismarck's manoeuvers, the French government had not asked the ambassador to step out of his role of a silent but interested observer; the state of negotiations between Austria and Prussia was as yet too inconclusive to warrant other measures.[1]

While the Prussian government had taken steps to advance the negotiations with Austria, it had also begun to show great interest in the attitude of the French government.[2] A statement about the views of the imperial government was made on 6 March by Ambassador Benedetti: annexation of the duchies would meet with no objection, he told Bismarck, provided the retrocession of northern Schleswig would take place. In stressing this last point, Benedetti reiterated once again the wishes of the imperial government:

Without doubt, if Schleswig were incorporated into Prussia and no account were made of either race or national aspirations, such a solution, resting solely on force, could not obtain our sympathies. But if the Berlin cabinet consents to trace a line of demarcation between the two populations of different origin... and the Germans in Schleswig, honestly consulted, express the desire to unite their destinies with those of the subjects of the Prussian monarchy, we shall hardly be in a position to raise objections, or to refuse our assent to a settlement which would contain nothing contrary to the maxims of our public law.[3]

To the minister-president's claim that at the present time public opinion would not permit the return of the northern districts to Denmark, the ambassador suggested that the annexation and retrocession take place simultaneously. Bismarck sidestepped this eminently reasonable advice by pleading his inability to make a decision without the participation of the Austrian government. As long as the relations between Austria and Prussia remained friendly, he could not proceed

---

[1] Drouyn de Lhuys to Benedetti, Paris, 25 February 1865, *ibid.*, no. 20.

[2] Goltz to Bismarck, Paris, 4 March 1865, *APP*, V, 708–710. Drouyn de Lhuys had told Goltz that France would accept the borderline Flensburg-Tonderen as Prussia's minimum demand if the northern districts of Schleswig were returned to Denmark. Goltz gained the impression that the French government was far more engrossed with the retrocession of the northern districts than with a plebiscite and incorporation of the southern districts.

[3] Drouyn de Lhuys to Benedetti, Paris, 4 February 1865, FAE CP, Prusse/351, P. Cf. Goltz to Bismarck, Paris, 3 February 1865, *APP*, V, 647. Bismarck thought it premature to seek a formal statement of policy from the imperial government (Bismarck to Goltz, Berlin, 5 February 1865, *ibid.*, 647–648, ft. 1 to no. 448).

alone in that matter.[1] When the subject was again discussed on the following Wednesday, 8 March, Benedetti found that Bismarck considered the retrocession of North Schleswig far more difficult than he had claimed in the previous December.[2] Perhaps he was seeking to magnify the Prussian sacrifice for reasons not yet apparent. Benedetti also observed that Bismarck was showing increased confidence that a discussion of the Schleswig-Holstein issue in the diet would not harm the Prussian cause. Adroit handling of the diet's legislative machinery would, in any case, lead to prolonged debates which, according to Bismarck, could only harm the Austrian position. Benedetti was not at all convinced by the minister-president's comments on the situation; he did think that the conciliation efforts of the Bavarian government had promoted a more benevolent mood on the part of Prussian statesmen.[3]

On March 2, while dining with the minister-president, Benedetti learned that Austria considered the demands incompatible with the prerogatives of sovereignty and in definite contradiction with the rights and obligations of the federated states. Bismarck could be pleased with the Austrian reaction, a reaction which his demands had been calculated to produce. Austrian acceptance would have checked the Prussian annexationist hopes. For Austria, the rejection of the demands meant a reorientation of her policy. By standing against Prussian expansionism, the Austrian government could hope to regain the goodwill of the secondary states in the forthcoming diet debates. Should one of the secondary states press the issue in the diet, however, Bismarck felt certain that no decisive vote would be mustered against Prussia.[4] The fluctuating nature of the Austro-Prussian negotiations convinced Ambassador Benedetti that France should continue her reserved attitude of the past. He himself did not consider the relations between France and Prussia to be on an intimate footing as yet, and at no time did he think the French government in any way committed.[5]

---

[1] *Aufzeichnung des auswärtigen Amtes. Resumé einer Unterredung Bismarcks mit Benedetti am 6. März,* Berlin, *ibid.,* 719–721.

[2] Benedetti to Drouyn de Lhuys, Berlin, 8 March 1865, FAE CP, Prusse/351, no. 34. "He [Bismarck] will invite the ambassador of Prussia at Paris to declare to Your Excellency that the government of the king desires to keep in mind the observations of the emperor's government on this point, but that it will not be able to consider them before having prepared public opinion in Prussia and in Germany, and after having reached an accord with Austria" (*ibid.*).

[3] Same to same, Berlin, 7 March 1865, *ibid.,* no. 33.

[4] Same to same, Berlin, 2 March 1865, *ibid.,* n. 30. See also C. CLARK, *Franz Joseph and Bismarck. The Diplomacy of Austria Before the War of 1866,* "Harvard Historical Studies," XXXVI (Cambridge, 1934), pp. 196–198.

[5] Zuylen to Cremers, Berlin, 11 March 1865, RBZ, Pruisen/1865, no. 753. "I said that

He was further convinced of this when he learned that the Vienna cabinet had formally rejected Bismarck's demands *in toto*. The immediate effect of the development was a temporary suspension of all negotiations between the two powers. As to the motive for the Austrian decision, Benedetti discounted the belief held by many observers in Berlin that Austria simply did not consider the time auspicious for demanding and obtaining from Prussia compensation commensurate with an Austrian renunciation of all claims and titles in Schleswig-Holstein. These observers presumed that the Austrian government counted on a situation in the future when Prussia, desiring at once to take over the duchies, perhaps because of public pressure, might agree more willingly to compensation demands. While rejecting this thesis, Benedetti admitted that he was unable to offer another explanation. He doubted that Austria seriously considered opposing Prussia's claims, in view of Prussian military and naval preponderance in the duchies. Should Prussia decide to terminate the situation by unilateral action, which could conceivably lead to conflict, Benedetti thought it imperative that the French government carefully assess the entire situation and formulate its policy in the light of the findings.[1] Nonintervention, as Benedetti recommended, was by and large the attitude of the imperial government, until the Sadowa *dénouement* demanded a decision.

In late March 1865, Ambassador Benedetti witnessed a new phase opening in the Schleswig-Holstein issue when the secondary states, in particular Bavaria, were making plans to bring the problem before the diet.[2] It was expected in Berlin that a motion would be made to invite Austria and Prussia to indicate the stage of the negotiations between them and to declare their intentions. Bismarck expected that a subsequent motion would then be passed recommending that the two powers come to an understanding and settle the future status of the duchies. He gave Benedetti every reason to assume that the Prussian government would not oppose such a development and that it would emphasize its conciliatory attitude at Frankfurt; indeed the ambassador thought that Bismarck had already begun to lend a more peaceable character

France was waiting for the moment in which Prussia annexes the Elbe-Duchies whole or in part in order to ask for compensation on the Rhine" (R. von DALWIGK ZU LICHTENFELS, *Die Tagebücher... aus den Jahren 1860–1871*, ed. W. Schüssler, "Deutsche Geschichtsquellen des 19. Jahrhunderts," II [Stuttgart, 1920], p. 172). For an account of French efforts in Vienna to sharpen the Austro-Prussian differences, see GEUSS, p. 119.

[1] Benedetti to Drouyn de Lhuys, Berlin, 13 March 1865, FAE CP, Prusse/351, no. 37.
[2] CLARK, pp. 206–215.

to his comments on the controversy with Austria. He cautioned, however, that Bismarck would not agree to a settlement suggested by the diet which would run counter to the aspirations of the Prussian government. Apart from the arguments which the minister-president would muster to reject an adverse vote, Benedetti noted that Bismarck was contemplating the introduction of a new factor into the controversy. Apparently satisfied with the popular reaction to Prussian propaganda in the duchies,[1] he might present a proposal calling for a meeting of the diets of the two duchies, in order to let them intervene in the debates. Far from regarding this as a concession to the principle of national self-determination, Benedetti labeled it a political weapon, to be used only if propitious to Bismarck's ambitions.[2] Despite the minister-president's public manifestation of his conciliatory attitude, the ambassador at no time discounted his resolution to pursue his goal, even in the event of an armed conflict in Germany. He was convinced that Bismarck was not alone in his determination; he believed that the king, influenced by the members of his military cabinet, would support Bismarck to the limit.[3]

As soon as the exact text of the Bavarian motion was known in Berlin,[4] Benedetti realized that Bismarck had misjudged the determination of the Bavarian government. Rather than simply calling for a statement from Prussia and Austria, the motion requested that the administration of the duchies be at once turned over to the duke of Augustenburg. Despite the fact that it did not touch on the claims of the various pretenders, the motion was clearly directed against Prussia's pretensions. The very fact that the administration of the duchies was to be turned over to a third party, one openly supported by Austria to boot, was sufficient to arouse the unrelenting opposition of the Prussian cabinet. Already on the following day, Sunday, 26 March, Benedetti was in a position to relate to Drouyn de Lhuys the first indication of Bismarck's reaction to the Bavarian motion.[5] Not

---

[1] *Ibid.*, pp. 200–206.

[2] Benedetti to Drouyn de Lhuys, Berlin, 22 March 1865, FAE CP, Prusse/351, no. 39.

[3] Same to same, Berlin, 24 March 1865, *ibid.*, no. 40. Benedetti probably gained this conviction in conversation with the king during the birthday reception at the palace (Napier to Russell, Berlin, 23 March 1865, PRO FO 64/574, no. 74).

[4] On 19 March, Mensdorff informed Bismarck of the Austrian plan. He revealed the substance of the Bavarian motion, calling for the endorsement of Augustenburg. He also indicated that an Austrian resolution would propose the transfer of the duchies to Augustenburg, subject to Prussian acquiescence (CLARK, p. 208).

[5] Bismarck insisted that he had been misled by the Austrian government, that the diet in dealing with the resolution would exceed its competency, and that Austria had violated

only had the minister-president criticized the action of the Bavarian cabinet, but he had also denied the authority of the diet to dispose of the administration of the duchies. He had informed Károlyi that the Prussian government would combat the Bavarian motion step by step. Benedetti also knew that the legislative machinery would lend itself to Bismarck's designs of procrastination. Moreover, the presence of Prussian military forces in the duchies would make it virtually impossible for the diet to impose its decision upon the Berlin cabinet. Whether the Austrian government would persist in the course initiated by the Bavarian motion was a consideration which he did not feel qualified as yet to evaluate.[1]

On Saturday, 8 April, Benedetti had occasion to discuss with the minister-president the adoption of the Bavarian motion by the diet two days earlier.[2] Bismarck seemed little concerned over the event which he considered a sterile attempt and one which could not harm the interests of Prussia. More important, according to Benedetti, was the question whether the move in the diet was a prelude to new and more cogent attempts to force Prussia to heed Austria's wishes. While Bismarck did not expect the Vienna cabinet to assume an outright hostile attitude, he did fear that anti-Prussian influences might gain the support of Francis Joseph for a more determined policy toward Prussia.[3] It might be possible, Benedetti thought, that Austria was hopeful of re-establishing her ascendancy over the German secondary states. Yet the attitude of these governments was far from unanimous in support of Austria.[4] He knew from Bismarck that the Berlin cabinet was prepared to see the issue transferred to the field of battle. The minister-president expected to win Italy's support in such an event, and he apparently had already intimated as much in Turin.[5] Benedetti felt that Bismarck's indifference to the diet proceedings was shared by King William and the possibility that the latter might go to Schleswig for the inauguration of monuments to the Prussian dead could be considered a public manifestation of that attitude.[6]

her agreements with Prussia by entering into combinations with other parties (ibid., pp. 208–209; BGW, V, 137–138, 144, 145).

[1] Benedetti to Drouyn de Lhuys, Berlin, 25 March 1865, FAE CP, Prusse/351, no. 44; same to same, Berlin, 26 March 1865, ibid., no. 45; same to same, Berlin, 5 April 1865, ibid., no. 53.

[2] CLARK, pp. 209–210.

[3] For a summary of the conflicting schools of thought relative to Austria's policy, see ibid., pp. 211–215.

[4] Ibid., pp. 216–217.

[5] Benedetti to Drouyn de Lhuys, Berlin, 9 April 1865, FAE CP, Prusse/351, no. 57.

[6] Same to same, Berlin, 15 April 1865, ibid,. no. 59.

The short lull in the affairs of the duchies was about to end. On Wednesday, 19 April, Bismarck informed Benedetti that he had proposed to Austria the convocation of a representative assembly of Schleswig-Holstein. The ambassador received the news with the expected satisfaction, believing that it demonstrated a desire to respect the wishes of the population, a course continuously urged by the imperial government. He assured Bismarck that the proposal would meet with support in France. Bismarck told the ambassador that he would reserve his detailed plans until he had received an answer from the Austrian government. Benedetti was apparently concerned over the possibility that Bismarck might think the simple convocation of an assembly enough to satisfy French wishes. He found it difficult to assess Bismarck's intentions with accuracy. It was indeed difficult to decide whether Bismarck was merely trying to keep Austria off balance, and conceivably exploit Hungarian demands on Vienna, or whether he hoped to influence France and the secondary states. The ambassador was not certain either as to the possibility that British and Russian pressure was influencing Prussia's attitude. For, in spite of the minister-president's remarks about Prussian determination, Prussia could not afford to ignore the views of the great powers relative to the duchies issue.[1] Only recently had Benedetti received another indication of his own government's attitude.

We remain convinced that the only means to conciliate the interests which appertain to the question of the duchies would be to keep in mind the desires of the populations. It is well understood, moreover, that this project would imply the division by nationalities and the restitution of the Danish part of Schleswig to Denmark. To the extent that the final solution would satisfy this principle, we could acquiesce in the arrangements which would result. Our language in this respect has not varied.[2]

When Bismarck had informed Benedetti of his proposal to Vienna for the convocation of an assembly he had not discussed its role in detail. He remedied the omission soon after and told the ambassador that the assembly would determine, together with Austria and Prussia, the conditions under which these two powers would abjure the rights obtained through the defeat of Denmark. This determination would also cover the manner in which the two powers were to be given indemnities and, in the case of Prussia, concessions to protect Germany against attacks from the north. This proceeding would necessitate a prior accord on the manner in which the assembly would be convoked

---

[1] Same to same, Berlin, 21 April 1865, *ibid.*, no. 63.
[2] Drouyn de Lhuys to Benedetti, Paris, 27 April 1865, *ibid.*, no. 37.

and on the propositions to be put before it. Benedetti was aware of the fact that Bismarck's proposal did not assure an immediate solution, but he was genuinely disturbed about the minister-president's apparent conciliatory spirit. Indeed, Bismarck had even renounced his ambition to annex the duchies. He had told Benedetti that Prussia could not risk a war which she would have to enter under unfavorable conditions. He had attributed the new policy to a change of attitude on the part of France. He allegedly had been told that France, in case of a conflict between Austria and Prussia, would side with the former in order to obtain a settlement of the Italian question, *i.e.*, the peaceful transfer of Venetia to Italy. Benedetti preferred to ignore Bismarck's trial balloon and asked for instructions from the foreign office.[1]

On 30 April Benedetti learned that the Austrian government had accepted Bismarck's overture in principle.[2] However, the acceptance was made conditional upon the mutual approval of the propositions to be submitted to the assembly of the duchies. Bismarck did not raise any objections; he merely indicated that the arrangements to be eventually concluded between Prussia and the duchies should not require, like the propositions, Austria's consent and should be treated as an entirely different matter. The possibility of an Austro-Prussian *rapprochement* did not fade in spite of the controversy engendered, in late April, by the transfer of the Prussian naval station to Kiel.[3]

Committed to a policy which endeavored to separate Austria and Prussia, Benedetti looked with little favor upon the *rapprochement* between the two powers. The ambassador was also apprehensive about the future of North Schleswig, because he feared that Bismarck was now far more interested in a settlement with Austria than in the wishes of the French government.[4] Only a short time ago Bismarck's course had been such as to dispel all fears of an *entente* with Austria – now such a development threatened to become reality. Still, the minister-president's position was not a brilliant one; he was not likely to find the Austrian cabinet disposed to grant all the con-

[1] Benedetti to Drouyn de Lhuys, Berlin, 28 April 1865, *ibid.*, no. 66; same to same, [Berlin], 30 April 1865, *ODG*, Vl, 191–193. Cf. Drouyn de Lhuys to Benedetti, Paris, 3 May 1865, *ibid.*, 199–203; Nothomb to Rogier, Berlin, 29 April 1865, BAE CP, Prusse/23, Pt. I, no. 48. The pessimistic report of 18 April, presaging a change in the attitude of France toward Prussia, may have caused Bismarck's remarks (GEUSS, p. 125).
[2] The Austrian decision was made after France and the secondary states had urged acceptance (CLARK, p. 219).
[3] Benedetti to Drouyn de Lhuys, Berlin, 30 April 1865, FAE CP, Prusse/351, no. 68. For a brief account of the issue, see CLARK, pp. 220–225.
[4] Benedetti to Drouyn de Lhuys, [Berlin], 30 April 1865, *ODG*, VI, 191–193.

cessions necessary to strengthen his own position in Prussia. In any event, it seemed to Benedetti that the French government could still wait a while longer before seeking an arrangement of its own with Prussia and thereby preventing an alliance between the two German powers. He hoped that Bismarck's ambition might soon again involve him in a controversy with Austria which would inhibit the development of an alliance.[1] The repeated references of the ambassador to the fluctuating nature of the Austro-Prussian negotiations may perhaps point to an over-cautious trait in Benedetti's character; he appeared to model his observations along the lines of those expressed by his government, in the tradition of the disciplined bureaucrat. However, imagination or bold suggestions might have precipitated a less fortuitous result – at a time when France hoped to profit from an Austro-Prussian dispute without stepping out of her passive role.

Benedetti was to discover in a note from the imperial foreign office that the spectre of Austro-Prussian collaboration was indeed taken seriously in Paris. Assuming that Goltz must have warned Bismarck about a change in French policy,[2] the foreign minister took issue with Bismarck's claim that the shift of the French cabinet had forced him to alter his stand. Drouyn de Lhuys saw in the determined opposition in Vienna to the Prussian aspirations the real reason for Bismarck's new course. He asked the ambassador to present those observations to him, so as to leave no doubt in the minister-president's mind about the attitude of the imperial government.[3]

During an interview with Bismarck on Saturday evening, 6 May, Benedetti invited Bismarck to read the text of Drouyn de Lhuys' letter. The minister-president followed the ambassador's suggestion and, in reply to the unequivocal language of the letter, he insisted that he personally had never doubted the friendly disposition of France but that Goltz's allegations had been so ominous that it had become imperative for the Prussian government to reappraise its position. Yet, apart from the letter of the minister, Benedetti had still another communication to make.[4] He announced, "I am authorized in effect to ask you

---

[1] Same to same, Berlin, 30 April 1865, FAE CP, Prusse/351, no. 69; same to same, Berlin, 30 April 1865, ODG, VI, 191–193.

[2] See above p. 22.

[3] Drouyn de Lhuys to Benedetti, Paris, 3 May 1865, ODG, VI, 199–203. It is interesting to note that Thiers, on 13 April, had sharply criticized French policy toward Prussia. Thiers warned against Prussian ambitions in Germany and emphasized the likelihood of a change in the balance of power which might adversely affect French interests.

[4] He was authorized to make this statement by a telegraphic dispatch from Drouyn de Lhuys, on the previous evening, 5 May; no record of this telegram exists either in the

to tell us plainly what you ask of us and what you offer us; we are ready to listen to you and to examine with you what could or should be our relations in all these eventualities." [1] This overture of the French government apparently caught Bismarck by surprise, although he may have hoped for as much from his trial balloon a week earlier. To Benedetti's startling remarks he finally replied ,"We ask you for benevolent neutrality, both during the negotiations with Austria and later, should they lead to a rupture." [2] When the ambassador asked him if he had no proposition to offer to France, Bismarck replied that he was not prepared at the moment to do so. In the light of the frankness with which the French government sought to demonstrate its friendly disposition, the minister-president evidently felt obliged to offer a further explanation. He told Benedetti that the Prussian government had concluded that the advantages of an outright annexation of the duchies did not warrant a war which might be difficult to justify. Benedetti had predicted the possibility of such a development and had stressed that the naval, military and commercial concessions now demanded by the Prussian government would equal the benefits to be derived from complete incorporation. At the same time, he emphasized Prussia's determination to gain these concessions at all cost. Should Austria refuse to approve them, then the French government might find Prussia ready to submit certain propositions to it. Bismarck then added:

In that case, everything would authorize us to make overtures to you, and we would probably ask you to make an accord with us. We know that we would have to pay the price for the assistance which you would lend us; but you realize that the king refuses to envisage that or to debate an eventuality which might place him in the obligation to abandon German populations and territories [i.e., the Rhine].[3]

The fact that Bismarck made a future offer to France contingent upon the king's views illustrates again the problem Benedetti faced when dealing with Bismarck on hypothetical questions. The problem of verifying the king's attitude was always confronting the ambassador and he was usually reduced to conjectures. He thought that the king was as yet unprepared to assume the responsibility for a war with Austria

---

archives in Paris or in the embassy. The content is clearly indicated by Benedetti's report (ibid., 212, ft. 1).

[1] Benedetti to Drouyn de Lhuys, Berlin, 7 May 1865, ibid., 210–217.

[2] Ibid. Bismarck's caution was justified, for he feared that Napoleon would use a treaty document to precipitate an Austro-Prussian conflict. He indicated that only in case of adverse developments in a war against Austria would Prussia be prepared to sign a pact with France and pay the price (GEUSS, p. 129).

[3] Benedetti to Drouyn de Lhuys, Berlin, 7 May 1865, ODG, VI, 210–217.

and for the sacrifices which such a conflict would ask of the Prussian people.[1] Benedetti agreed with the foreign minister that it was the realization of this difficulty and the determination of the Vienna cabinet which had prompted the change in Bismarck's attitude. The ambassador believed that the reversal was thus fully sanctioned by the monarch, and he did not think that Bismarck was merely using the king's attitude as a screen to veil his own designs. In reference to the overture Benedetti felt that King William would show little enthusiasm to collaborate with France and isolate Austria; the ambassador was under no illusion that William would think the price too high. No doubt the fear that France might demand the Rhineland was enough to arouse William's opposition. Benedetti believed that it was not at all certain that the king would support his minister if the latter adopted a policy of collaboration with France.[2] A war between the Hapsburg and Hohenzollern dynasties might be considered a fratricidal struggle, benefitting only non-German powers, and William might be reluctant to give the signal for it. Although Benedetti was aware of the rivalry between the two houses, as well as of the past conflicts between them, he wished that his government might not minimize those factors and traditions which bound the two powers together.

Benedetti's observations may be considered a slight critique of the overture, which he had been instructed to make. No friend of Austria, he did exhibit nevertheless impartiality of mind by his advice that a *hasty* offer to Prussia might do far more harm than good for the goal France was pursuing. Instead he continued to think it best for France to maintain her vigilance without going beyond it:

If I dared express my advice, I would say that we should give satisfaction to Bismarck's desire, which binds us in no way to his policy, to observe the strictest neutrality while showing ourselves benevolent to Prussia [and] which would not oblige us to be ill-disposed toward Austria, and to await events. As modest and loyal as its motive may be, every effort which we tender to influence the resolutions of the court at Berlin would awaken at once in its mind, as in all of Germany, defiance and uneasiness; our abstention, I would say even our indifference, can by itself contribute to the development of the dissentions which separate the two great Germanic powers.... Before thinking of making an accord of any kind with Prussia, we must wait until she is fatally condemned to it by her ambition or by her mistakes; I add that the most essential interests of Austria safeguard us against the success of her rival, with whom we would then have to preoccupy ourselves.[3]

---

[1] As of March, Bismarck had won over William to the idea of annexation (PFLANZE, p. 257).
[2] Benedetti to Drouyn de Lhuys, Berlin, 7 May 1865, *ODG*, VI, 210–217.
[3] *Ibid.*

At no time had Benedetti disavowed the course his government was following nor the ambition it harbored to see the 1815 treaties destroyed. Furthermore, he did not deny the fact that to obtain the coveted Rhine frontier France might find it expedient to make an alliance with either of the German powers, his preference being of course obvious. His objection to the present overture was one touching only upon the timing of the move. It seemed preferable to Benedetti that his government retain its freedom of action as long as possible, when its conditions for making an alliance might be readily acceptable to the alliance partner. The fluctuations in the Prussian policy toward Austria emphasized the need for caution. Alarm at what he considered tactical shifts on the part of Bismarck was as out of place in his opinion as relaxation of French vigilance.[1] One can assume that he was pleased about Bismarck's decision not to pursue the French overture any further at this time.

Benedetti was not disturbed to see the Austro-Prussian efforts for a settlement continue. On 9 May, he learned that the two powers were exchanging views regarding the constitution of a representative assembly destined to participate in the search for a solution of the duchies question. Bismarck favored inviting the estates of the two duchies to recommed first whether a special assembly should be convoked and to advise on the election of such an assembly. He apparently was also anxious that the duke of Augustenburg leave the duchies during the prospective election period.[2] The ambassador pointed out, however, that thus far Bismarck had refused to promise not to offer to, and solicit from, the assembly any proposition or combination outside an Austro-Prussian accord on that question. Benedetti expected this point of controversy to remain for some time an obstacle to concerted action on the duchies problem.[3] Indeed, ten days later he learned that the negotiations had not been fruitful thus far. Bismarck's views on the election of the assembly had not been accepted in Vienna, and Mensdorff had refused to invite the duke of Augustenburg to withdraw from the duchies. He had not denied Prussia's right to solicit arrangements with an assembly outside an Austro-Prussian accord. While the ambassador's prediction was upset on this particular point, it did not shake his belief that a lasting accord was as distant as ever. The dis-

---

[1] *Ibid.*

[2] Bismarck's demand for the expulsion of Augustenburg from the duchies was calculated to embarrass the Austrian government, which had supported his cause in the diet. (CLARK, pp. 237–238; *BGW*, V, 178 ff.).

[3] Benedetti to Drouyn de Lhuys, Berlin, 9 May 1865, FAE CP, Prusse/352, no. 72.

trust demonstrated by both cabinets so far had made for an atmosphere ill-suited for the evolution of a settlement involving major interests of both parties.[1] On 25 May the Prussian government rejected the Austrian counter-proposals and renewed its demands that the duke of Augustenburg leave the duchies during the election period. To emphasize his determination of maintaining Prussia's interests, Bismarck also notified the Austrian government that he would also submit a list of the war expenditures, which the duchies presumably would have to pay, to the proposed assembly. Benedetti suspected that Bismarck hoped to strengthen support for union with Prussia, since the prospect of escaping heavy reparations would increase the sympathies for annexation.[2]

While the situation seemed now to be deteriorating Benedetti heard of rumors about a summer meeting between William and Francis Joseph, to take place at Carlsbad, for the settlement of the duchies question. Bismarck, however, claimed that the hostile attitude of the Austrian government would not permit the Prussian monarch to accept an invitation to such a meeting. His intransigent stand persuaded Benedetti, and his colleagues as well according to the ambassador, that no accord between the two powers was near at hand.[3] The accuracy of Benedetti's report on the attitude of the Prussian government was to some extent substantiated by other revelations.[4] For instance, as early as 19 May Bismarck had planned to use General Edwin von Manteuffel's courtesy visit to Vienna to impress upon the Austrian cabinet the seriousness of the situation.[5] The general's visit had now been postponed until after the crown council meeting which took place in Berlin on Monday, 29 May, and in which the possibility of war was considered at length. Most of the king's advisers demanded that the February conditions be met, or that Prussia annex the duchies, if necessary by war.[6] Bismarck argued that war with Austria was inevitable, that the present situation favored Prussia, and that a military victory would bring her the duchies as well as hegemony in North Germany. However, Bismarck preferred to leave the decision entirely to the king, who decided against force, lest it would precipitate Ger-

---

[1] Same to same, Berlin, 20 May 1865, *ibid.*, no. 80.
[2] Same to same, Berlin, 27 May 1865, *ibid.*, no. 83.
[3] *Ibid.*
[4] H. VON SYBEL, *Die Begründung des deutschen Reiches durch Wilhelm I.* (Munich, 1892), IV, 116–120.
[5] Manteuffel was to assume command of the occupation forces in Schleswig-Holstein.
[6] The bellicose attitude of Roon and Moltke is less pronounced in their private correspondence (CLARK, p. 239, ft. 17).

many into civil war.[1] Yet, the signs pointing toward a crisis continued to increase. What the outcome would be not the most careful observer could predict; the issues at stake contained far too many imponderables. Reviewing the past recrimination between Berlin and Vienna, Benedetti drew attention to Bismarck's contention that the Austrian government was actively furthering the candidacy of the duke of Augustenburg in order to frustrate the advantages the Prussian government was seeking to obtain in the duchies. His claim that the Prussian government could consider itself released from the obligation to reach a prior accord with Austria on the duchies question was not accepted in Vienna. Although the ambassador had been informed that the acrimonious correspondence of late between the governments would cease, he did not think that its effects could be eradicated quickly.[2] The abandonment of all intention to send Manteuffel on a visit to Vienna, lest it be interpreted as a sign of Prussian weakness, was taken as another indication that the situation was beginning to reach a critical point.[3]

The tension between Austria and Prussia and the spectre of war also provoked rumors of French expansionist schemes, presumably on the basis of a Franco-Dutch accord. Bismarck questioned Benedetti concerning reports from The Hague and Brussels that France and Holland had come to an agreement on the division of Belgium. The ambassador speculated whether the minister-president was now entertaining plans for an agreement with France, in view of the tense situation in Germany, which might compensate France for Prussian expansion. Benedetti was particularly interested in the fact that Bismarck was hopeful of French expansion northward rather than toward the Rhine. The minister-president had remarked:

I conceive... among other things, that France might think about annexing countries which would be easy for her to assimilate, like Belgium or the French part of Switzerland, [and] the possession of which would assure her of much more suitable frontiers to cover her against all aggression.[4]

---

[1] *Aufzeichnung Moltkes über die Ministerkonferenz am 29. Mai 1865, APP*, VI, 179–180. "Bismarck sought 'for now'... the peaceful solution, but counted on war in the future – not over Schleswig-Holstein, but over the German question" (A. O. MEYER, "Der preussische Kronrat vom 29. Mai 1865," *Gesamtdeutsche Vergangenheit. Festgabe für Heinrich Ritter von Srbik* [Munich, 1938], p. 318); CLARK, p. 240, ft. 20; STADELMANN, pp. 29–31.

[2] Benedetti to Drouyn de Lhuys, Berlin, 3 June 1865, FAE CP, Prusse/352, no. 87.

[3] *Ibid.*, no. 88 The Austrians indeed had interpreted the projected Manteuffel visit to Vienna as a Prussian olive-branch (CLARK, p. 241).

[4] Benedetti to Drouyn de Lhuys, Berlin, 29 May 1865, *ODG*, VI, 266–267. Cf. Magnus to Bismarck, St. Petersburg, 25 May 1865, *APP*, VI, 163–164; GEUSS, pp. 130–133.

Benedetti was not prepared to discuss the question of French expansion or compensation and advised the minister-president that he could not take up the topic without having instructions from his government.[1]

Ambassador Benedetti interrupted his duties in Berlin in early June to make a short trip to Corsica. He arrived in Paris on Monday, 5 June, coming from Cologne, and continued his journey the very next day.[2] He was again back in Paris by 19 June, when he had an audience with the emperor,[3] an interview undoubtedly devoted to the affairs in Germany. Although no record of their conversation has been found, there is no reason to assume that it was more than a routine consultation. The ambassador returned to Berlin on 22 June, and his subsequent activities do not suggest that he had been given new and different instructions.[4]

From the *chargé d'affaires*, Edouard Lefèbvre de Béhaine, Benedetti learned that Bismarck had lately appeared very confident about prospects of an advantageous settlement with Austria on the duchies question. The fact that the Vienna cabinet had asked to be informed about William's arrival at Carlsbad seemed to be the cause for Bismarck's optimism.[5] He apparently thought that the Austrian cabinet was prepared to compose its differences with Prussia, and he expected Prussia to reap all the advantages. The minister-president had also indicated that he hoped to win French support through giving his assent to retrocession of North Schleswig.[6] Benedetti met Bismarck later in the day and discovered nothing that in any way altered the impressions of the *chargé d'affaires*.[7] The minister-president left Berlin on the following Sunday, 25 June, and it became increasingly difficult for the ambassador to keep abreast of the course the Prussian cabinet was following in these critical times. A conversation with Hermann von Thile, undersecretary of state, on 29 June, was spent in a repudiation of Prussian charges that Drouyn de Lhuys had been highly critical of Prussia's attitude on the duchies question. Benedetti insisted that the

---

[1] Benedetti to Drouyn de Lhuys, Berlin, 29 May 1865, *ODG*, VI, 266–267. "The famous secret treaty between France and Holland for the partition of Belgium is a vision" (Drouyn de Lhuys to Benedetti, Paris, 3 June 1865, *ibid.*, 269).

[2] *Ibid.*, 266.

[3] E. D'HAUTERIVE, *Napoléon III et le Prince Napoléon* (Paris, 1925), p. 381.

[4] Benedetti to Drouyn de Lhuys, Berlin, 27 June 1865, FAE CP, Prusse/352, no. 101.

[5] For the exchange of notes, initiated by Austria on 5 June, see SYBEL, IV, 96 ff.; CLARK, pp. 242 ff.

[6] Lefèbvre de Béhaine to Drouyn de Lhuys, Berlin, 12 June 1865, FAE CP, Prusse/352, no. 92; same to same, Berlin, 19 June 1865, *ibid.*, no. 99.

[7] Benedetti to Drouyn de Lhuys, Berlin, 27 June 1865, *ibid.*, no. 101.

French government was not in the least hostile or critical of Prussian policy. "He added... that France was still determined to leave the solution of the Schleswig-Holstein question exclusively to Prussia, and that it would be pleased if such [a solution] would result in a fashion as much as possible in accordance with Prussia's interest." [1]

Although the situation was rather serious in Germany, the departure of Bismarck for Carlsbad had become the signal for the exodus of the diplomats from the capital. A few days after the minister-president, Benedetti left for Bad Kissingen where he planned to spend his summer vacation. The fact that all Prussian diplomatic correspondence was being transmitted directly to Bismarck made it very difficult to follow events from Berlin. Moreover, Bismarck's stay at Carlsbad was expected to be rather short; thus Benedetti's decision not to follow him seems to have had some justification. The zeal with which Austria and Prussia sought adoption of their respective points of view had kept them still apart, and Bismarck had given no indication before his departure that he would yield to Austrian pressure. Indeed, conversations between the minister-president and the Italian envoy had caused Benedetti to suspect that Bismarck was making preparations in case the talks with Austria should lead to a rupture between them.[2] However, he did become convinced that a meeting between William and Francis Joseph would take place, despite the assertions of Bismarck.[3] The ambassador had by now ample reason not to accept statements by the minister-president at face-value in each and every case. In conversation with a friend he gave vent to his impatience with Bismarck's unreliability and self-assurance. He minimized the Prussian threats against Austria and rejected Bismarck's apparent belief that the Italian government would quickly enter into an Austro-Prussian conflict: "He [Bismarck] counts on an attack by Italy on Austria, but he is mistaken in that matter. I tell him that [Italy] will not move." [4] As events were to prove the following year, the Italian government insisted very decidedly on a precise arrangement with Prussia relative

---

[1] *Promemoria des auswärtigen Amtes*, Berlin, 29 June 1865, *APP*, VI, 218–219. "He [Benedetti] asserts that the affairs of Mexico, Algiers, and the internal conditions absorb Paris so much that hardly any attention is being paid anymore to the duchies question, and he doubts that his Berlin reports are being read with attention (Watzdorff [Saxon *chargé d'affaires*] to Beust, Berlin, 26 June 1865, *APP*, VI, 219, ft. 4).

[2] Benedetti to Drouyn de Lhuys, Berlin, 27 June 1865, FAE CP, Prusse/352, no. 101. For Prussian military preparations, see STADELMANN, pp. 31–37.

[3] Benedetti to Drouyn de Lhuys, Berlin, 27 June 1865, FAE CP, Prusse/352, no. 101.

[4] Werner to Mensdorff, Dresden, 5 July 1865, *QDPO*, IV, 767–768.

to a war against Austria. One can assume that the ambassador would not have been found wrong in 1865 had war broken out.[1]

It was during Benedetti's vacation at Bad Kissingen that a compromise on the Schleswig-Holstein question was worked out between Prussia and Austria.[2] The resignation of the Austrian cabinet on 27 June, with the exception of Mensdorff, and Bismarck's note à bref délai of 12 July to Vienna constituted the initial steps in the settlement of a dispute which had been steadily mounting toward a crisis.[3] On Thursday, 20 July, the Prussian monarch had arrived in Regensburg on his way from Carlsbad to Gastein and had summoned Goltz, who was also vacationing at Bad Kissingen, for a conference. On his return Goltz told Benedetti that William expected to meet Francis Joseph toward the end of July. The king and his entourage, especially Manteuffel and Gustav von Alvensleben, were firmly resolved to maintain all the demands formulated in the past by Bismarck. Benedetti heard with great interest Goltz's statement that the meeting with the king, on 21 July, had also been devoted to a consideration of measures to be taken if the coming Gastein meeting were to be fruitless.[4] Apparently the optimism shown publicly in Berlin before Benedetti's departure had given way to a more realistic estimate of future developments. Should it become apparent that no accord could result from the Gastein meeting, the first step of the government would be to provide the basis necessary for a mobilization of the entire Prussian army. Goltz did not minimize the significance to be attributed to the Gastein meeting; apparently no possibilities had been overlooked at Regensburg and Goltz was requested to be back in Paris by the time William and Francis Joseph were to meet, in case the situation called for talks with the French government.[5] Should no accord be reached with Austria, Goltz was to open negotiations for a neutrality pact between France and Prussia and, if deemed advisable, negotiate for an alliance between the two powers. Benedetti did not neglect to relay Goltz's remarks to the foreign ministry. In itself a commendable fact, he did not seem to think it necessary, however, to break off his vacation and return to

---

[1] Note below Benedetti's role in this respect during March-April 1866.

[2] For a full account of the Austro-Prussian negotiations culminating in the Bad Gastein convention, see CLARK, pp. 257–297.

[3] Lefèbvre de Béhaine to Drouyn de Lhuys, Berlin, 13 July 1865, FAE CP, Prusse/352, no. 107; same to same, Berlin, 15 July 1865, ibid., no. 108.

[4] Benedetti to Drouyn de Lhuys, Bad Kissingen, 22 July 1865, ODG, VI, 347–348. Cf. QDPO, IV, 151–154.

[5] Benedetti to Drouyn de Lhuys, Bad Kissingen, 22 July 1865, ODG, VI, 347–348.

Berlin to await developments. It is surprising that he should have minimized the significance of the coming events by remaining at Bad Kissingen but his return to Berlin might not have placed him in any better position.[1]

The attitude of the French government during this period was of course an important element in Bismarck's considerations. He was anxious to check the views of the imperial cabinet and ascertain whether or not Benedetti's assurance of French sympathy was still valid. In his inquiry, addressed to Goltz, Bismarck made reference to a very promising statement by Benedetti, without indicating to Goltz the time he had made it:

> Benedetti said to me while I was still in Berlin, "The benevolent neutrality of the emperor is assured to you without any compensation." He had received a telegram from Paris which he read to me, and in which the readiness of France to make an alliance with us and to receive our propositions in that respect was pronounced.[2]

Bismarck's reference was to Benedetti's overture of 6 May, but Goltz was unable to evaluate Benedetti's act properly. His supposition that the emperor might have empowered the ambassador to stress France's benevolence toward Prussia, without having informed his foreign minister, is negated by the fact that Benedetti reported on 9 May to Drouyn de Lhuys on the overture to Bismarck. The content of that same communication denies Goltz's other tentative explanation that Benedetti, in an effort to widen the breach between the two Germanic powers, might have offered the assurance on his own authority. Unable to verify the facts, Goltz could not decide whether Benedetti's remarks did agree with the views of the imperial government.[3] His implied skepticism suggests that since his return to Paris he had reason to doubt the continued friendship of France. But while he pondered Benedetti's remarks to the minister-president, the Schleswig-Holstein compromise was being worked out between Bismarck and Gustav Blome, the Austrian negotiator. The Gastein convention brought to an end, at least temporarily, the long and fluctuating negotiations between

---

[1] *QDPO*, IV, 153. Usedom wrote that according to Nigra: "The chances have never been so favorable for Prussia and for all the plans she might be making for her military, political and territorial grandeur; because never will one see on the French throne a sovereign more disposed to remain quiet, or who would sell his neutrality at a more modest price to Prussia" (Usedom to William I, Florence, 28 July 1865, *APP*, VI, 278–280).

[2] Bismarck to Goltz, Gastein, 4 August 1865, H. ONCKEN, *Die Rheinpolitik Kaiser Napoleons III. von 1863 bis 1870 und der Ursprung des Krieges von 1870/71* (Stuttgart, 1926), I, 49, ft. 1.

[3] Goltz to Bismarck, Paris, 4 August 1865, *ibid.*, 49.

the two Germanic powers. The agreement received its final approval when William and Francis Joseph ratified it in Salzburg on 20 August 1865.[1]

The rapid, if temporary, settlement of the duchies issue was unexpected in Paris, despite the letter of Ambassador Benedetti from Bad Kissingen announcing that a *dénouement* was in the offing. News of the accord found Benedetti still on vacation. He was unable to inform his government as to the details of the talks and the convention. The fact that the scene of the negotiations was a small mountain resort made it even difficult for the *chargé d'affaires* in Berlin to relay all the desired facts. His main source of information was Count Friedrich Albert Eulenburg, minister of the interior, who was unacquainted with all the details himself. However, information on the accord made it obvious that Gastein represented a Prussian victory. While joint sovereignty over the duchies was continued, Prussia obtained the exclusive right to administer Schleswig, while her possession in Holstein of Kiel, Friedrichsort, two military routes, the postal and telegraphic services along the main communication artery, as well as the right to a canal, gave her the means to exercise a certain degree of influence in the affairs of that duchy. Moreover, Austria was obligated not to alienate her rights in Holstein without the approval of Prussia. In addition, Prussia had now complete possession of Lauenburg, subject to an indemnity to Austria. The principles of the indivisibility and of the union of the duchies were to be maintained. Eulenburg had made it apparent that sooner or later Prussia would use this doctrine to absorb Holstein in turn. Relative to the retrocession of North Schleswig he had maintained an ominous silence.[2]

Despite the highly important developments of the late summer, Ambassador Benedetti had not considered it necessary to break off his vacation. Unlike Goltz he remained on his vacation and apparently went to Paris in mid-October before resuming his duties in Berlin. He was no doubt informed, during his stay in Paris, of the developments subsequent to the Austro-Prussian accord. The fact that this compromise represented a setback for imperial policy and for Benedetti's

[1] For the text of the Gastein convention, see *ODG*, VI, 463–466. It is rather revealing of Bismarck's unjustified criticisms of Goltz, that the latter was blamed for the necessity to conclude the convention. Bismarck claimed that Goltz's uncertain estimate about the course of French policy toward Prussia had forced William to come to terms with Austria and continue an undesirable arrangement in the duchies (GEUSS, pp. 133–135). Cf. *BGW*, V, 233 ff., 242 ff., 282 ff.; STADELMANN, pp. 43 ff.

[2] Lefèbvre de Béhaine to Drouyn de Lhuys, Berlin, 21 August 1865, FAE CP, Prusse/352, no. 121. Cf. E. KESSEL, "Gastein," *HZ*, Heft 3, CLXXVI (December 1953), 544.

mission makes it desirable to discuss briefly the French official reaction. In a now famous circular of 29 August,[1] for the benefit of French diplomatic agents, Drouyn de Lhuys censured the two powers for having broken the treaties of Vienna and London which had regulated the *conditions d'existence* of the Danish monarchy. Instead of restoring to the most qualified pretender the heritage in question, Prussia and Austria had pre-emptively divided its administration between themselves. He indicted both powers equally for having ignored the wishes of "Germany," which had hoped to see the creation of an indivisible state of Schleswig-Holstein, separated from Denmark and ruled by a prince whose cause the secondary states had espoused. The popular candidate had been dismissed while the duchies, instead of being united, came under two separate administrations. Drouyn de Lhuys depicted the convention as being not only in conflict with the true interests of the duchies but also as preventing the self-determination of the peoples involved. The wishes of the population had been ignored and the convention carried the odium of force:

We regret to find [in the convention] no other basis than force, no other justification than the reciprocal convenience of the two shareholders. It is a practice to which Europe is no longer accustomed, and one had to look for the precedents in the worst ages of history. Violence and conquest pervert the notion of law and the conscience of peoples. Substituted for the principles which regulate the life of modern societies, they are an element of trouble and dissolution and can only upset the old order without establishing solidly any new order.[2]

The obdurate language employed by Drouyn de Lhuys left no doubt that the imperial government was violently opposed to the solution worked out at Gastein. Disappointment over the *rapprochement* between Austria and Prussia rather than moral indignation motivated the bitter condemnation; after all the encouragement given to Bismarck's annexation schemes France could scarcely qualify as the defender of the rights of the pretender, the wishes of the people and the opinions of the German secondary states. Only the remarks concerning the self-determination of the people can be admitted as being in accord with the position of the French government for, in fact, Benedetti had

---

[1] Drouyn de Lhuys to diplomatic agents, Paris, 29 August 1865, *ODG*, VI, 453–454. Only after the foreign minister had given his report on the convention was permission for issuance of the circular granted by the emperor at Fontainebleau on 27 August (see H. ROTHFRITZ, *Die Politik des preussischen Botschafters Grafen Robert von der Goltz in Paris, 1863–69*, "Abhandlungen zur mittleren und neueren Geschichte," LXXIV [Berlin, 1934], pp. 71–72).

[2] Drouyn de Lhuys to diplomatic agents, Paris, 29 August 1865, *ODG*, VI, 454. For the reaction of French public opinion, see L. CASE, *French Opinion on War and Diplomacy during the Second Empire* (Philadelphia, 1954), pp. 193–194.

constantly maintained to Bismarck the condition that North Schleswig be retroceded to Denmark.

During his stay in Paris, Benedetti also learned from the dispatches of the *chargé d'affaires* that Bismarck had reasserted his determination to retrocede North Schleswig but that he had remained vague as to the time for such a step.[1] Bismarck had also stressed the temporary nature of the convention and had voiced the hope that Prussia could ultimately annex both duchies and bring about her hegemony in Germany.[2] It was obvious that he was endeavoring to efface the adverse reaction to the Gastein convention in France and to regain French support for his aims. Trying to conciliate the imperial government, he also used the stratagem of encouraging expansion on the part of France. "[Bismarck] added that he... wished that we... would give our policy a better impetus by seeking in the sphere of action which similarity of language and race assigns us expansion of territory and influence."[3] He even hinted at an alliance between France and Prussia in exchange for which Prussia would recognize the right of France to expand "anywhere in the world where French is spoken."[4] The perusal of the *chargé d'affaires'* communications made it clear to the ambassador that the immediate future would witness efforts on the part of the Prussian government to win back the confidence and friendship of the French emperor.[5] The success or failure of these attempts, marked by the scheduled visit of Bismarck to Biarritz and Paris, would be of decisive influence on the mission he himself had been charged with.

Superficial reflection upon the Austro-Prussian accord suggests that Ambassador Benedetti had been unsuccessful in his mission thus far. The Gastein convention had brought Austria and Prussia together in a compromise of their differences over Schleswig-Holstein. However, the truce was an uneasy one and, in character with the fluctuating negotiations it concluded, it did not hold the promise of a final solution of the problem. Gastein represented only a temporary setback for French policy and therefore should not have an overriding influence on the evaluation of Benedetti's effectiveness.

---

[1] Lefèbvre de Béhaine to Drouyn de Lhuys, Berlin, 12 September 1865, FAE CP, Prusse/353, no. 129. Bismarck referred to the taking of Schleswig as "cutting ourselves a slice of the big toe" (*ibid.*).

[2] *Ibid.*, no. 130.

[3] Same to same, Berlin, 14 September 1865, *ODG*, VII, 64.

[4] Same to same, Berlin, 27 September 1865, FAE CP, Prusse/353, no. 137.

[5] Drouyn de Lhuys did accept the Prussian explanation of the provisional character of the Gastein convention (Drouyn de Lhuys to Lefèbvre de Béhaine, Paris, 23 September 1865, *ibid.*, no. 66).

Charged with the mission of preventing an *entente* between Prussia and Austria, Benedetti had entered upon his duties in Berlin with marked caution and reserve, an attitude in accord with his instructions. He made it his first task to become acquainted with the aspirations and ambitions of the Prussian government. To this end he devoted much of his time to Bismarck who, as the minister-president, was the spokesman for the hopes of Prussia. Benedetti soon learned that in regard to Schleswig-Holstein the Prussian government aspired to the annexation of the duchies, a scheme which was vigorously opposed by the Austrian cabinet. Benedetti recognized that the duchies question was, along with the federal reform plan, a means to an end – the establishment of Prussian hegemony in Germany. This basic issue was not likely to be settled by compromise, and Benedetti did not fail to convey his impression to the foreign ministry in Paris. His instructions did not call for positive action and he himself felt that the ends of French policy were admirably served by the dispute which had arisen without any special efforts on his own part. He limited himself to assuring Bismarck of the sympathy of France and of her benevolent neutrality during the controversy. The manner in which the situation developed was quite satisfactory to the ambassador, and he cautioned his government against any unnecessary demonstrations of French support for Prussia. He was decidedly opposed to the overture of 6 May and considered it premature.

In conformity with his belief that the imperial government should maintain its freedom of action, Benedetti never followed Bismarck into discussions on compensation. He was not opposed to French expansion but he preferred not to prejudice the position his government would take on the matter. He was prepared to accept an overthrow of the 1815 treaties which thus far had prevented French expansion but he was unwilling to advise a hasty agreement with Prussia on that question. The fluctuations in the Austro-Prussian negotiations did not exclude the possibility of a temporary agreement and thus pointed up the importance of time in reference to compensation or alliance talks with Prussia. The ambassador's caution was well taken and the course which he thought best to follow was indeed the one which the imperial government did follow up to the Sadowa crisis.

The significance of the Austro-Prussian dispute for French foreign policy was fully realized by the ambassador. He constantly endeavored to keep abreast with new developments, and his regular dispatches bear witness to the commendable manner in which he accomplished this task.

Although he largely confined himself to reporting and analyzing events, he did not hesitate to make recommendations as to the course or attitude the imperial government should adopt. The remarkable sense of duty which Benedetti demonstrated during the winter and the spring makes it difficult to comprehend his behavior during the critical summer weeks when the Austro-Prussian crisis was moving toward a *dénouement*. His failure to take the initiative to remain in contact with the Prussian minister-president and to arrange for the transmission of the details of negotiation contrasts sharply with his attentiveness of the preceding months. His indifference suggests a lack of responsibility and good judgment at a time when the interests of France demanded the utmost attention on the ambassador's part.

CHAPTER III

PRELUDE TO SADOWA

Ambassador Benedetti, upon arrival in Paris from Kissingen in mid-October, learned that the Prussian minister-president had passed through the capital on his journey to Biarritz, where he was to vacation and meet with Emperor Napoleon. As imperial envoy to the Prussian court he was no doubt interested in the forthcoming meetings on the Bay of Biscay, for they might have repercussions which could greatly influence the ambassador's mission. Not only was Bismarck expected to try to erase the adverse effect the Gastein convention had had in France, but, more important, the talks would most likely cover future developments in the affairs of Europe. Bismarck's courtesy calls on Rouher and Drouyn de Lhuys gave no indication as to his political projects,[1] and thus Benedetti, like everyone else in Paris, could only hope ultimately to be acquainted with the content of the talks at Biarritz. Benedetti probably was disappointed by the fact that Ambassador Goltz had been invited while he himself had not been summoned to Biarritz.[2] His exclusion only serves to illustrate the pronounced handicap under which he carried out his duties in Berlin. In effect, the curious methods of the emperor almost exploded the Nothomb-sponsored myth of the preceding fall that Benedetti was the emperor's personal agent.

In the light of the events of 1866, efforts have been made to give the Biarritz and Paris talks either the same significance as the Plombières interview or else strip them almost entirely of political importance.[3] An accurate appraisal is most difficult. It is true that Bis-

---

[1] Cf. Bismarck to Goltz, Berlin, 26 November 1865, *BGW*, V, 327, in which Bismarck states that his calls in Paris were only made, reluctantly, for reasons of courtesy.

[2] Both Ambassador Goltz and the legation secretary, Radowitz, accompanied the emperor as his guests to Biarritz. Cf. J. M. VON RADOWITZ, *Aufzeichnungen und Erinnerungen*, ed. H. Holborn (Stuttgart, 1925), I, 79, for Goltz-Bismarck dispute in Biarritz.

[3] Perhaps as many as nine conversations constitute the Napoleon-Bismarck exchange of views.

marck endeavored to dispel French hostility to the Gastein convention. In his short report of 5 October to King William, he announced success in this respect and also stated that the emperor would not object to a peaceful Austro-Prussian agreement on a Prussian monetary compensation for Holstein.[1] As for a consideration of future plans it may be assumed that the possibility of an Austro-Prussian war was mentioned and that Bismarck tried unsuccessfully to gain a definite statement from the emperor as to the attitude France would assume in such an event. It does not seem that Napoleon claimed specific territorial compensation, in Germany, Belgium, Luxemburg, or Switzerland, in return for French neutrality. However, Bismarck was probably not left in doubt about the likelihood of such an eventuality. It is possible that the emperor agreed to support efforts toward a Prusso-Italian alliance and that the future of Germany was discussed with reference to the changes in the balance of power war might bring in its wake. Although both parties later denied having discussed French compensation, and although no written agreement had been drawn up, there is little doubt that the talks gave both participants definite impressions as to their mutual intentions.[2] It is important

[1] Bismarck to William I, Biarritz, 5 October 1865, *APP*, VI, 403–404; SYBEL, IV, 213–221.

[2] "Bismarck had come with the intention 'to shift Napoleon's eyes from the Rhine to Belgium.' This attempt failed completely. Napoleon remained steadfast in his demand for compensation on the Rhine and indicated that in a form clearly comprehensible to Bismarck but without showing any interest in an understanding with Prussia. Bismarck took care not to advance further than he had to in order to recognize how Napoleon would react to overtures going further" (F. FRAHM, "Biarritz," *HVj*, XV, Heft 3 [1912], pp. 352–353); "It was no more a question of Belgium than of the Rhine provinces or any other country where French is spoken. Bismarck, despite all his ingenuity, received nothing but compliments and vague phrases" (E. OLLIVIER, *L'Empire libéral* [Paris, 1895–1918], VII, 480); "A grand conversation took place between the emperor and Bismarck, but neither one nor the other said anything to me about it. My impression is that he was received politely but quite coldly"(MÉRIMÉE, II, 141); "Bismarck reached his first political aim completely [to dispel the emperor's reservation on the Gastein convention]. Regarding the second one [to ascertain the emperor's intentions in case of an Austro-Prussian war], the emperor maintained an attitude of benevolent reserve toward the minister. Nonetheless, Bismarck discerned that the emperor would adopt a friendly attitude *vis-à-vis* a Prusso-Italian alliance against Austria as well as toward the acquisition of the Elbe duchies.... The minister also had the correct impression that the emperor counted on the superiority of the Austrian army and that he reserved for himself the role of arbiter at the appropriate moment" (W. VON LOË, *Erinnerungen aus meinem Berufsleben, 1849 bis 1867* [2nd ed.; Stuttgart, 1906], pp. 78–80); "Emperor Napoleon himself told me several years later that Bismarck had promised him various compensations, but that it came to no written agreement concerning them" (K. VITZTHUM VON ECKSTÄDT, *London, Gastein, Sadowa, Denkwürdigkeiten 1864–1866* [Stuttgart, 1889], p. 318); *Aufzeichnung von Goltz über Bismarcks politische Gespräche in Paris und Biarritz*, OTTO GRAF ZU STOLBERG-WERNIGERODE, *Robert Heinrich Graf von der Goltz, Botschafter in Paris 1863–1869* (Oldenbourg, 1941), pp. 403–408; Goltz to Bismarck, Paris, 18 October 1865, *APP*, VI, 406, ft. 4; SYBEL, IV, 213–221; J. G. DE PERSIGNY, *Mémoires*, ed. H. d'Espagny (Paris, 1896), p. 376; ONCKEN, I, 69–76; *BGW*, V, 308–311; P. BERNSTEIN, "Biarritz," *Year Book of the American Philosophical Society, 1960* (Philadelphia, 1961), pp.

to note, however, that Bismarck's exaggerated reports about French sympathies had the desired effect on King William. Bismarck could hope now for less royal opposition to his determined policy toward Austria.[1]

Ambassador Benedetti had occasion to call on Count Bismarck during the latter's return journey. The minister-president stopped off in Paris on 2 November, expecting to continue his journey on Monday, 6 November, after a week-end of visits and entertainment.[2] Benedetti's call, at the *Hôtel du Douvres*, was apparently a courtesy call, and it does not appear that Bismarck discussed his conversations with the emperor. The ambassador was not present at the calls which Bismarck paid to Napoleon, who had returned ahead of him from Biarritz, to Rouher and to Drouyn de Lhuys. Like the talks in Biarritz, so these conversations gave rise to speculations about Franco-Prussian alliance and compensation schemes. No written agreement resulted, and the talks did nothing more than confirm the impressions gathered at the other meetings.[3] Benedetti was informed to some extent about the last conversations by either Rouher or Drouyn de Lhuys. It was his belief that the imperial government had retained its freedom of action regarding future developments in Germany and that Bismarck had failed to gain *a priori* and unconditional assurances.[4] In order to be in Berlin by the time Bismarck arrived, Benedetti departed from Paris early on Monday morning, 6 November.[5] A rail accident near Charleroi delayed him and he continued the journey with Bismarck and his family, who had left the French capital after him, arriving in Berlin on 7 November.[6]

The diplomatic colony in Berlin was of course anxious to obtain every bit of information regarding Bismarck's meeting with the emperor and his ministers. A few days after his return Benedetti told Nothomb: "Bismarck did nothing in Paris, for a simple reason:

365–366; R. FESTER, "Biarritz, eine Bismarck-Studie," *Deutsche Rundschau*, CXIII, Heft 2 (November 1902), pp. 212–236; GEUSS, pp. 142–151; E. EYCK, *Bismarck. Leben und Werk* (Erlenbach-Zürich, 1944), II, 98 ff.; *ODG*, VII, 114, ft. 1.

[1] GEUSS, p. 151.
[2] KOHL, I, 265.
[3] Bismarck to foreign office, Paris, 3 November 1865, *BGW*, V, 315.
[4] See above ft. 2, p. 39. "At the French embassy [in Berlin, Bismarck's] sojourn in Paris is summarized with the words: 'They have been very polite to Count Bismarck. They have played games with him, but he has brought nothing back, and the bad impression of the Gastein convention has not been swept away at all'" (Hohenthal to Beust, Berlin, 10 November 1865, *APP*, VI, ft. 2 to no. 349).
[5] Zuylen to Cremers, Berlin, 9 November 1865, RBZ, Pruisen/ 1865, no. 934.
[6] Nothomb to Rogier, Berlin, 9 November 1865, BAE CP, Prusse/23, Pt. I, no. 70.

because there was nothing that could be done." [1] The French government, he added, planned to observe events as they took place. Nothomb reported: "Benedetti therefore resumes his attitude of expectancy, but without approving, without encouraging, as his ex-colleague from England did." [2] The ambassador continued to maintain his careful observation of Prussian policy in order to discover how Bismarck would move to decide the rivalry with Austria and establish Prussian hegemony in Germany. Having adduced the basic motives in Bismarck's activities, he now had to witness the implementation of his plans.[3] Benedetti expected that the Gastein convention would produce but a temporary improvement in the relations between Austria and Prussia, an improvement for which the Austrian government was particularly anxious.[4] He detected a clue to Bismarck's pressure on Austria in the Prussian commercial negotiations with Italy – the first step toward closer association.[5]

Toward the end of November the relations between Berlin and Paris were slightly disturbed by Bismarck's scarcely concealed annoyance with French press reports asserting that he had made several abortive overtures to the imperial government. Benedetti had twice sought to discourage a discussion of those press statements by reminding the minister-president that he could not admit that the imperial government approved of views expressed in misinformed newspapers. Bismarck forestalled his objections on the second occasion, however, by citing reports from the Prussian ambassador in Paris claiming that the unfriendly press reports emanated from journalists considered close to the French foreign ministry. Goltz maintained that the articles bore the approval of Drouyn de Lhuys: that is, tacit approval was implied by the failure of the foreign minister to repudiate them. Benedetti was rather displeased with Goltz's allegations and insinuations; he thought them quite improper and cautioned Bismarck against accepting them at face value.[6] Speculating as to Goltz's motives, Benedetti pointed out to Drouyn de Lhuys that Bismarck's position was not above the attacks of an opposition which, even Bismarck conceded, included Queen Augusta, Crown Prince

---

[1] *Ibid.*
[2] *Ibid.*
[3] Cf. SCHOEPS, pp. 39–40.
[4] Benedetti to Drouyn de Lhuys, Berlin, 11 November 1865, FAE CP, Prusse/353, no. 154.
[5] Same to same, Berlin, 15 November 1865, *ibid.*, no. 155.
[6] Same to same, Berlin, 26 November 1865, *ODG*, VII, 197–202.

Frederick, Crown Princess Victoria, as well as Goltz.[1] Bismarck had
to be constantly on guard to maintain his influence over the monarch
and to prevent any effort, such as Goltz's reports might constitute,
to undermine the king's confidence in Bismarck and his policies.
Benedetti indicated that he had also shown Bismarck that the interests of French policy made it advisable not to give Prussia cause to
doubt the sincerity of France and that he had repeatedly and vehe-
mently denied any official sanction of the press reports.[2] His refutation seemed to allay the minister-president's misgivings, and the
ambassador felt sure his words would be used to convince the king
that no obligations had been assumed toward France.[3] An article
in the *Constitutionnel* in early December which refuted the earlier
press accounts of Bismarck's talks in France further assuaged the
irritation of the minister-president. He was convinced that Benedetti's
remonstrances in Paris had led to the article which carried with it the
approval of the foreign ministry.[4]

The relative quiet which had enveloped the Schleswig-Holstein
question was an indication of the relaxed political atmosphere which
had prevailed since the meeting between the emperor and Bismarck.[5]
Benedetti's correspondence contained only general references to the
duchies question and Bismarck apparently had the firm intention
to *"faire le mort"* for the time being. He did, however, tell the ambassador that he complained rather regularly, once or twice a week,
to Vienna relative to the Austrian administration in Holstein.[6] The
Prussian government did become agitated at the time of the death
of Leopold I of Belgium;[7] should the French attempt an annexation
coup in Belgium, Prussia might be forced to tolerate it in order to con-
sumate eventually the annexation of Holstein.[8] Bismarck perhaps
preferred not to touch upon this subject with the ambassador, for
there is no reference to it in his correspondence. Benedetti, on the

---

[1] *Ibid.*

[2] "Benedetti assures me that if Drouyn de Lhuys had earlier been pro-Austrian he now is
cured thereof" (Bismarck to Goltz, Berlin, 26 November 1865, *BGW*, V, 328).

[3] Benedetti to Drouyn de Lhuys, Berlin, 26 November 1865, *ODG*, VII, 197–202.

[4] Bismarck to Goltz, Berlin, 12 December 1865, *APP*, VI, 477, ft. 4 to no. 373.

[5] The friendly relations between Bismarck and Benedetti became momentarily strained
over a protocol matter on the occasion of the marriage of Princess Alexandrine, daughter of
Prince Albert of Prussia, to Duke William of Mecklenburg-Schwerin. Both the French and
the British ambassadors left the wedding banquet as the result of differences over the seating
arrangements (FRIEDRICH III., p. 404).

[6] Benedetti to Drouyn de Lhuys, Berlin, 14 December 1865, FAE CP, Prusse/353, no. 169.

[7] King Leopold I had died at Laeken on 10 December.

[8] Goltz to Bismarck, Paris, 9 December 1865, *APP*, VI, 483–485.

other hand, seemed to believe that Bismarck had suffered a few light reverses during the early days of December, which had induced his more pacific frame of mind. To Count Bohuslav Chotek, he mentioned in particular the recall of Lord Napier, the marriage of a British princess with the brother of the duke of Augustenburg, and even that slight disaffection – the protocol incident of 9 December.[1]

The air of expectancy which hung over Berlin continued into the new year. The opening of the Prussian *Landtag*, scheduled for 15 January, was not anticipated with great interest by Benedetti, since Bismarck's parliamentary plans were essentially concentrated upon Prussian internal affairs. The advantages expected from the Gastein convention had initially strengthened Bismarck's position *vis-à-vis* the legislature, but Austrian failure to cede Holstein had begun to raise doubts in Prussia regarding the efficacy of the convention. In view of the struggle between the minister-president and the chamber, Benedetti foresaw no marked decrease in the parliamentary opposition to Bismarck's legislative program.[2] The political future of Bismarck, in Benedetti's opinion, was inextricably bound up with the solution of the duchies question. Resolved to achieve his aim, Bismarck was believed to be in contact with the Italian cabinet as well as with Hungarian elements considered to be anti-Austrian. The king's support of his policy was always an uncertain factor: only definite international engagements could prevent William from retreating at the last minute.

Benedetti advanced a rather interesting suggestion to Drouyn de Lhuys on the intimate connection between the duchies question and the Venetian problem, and the role France might play:

> With the possession of Venetia, Austria remains exposed to temptations which put obstacles in the way of the relations she could establish with us and cause her to show complaisance to Prussia to which we could not remain indifferent. Rid of Venetia, she recovers, on the contrary, her entire freedom of action, and in bringing her back, because of the nature of things, onto the federal terrain, she becomes for us a counterweight to the ambitions of Prussia. But would we not pay this double advantage with a price too high by facilitating the annexation of the duchies to the Prussian monarchy? It is not for me to touch upon this question; what I want to call to your attention is that a moment can come in a future more or less near when Prussia, if she were assured of our neutrality, could want seriously to make an agreement with Italy to force Austria to concede her sovereign rights over the territories which they wish to acquire, through a money compensation which would help [Austria] redress her financial situation;

---

[1] Chotek to Mensdorff, Berlin, 16 December 1865, HHStA, Preussen/89, no. 75; see above ft. 5, p. 42.

[2] Benedetti to Drouyn de Lhuys, Berlin, 4 January 1866, FAE CP, Prusse/354, no. 1.

what I want to say further is that it would not be impossible to hasten the ma-
turity of such a project through our manifestly sympathetic and, if necessary,
armed neutrality, with the understanding of leaving to Prussia and to Italy
the job of starting the affair and pursuing the solution.[1]

In view of the *dénouement* which was to occur six months later, Benedetti showed some perspicacity and discernment in this evaluation
of the situation. The opinions demonstrate his unwavering loyalty
to the Italian cause, conditioned by traditional French policy toward
Germany of sustaining the Austro-Prussian rivalry. The role assigned
to Austria bespeaks a sense of realism bordering on cynicism: Austria
was to be robbed of a province in Italy in order to strengthen her vigor
in Germany, where her activity would be of definite advantage to
France. The picture, as drawn by Benedetti, was indeed an enticing
one: Italy in possession of Venetia, Prussia sole arbiter in the duchies,
Austria in a position of added strength in Germany, and the continuation of rivalry between the two German powers. The specific absence of
a reference to territorial gains for France postulates that the solution
presupposed compensation. France could never be reconciled to a change
in the balance of power without proportionate benefit to herself.
Neither the prevention of an Austro-Prussian alliance nor the satisfaction
of Italian irredentism would provide sufficient consolation: perhaps
uncontested French expansion in Belgium could be the payment.
While Benedetti did not enter into considerations regarding the attitudes Russia and Britain might assume, in view of the likely repercussions of his plan, he emphasized the need to return the French
expeditionary corps from Mexico before such a solution could be
attempted.[2] In relation to the events which were to develop in the
spring, he made an accurate prediction: in particular, the conclusion
of the Prusso-Italian alliance represents a vital element for the violent
and simultaneous solution brought to the two questions, between
which he saw a definite relationship.

The opening of the Prussian legislative session on 15 January passed
without fanfare. The throne speech insinuated that the Prussian
government had not abandoned its hope of annexing the duchies,
and no amelioration of the existing relationship between Bismarck

---

[1] Same to same, Berlin, 14 January 1866, FAE MD, Autriche/67.

[2] It is rather interesting to note that during January Bismarck, in his correspondence
with Goltz, stressed the difficulties which might develop for France in her relations with the
United States over the Mexico affair. For Prussia it would spell less concern over French
intervention in Germany, while forcing France to cultivate Prussian sympathies. Bismarck
expressedly forbade Goltz to exert a restraining influence upon the American minister in
Paris (GEUSS, p. 152).

and the chamber could be expected.[1] The preoccupation with internal affairs in Berlin during January as well as the temporary lull in international affairs gave Benedetti less frequent occasion to report upon political developments in the Prussian capital.

While international affairs were in abeyance, the social season was in full swing: the French embassy, noted for its highly successful receptions and *soirées*, was frequently the center of gaiety during the winter season.[2] The political significance which the role of the French government had assumed in Bismarck's plans exercised a direct effect upon the success of these *soirées;* it was not surprising to find the minister-president strongly endorsing invitations tendered to the king and queen and recommending the attendance of the royal family.[3] He was probably also desirous of soothing Benedetti's ruffled feelings, which had again been tried by a new protocol issue early in the month. The absence of the French ambassador from a royal reception on 18 January and again at the first court ball on 1 February had been interpreted by King William as a deliberate breach of courtesy. The intentional failure of the monarch to dance the customary polonaise with Mme Benedetti, who was in attendance at the ball, was considered an expression of the king's annoyance and became the subject of much comment among the guests. When it became apparent, however, that the ambassador had indeed been prevented by illness from attending the social functions, the minister-president was anxious to make amends for the inconsiderate treatment of the ambassador's wife.[4] The gala evening of 6 February at the French embassy provided a suitable occasion and the entire royal family was in attendance.[5] This signal honor to the French ambassador apparently re-established the friendly relation between court and embassy, and the social season was expected to come to a close without further *contretemps*. Such an expectation was not destined to be fulfilled: at the court ball of 8 February, the highlight of the season, a new protocol conflict ruffled the feelings of Benedetti.[6]

---

[1] Benedetti to Drouyn de Lhuys, Berlin, 15 January 1866, FAE CP, Prusse/354, no. 5.

[2] H. von Chappuis, *Bei Hof und im Felde* (Frankfurt, 1902), p. 45.

[3] Bismarck to William I, Berlin, 31 January 1866, Wilhelm I., *Kaiser-und-Kanzler-Briefe*, ed. J. Penzler (Leipzig, 1900), pp. 67–68.

[4] Bylandt to Cremers, Berlin, 12 February 1866, RBZ, Pruisen/ 1866, no. 33.

[5] "Both Benedettis have the best of intentions, but cannot overcome their *parvenu* airs" (Friedrich III., p. 409). Cf. C. Tschudi, *Augusta, Empress of Germany*, tr. E. M. Cope (London, 1900), p. 153, who states that the queen was always very favorably disposed toward the French ambassador.

[6] According to Benedetti, the breach of protocol occurred when the guests were passing

While social affairs had almost taken precedence in the activities of the foreign representatives in Berlin and a temporary stagnation prevailed in the political life of the capital during the early weeks of the year, Benedetti nonetheless remained in close contact with the minister-president. He found Bismarck still determined to obtain the cession of Holstein, and the Prussian policy of harassment was not likely to abate in the near future. Indeed, the conviction that the Austrian government would not cede the duchy of Holstein to Prussia had become more pronounced. Bismarck suspected that Austria was deliberately encouraging the ambitions of the duke of Augustenburg in order to frustrate efforts to attach Holstein to the Prussian monarchy. Benedetti thought that Bismarck might well reinaugurate the policy he had pursued during the preceding July to induce the Austrian cabinet to accede to his wishes.[1] The minister-president told him that continued evasive replies to his complaints might force Prussia to take swift and perhaps far-reaching measures;[2] such a course could quickly place Prussia before the alternatives of "temerity or weakness." [3] The ominous tension was not relieved by a reply from Vienna refuting Bismarck's complaints and asserting that Austria's policy in Holstein was in conformity with the Gastein convention.[4] In commenting to Benedetti on the Austrian note, Bis-

from the reception room into the ballroom. He insisted that, since he was the highest ranking foreign envoy, his wife should have been escorted to the ballroom immediately following the royal family and ahead of the ladies of the realm. Negligence on the part of the master of ceremonies had left Madame Benedetti without an escort, until Prince August of Württemberg had come to her rescue. When Benedetti inquired later in the evening of the master of ceremonies, Count Rudolf Stillfried d'Alcántara, if there had not occurred a breach of protocol, the count averred that Madame Benedetti was ranked *with* and not necessarily *ahead* of the ladies of the realm. The ambassador felt insulted by this remark and, next day, addressed an official note to Bismarck, setting forth the occurrence of the previous evening and announcing his decision to remain absent from court ceremonies until apologies had been tendered. Bismarck was disturbed by this new incident, and he informed the king of the contents of the note. William, acknowledging the slight to Madame Benedetti, disavowed the actions and remarks of the master of ceremonies and asked the minister-president to present his personal apologies to the ambassador. He was to tell Benedetti that the master of ceremonies would be reprimanded and ordered to apologize. Although Count Stillfried never did tender his personal apologies, Benedetti attended the last major ball at the court. Perhaps the sensitive ambassador was mollified by the fact that Madame Benedetti, attending the ball of Prince Charles alone on the previous evening, had been offered the arm of the prince himself (Bylandt to Cremers, Berlin, 12 February 1866, RBZ, Pruisen/1866, no. 33; same to same, 16 February 1866, *ibid.*, no. 36).

[1] Benedetti to Drouyn de Lhuys, Berlin, 11 February 1866, FAE CP, Prusse/354, no. 20.
[2] Same to same, Berlin, 14 February 1866, *MMP* (2d ed.; Paris, 1871), p. 30.
[3] *Ibid.*, p. 31. Cf. Prince Napoleon to Queen Sophie of Holland, Paris, 11 February 1866, FRANCE. COMMISSION DES PAPIERS SAISIES AUX TUILERIES, *Papiers et correspondance de la famille impériale* (Paris, 1870), I, 389–390. The prince wrote that Benedetti believed a serious conflict between Prussia and Austria was near.
[4] Benedetti to Drouyn de Lhuys, Berlin, 14 February 1866, FAE CP, Prusse/354, no. 22.

marck touched upon the possibility of war, but the ambassador did not predict such a drastic event in the immediate future, for Prussia was not yet in a position to justify such a radical step.[1] Bismarck would be reluctant to unleash a war before having made preparations assuring him of the success of the undertaking.

The dissension which seriously began to trouble the relations between Vienna and Berlin prompted the calling of a Prussian crown council, preparatory to which Prussia made efforts in Paris to sound out the French government as to its attitude in case of armed conflict.[2] Benedetti felt some displeasure at not being directly consulted concerning French intentions:

> If Count Bismarck wished to know what the [French] cabinet thought regarding the event of a war between Austria and Prussia, he need not have recalled Count Goltz; I could have told him with the greatest certainty that in such an event France would observe the strictest neutrality – contrariwise to the peace which would follow, for there she too would add her weight to the deliberations.[3]

In a subsequent meeting with Bismarck, Benedetti found his own observations to be in accord with those which Goltz had brought back from Paris. Assurances of French benevolence apparently prompted the minister-president to continue the course thus far pursued toward Austria.[4] At a dinner which he offered in honor of Count Goltz, Benedetti learned that Bismarck contemplated sending a comminatory note to Vienna, setting forth Prussian pretensions which would form the basis for a new agreement relative to the duchies. He speculated whether Bismarck was not seeking, through new

---

[1] *Ibid.* The adverse resolution of the chamber on 3 February regarding the acquisition of Lauenburg had probably strengthened Bismarck's desire for a diplomatic victory (same to same, Berlin, 20 February 1866, *ibid.*, no. 25).

[2] Goltz to Bismarck, Paris, 17 February 1866, ONCKEN, I, 90. In his interview with Goltz, Drouyn de Lhuys remarked that at present France would continue her attitude of neutrality but would have to consult her own interests at all times (Drouyn de Lhuys to Benedetti, Paris, 22 February 1866, FAE CP, Prusse/354, no. 10).

[3] Türckheim to Edelsheim, Berlin, 20 February 1866, *APP*, VI, 570–571. Cf. a remark made by the emperor to Goltz: "Only I alone know what the foreign policy of France will be, I and my minister of foreign affairs, naturally" (Goltz to Bismarck, Paris, 17 February 1866, ONCKEN, I, 90). Cf. E. BRANDENBURG, *Untersuchungen und Aktenstücke zur Geschichte der Reichsgründung* (Leipzig, 1916), pp. 475–476, who states that Bismarck knew that France hoped for an Austro-Prussian war and would endeavor to benefit from it. He repeatedly sought to ascertain Napoleon's plans because William's suspicion of France was a constant obstacle to Bismarck's plans for war.

[4] Benedetti to Drouyn de Lhuys, Berlin, 24 February 1866, FAE CP, Prusse/354, no. 28. Benedetti thought it probable that the legislative session would soon be closed by the king at the behest of his minister-president, who preferred not to have to reckon with the opposition of the *Landtag*. For the Austrian reaction to Bismarck's pressure, see CLARK, pp. 333–343

negotiations, to find the proper occasion for deciding the question of war against Austria.[1] He was sure that the king, as in previous situations, was the unknown factor in all speculations and that the struggle to win the monarch over to Bismarck's course leading to war had begun. He regretted the fact that Prussian court usages made it so difficult to observe more closely the course of the struggle; all that he had learned thus far indicated that William was still anxious to annex the duchies, and efforts to depict an Austro-Prussian conflict as a necessity had not altered his resolution. He cautioned Drouyn de Lhuys that all the information on the king's attitude could not be controlled and therefore might prove unreliable.[2] He also emphasized the futility of speculating on the outcome of the crown council of 28 February. He knew that Bismarck's views would be supported by the cabinet and that the opposition would be led by the crown prince. He was not sure whether General Manteuffel, an ardent supporter of Austro-Prussian collaboration in the past, would remain on the side of Frederick, since his stay in Schleswig might have caused a revision in attitude. The king was expected to enter the meeting more or less undecided on the course to be followed; pride and apprehension made him hesitate between a retreat and a war against Austria. No extreme measure was expected to result from the deliberations, for Bismarck had told Benedetti that he would not submit a decisive proposition. He was as yet undecided between an eventual course calling for the reconstitution of Germany or for a polemic which would lead to a rupture with Austria. The possibility of concentrating troops along the Holstein-Schleswig border would be considered as a development in which Austria might see a commencement of hostilities.[3]

Despite the fact that the participants had been pledged to utmost secrecy, Bismarck appeared almost anxious to relate certain details to the ambassador and revealed that none of the adopted measures enjoined immediate action. It had been agreed that the annexation of the duchies be actively pursued, but it had been decided to send no communication at present to Austria. Goltz had convinced all those in attendance of the friendly dispositions of the French government. Even General Manteuffel, one who might have counterbalanced

[1] Benedetti to Drouyn de Lhuys, Berlin, 26 February 1866, FAE CP, Prusse/354, no. 30.
[2] Same to same, Berlin, 26 February 1866, *MMP*, pp. 34–35.
[3] Same to same, Berlin, 28 February 1866, *ibid.*, pp. 35–37. Cf. I.A.A.a. 27; W. Busch, "Bismarck und die Entstehung des Norddeutschen Bundes," *HZ*, CIII, Heft 1 (1910), pp. 52–78.

Bismarck's influence with the king, had supported the view that the interests of Prussia demanded the annexation of the duchies and General Albrecht von Roon and General Alvensleben, the king's aide-de-camp, had concurred with him. Only with great difficulty could the king have opposed the common opinion of his advisers.[1]

The wealth of information relative to the crown council which Benedetti had received from Bismarck[2] permitted him to transmit to his government an accurate resumé of the meeting. During the following week he obtained further details which enabled him to control his information. General Manteuffel had expressed views to general staff officers which were in accord with those Bismarck had related to him two days earlier. Although he had no specific information about a Prussian time-table, Benedetti felt that Prussia would proceed with extreme caution – an indication that the Prussian government was aware of the gravity of the complications which could arise as a consequence of its policy toward Austria. He expected Goltz to shed further light on this in communications he would probably make to the emperor upon his return to Paris.[3]

On the eve of Goltz's departure, Thursday, 2 March, the Benedettis were invited to a dinner which the king gave in honor of the Prussian ambassador. Referring to Goltz's impending return to the French capital, William implied the nature of the ambassador's instructions: "Goltz returns to Paris under circumstances which are very serious for us, and we reach the moment when we shall have to find out who our friends are."[4] Benedetti assigned great importance to these remarks since he believed (quite wrongly) that the king had the habit of *never* discussing political questions with the representatives

---

[1] Benedetti to Drouyn de Lhuys, Berlin, 1 March 1866, *ODG*, VII, 358–360. Bismarck, on the basis of the inevitability of war with Austria, had urged that Helmuth von Moltke be sent to Italy to negotiate an alliance, the conclusion of which would not be a signal for war but a cause for increased apprehension in Vienna, forcing Austria to realize the gravity of the situation. King William approved this program and the diplomatic steps necessary to promote Prussia's preponderance. In accord with this decision, Goltz was to convey a letter from the king to Napoleon, requesting an exchange of views between France and Prussia with the expectation of concluding an *entente* (*Kronratsprotokoll*, 28 February 1866, APP, VI, 611–616; cf. *BGW*, V, 386, ft.); FRIEDRICH III., pp. 541–544; GEUSS, pp. 153–154; PFLANZE, p. 284.

[2] Cf. V. VALENTIN, *Bismarcks Reichsgründung im Urteil englischer Diplomaten* (Amsterdam, 1938), p. 279, whose belief that Benedetti, up to the time of the Luxemburg crisis, was far better informed than his British colleagues is strongly seconded by the research of the present writer.

[3] Benedetti to Drouyn de Lhuys, Berlin, 3 March 1866, FAE CP, Prusse/355, no. 34.

[4] Same to same, Berlin, 3 March 1866, *ODG*, VII, 368.

of foreign courts.[1] He did not know, however, the content of William's letter to Napoleon:

When my minister for foreign affairs [wrote William] had the honor of being received by Your Majesty last year in Biarritz and in St. Cloud, you kindly charged him to tell me that you, like myself, were of the opinion that in order for us to have an understanding concerning the future of our political relations the development of the situation ought not to be precipitated but its progress should be awaited in order to adapt our resolutions to it. After the exposé of your opinion Your Majesty added the invitation to write to you confidentially as soon as the circumstances were to indicate to me the need for a more intimate and more special *entente* between our two governments. This moment, I believe has come and, guided by the memory of the assurances of political sympathy and personal friendship which Your Majesty caused to be transmitted to me on the same occasion, I have charged Count Goltz to develop to you, with the frankness and loyalty which have always presided over our mutual relations, the manner in which I envisage the actual situation of Europe and the attitude which in my opinion results from it for Prussia. If Your Majesty will kindly acquaint me with the appreciations suggested to you by the views my ambassador will submit, I beg you to believe that I will receive the communications which you will have transmitted to me with the discretion conforming entirely to the personal character which Your Majesty will kindly give to this exchange of ideas.[2]

This letter signalled the opening of a Prussian diplomatic effort, lasting to the outbreak of the Austro-Prussian war, to come to an agreement with France over Prussian expansion and French compensation. The aspirations of Prussia in Germany made an *a priori* understanding with France desirable, for her position might have a decisive influence on the outcome of a conflict between the German powers. The Prussian government had reason to expect success, for the continual French vows of sympathy pointed to an ideological solidarity relative to the international order in Europe. The king's letter was written under such an impression, and the explanations of Ambassador Goltz were to be given in the same vein.

King William's mission to Goltz had momentarily made Paris the focal point for Franco-Prussian *entente* talks. The overture of the Prussian ambassador had found the emperor embarrassed regarding the definition of a compensation project, because the Belgian question had not matured, although French sympathies were supposedly noticeable in the Bavarian Palatinate and in Luxemburg.[3] After Goltz had

---

[1] *Ibid.*

[2] William I to Napoleon III, Berlin, 3 March 1866, *BGW*, V, 386–387.

[3] Goltz to Bismarck, Paris, 5 March 1866, *ibid.*, p. 389; "Regarding sympathies in the Bavarian Palatinate the emperor must be wrongly informed. In Luxemburg the sympathies of the rich in particular are perhaps oriented more toward Paris. If we start by ceding federal territory with German inhabitants, we cut off the national development of our plan" (Bismarck to Goltz, Berlin, 6 March 1866, *ibid.*; same to same, 9 March 1866, *ibid.*, p. 394).

defined Prussia's aims as acquisition of the duchies and formation of a North German Confederation,[1] the emperor had asked for more time before replying and had insisted on secrecy toward Drouyn de Lhuys.[2] This exclusion was, however, temporary, for it was the foreign minister who communicated the evasive reply of Napoleon:

If serious events appear in Germany, my formal intention is to observe neutrality while maintaining the friendly relations which have already existed for a long time with the government of Your Majesty. If later extra-ordinary circumstances were to change the European equilibrium, I would ask Your Majesty to examine with me the new bases upon which to guarantee the interest of my country.[3]

This equivocation could hardly be satisfactory to the Prussian government. It meant the rejection of an *entente* at this time, while it clearly indicated that France would expect compensation if the balance of power were to be upset by Prussian machinations. Nonetheless, Goltz continued his efforts, but by 17 March he realized that his exertions had been futile. "Emperor Napoleon talked with me in a manner which does not directly encourage the initiation of [war with Austria], but does not discourage it either." [4]

While the talks between the emperor, Goltz, and Drouyn de Lhuys were occurring in Paris, Benedetti continued to pay close attention to developments in Berlin, although he realized that some time would elapse before tangible evidence of the crown council resolutions could be observed. Still unaware of the exact nature of Goltz's mission, he did surmise, however, that political activity would be in abeyance until the French reaction to the king's communications would be known in the Prussian capital.[5] In view of this uncertainty he decided to maintain "the most rigorous reserve" in his contact both with Bismarck and the diplomatic representatives in Berlin.[6] The failure of his government to inform him about Goltz's mission prompted Benedetti to abstain from remarks which might compromise him later, and it left him in some doubt regarding the inaction on the political scene.[7] By 9 March he seemed to have gained more certitude and suspected that the Prussian ambassador had again "taken our pulse" and that he had found it "beating neither slower, nor faster." [8]

---

[1] SYBEL, IV, 285–288; OLLIVIER, VIII, 23.
[2] Goltz to Bismarck, Paris, 5 March 1866, *BGW*, V, 389.
[3] Napoleon III to William I, Tuileries, 7 March 1866, ONCKEN, I, 98–99.
[4] Goltz to William I, Paris, 17 March 1866, *ibid.*, 111.
[5] Benedetti to Gramont, Berlin, 9 March 1866, *MMP*, pp. 49–50.
[6] Benedetti to Drouyn de Lhuys, Berlin, 8 March 1866, FAE CP, Prusse/355, no. 38.
[7] Károlyi to Mensdorff, Berlin, 8 March 1866, HHStA, Preussen/89, no. 15.
[8] Benedetti to Gramont, Berlin, 9 March 1866, *MMP*, p. 49.

Nevertheless, he had become impatient with the manner in which he was left ignorant of events in Paris: "[Drouyn de Lhuys], while thanking me with the greatest kindness in the world, limits himself to acknowledging the reception of my correspondence."[1] He should have known that Drouyn de Lhuys, too, had been for a time uninformed of the emperor's plans.

Benedetti's ignorance concerning the consultations between William and Napoleon was cleared up when he received the official reply of the French emperor and was charged to solicit a royal audience for its transmission to the king. He delivered the letter on 11 March, and despite the king's expressions of satisfaction, Benedetti noted a tone of regret in his remarks. Instead of benevolent neutrality the monarch had hoped for an *entente*, which he thought might yet be concluded with the emperor at a future date. William assured the ambassador that at the outset of the discord with Austria the Prussian government had entertained no purely ambitious designs and that Austria's refusal to grant Prussia the guarantees necessary to her interest had led to the present troubles. He claimed that at the time of the Gastein convention he had hoped that with the passage of time Austria would show herself more conciliatory and contribute all her efforts to a satisfactory solution. But this hope had not materialized and, according to the monarch, the Austrian cabinet had used the stipulations solely to further its attacks and designs against Prussia. Benedetti had little opportunity to reply to the observations of the king but, when the occasion did present itself, he expressed his views with great circumspection. The convictions which the king professed relative to the justice of his complaints caused the ambassador to choose his words with caution. William insinuated that the Austrian attitude was evidence of the fact that she hoped to debase the honor of Prussia and treat the Brandenburg dynasty as *parvenu*. His remarks gave Benedetti again occasion to note his indecision between policies which would lead to either war or peace.

Upon the termination of his audience with the king, the ambassador called on the minister-president, who informed him of developments which further explained William's indecision. Reports from the Prussian ambassadors in London and St. Petersburg stressed that these powers were hopeful that the peace in Germany would not be broken. Both ambassadors, Albrecht Bernstorff and Count Heinrich Redern, advised that war be averted in view of the attitude in the respective

[1] *Ibid.*

capitals.[1] Benedetti believed that these reports had decided the Berlin cabinet to make federal reform the terrain upon which Prussia would force Austria to a decision between war and peace. Bismarck expected to propound a federal reform, on the basis of the proposed constitution of 1849, which would provide a national representation elected by direct popular vote, as one of the branches of federal government.[2] The real intent of this proposition was not hidden by the minister-president, and Benedetti emphasized it:

> I call your attention to this combination; and in the mind of Bismarck it is exclusively destined to become a weapon of war, an expedient to sow confusion in all of Germany; but if he were to miscalculate, and if this central authority, chosen by the German people, should succeed in constituting itself despite him, he would have involuntarily laid the bases for the German union. I do not wish to have suspected him of having calculated on this eventuality and having accommodated himself to it in advance, in the conviction that it could not but further the elevation and aggrandizement of his state and realize Prussian hegemony; I must however bring to your attention an attempt whose consequences could touch us in a most regrettable fashion.[3]

The significance of the federal reform plan was crucial, as time was to demonstrate, and Benedetti was immediately aware of its possible consequences. The manifest frankness with which the Prussian minister-president initiated him into his plans implied that Bismarck hoped to win the envoy's personal and official sympathy for his aspirations and thus promote their acceptance by the imperial government. Benedetti's known sympathies for the Italian cause and his antipathy to Austria made him a most acceptable figure to Bismarck at this particular time.

Yet the candor with which Benedetti was treated in Berlin was not without its disadvantages. In a pointed letter of 11 March Benedetti explained to the minister of foreign affairs in a tone of polite restraint that the frankness with which Bismarck revealed his plans had proved time and again embarrassing to him because of lack of information from Paris:

> You will see that one is so frank with me here that you can easily imagine for

---

[1] In hopes of seeing his policy of moderation prevail, Mensdorff made a great effort in late March to bring the influence of Queen Victoria and others to bear on King William. The so-called "Coburg intrigue" failed to achieve the desired result of driving a wedge between William and his bellicose minister-president (*QDPO*, V/1, 240, 292 ff., 298–299, 302–323, 380–395; *BGW*, V, 410–411, XIV, 710–711; HEINRICH RITTER VON SRBIK, *Deutsche Einheit. Idee und Wirklichkeit vom Heiligen Reich bis Königgrätz* [Munich, 1935–1942], IV, 335 ff.; CLARK, pp. 374 ff.; STOLBERG-WERNIGERODE, pp. 146 ff.).

[2] Benedetti to Drouyn de Lhuys, Berlin, 11 March 1866, *ODG*, VII, 407–411.

[3] *Ibid.*, p. 412.

yourself my embarrassment when I am being told of things about which I am supposed to be informed but of which I know nothing. I remained silent with the king, but it was necessary for me to declare to Bismarck that I did not know either what Goltz had been charged to tell the emperor or you, or what had been the reply to him. He certainly did not believe my word.... You will judge for yourself, I hope, that under these circumstances it is difficult to be an intelligent auditor of what is being confided to me, a valuable appreciator of impressions produced here as a result of advice from Paris of the judgment made of our attitude and our intentions, finally, an exact reporter of what I learn.... Do you not yourself think I would be a poor servant if the persuasion developed that I am completely forgotten here? [1]

Just as the ambassador was kept ill-informed so his value as an observer declined. Without knowledge of the actions and intentions of his own government it was difficult to question Bismarck with adroitness, to elicit precisely that information which the foreign ministry would most keenly appreciate. The uncommunicative habits of the emperor and the uneasy truce between the French foreign minister and his envoy were evident in the flow of information between the embassy and the *Quai d'Orsay*, and the combined effects could only be detrimental to the interests of French policy in Germany. In this light, the ignorance in which Benedetti was kept, notably in regard to the Goltz mission, was a lamentable and glaring shortcoming.[2]

An indiscreet revelation permitted Benedetti to report the imminent arrival of General Guiseppe Govone in Berlin. This news had made a deep impression in political circles and the appearance of an Italian general, ostensibly to study Prussia's military organization, had been immediately connected with an alliance project between the two courts, in anticipation of a war between the two German powers.[3] General Govone had arrived Wednesday, 14 March, and had his first conversation with Bismarck at the Italian legation.[4] Later in the evening Benedetti met him at a party given by the minister-president, where the ambassador contented himself with merely alluding to the un-

---

[1] *Ibid.*

[2] "With laudable care, Benedetti reports to Paris everything the Prussian minister-president is willing to tell him. His numerous dispatches remain most of the time unanswered" (LA GORCE, *Études*, p. 322). Cf. OLLIVIER, VIII, 438, who attributes Benedetti's ignorance about some of the emperor's diplomatic moves to a lack of confidence in him on the part of the emperor and Drouyn de Lhuys. His analysis seems rather biased and reflects a desire to overlook serious flaws in the methods of imperial diplomacy. Cf. VALENTIN, p. 279; ft. 3, p. 47 above.

[3] Benedetti to Drouyn de Lhuys, Berlin, 14 March 1866, FAE CP, Prusse/355, no. 42; see also F. BEICHE, *Bismarck und Italien. Ein Beitrag zur Vorgeschichte des Krieges, 1866*, "Historische Studien," Vol. 208 (Berlin, 1931), *passim*.

[4] *BGW*, V, 412, explanatory ft.

intentional publicity connected with the Italian's presence.[1] The renewed activity in Prussian diplomacy, inaugurated with the Paris consultation and now intensified by the appearance of the Italian general, persuaded Benedetti that Bismarck's influence over the king was in the ascendancy and that the course he had traced for Prussia was to be taken without reservation.[2] His latest impression gathered in conversation with Bismarck, Károlyi, and others, was that Austria could ill-afford to tolerate the preparation, both military and diplomatic, which the Prussian government pursued.[3] On 16 and 17 March, Benedetti conferred with both Bismarck and Camillo Barral de Monteauvrad, the Italian envoy, relative to Govone's activities in Berlin.[4] The following day he remarked to General Govone that he considered the situation far more serious than during the Olmütz crisis, but that Prussia did not as yet dare to precipitate a war.[5] He wrote Drouyn de Lhuys that Prusso-Italian negotiations for an alliance had begun in Berlin. Italy was not pressed to conclude an accord but was willing, however, to sign an alliance with its objects well defined and its execution set for an early date. Bismarck had pointed out to Govone that he could not yet negotiate upon such a basis; relations with Austria would have to become far more aggravated, offering no alternative but recourse to war, before Prussia could engage herself in such a definite commitment. He had hoped that an alliance could be agreed upon on a basis of eventual execution.[6]

Not long afterwards the negotiations with General Govone led Bismarck to complain to the French ambassador of the difficulties which hampered the alliance he hoped to conclude. The Italian insistence upon war by a certain date in the near future had not relented, while the minister-president had remained steadfast in his assertion that Prussia could only enter into an agreement which called

---

[1] Govone to La Marmora, Berlin, 15 March 1866, G. GOVONE, *Mémoires, 1848–1870*, tr. M. H. Weil (Paris, 1905), p. 437; CLARK, p. 344.

[2] Cf. Bondy to Reiset, Cassel, 16 March 1866, G. REISET, *Mes souvenirs*, Vol. III, *L'unité de l'Italie et l'unité de l'Allemagne* (Paris, 1903), p. 389. Bondy had visited Benedetti in Berlin where he had been informed by the ambassador of the developments and the issues engaged between Prussia and Austria, which convinced him that Bismarck would not turn back.

[3] Countess Gabriele Hatzfeld-Weisweiler to Mensdorff, on the railroad between Berlin and Dresden, 17 March 1866, *QDPO*, V/i, 313. Cf. Bylandt to Cremers, Berlin, 16 March 1866, RBZ, Pruisen/1866, no. 61, who reports that Benedetti had had very long conversations with both Bismarck and Károlyi after a party at Bismarck's residence. Cf. Károlyi to Mensdorff, Berlin, 17 March 1866, *QDPO*, V/i, 308.

[4] KOHL, I, 274.

[5] Govone to La Marmora, Berlin, 18 March 1866, GOVONE, p. 443.

[6] Benedetti to Drouyn de Lhuys, Berlin, 18 March 1866, *ODG*, VIII, 15–17.

for an eventual implementation.[1] By now completely in the confidence of the Italians,[2] Benedetti informed Drouyn de Lhuys that they feared an indefinite period would permit Bismarck, by placing Italy in his camp for an unlimited time, to intimidate Austria into conceding his demands and at the same stroke rob Italy of her chance to obtain Venetia. By the same token the Prussian government feared that if an alliance were concluded at once and for a definite date, Italy could use it as a lever against Austria for the outright cession of Venetia and, consequently, repudiate the engagement *vis-à-vis* Prussia. Mutual distrust had caused an *impasse* which was only overcome by a modification which Bismarck suggested – an alliance stipulating that for Italy to be obligated war must come within three months. Satisfied with this proposition, General Govone had agreed, after consultation with his government, to the drafting of a text to be submitted to the cabinet in Florence.[3] Yet, Bismarck's fear that the Italian government might show the text in Vienna before returning it to Berlin had led him to postpone presenting his draft to the Italian negotiator. Pressed by Count Barral, who took up the negotiations with Bismarck, a draft was agreed upon and immediately communicated to the Italian cabinet.[4] The degree to which the French ambassador was privy to these negotiations is revealed by Barral's dictation to him of the provisions of the draft treaty as soon as it had been agreed upon by Bismarck.[5] The apparent intimacy of Benedetti with the details of the negotiations during the first phase was probably due to his professed Italian sympathies as well as to his official position with the French government which enhanced his value as an adviser to the Italians. Regardless of his attitude toward purely Prussian schemes, he undoubtedly supported an alliance which would, if implemented, bring closer to its goal Italian irredentism.[6] The correspondence between the am-

---

[1] Same to same, Berlin, 27 March 1866, *ibid.*, pp. 81–82.

[2] *Ibid.*, p. 84. "I think I should tell you that the president of the council [Bismarck] keeps Benedetti exactly informed of the negotiations with us" (Govone to La Marmora, Berlin, 28 March 1866, GOVONE, p. 450).

[3] Benedetti to Drouyn de Lhuys, Berlin, 27 March 1866, *ODG*, VIII, 81–82. For text of the draft treaty, see same to same, Berlin, 28 March 1866, *ibid.*, pp. 101–102.

[4] Same to same, Berlin, 27 March 1866, *ibid.*, pp. 81–92. The interview took place on the 27th and Bismarck treated with Barral because Govone did not have full powers of negotiation (*ibid.*, p. 82, ft. 3).

[5] Benedetti to Drouyn de Lhuys, Berlin, 27 March 1866, *ibid.*, p. 84.

[6] "Although the French ambassador states that he has no instructions, it is evident that he pushes with all his force our offensive and defensive alliance with Prussia (Barral to La Marmora, Berlin, 27 March 1866, L. CHIALA, *Ancora un po' più di luce sugli eventi politici e militari dell'anno 1866* [Florence, 1902], p. 90).

bassador and his government does not indicate that he had recently received instructions by which to guide himself relative to the Prusso-Italian negotiations. His past experience, his awareness of imperial sympathies for the Italian cause probably justified, at least to himself, the attitude which he had assumed thus far.[1]

The new situation as depicted in Benedetti's last dispatches prompt-ed the foreign minister to remind the ambassador of the policy which the imperial government was following relative to German affairs. While confessing that France could not be indifferent to the course of events, he did not think it necessary or advisable to modify the neutral position thus far maintained:

> You have very well understood that the natural development of an expected situation did not entail modifications of the instructions which you have re-ceived and, that in taking them as you have done for the rule regarding your statements and your conduct, you have conformed exactly to the intentions of the government of His Majesty. You have also had a presentiment that the loyal neutrality which we have imposed upon ourselves forbade us to mix into the schemes and the alliances which Prussia or Austria could seek and pursue in anticipation of the war which might break out between them. We remained therefore absolutely ignorant of the treaty of alliance, offensive and defensive, the draft of which has been made between Bismarck and the minister of Italy . . . . We have no right to intervene in similar arrangements. . . . We had to abstain thus from any advice, any incitation, and from all influence.[2]

While the French government had not officially participated in the negotiations, there was little doubt about its sympathies. The en-couragement given to Prussia's annexation policy and the support of the Prusso-Italian *rapprochement* gave ample proof of a neutrality which continuously remained benevolent to the aspirations of one party to the dispute. Just as the French government had not hidden its sympathies, so the French ambassador in Berlin had not remained indifferent to the alliance between Prussia and Italy.[3] Neither he

---

[1] "I was well received by the emperor. . . . He thinks the signing of the treaty with Prussia useful" (Arese to La Marmora, Paris, 30 March 1866, J. GRABINSKI, *Un ami de NapoléonIII*; *le comte Arese et la politique italienne sous le Second Empire* [Paris, 1897], pp. 225–226); Goltz to Bismarck, Paris, 30 March 1866, ONCKEN, I, 121, ft. 1; OLLIVIER, VIII, 56.

[2] Drouyn de Lhuys to Benedetti, Paris, 30 March 1866, FAE CP, Prusse/355, no. 20.

[3] Benedetti was able to hide for a time his intimate knowledge about the Prusso-Italian negotiations from some of his colleagues. "I have alluded once or twice in a conversation with Benedetti to the existence of the supposed treaty between Prussia and Italy, but he gave me no information which could induce a belief that he was cognizant of the terms of the treaty, or of the nature of any negociations between Count Bismarck and General Govone; on the contrary, he spoke with some sensitiveness as if the Italian envoy [Count Barral] and General Govone had withheld from him all the information on the subject of their negociations with Count Bismarck. Be this as it may, whether Benedetti has been informed or not of the negociations carried on between Count Bismarck and General Govone, or whether he has cognizance of said treaty or not, being of Italian origin, and devoted to the

nor the emperor had acted according to Drouyn de Lhuys' concept of neutrality. Indeed, Napoleon admitted to Nigra that he had not taken the foreign minister into his confidence and for that reason must also exclude his ambassador in Berlin.[1] Although Benedetti had reported to the *Quai d'Orsay* on the alliance, he had not indicated the extent of his own role in the negotiations. It is obvious that Drouyn de Lhuys had been deliberately kept ignorant on the issue, and the incident serves to illustrate Napoleon's peculiar conduct of diplomacy. It also shows the distrust between foreign minister and ambassador and explains, in part, the neglect with which Drouyn de Lhuys treated Benedetti in turn.

The remarks from the foreign ministry did not cause Ambassador Benedetti to lessen his interest in Prusso-Italian collaboration when the second phase of the alliance negotiations opened in Berlin. Drouyn de Lhuys' reminder that the imperial government would abstain from giving any advice or exercising its influence was promptly violated by the ambassador. It is apparent that in this he acted as agent of the emperor and that as such, it must be assumed in the absence of written instructions, Benedetti acted in accord with earlier oral instructions from Napoleon.

When he heard that authorization to conclude the alliance had been delayed by the Italian king's absence from Turin, Benedetti suggested to Govone that Italy postpone the final signature until Prussia had completed her mobilization.[2] This would leave open the way for a bilateral agreement with Austria, while it would prompt Prussia to accelerate her preparations for war. Govone replied that in that case it would be better not to enter into any agreement until hostilities had commenced. However, he felt that a war between Prussia and Austria would be so short – not more than two major battles or a six weeks' campaign – that it would be virtually impossible to conclude an alliance, mobilize, and participate in the action. It was for these reasons that the Italian government desired to make the accord and follow up with war preparations. Govone also pointed out that the

---

Italian cause, – it may be surmised that he would not view with a jealous eye any event calculated to promote the ambition of the Italian nation to acquire possession of Venetia" (Loftus to Clarendon, Berlin, 9 May 1866, PRO FO 64/594, no. 190). "Being a Corsican by birth, patriotism led him [Benedetti]to espouse the cause of Italian unity and independence, and he was probably the more anxious and ready to do so knowing they were the sentiments of his Imperial master" (A. LOFTUS, *Diplomatic Reminiscences, Second Series* [London, 1894], I, 52). Cf. Metternich to Mensdorff, Paris, 31 March 1866, ONCKEN, I, 123.

[1] Goltz to Bismarck, Paris, 23 March 1866, *ibid.*, 121, ft. 1.

[2] Benedetti to Drouyn de Lhuys, Berlin, 1 April 1866, *ODG*, VIII, 135–136.

alliance in itself was an important element for expediting the outbreak of the war, namely, a means to dispose King William toward a rupture with Austria. Lastly he considered it improbable that Italy would care in any case to come to an agreement with Austria.[1]

Benedetti did not doubt Bismarck's desire for war, but he was not as yet convinced that it could be implemented. He told Govone: "War will only become probable if the mistakes made on the opposite side legitimatize the considerable and persistent armaments of Prussia and if things come to such a point as to make another Olmütz necessary to both parties." [2] Extending his analysis to the personalities involved in the issues demanding a solution in Germany, Benedetti pictured King William as being, in a sense, a fanatic who at the bottom of his heart harbored theories of divine right and who had an unshakable belief in the providential mission of kings. The ambassador did not think William a complicated personality, nor that his philosophy was steeped in mysticism: his views and opinions were predetermined by the interpretation he had given to kingship, and which had a philosophical resemblance to that of his illustrious ancestor Frederick the Great. As for Bismarck, Benedetti considered him, like William, uncomplicated in philosophical outlook and possessed of one mania: to relegate Austria to the rank of a secondary power and to assure the preponderance of Prussia in Germany. Although he expressed no sympathy for Bismarck's aims, Benedetti paid tribute to his perseverance and adroitness. He told Govone that the king was dependent upon his minister to safeguard his prerogatives in the struggle with the Prussian parliament and that this factor was perhaps decisive in the ultimate reaction of the king to Bismarck's plan.[3]

Benedetti's recommendation that Italy sign an alliance only after the completion of the Prussian mobilization was based on valid considerations. The ambassador was anxious that Italy should not prejudice her chances to obtain Venetia by means other than war. He did not share the belief that the unity of Italy must of necessity be forged in heroic battle, and he would have been satisfied to see Italian aspirations furthered by peaceful means. Furthermore, he was not absolutely convinced of the inevitability of war. The secondary

---

[1] Govone to La Marmora, Berlin, 6 April 1866, GOVONE, p. 457.

[2] *Ibid.*, p. 458. Cf. "There were no real grounds nor justification for a war between Austria and Prussia as regarded the question of the Elbe Duchies.... So much was this the case that the French ambassador Count Benedetti... said to me, '*Je défie à M. de Bismarck d'arriver au champs de bataille*'" (LOFTUS, I, 43).

[3] Govone to La Marmora, Berlin, 6 April 1866, GOVONE, pp. 457–458.

states, replying to Bismarck's declared intention to reform the compact,[1] were stressing the use of federal machinery to solve controversies between members of the Germanic Confederation.[2] Despite Bismarck's assertion that he would nevertheless proceed with his plans and that he had the king's support, Benedetti was less certain of the consequences. But apart from the growing efforts in Germany to prevent war, the ambassador had also been informed of Russian peace efforts. Indeed, his recommendation to Govone was made the very day Bismarck told him that Tsar Alexander had addressed a letter to Francis Joseph, a copy of which, with explanations, had been sent to William. The tsar proffered his good offices to bring the discord to a close. Bismarck had expressed doubt about Austria's willingness to reverse her military dispositions, thus making a consideration of the tsar's advice impossible. Benedetti, however, was not prepared to discount entirely the Russian intervention. If the tsar were serious in his efforts to prevent a war, the Austrian emperor might interpret his advice as a guarantee against a Prussian attack and therefore relent the pace of military preparations.[3] Moreover, the letter could be the beginning of prolonged mediation efforts which might postpone the Italian expectations by leading to a new Gastein.

The observations of Ambassador Benedetti did not influence the determination of the Italian negotiator and, as soon as authorization to conclude the alliance had arrived, he and Bismarck signed on Sunday, 8 April, the treaty of alliance. The text conformed almost exactly to the draft text. In addition, the contracting parties signed a protocol stating that the treaty was to remain secret.[4]

While the Prusso-Italian negotiations had been carried on, Benedetti had not neglected to keep abreast of developments in Germany. Reports of extensive military preparations had been reaching Berlin from Vienna since the end of March, and Benedetti had learned that a council of ministers had been convoked to consider measures preliminary to a military mobilization.[5] These measures might provoke

---

[1] Benedetti to Drouyn de Lhuys, Berlin, 26 March 1866, FAE CP, Prusse/355, no. 49.

[2] Same to same, Berlin, 1 April 1866, *ibid.*, no. 55.

[3] Same to same, Berlin, 6 April 1866, *ibid.*, no. 60.

[4] Same to same, Berlin, 9 April 1866, *ODG*, VIII, 200, T. For text of alliance see *ibid.*, pp. 462–463.

[5] Cf. Loë, p. 85. Loë, Prussian military attaché in Paris, had been recalled to Berlin in the latter part of March to report on the ability of the French army to launch a war. Asked how strong Prussian forces on the Rhine would have to be to deal successfully with any French intervention attempt, he replied that the French army would not be able to concentrate a large force in that area. Loë writes that Moltke agreed with his view and that Berlin was fully aware of French military weakness in 1866.

a large-scale Austrian preparation and give Bismarck the chance to accuse the Vienna cabinet of harboring bellicose intentions.[1] It would be necessary to gauge the extent of Prussian preparations after the council meeting, but Benedetti thought "the situation was in fact too dangerous to let go unchecked and that it should be ended." [2]

On 26 March Benedetti found Bismarck preoccupied with Austrian military preparations – extensive preparations which the Prussian government could not ignore.[3] In Prussia all steps necessary for a mobilization had been taken, and he predicted that a change-over to a state of war could be accomplished swiftly. He did not believe Bismarck ready to take the initiative in ordering such an extreme measure as full mobilization; these preliminary steps constituted an effort to force such a decision instead upon Austria. He did not discount the possibility that Bismarck hoped, through a series of menacing manoeuvers, to win the annexation of the duchies without bloodshed.

In fact, the Prussian government was reluctant to use the duchies as a pretext for war, an observation repeatedly made by the ambassador; instead, great emphasis was given to the opinion that the defects of the federal compact made a lasting agreement between Prussia and Austria impossible. However, Benedetti suspected that the minister-president would clothe his reform proposal in a form radical enough to assure its rejection by the Austrian government. This plan was designed to develop a constitutional discord with Austria on the level of an national German issue; it would indeed move the entire political future of Germany into the arena and give Bismarck the possibility of attempting a union of the members of the Confederation against Austria. Benedetti expected that the proposal would not be presented to the diet until Prussia had ascertained

---

[1] Benedetti to Drouyn de Lhuys, Berlin, 21 March 1866, FAE CP, Prusse/355, no. 47. For Austrian military measures and the Károlyi *démarche* in Berlin in March, see CLARK, pp. 363–370.

[2] Károlyi to Mensdorff, Berlin, 22 March 1866, HHStA, Preussen/ 91, no. 21. Cf. LoË, pp. 84–85, who states that King William told him in an interview that he would go to war if the Austrian government retained its anti-Prussian attitude relative to the duchies question. Benedetti's speculation that Prussia might use Austrian military preparations as a pretext to blame the tension in Germany on Austria and to accuse her of hostile intent was borne out by a circular sent to Prussian diplomatic representatives in Germany, in part of which Bismarck asked the envoys to denounce Austria's military preparations and to inform the governments to which they were accredited that Prussia might be forced to take military measures for her own security (Benedetti to Drouyn de Lhuys, Berlin, 26 March 1866, FAE CP, Prusse/355, no. 49).

[3] About this time, Bismarck had told Lord Loftus that the alliance between Austria and Prussia was at an end, and added, "I might... use the words of Richelieu to his discarded mistress: '*Nous ne sommes pas enemies: mais nous ne nous aimons plus*'" (LOFTUS, I, 45).

the attitude of the secondary states, or until Prussia was prepared militarily to deal with the consequences of the planned steps.[1]

Two days later, on 28 March, Bismarck told Benedetti that military units belonging to the Guard were being mobilized and that the purchase of horses for the artillery had been decided upon. Yet, while the activities and measures of the Prussian government were all oriented toward war, the proponents of peace were still trying to influence the king. To this the minister-president commented, "I hope that my master will hold fast, but I would not want to be obliged to guarantee it." [2]

The armament race between Austria and Prussia had occasioned a Bavarian intervention to check the trend toward war. When the Austrian government had requested the repeal of the Prussian mobilization orders announced in the *Staats-Anzeiger* of 28 March, Count Pfordten suggested that the Prussian government postpone its reply,[3] and on 13 April he sent identical notes to the Prussian and Austrian governments proposing that the two powers repeal their war preparations simultaneously. Ambassador Benedetti, to whom Count Ludwig Montgelas had shown the text, was pessimistic about the Pfordten efforts. Bismarck as well as the king had resented the tone of the Bavarian demand,[4] and Benedetti thought they would consider Pfordten's suggestion incompatible with Prussia's dignity. The ambassador did believe, however, that if Austria agreed to the proposition the Prussian government would be forced to go along.[5] Bismarck's reply to the Austrian demand, sent to Vienna on 15 April, presaged the failure of Pfordten's effort. The minister-president told Benedetti that Prussia would not take the initiative in reversing the trend.[6] The two powers were reaching a point at which disarmament was no longer a matter of integrity but a question of security.

In addition to keeping a close check on this phase of the dispute, Benedetti had not lost sight of Bismarck's reform plan which was beginning to achieve consistency. In a special session on 9 April the

---

[1] Benedetti to Drouyn de Lhuys, Berlin, 27 March 1866, *ODG*, VIII, 77–79.
[2] Same to same, Berlin, 28 March 1866, FAE CP, Prusse/355, no. 51.
[3] Same to same, Berlin, 11 April 1866, *ibid.*, no. 64.
[4] Same to same, Berlin, 9 April 1866, *ibid.*, no. 63. Bismarck later characterized the note as sounding like a communication from the emperor of Germany to the margrave of Brandenburg, a phrase no doubt employed to wound further the intimate susceptibilities of the king and strengthen his resolve (same to same, Berlin, 10 April 1866, *ODG*, VIII, 204); CLARK, pp. 370–372.
[5] Benedetti to Drouyn de Lhuys, Berlin, 14 April 1866, FAE CP, Prusse/355, no. 66.
[6] Same to same, Berlin, 15 April 1866, *ibid.*, no. 68.

Prussian delegate in Frankfort proposed that a reform project, agreed upon by the members, should be submitted to a parliament of the Confederation elected by universal and direct suffrage.[1] Although Bismarck planned to reveal his specific proposals only after acceptance of the proposition, the importance of the contemplated step was fully appreciated by Benedetti.[2] While he considered constitutional reform a means to hasten hostilities with Austria, he knew that France could not remain indifferent to a proposal which, if implemented, might transform the relationship of the powers within the Confederation as well as between the two German powers and the great powers. Greater cohesion and unity, politically and militarily, within Germany would touch directly upon French interests. Acting on instructions, Benedetti on Monday, 16 April, engaged Bismarck in a discussion of France's position in regard to the proposed reforms, and he asked for more precise information relative to the minister-president's intentions. He stressed in particular the distinction regarding the exercise of sovereignty in internal affairs and in external affairs. While the member states had a right to reform their compact, the other powers had a legitimate interest in such a reform. Bismarck assured the ambassador that the Prussian government was fully cognizant of such considerations and would pay due attention to them. Benedetti considered it premature to go beyond this reminder for the details of the reform plan were as yet unknown.[3] However, he was convinced by now that only an outright rejection of the Prussian proposition would stop the minister-president from carrying forward his plans. Not even the fear that a constituent parliament might claim exaggerated attributes from the member governments was likely to change Bismarck's intentions. Should such a development come about, it could only lead to a break-up of the Confederation, a pleasant prospect, Benedetti thought, for Bismarck to contemplate. The political sa-

---

[1] Same to same, Berlin, 9 April 1866, *ibid.*, no. 63; Reculot to Drouyn de Lhuys, Frankfort, 9 April 1866, *ibid.*, Confédération Germanique/842, T.

[2] "I note furthermore... that Benedetti is supposed to have designated the proposals in question a 'joke.' If this were true, which I still doubt, that report must have been made some time ago, before the formulation and official presentation of the proposal" (Goltz to Bismarck, Paris, 10 April 1866, ONCKEN, I, 131). Metternich claims that Drouyn de Lhuys stated that Benedetti's dispatch on the Prussian reform proposal had been written with an *indifférence étonnante* and that Benedetti viewed the proposal as simply a *coup d'épée dans l'eau* (Metternich to Mensdorff, Paris, 9 April 1866, ONCKEN, I, 126). Both reports are refuted by the evidence of Benedetti's very meticulous analysis of Bismarcks' moves in the reform issue.

[3] Benedetti to Drouyn de Lhuys, Berlin, 17 April 1866, FAE CP, Prusse/355, no. 70. Cf. Nothomb to Rogier, Berlin, 19 April 1866, BAE CP, Prusse/23, Pt. I, no. 121.

gacity of the minister-president made a proposal which appeared to consolidate German unity the weapon for destroying the Confederation and for creating upon its ruins Prussia's hegemony in Germany.[1]

Since the Frankfort debates could only heighten the tension, Ambassador Benedetti saw little hope for an amelioration in the diplomatic relations between Austria and Prussia. The latest Austrian proposal on disarmament, submitted 20 April in Berlin, under which Prussia would follow in twenty-four hours the Austrian revocation of military measures had not been accepted by the Berlin cabinet.[2] While the Prussian counterproposal, submitted next day, had been favorably received in Vienna, the entire issue was greatly complicated by the Italian war preparations.[3] Benedetti, who dined that evening with the minister of war, General von Roon, learned that the Prussians, in case of an agreement on disarmament, intended to sell the least possible number of horses, "because," the general added, "in fifteen days we have to start again to buy them back."[4] From this Benedetti concluded that even with disarmament the conflict would soon again fester, perhaps in consequence of the proposed federal reform. But he told Govone that the solution of the armament crisis would be a strong symptom against the possibility of war, for the king, "who escaped Bismarck on this occasion could very well escape him again." [5]

In view of the Italian war preparations, the Austrian government now insisted that her military preparations could only be revoked in the north. It seemed to Benedetti that the minister-president welcomed this new development which would lead to a further deterioration of relations with Austria. He found Bismarck almost eager to vouchsafe Prussia's determination to come to Italy's aid in case of an Austrian attack against her. His momentary fear, when the Austrian proposal

---

[1] Benedetti to Drouyn de Lhuys, Berlin, 18 April 1866, FAE CP, Prusse/ 355, no. 72.

[2] Same to same, Berlin, 21 April 1866, *ibid.*, no. 74, "England and France have acted in this sense [a return to the *status quo*] in Vienna; in view of the urgency, Benedetti has even taken it upon himself to write to the duke of Gramont to have him advise Count Mensdorff to take the initiative in this sort of disarmament" (Nothomb to Rogier, Berlin, 19 April 1866, BAE CP, Prusse/23, Pt. I, no. 121).

[3] Benedetti to Drouyn de Lhuys, Berlin, 25 April 1866, FAE CP, Prusse/355, no. 77. News of the Italian military preparations strengthened the hand of Francis Joseph's military advisers, who were concerned already over the military advantages conceded to Prussia since 28 March by Mensdorff's conciliatory diplomatic efforts (CLARK, pp. 379 ff.). For an account of the April mediation efforts of the Gablenz brothers, see *ibid.*, pp. 414 ff.

[4] Govone to La Marmora, Berlin, 23 April 1866, GOVONE, p. 470.

[5] *Ibid.*

of 20 April had been received, that a peaceful solution was in the offing had given way to a more bellicose attitude.[1]

Ambassador Benedetti's concern over the new complications and over Bismarck's provocative attitude was further justified when he learned in a new meeting with the minister-president that the Austrian government had been informed that Prussia would not disarm if Austrian preparations were maintained on the Italian border. Furthermore, the Prussian envoy in Vienna had been ordered to declare that Prussia would not remain indifferent to an attack on Italy. Benedetti expressed the belief that such an announcement could only create uneasiness in Vienna and provoke additional military measures. He was under no illusion as to Bismarck's plan and he did not believe that warnings would impede the progress toward war.[2] Although Benedetti had warmly supported the Prusso-Italian alliance negotiations in hope of furthering Italian unification aspirations, he seemed concerned over the deliberate and methodical preparations for war which Bismarck now pursued. The prospect of war might also have raised doubts in his mind as to the consequences of the struggle. An Austrian victory could have a tremendously adverse effect upon the Italian cause. Yet, Benedetti was far from supporting Austria in the disarmament issue:

> Can the.... [Austrian] cabinet... pretend that it acted with all sincerity when it proposed to the [Prussian] cabinet... to renounce gradually military preparations? It seems no longer doubtful today that in that very moment it employed all its efforts to extend its armaments on one side, and on the other, to come to an agreement with the secondary courts; ... the resolution it has taken to turn the duchies affair over to the diet is the pledge for the *entente* which it has succeeded in making with the majority among them and which assures it of their support in all eventualities.[3]

Although the seriousness of the situation was pronounced, Ambassador Benedetti must have been surprised to learn from Bismarck that Emperor Napoleon had proposed the convocation of an international congress in a talk with Goltz on 23 April.[4] As on other oc-

---

[1] Benedetti to Drouyn de Lhuys, Berlin, 25 April 1866, FAE MD, Allemagne/171.

[2] Cf. Bylandt to Cremers, Berlin, 28 April 1866, RBZ, Pruisen/ 1866, no. 104, who heard that Benedetti had written a private letter to the duke of Gramont saying that the "inflexible and precipitate decision of the Vienna cabinet" favored the aims of Bismarck and the only way for Austria to paralyze those aims would be to show herself *partout* sincerely and frankly peaceful, and not to admit that she could be anymore attacked in the south than in the north.

[3] Benedetti to Drouyn de Lhuys, Berlin, 29 April 1866, FAE CP, Prusse/355, no. 80.

[4] A. KULESSA, *Kongressidee Napoleons III. im Mai 1866* (Leipzig, 1927), pp. 23–24; cf. SYBEL, IV, 364–365.

casions, Benedetti had not been informed of this development which carried with it the possibility of a change in policy relative to affairs in Germany. The emperor's affinity for international conferences was known to Benedetti, but thus far he had had no indication that such a prospect was being entertained in Paris. His main task had been the prevention of an Austro-Prussian coalition and now, when these two powers were at the breaking point, the emperor suggested a conference to settle the dispute between them. The instructions from Drouyn de Lhuys, who usually was not in the emperor's confidence, also had failed to indicate a possible shift in policy. Benedetti did not comment upon the matter but confined himself to a report on Bismarck's reaction to the congress idea. The minister-president did not favor it and had expressed the view that only war could prepare the ground for a successful congress. He thought it best to wait until disarmament had become a *fait accompli*, in any case, and had intimated that for the moment Prussia preferred war.[1] Bismarck feared that a congress would postpone indefinitely the decision with Austria and perhaps lead to a regrouping of the powers which might be detrimental to Prussia's interests. He preferred accords with the individual powers and, having concluded the Italian alliance, he now desired an understanding with the imperial government. Thus, rather than reject the congress proposal outright, he made Prussia's acceptance conditional upon a prior accord with France.[2]

It was not until 3 May that Benedetti was directly and officially notified of Napoleon's suggestion for a congress. A circular of the foreign ministry communicated the proposal which Drouyn de Lhuys had meanwhile discussed with Goltz, Metternich and Cowley and requested that the respective governments be asked to give their views on this new development.[3] Although Benedetti had already relayed Bismarck's reaction, he now officially informed the minister-president and was told again that Prussia would make her acceptance dependent upon a prior agreement with the French government.[4] Benedetti had hardly fathomed the meaning of the new proposal, when he received word from Drouyn de Lhuys that the congress idea had been abandoned for the time being.[5] The proposal did arouse of course

---

[1] Benedetti to Drouyn de Lhuys, Berlin, 25 April 1866, FAE MD, Allemagne/171.

[2] KULESSA, pp. 25–26.

[3] Drouyn de Lhuys to diplomatic agents, Paris, 2 May 1866, FAE CP, Angleterre/737, T. Cf. SYBEL, IV, 365–366. Drouyn de Lhuys supposedly told Goltz that France had enough influence and desired, like the other powers, to gain more territory.

[4] Benedetti to Drouyn de Lhuys, Berlin, 3 May 1866, FAE MD, Allemagne/171.

[5] Drouyn de Lhuys to Benedetti, Paris, 6 May 1866, FAE CP, Prusse/356, T. The con-

a great deal of speculation. Both Prussian and Austrian diplomats saw it as a threat to their respective plans. Bismarck was convinced that Napoleon sought to postpone war in order to see Austrian preparations completed and Italian obligations *vis-à-vis* Prussia terminated – as stipulated in the alliance of 8 April. It meant, so Bismarck reasoned, that France expected Prussia to find herself in a precarious position and, hence, forced to accept the ambitious compensation demands of Napoleon.[1]

The obvious lack of co-ordination and information was even more pronounced, at this same time, in a development relative to the Prusso-Italian alliance. The armament crisis had awakened fears in Bismarck that Italy might precipitate a clash with Austria in order to realize her schemes. He told Benedetti that the alliance did not formally obligate Prussia to go to Italy's aid should the latter alone become the victim of Austrian aggression.[2] Benedetti warned Govone about Bismarck's apprehensions, and the general, on 2 May, discussed the propriety and justifiability of the Italian measures with the minister-president.[3] Already next day Benedetti learned that Bismarck had agreed that Prussia was morally, if not formally, bound to assist Italy in case of an Austrian attack.[4] Benedetti's efforts to prevent a rift in the alliance contrasted sharply with the activities of the emperor at this time.[5] A conditional Austrian offer to cede Venetia was made to Napoleon between 3 and 4 May and prompted him to try to exploit the slight rift between Prussia and Italy, news of which had just reached him through Nigra.[6] However, his endeavor to get the

---

jecture can be advanced that the emperor had not yet abandoned hope of persuading Italy to accept the cession of Venetia in spite of her obligations under the treaty of alliance with Prussia. Such an event would satisfy Italian grievances toward Austria, while at the same time create for Prussia a disadvantage in Germany. Napoleon could hope to exploit the Prussian dilemma to the fullest. However, La Marmora's rejection was wired to Nigra in Paris on Saturday, 5 May, and perhaps was not known to the emperor when he delivered a speech in Auxerre on Sunday, 6 May. The telegram to Benedetti was evidently sent in ignorance of the Italian rejection and in anticipation of favorable arrangements with Austria and Italy. Cf. Drouyn de Lhuys to Gramont, Paris, 11 May 1866, *ODG*, IX, 95–97; *ibid.*, 95–97, ft. 1; CASE, pp. 200 ff.

[1] GEUSS; pp. 157 ff.

[2] Benedetti to Drouyn de Lhuys, Berlin, 2 May 1866, FAE MD, Autriche/67.

[3] Govone to La Marmora, Berlin, 2 May 1866, GOVONE, p. 473.

[4] Benedetti to Drouyn de Lhuys, Berlin, 3 May 1866, FAE MD, Allemagne/171.

[5] See *ODG*, IX, 95–97, ft. 1. "The Emperor Napoleon was a mystic dreamer, and, being a fatalist, believed that his dreams were destined to be fulfilled; and the secret means he employed for carrying out his ambitions and tortuous policy ended disastrously to himself and to France" (LOFTUS, I, 84).

[6] See Metternich to Mensdorff, Paris, 5 May 1866, ONCKEN, I, 160. The prince reports a proposal of the emperor to remain neutral and to guarantee Italy's neutrality in case of an

Italians to accept – and desert Prussia – failed when a Marmora, in reply to Nigra's communication of the offer, telegraphed on 5 May that it was a question of honor and loyalty not to break the pledge to Prussia.[1] This episode of imperial vacillation illustrates the difficulties of representing the emperor abroad.

To make matters worse Benedetti was also ignorant of still another consideration which had prompted the message. On 1 May the emperor had confided to Goltz that the Austrian government was anxious to come to an agreement with France but that he personally preferred an understanding with Prussia.[2] When Goltz had inquired about the basis for such an accord, the emperor had replied that the eyes of France were directed toward the Rhine.[3] Anxious to keep this overture secret he also asked that Benedetti be kept ignorant of it.[4] The isolation of Benedetti is impossible to comprehend, particularly when related to his mission of preventing an Austro-Prussian *entente* and of furthering a *rapprochement* between France and Prussia. It implied a lack of confidence which was totally unwarranted in the light of Benedetti's own views.

It was not until mid-May that Benedetti gained some indication of the emperor's plans. Again the information came to him indirectly and through Bismarck. During an interview with the minister-president on 14 May, the ambassador found that Bismarck, and apparently Goltz as well, were disturbed about changing and conflicting attitudes on the part of the French government. Not only did Benedetti hear about a supposedly pro-Austrian attitude in Paris, but he also learned about the overtures which had been made to Goltz relative to the Rhine. As for the fear in Berlin that France was drawing closer to Austria, the ambassador could only state that

---

Austro-Prussian war. The date of this report indicates that Napoleon was still ignorant of La Marmora's refusal to accept Venetia. Cf. PERSIGNY, pp. 358–361; KULESSA, pp. 28–29, who shows that La Marmora was advised of the Austrian offer by Nigra on 5 May. CLARK, pp. 403 ff.

[1] A. DE LA MARMORA, *Un peu plus de lumière sur les événements politiques et militaires de l'année 1866*, trans. Niox and Descoubes (Paris, 1874), pp. 215–226. To his refusal La Marmora appended: "But since the treaty expires 8 July one can arrange the thing at a congress."

[2] Goltz to Bismarck, Paris, 1 May 1866, ONCKEN, I, 145–150. Cf. Bismarck to Goltz, Berlin, 5 May 1866, *BGW*, V, 482–484, in which Bismarck informed the ambassador that Prussia could not offer the left bank of the Rhine to France. GEUSS, pp. 160 ff.

[3] See above ft. 2. The speculation can be allowed that, as in the case of Italy, the emperor was unaware at the time of the Auxerre speech of Bismarck's denial of his bid for the left bank of the Rhine; the explanation of the telegram of Drouyn de Lhuys offered above may now be extended to the *entente* feelers toward Prussia.

[4] Goltz to Bismarck, Paris, 1 May 1866, ONCKEN, I, 147–148.

the intentions attributed to the imperial government were irreconcilable with his own impressions.[1] Embarrassed no doubt, Benedetti preferred not to reveal to Bismarck that he was completely ignorant of the confidential talks of Napoleon and Drouyn de Lhuys with Goltz, Metternich and Nigra. He probably welcomed the news that a Prussian officer, Major von Burg, had been sent to Paris with a letter from the king to the emperor in an effort to ascertain the position of the French government. Despite this humiliating experience Benedetti did not complain at once to the foreign ministry. Perhaps he did not quite believe that he had been grossly neglected, or perhaps he preferred to await the return of the officer before deciding what to do. He again met with Bismarck on Friday, 18 May, and was told that Major von Burg had returned without having delivered the letter. Goltz claimed that the emperor was preparing a conciliation program with the Russian and British ambassadors,[2] and that he himself had failed to win Napoleon over to a tripartite accord between France, Italy and Prussia. For this reason he had thought it best not to communicate the king's letter.[3] Benedetti could do little to counter the bitter recriminations which Bismarck directed at the imperial government.[4] Speaking "not without regret and pain" Bismarck asserted that Prussia, despite French perfidy, would not submit to Austria but would fight. He told Benedetti that the Prussian army was at peak condition and that at worst it would obtain an honorable peace with the enemy.[5]

Benedetti did not consider the neglect with which he had been treated by his government as simply a personal slight. He was far more concerned about the fact that his ignorance about the emperor's aims had been misconstrued by Bismarck. The minister-president had suspected that the ambassador was aware of the emperor's intentions and that his reserve during their conversations was designed to shield them from him. Benedetti knew that such a belief on Bismarck's part could have serious repercussions and cost him Bismarck's confidence.

[1] Benedetti to Drouyn de Lhuys, Berlin, 15 May 1866, FAE MD, Allemagne/171.
[2] France had entered into such consultation on the initiative of the British government (Drouyn de Lhuys to diplomatic agents, Paris, 18 May 1866, FAE CP, Autriche/491, no. 52).
[3] Benedetti to Drouyn de Lhuys, Berlin, 19 May 1866, FAE MD, Allemagne/171.
[4] Bismarck insisted that the consultation of the French government with Russia and Britain was a deliberate attempt to give Austria a free hand to seek the annexation of Silesia in compensation for a renunciation of Venetia (ibid.). Drouyn de Lhuys had rejected such a proposition from Metternich (Drouyn de Lhuys to Gramont, Paris, 11 May 1866, ODG, IX, 95-97).
[5] Benedetti to Drouyn de Lhuys, Berlin, 19 May 1866, FAE MD, Allemagne/171.

I would certainly neglect my duty toward you [he wrote to Drouyn de Lhuys] if I did not tell you that the ignorance in which you leave me places me in a false position. The majority of my colleagues are more or less informed, those of England and Russia [are] exactly [informed], and you will easily judge how difficult it is for me therefore to accept any discussion at all with them. Nobody wanting to believe it is so... they all imagine, and Bismarck with them, that I am in the possession of all your secrets; only they conclude from my silence that these secrets are of such a nature that it is necessary for us to hide them in Berlin.... Bismarck pretends, rightly or wrongly, that the majority of our ministers in Germany are not as discreet and that everywhere their language is hostile to Prussia. 'The contrast with your reserve,' he told me yesterday, 'is at least as strange, and how can one believe that they are authorized to speak while you are asked to remain silent.'... I am not motivated by vain curiosity or misplaced susceptibility. I do not have the ridiculous pretension to reverse the roles and to be informed, instead of remaining an informer; but even in this capacity I owe it to you not to let you ignore the inconveniences of my personal situation.[1]

The mystery of imperial policy was somewhat clarified for the ambassador when next day he received a circular informing him of the renewed discussions relative to the proposed congress.[2] Drouyn de Lhuys made also a point of paying his respects to the initiative and accuracy of Benedetti's efforts to keep the ministry informed, a compliment which the ambassador could hardly return. The minister brought him up to date on news which had reached Paris from Benedetti's colleagues and promised definite information on the congress proposal as soon as available.[3] Benedetti was still in the dark on various points and, worse, he had noticed a definite reserve on the part of Bismarck. When he had sought to obtain the facts on the sudden return of Govone to Berlin, he had found the minister-president tight-lipped.[4] Rather than reply to his question, Bismarck had shown his disapproval of the haste with which France proceeded to arrange a congress. He had reminded Benedetti that Prussia would continue to insist upon a prior agreement with France and he pointed out that he was still waiting for talks with the imperial government on that point.[5]

Preparations for the congress had indeed progressed rapidly. On 27 May Benedetti was instructed to meet with Loftus and Oubril and

[1] Same to same, Berlin, 19 May 1866, *MMP*, pp. 151–152.

[2] Drouyn de Lhuys to diplomatic agents, Paris, 18 May 1866, FAE CP, Autriche/491, no. 52.

[3] Drouyn de Lhuys to Benedetti, Paris, 22 May 1866, *ibid.*, Prusse/356, no. 38, no. 39.

[4] Benedetti to Drouyn de Lhuys, Berlin, 22 May 1866, *ibid.*, T. For the movements of Govone, see *ODG*, IX, 223, ft. 1. The Italian general did not discuss any political issues during his stay in Berlin the purpose of which was to pay a farewell call to the king (Benedetti to Drouyn de Lhuys, Berlin, 23 May 1866, FAE MD, Autriche/67).

[5] Same to same, Berlin, 22 May 1866, *ibid.*, Allemagne/171.

arrange for the transmission of a common invitation to the Prussian government.[1] The situation in Germany had decidedly deteriorated since the beginning of the month. King William had given his approval for the mobilization plans,[2] while the Saxon government had petitioned the diet for support after the Prussian government had inquired about Saxon troop activities on her borders.[3] Prussian mobilization on 8 May had heightened the tension [4] and reports of military preparations by the secondary states were reaching Berlin from everywhere. In the diet the opposition to Prussia had crystallized, and the delegate of the Prussian government had made it clear that Prussia would place her own interests ahead of her relationship with the Confederation.[5]

After a short consultation with his two colleagues, Benedetti asked for an appointment with the minister-president which was granted for 28 May. At this meeting, Benedetti stated the purpose of the request and communicated the dispatch which invited the Prussian government to attend a conference for the consideration of the duchies question, the Venetian problem, and the federal reforms insofar as they might affect the European balance of power. His declaration was followed by similar ones on the part of Loftus and Oubril. While indicating the probable acceptance of the invitation by the king, Bismarck noted that the duchies question, in his opinion, was not a threat to the peace; instead he pointed to the armament race, the consequence of the Austro-Prussian dispute, as a likely cause for war. He also expressed the view that the Germanic Confederation would be adequately represented by Austria and Prussia, thus making a special representation of the diet, as planned by the three powers, superfluous.[6]

After the invitation had been tendered to the Prussian government, Benedetti presented his observations to Drouyn de Lhuys relative to the reaction in Berlin. Recalling the past reluctance of the king

---

[1] Drouyn de Lhuys to diplomatic agents, Paris, 24 May 1866, *ibid.*, France/Circulaires politiques, 1863–1869, V, 2128; same to same, Paris, 26 May 1866, *ibid.* Cf. *Projet d'allocution pour l'ouverture du congrès* [Paris], 29 May 1866, FAE CP, Autriche/491.

[2] Benedetti to Drouyn de Lhuys, Berlin, 3 May 1866, *ibid.*, Prusse/356, T. The first orders called for the mobilization of the 3rd, 4th, 5th and 6th corps; the 8th was mobilized on 6 May, followed by the 1st, 2nd and 7th corps on 8 May.

[3] Same to same, Berlin, 5 May 1866, *ibid.*, no. 85.

[4] Same to same, Berlin, 7 May 1866, *ibid.*, no. 88; same to same, Berlin, 8 May 1866, *ibid.*, no. 89.

[5] Same to same, Berlin, 12 May 1866, *ibid.*, no. 94; *AD* (Paris, 1861–1914), 1866, II, 425–428.

[6] Benedetti to Drouyn de Lhuys, Berlin, 28 May 1866, FAE CP, Prusse/356, no. 109.

to start a war against Austria, Benedetti reported that William
would accept the proposal favorably. Concessions which he would
refuse to make to Austria outright, William might be disposed to
make to Europe instead. However, Benedetti did not believe that
the minister-president shared the attitude of the monarch. Bismarck,
hopeful to disrupt the 1815 system, had accepted war as the supreme
and the best means for attaining his ends. A congress would only
upset his plans and check the ambitions of the Prussian cabinet.
Only fear of isolation would, in Benedetti's belief, bring Bismarck
to accept the congress idea. The ambassador cautioned the minister
against expecting a Prussian contribution to an actual solution;
he rather expected Bismarck to place obstacles in the path of a
congress success. He also warned that internal conditions in Prussia might strengthen the arguments for war; the peculiar financial
situation of the Prussian government could place it soon before a
decision for or against war. Moreover, the fact that armaments
of the secondary states, which showed very definite tendencies of
supporting Austria, were as yet incomplete might cause a desire
in Berlin to strike against those states before their forces could take
the field. These factors could permit Bismarck a decisive influence
upon the king's disposition; supported by the military he could
perhaps bring about the war even though a congress were in session.[1]
While not unduly pessimistic, Benedetti did make it clear that the
danger was not removed simply by the convocation of an international
congress.

Bismarck, in his dispatch to Goltz, did not go beyond the reservations made earlier to the three envoys and merely stated that the
Prussian government would accept the invitation.[2] However, he
told Barral "with a mark of deep discontent, 'The French emperor
now wants peace at all cost.'"[3] He also expressed his hope that the
congress would be of short duration, giving no hint as to whether he
foresaw failure or success.[4] His anxiety regarding the convocation
of a congress and the prolonged uncertainty it might create prompted
the minister-president to point out that the date for the convocation,
12 June,[5] was far too distant. He told Benedetti that every delay
would prejudice the position of Prussia and implied that the Prussian

---

[1] Same to same, Berlin, 29 May 1866, *ibid.*, no. 110.
[2] Bismarck to Goltz, Berlin, 29 May 1866, *ibid.*, copy.
[3] Barral to La Marmora, Berlin, 29 May 1866, LA MARMORA, p. 269.
[4] Same to same, Berlin, 30 May 1866, *ibid.*, p. 270.
[5] Drouyn de Lhuys to diplomatic agents, Paris, 31 May 1866, FAE CP, Angleterre/737, T.

government "might have to examine to what point it could adhere to adjournments which assure its adversaries advantages equal to a battle won." [1] Benedetti's dispatches to Drouyn de Lhuys show that he had expected similar reservations from the minister-president and that he had drawn the foreign minister's attention to such a possibility.[2]

Drouyn de Lhuys informed Benedetti on 1 June that the acceptance of Prussia had been communicated by Goltz and that favorable replies were expected from the Confederation and the Italian government as well. He reported that no indication of Austria's decision had as yet been received, but he voiced the hope that the foreign ministers of all the invited states would attend.[3] Drouyn de Lhuys' expectation that Austria, like Prussia, would give its unconditional acceptance did not materialize. Instead the conditions formulated in the reply became an effective aid to the designs of Bismarck. On 3 June he had told Benedetti that reports from Vienna and St. Petersburg pointed toward a conditional Austrial acceptance,[4] and on the following day, when the ambassador was at Bismarck's office, a telegram from the Prussian embassy in Paris announced the conditions which the Austrian government had attached to its acceptance of the congress invitation: the participating powers were not to debate any territorial questions and were to renounce, a priori, territorial aggrandizement.[5] These demands became an insurmountable obstacle to an international congress; the hopes of resolving the issues in this fashion were indeed shattered by the Austrian reply.

The failure of the international mediation attempt removed the last barrier to war. On 5 June General Ludwig von Gablenz, the Austrian commander in Holstein, ordered the convocation of the estates of the duchy.[6] Prussia seized upon this step as the needed pretext for launching military efforts to safeguard her own interests.[7] On 7 June General Manteuffel was ordered into Holstein to

---

[1] Benedetti to Drouyn de Lhuys, Berlin, 1 June 1866, *ibid.*, Prusse/357, T.

[2] Same to same, Berlin, 1 June 1866, *ibid.*, no. 112. "There is no doubt, the French ambassador told me, that Count Bismarck goes [to the congress] with the decided wish to touch off the powder keg" (Barral to La Marmora, Berlin, 1 June 1866, LA MARMORA, p. 291); Nothomb to Rogier, Berlin, 1 June 1866, BAE CP, Prusse/23, Pt. II, no. 184.

[3] Drouyn de Lhuys to Benedetti, Paris, 1 June 1866, FAE CP, Prusse/357, no. 46. The plenipotentiary of the Confederation, Pfordten, was designated on 1 June (*AD*, 1866, III, 29–30).

[4] Benedetti to Drouyn de Lhuys, Berlin, 3 June 1866, FAE CP, Prusse/357, no. 116.

[5] Same to same, Berlin, 4 June 1866, FAE MD, Allemagne/171. Benedetti added that Bismarck, on reading the telegram, exclaimed, "Long live the king."

[6] *ODG*, IX, 337.

[7] *MMP*, pp. 132–133.

prevent the convocation of the estates. Surprisingly enough, Gablenz withdrew across the Elbe into Hanover and for the moment a clash of arms was avoided. The Austrian government demanded, on 11 June, immediate military action by the diet against Prussia and ordered its envoy in Berlin to request his passports.[1] Károlyi left the Prussian capital late the following evening, while two days later, 14 June, the diet adopted the Austrian proposal by a vote of nine to five.[2] In the face of this adverse vote, the Prussian delegate declared the Confederation dissolved and withdrew. The Prussian government next day followed up with ultimatums to, and subsequent invasion of, Hanover, Saxony, and Hesse.[3] The defenses of these states could not stem the Prussian tide, and Germany became the scene of impressive Prussian military performances, clearing the way for the decisive battle yet to come between Austria and Prussia. Austria's treaty with France of 12 June, by which she ceded Venetia for French neutrality, was a desperate gesture.[4] It did not prevent a two-front war against Austria, for on 20 June the Italian government declared war. Austria was beleaguered by foes who intended to make her defeat the basis for their rise to political and military power.

Ambassador Benedetti followed the developments in Germany closely. Since war had become inevitable he took great pains to learn of the reform plans Bismarck was hoping to put into effect once the war had been decided. In a meeting on 6 June, he had been able to draw out of the minister-president the basic changes the Prussian government hoped to see achieved: the exclusion of Austria from the Confederation; the creation of a parliament which was to deal with economic matters only; the organization of the military forces of the new Confederation into two armies, over which Prussia and Bavaria were to divide the command in time of peace. Bismarck assured Benedetti that the reform plan had been evolved in full consideration of French security interests. While the ambassador followed Bismarck's exposé with great attention, he did not express his opinion in respect to the effects of the proposed change upon

[1] Benedetti to Drouyn de Lhuys, Berlin, 12 June 1866, FAE CP, Prusse/357, T.

[2] ODG, IX, 337–338. For the proceedings in the diet see CLARK, pp. 466 ff.

[3] C. zu HOHENLOHE-SCHILLINGSFÜRST, Denkwürdigkeiten, ed. F. Curtius (Stuttgart, 1906), I, 160–161.

[4] For the Austro-French negotiations see HEINRICH RITTER VON SRBIK, "Der Geheimvertrag Österreichs und Frankreichs vom 12. Juni 1866," Historisches Jahrbuch, Vol. 57 (1937), pp. 454–507; G. RITTER, "Bismarck und die Rheinpolitik Napoleons III.," Rheinische Vierteljahrsblätter, XV–XVI (1950–1951), pp. 339–370; ODG, X, 145, 257–260; ONCKEN, I, 265–268; CLARK, pp. 428 ff.

the European equilibrium. He explained his reserve by stating that he did not wish to prejudice the reaction of his government.[1] Four days later Benedetti informed Drouyn de Lhuys that Luxemburg and Limburg were not to be members of the new Confederation.[2] The importance of this announcement, particularly in reference to Luxemburg, had been realized by the ambassador, who no doubt was already considering the territorial readjustments the war would bring in its wake.

Considerations about the aftermath of the war were now in order and, in the circular of 12 June, Ambassador Benedetti could see that his superiors in Paris were deeply interested in the consequences of the war. The policy which the imperial government planned to follow during the conflict in Germany also looked ahead to eventual peace negotiations.

In the face of these eventualities, which is the attitude which suits France? Must we manifest our displeasure because Germay finds the treaties of 1815 lacking the strength to satisfy her national tendencies and to maintain her tranquility? In this struggle which is about to explode we have only two interests: the conservation of the European equilibrium and the preservation of the work to which we have contributed to build Italy. But in order to safeguard these two interests, is not the moral strength of France enough? In order that her word might be heard, will she be obliged to draw the sword? I do not think so. If in spite of our efforts the hopes for peace will not be realized, we are nonetheless assured by the declaration of the courts engaged in the conflict that, whatever the results from war, none of the questions which affect us shall be resolved without the consent of France. Let us remain in attentive neutrality and, strong in our disinterest, animated by the sincere desire to see the peoples of Europe forget their disputes and unite in a goal of civilization, liberty and progress, remain confident in our right and calm in our strength.[3]

---

[1] Benedetti to Drouyn de Lhuys, Berlin, 8 June 1866, *MMP*, pp. 134–137.

[2] Same to same, Berlin, 12 June 1866, FAE CP, Prusse/357, no. 128. "Through the exclusion of Luxemburg one makes this land, the only one on the left bank of the Rhine which remains *French*, available for future arrangements; one can in that case, as has been done in Savoy, sanction there the annexation to France through universal suffrage. I do not pretend that there is a pact with the emperor of the French but Bismarck knows that without compensation for France he cannot, if he is victorious, make the territorial aggrandizement and increase in power of Prussia acceptable to the French emperor" (Nothomb to Rogier, Berlin, 12 June 1866, BAE CP, Question du Grand-Duché de Luxembourg/I, Pt. I, no. 18 bis). "The imperial government has a consul in the grand-duchy... who always takes care to note in his reports that the house of Orange has no adherents in the land but that there exists a French party.... Benedetti who was for a long time in the *Direction politique* told me that these reports often impressed him" (*ibid.*, no. 19). Cf. Govone to La Marmora, Berlin, 3 June 1866, GOVONE, pp. 491–492. Govone writes that Bismarck was willing to cede the entire area between the Moselle and the Rhine to France as compensation if necessary. He told Govone that he was more Prussian than German and thus felt no compunction concerning that area.

[3] Napoleon III to Drouyn de Lhuys, Tuileries, 11 June 1866, FAE CP, Angleterre/738. The letter, read to the chamber by Rouher on 13 June, had been sent to French diplomatic representatives abroad on the preceding day.

According to Benedetti it was felt in Berlin that the emperor, in rather veiled language, was filing nothing less than a claim for territorial compensation. The press in particular speculated upon the meaning of the emperor's remarks and raised the question of a relinquishment of German territory to France, an event likely to arouse vehement protest in Germany. Official reaction was more reticent and difficult to evaluate:

Bismarck merely spoke to me of the emperor's letter in order to recognize that the opinions expressed in it were completely in conformity with the sentiments which the emperor has invariably expressed to him on all occasions... and he paid homage to the sincerity of his intentions. The minister-president has given me the assurance that such was also the impression of the king. [1]

Just as the declaration of the emperor cast an air of apprehension over Berlin, so it failed to dispel rumors of a Franco-Prussian *entente*. The very wording of certain phrases caused anxiety in Vienna,[2] while the *Nieuwe Dagblad* in The Hague published the supposed terms of a convention which envisaged a partition of Luxemburg and a rectification of French claims along the Belgian border.[3]

Speculations on the outcome and consequences of the clash of arms rose to new heights in Germany, while conjectures on future developments rapidly multiplied. On 24 and 25 June, Benedetti offered his views on the effects which a Prussian victory would have upon German unification. Apart from a discussion of possible ways in which the unity of Germany might emerge under Prussian guidance, he did not offer any suggestion for dealing with such an eventuality. He limited himself to the presentation of a relative balance sheet, in geographic and demographic terms, which clearly portrayed the full meaning of German unification for France.[4] The foreign minister's reply is indicative of the effect Benedetti's statistical evaluation had in Paris:

His Majesty admits up to a certain point a greater cohesion and greater strength for Prussia in the north of Germany; but the emperor has also indicated the limit beyond which the changes which could occur in this respect in the situation of Prussia could not be viewed with indifference by the French government.[5]

---

[1] Benedetti to Drouyn de Lhuys, Berlin, 15 June 1866, *ibid.*, Prusse/357, no. 134.

[2] Gramont to Drouyn de Lhuys, Vienna, 16 June 1866, *ODG*, X, 197–198.

[3] Baudin to Drouyn de Lhuys, The Hague, 15 June 1866, FAE CP, Hollande/665, no. 28.

[4] Benedetti to Drouyn de Lhuys, Berlin, 24 June 1866, *ibid.*, Prusse/357, no. 141; same to same, Berlin, 25 June 1866, *ibid.*, no. 143.

[5] Drouyn de Lhuys to Benedetti, Paris, 2 July 1866, *ibid.*, Prusse/358, no. 66; cf. Drouyn de Lhuys to La Tour d'Auvergne, Paris, 26 June 1866, *ibid.*, Angleterre/738, no. 76, regarding the foreign minister's views on the possible dissolution of the Confederation.

While Drouyn de Lhuys' dispatch was on the way to Berlin, the decisive battle of the war was preparing in Bohemia. The entire northern forces of Austria were concentrated near Königgrätz while units of all eight Prussian corps were marching on the area. The major engagement on Tuesday, 3 July, lasted throughout the day and by evening the Austrian army was in full retreat. The official news reached Berlin in a telegram from the king to the queen, copies of which were posted in the streets of the capital next morning, 4 July:

We fought to a complete victory over the Austrian army near Königgrätz, between the Elbe and the Bistritz, today in an eight-hour battle. The losses of the enemy and the trophies have not yet been counted, but are important, some twenty cannon. All eight corps have fought, but large sorrowful losses. I praise God for His grace, we are all fine.
The governor is to fire vitcory.[1]

The hundred and one rounds which announced the Prussian victory at Sadowa heralded a new era in the history of Germany and in the relations between Prussia and France.

Gastein and Sadowa represent two focal points and the period which lies between them was characterized by a diversity of activities on the German scene which had demanded Benedetti's constant attention. Yet, at the very beginning of this phase he had not been initiated in the very important talks between Napoleon and Bismarck. Although his impressions about Bismarck's visit in France had been essentially correct, his exclusion from the meetings had made it impossible for him to gain a precise idea regarding the emperor's intention toward Germany and Prussia in particular. Uncertainty about imperial aims as well as distrust toward Bismarck, as a result of the Gastein accord, actually had encouraged the reserve which Benedetti had maintained toward developments in Germany. Yet, it soon had become clear to him that Gastein meant nothing more than a temporary truce; conversations with Bismarck as well as observation had shown that the Prussian government was still determined to annex the duchies.

The prospect of an eventual break between Prussia and Austria had led Benedetti to offer his interesting suggestions for a simultaneous settlement of the duchies and Venetian questions. He desired Italian unification but he was not willing to pay for it in terms of unrestricted Prussian expansion. The merits of his proposal are clear and the tendency of French policy after Sadowa, to bring about an Austro-

---

[1] Benedetti to Drouyn de Lhuys, Berlin, 4 July 1866, *ibid.*, Prusse/ 358, no. 154, annex.

French *entente*, moved along lines suggested by Benedetti at this time. He had shown a definite awareness of the long-range consequences the German problem would have for French interests and security. Moreover, the role which he had assigned to Austria reveals the influence which old traditions of French foreign policy had upon his consideration.

The recurring failure of the imperial government to brief the ambassador without delay on important developments was demonstrated in respect to the Prussian overture in March. Although the interval was not long, it had nevertheless caused uncertainty and had hindered the ambassador in the exercise of his duties. This disadvantage, which his preoccupation with protocol made worse, had been very real and Benedetti's complaints had been fully justified. He had been particularly concerned, and rightly so, about the effect his enforced silence might have upon his relations with Bismarck – his most valuable source of information in Berlin. This lack of co-ordination had been pronounced during the Prusso-Italian negotiations; particularly so when in May neither the emperor, nor the foreign minister, nor the ambassador had pursued the same aim.

Benedetti's interest in the negotiations between Prussia and Italy had been motivated by his Italian sympathies. His advice to Govone had emphasized the fact that he did not think war a *sine qua non* to Italian unification. His support of Bismarck's aims had not been due to a pro-Prussian sentiment on his part but to interest in Italian unification and hostility to the old order.

The introduction of Bismarck's federal reform project was added assurance, in Benedetti's opinion, that the Prussian government was determined to bring about a decision in Germany. He was convinced that Bismarck would use it as a vehicle upon which to advance his plans for Prussian hegemony. His note of warning about the possible consequences of federal reform in terms of unification had been no empty gesture, for the prospect of a unified Germany was a development which haunted many a French diplomat.

The threat of the war preparations, which had been greatly accelerated in the spring, was undeniable, and Benedetti had successfully kept the foreign ministry informed of the latest developments. His belief that the Prussian government was not ready to take the initiative appears to have been a rather over-cautious estimate, especially since Bismarck's remarks were indicative of the bellicose mood in the Prussian capital. Thoughts of a second Gastein might well have been the reason for this guarded estimate. While the desire for a peaceful settlement of the Austro-Prussian dispute was not particularly strong in Berlin, a scheme for such a solution had been advanced in the least suspected quarter, from Benedetti's viewpoint, namely Paris.

The intervention of the emperor with a proposal for an international congress had been a double suprise for Benedetti. He had not only failed to receive an advance notice of the emperor's intention but the proposal itself had suggested a reversal of the policy and the aims thus far pursued by France. The desired break between Prussia and Austria at hand, the emperor had proposed to prevent it, and this without giving "his agent" in Berlin the slightest hint. It is not surprising, then, to find that the emperor also had neglected to inform Benedetti about his compensation talk with Goltz. The fluctuations of imperial policy had made it extremely difficult for the ill-informed ambassador to discuss the intentions of his government intelligently and adequately. Benedetti's problem had not been of his own making, and he could do little to correct the situation. He had merely remained steadfast in his opinion that his government should retain its freedom of action for the time being. Yet, the events suggest that the emperor had been keeping his own counsel.

The failure of the congress proposal removed the last barrier to war and Benedetti apparently expected a prolonged struggle. His correspondence does not contain suggestions for an immediate decision on the part of the imperial government. He did expect, however, a Prussian victory but there is no doubt that he would welcome neither a total defeat of Austria nor an unchecked expansion of Prussia. An idealist in regard to Italy, Benedetti was decidedly a realist in regard to Germany.

CHAPTER IV

MEDIATION AT NIKOLSBURG

The sudden and spectacular success of the Prussian arms at Sadowa caught Ambassador Benedetti by surprise.[1] He had not entered upon speculations as to the length of the Austro-Prussian hostilities but apparently he had not counted with such a rapid victory. While the outcome of the battle gave him reason to rejoice, in view of the promise it held for the Italian cause, he must have felt apprehensive about the prospective danger to the European power equilibrium. He has left no indication of his immediate reaction to Sadowa but one may assume that he had mixed feelings.

Before the situation had appreciably clarified in Berlin, Benedetti experienced yet another surprise when news was received through the unofficial wire bureau that Emperor Napoleon had offered his mediation.[2] French reaction to Sadowa had been swift, and at midnight on 4 July the emperor addressed a telegram to the victorious king of Prussia announcing his intentions:

The successes, so prompt and so spectacular, of Your Majesty have brought results which force me to give up my role of complete abstention. The Austrian emperor has informed me that he cedes Venetia to us and that he is ready to accept my mediation in order to bring an end to the conflict which arose between Austria, Prussia and Italy. I know the magnanimous sentiments of Your Majesty as well as your affectionate confidence in me only too well not to believe that, on your part, after carrying so high the honor of your arms, you do not receive with satisfaction the efforts which I am disposed to make to help you render to your states and to Europe the precious advantage of peace.

If Your Majesty accepts my proposition, you will judge it without doubt

---

[1] For official accounts of the military campaigns, see AUSTRIA. GENERALSTABS-BUREAU FÜR KRIEGSGESCHICHTE, *Österreichs Kämpfe im Jahre 1866* (Vienna, 1867), I, 254–386; PRUSSIA. KRIEGSGESCHICHTLICHE ABTEILUNG DES GROSSEN GENERALSTABES, *Der Feldzug von 1866 in Deutschland* (Berlin, 1867), pp. 251–345.

[2] Nothomb to Rogier, Berlin, 5 July 1866, BAE CP, Prusse/23, Pt. II, no. 252. Cf. Goltz's description of Napoleon as "...being shaken, almost broken... [having] lost his compass" (SCHNERB, p. 186).

convenient that an armistice concluded for Germany and Italy opens immediately the way for negotiations.[1]

Benedetti had not foreseen the action the imperial government now proposed to take, nor had he himself expressed any recommendations. The announced cession of Venetia to France – in trust for Italy – amazed Benedetti as well as the other diplomats in Berlin, and he thought that the cession must have been arranged by telegraph between the two emperors.[2] Although he himself had not yet received an official confirmation from Paris, he could not wait, on 5 July, to express his satisfaction that Venetia was to be now a part of Italy.[3] During a conversation with Thile he readily conceded that he was without official news as yet from the *Quai d'Orsay*, and hence unable to say much about the latest developments.[4] He could easily see that the French mediation proposal was deeply resented in Berlin, along with Austria's cession of Venetia. It appeared as though France were trying to prevent a complete Prussian victory by aiding Austria to free her forces in Italy and bolster the defense of Vienna against the expected Prussian attack.[5] Although the adverse reaction in Prussia to the French intervention was rather expected, Benedetti did not acquaint his government with the full extent of it; instead, he decided

[1] Napoleon III to William I, Paris, 4 July 1866, FAE CP, Prusse/358, T. A slightly different version of this telegram was sent to the Italian king. For an account of the scene when Napoleon heard from Metternich the news of the Austrian military disaster at Königgrätz, see A. VANDAM, *Undercurrents of the Second Empire* (New York, 1896), p. 316.

[2] Already on 2 July, Emperor Francis Joseph had informed Napoleon of his intention to cede Venetia, in hopes of obtaining an armistice. Next day, Napoleon told Ambassador Metternich that he would propose mediation to the parties at war upon cession of Venetia. The Austrian decision to give up Venetia was communicated late in the afternoon of 4 July to Paris, when news of the Austrian defeat at Königgrätz was reaching the French capital. (*ODG*, X, 314, ft. 3; Mensdorff to Metternich, Vienna, 2 July 1866, ONCKEN, I, 297; same to same, *ibid.*, 298; Metternich to Mensdorff, Paris, 2 July 1866, *ibid.*; same to same, Paris, 3 July, *ibid.*, 298–299; ft. 3, *ibid.*, 299; GEUSS, pp. 172–173).

[3] Nothomb to Rogier, Berlin, 5 July 1866, BAE CP, Prusse/23, Pt. II, no. 252. "The Venetia episode is difficult terrain for diplomacy. One has never seen anything like it, because of Austria's hate for Prussia! After a victory they cede a territory, hitherto held *à toute outrance*, to be able to go against Prussia with greater strength" (William I to Bernstorff, Pardubitz, 9 July 1866, K. RINGHOFFER [ed.], *Im Kampfe für Preussens Ehre: aus dem Nachlasse des Grafen Albrecht von Bernstorff* [Berlin, 1906], p. 590.)

[4] Thile to Balan, Berlin, 5 July 1866, J. SASS, "Hermann von Thile und Bismarck," *PJ*, CCXVII, Heft 3 (September 1929), p. 266. Thile regarded the cession of Venetia to France as a *deus ex machina* and foresaw either peace in a short time with very limited gains for Prussia or a war against France.

[5] Bismarck commented on the news: "After a few years Louis will probably regret having taken sides against us; it may cost him dearly" (R. VON KEUDELL, *Fürst und Fürstin Bismarck* [Berlin, 1902], pp. 294–295). For the effect of the French step in Germany, see A. RAPP, *Die Württemberger und die nationale Frage, 1863–1871*, "Darstellungen aus der württembergischen Geschichte," IV (Stuttgart, 1910), p. 169.

to await communications which would reveal how the emperor expected to implement his proposal.

 ·· The form which the imperial mediation was to take had found the cabinet sharply divided. The traditionalist and pro-Austrian group of Empress Eugénie, Drouyn de Lhuys, Marshal Jacques Randon and Pierre Magne favored, if necessary, armed mediation. They hoped to prevent a total defeat of Austria as well as her exclusion from Germany, and maintain the balance of power. They demanded the convocation of the chambers – to vote the credits necessary for mobilization – and a military demonstration on the Rhine. The Italian faction of Prince Napoleon, Rouher, and La Valette, to which Benedetti had always adhered, demanded that the imperial government do nothing more than mediate the war peaceably. They argued that the nation opposed war and that a hostile demonstration against Prussia and Italy would be a betrayal of those two powers. They contended, moreover, that friendship with Prussia would prove more conducive than threats to French annexation hopes on the Rhine. They insisted that an unqualified Prusso-Italian success would destroy the 1815 treaties and free France from the shackles that hindered her expansion. The program of the traditionalist group was accepted at the council meeting at St. Cloud, 5 July, and the necessary decrees were to be published next day in the *Moniteur officiel*. But during the evening hours of that same day the Italian faction succeeded in reversing the emperor's view; the decrees were not published and the die was cast for peaceful mediation.[1]

Benedetti was informed, on 6 July, by Drouyn de Lhuys[2] that the Prussian king had telegraphed his acceptance of the imperial mediation

---

[1] For various accounts of the meetings see B. D'HARCOURT, *Diplomatie et diplomates: les quatres ministères de Drouyn de Lhuys* (Paris, 1882), pp. 258–259; J. RANDON, *Mémoires* (Paris, 1875–1877), II, 145–146; J. DURIEUX, *Le ministre Pierre Magne, 1806–1879* (Paris, 1929), II, 176–177; OLLIVIER, VIII, 415–421; V. DURUY, *Notes et souvenirs, 1811–1894* (Paris, 1901), II, 126–127; H. FARAT, *Persigny. Un ministre de Napoléon III 1808–1872* (Paris, 1875), pp. 290–292; J. HANSEN, *Les coulisses de la diplomatie: quinze ans à l'étranger, 1864–1879* (Paris, 1880), pp. 97–99; C. DE GRÜNWALD, *Le duc de Gramont: gentilhomme et diplomate* (Paris, 1950), pp. 153–154; G. ROTHAN, *Les origines de la guerre de 1870. La politique française en 1866* (Paris, 1879), p. 190; —, *Souvenirs diplomatiques. L'affaire du Luxembourg. La prélude de la guerre de 1870* (Paris, 1872), pp. 44–47; ONCKEN, I, 176, ft. 1; Bamberg to Bismarck, Paris, 20 December 1868, I.A.A.b. 84. For the impact of French public opinion on the ultimate decision of the emperor, an impact which may have been decisive, see CASE, pp. 207–211; Goltz to Bismarck, Paris, 6 July 1866, ONCKEN, I, 309.

[2] "He [Drouyn de Lhuys] remained in power with the secret hope of repairing by his ability the failure he had sustained. The violence which he did to his own convictions only irritated his adversaries, increased the irresolution of the sovereign and removed from our policy its last chance for salvation: unity of views and direction" (ROTHAN, *Souvenirs*, I, 36–37).

proposal and that his conditions for an armistice were to be trans-mitted through Ambassador Goltz.[1] The minister enjoined Benedetti to do everything in his power to obtain from the Prussian govern-ment the collaboration necessary for the success of the emperor's efforts.[2] The absence of the king, the princes, Bismarck, and the leading military from Berlin made the execution of such a request virtually impossible. Under the circumstances he could only talk to Baron von Werther, who promised to inform the minister-president of the conversation.[3] Since neither the king nor Bismarck were ex-pected to return to the capital in the near future, Benedetti gave Werther a private letter for Bismarck, asking for the cooperation of the Prussian government in promoting a successful and expeditious mediation.[4] The tone of Benedetti's report to Drouyn de Lhuys indicates that he considered his presence in the Prussian capital at that moment of very little use to the imperial government, for his sources of information were restricted to news reaching him through the inter-mediary of the Prussian foreign office. The continual advance of the headquarters of the king made it difficult to maintain liaison and carry out the instructions of the ministry.

Although Ambassador Benedetti telegraphed Drouyn de Lhuys on Sunday, 8 July, that Prince Henry VII Reuss would arrive in Paris on Tuesday morning with a letter from the king to the emperor,[5]

---

[1] Although Moltke, as well as Loë, the Prussian military attaché in Paris, insisted that France was not prepared to wage war, King William decided to accept French mediation. He and Bismarck were guided by the possibility that Napoleon, carried along by press reports celebrating him as the peace-maker of Europe, might risk an armed clash. French military intervention, however minor, could also stiffen the resistance of Austria and her allies, while limiting at the same time Prussia's freedom of action against her foes. These considerations prompted Prussian acceptance in principle of the French mediation offer, although Bismarck hoped to gain precious time through procrastination. He also endeavored to create additional difficulties for Austria by giving aid and comfort to Hungarian separatists (GEUSS, pp. 173–176). For text of King William's telegram, see SYBEL, V, 229–230.

[2] Drouyn de Lhuys to Benedetti, Paris, 6 July 1866, FAE CP, Prusse/358, T.

[3] Benedetti to Drouyn de Lhuys, Berlin, 7 July 1866, *ibid.*, T.

[4] Benedetti to Bismarck, Berlin, 7 July 1866, FAE MD, Allemagne/171; Nothomb to Rogier, Berlin, 10 July 1866, BAE CP, Prusse/23, Pt. II, no. 258.

[5] Benedetti to Drouyn de Lhuys, Berlin, 8 July 1866, FAE CP, Prusse/358, T. The mission of Reuss was essentially designed to calm the apprehension of the emperor and to retard the conclusion of an armistice, in order to obtain further military advantages against the Aus-trians. The letter of William, dated 7 July, was couched in rather vague terms; however, it did allude to certain Prussian objectives: federal reform, annexation of the duchies of Schleswig-Holstein, and other related matters. Moreover, Reuss did not have authority to discuss an armistice (Goltz to Bernstorff, Paris, 28 August [24 October] 1866, STOLBERG-WERNIGERODE, pp. 449–450; Goltz to Bismarck, Paris, 11 July 1866, ONCKEN, I, 338–343). For the report of the Napoleon-Reuss interview on 10 July, see Reuss to William I, Paris, 10 July 1866, *ibid.*, 328–331. Cf. W. BUSCH, *HZ*, CIII, Heft I (1909), p. 72, who writes that Bismarck indicated already on 4 July that he would be satisfied with a unification limited to North Germany.

Napoleon nevertheless decided to send Benedetti to the Prussian headquarters. In view of the ambassador's wire of 7 July, and the delay already experienced, it appeared that efforts to obtain an armistice would prove more effective if seconded by a French representative on the scene.[1] Thus, Drouyn de Lhuys on 9 July ordered Benedetti to leave at once for the Prussian headquarters and press for a cessation of hostilities:

> Proceed at once to the headquarters of King William. You will explain to the king as well as to Bismarck that the cession of Venetia to the emperor places His Majesty in a position which cannot be prolonged and from which, nevertheless, His Majesty is resolved to emerge with honor. We have to give Venetia to Italy, but to do so it is necessary that Italy accept an armistice, and her acceptance is subordinated to the consent of Prussia.
>
> Use all your efforts for the attainment of this consent. Make it understood that a refusal would be vigorously resented in France and would entail the gravest of consequences.[2]

The urgent summons from the foreign ministry reached Berlin late on Monday afternoon. The determined tone of the telegram convinced Benedetti that it was imperative for him to reach the king's camp without delay; he replied that he would leave that very evening, taking along the code tables necessary for direct communication with the foreign ministry in Paris.[3] When informed of the ambassador's intention to join the Prussian headquarters, Baron Werther tried to dissuade Benedetti from such a hazardous undertaking. Only after Benedetti told him that he had received formal orders did Werther issue a safe-conduct to him.[4] Before leaving, Benedetti received a visit from Loftus to whom he had sent a hasty note about his impending journey. He confided to his British colleague that some difficulties with Italy over the armistice had arisen and that King William seemed to delay a settlement in order to gain possession of Frankfort. In view of the urgent circumstances of Benedetti's departure, Loftus assumed that the forthcoming negotiations would probably be extended to territorial readjustments, despite the ambassador's assertion that he had no further instructions than to hasten the conclusion of an armistice.[5] After the necessary preparations regarding the direction

---

[1] Eugénie to Metternich, n.p., 9 July 1866, ONCKEN, I, 326. The decision to send Benedetti reversed an earlier intention to send a general staff officer; it may have been made in the belief that peace preliminaries might be discussed simultaneously with the armistice negotiations (Loftus to Stanley, Berlin, 14 July 1866, PRO FO 64/597, no. 16).

[2] Drouyn de Lhuys to Benedetti, Paris, 9 July 1866, FAE CP, Prusse/358, T.

[3] Benedetti to Drouyn de Lhuys, Berlin, 9 July 1866, *ibid.*, T.

[4] Nothomb to Rogier, Berlin, 10 July 1866, BAE CP, Prusse/23, Pt. II, no. 258.

[5] Loftus to Stanley, Berlin, 14 July 1866, PRO FO 64/597, no. 16.

of the embassy had been completed, the ambassador and the first secretary, Lefèbvre de Béhaine, entrained at eleven o'clock for Reichenberg.[1]

Soon after Benedetti's departure from Berlin, Drouyn de Lhuys sought to have more resolute instructions issued to the ambassador. The veiled ambitions in William's letter, communicated by Reuss on Tuesday, 10 July, had caused considerable apprehension as to Prussia's intentions.[2] During a cabinet meeting that evening, Drouyn de Lhuys asked that Benedetti be permitted to threaten an Austro-French alliance if the Prussian government rejected the mediation efforts. The emperor, however, did not accept the proposal and preferred not to jeopardize the possibility of a peaceful arrangement with Prussia. Already next day he learned from Goltz that a courier with more specific Prussian conditions was on his way to Paris.[3] Apparently Bismarck had decided, on his part, to calm French apprehensions. Bismarck's decision might have been influenced partly by Benedetti's advice, given to Werther in Berlin and relayed to Bismarck, that Prussia restrain her demands, for in his letter to Goltz the minister-president made mention of Benedetti's remarks.[4] The conciliatory attitude of Bismarck apparently convinced the emperor that a quick armistice could be expected, and a telegram of the same day to Benedetti reads: "Come to Paris as soon as you can in order to give an account of your trip to the [Prussian] headquarters." [5]

[1] Nothomb to Rogier, Berlin, 10 July 1866, BAE CP, Prusse/23, Pt. II, no. 259. "Benedetti left yesterday for the headquarters, presumably without exact instructions, merely to recommend restraint [in the demands] and acceleration [in concluding an armistice]" (Werther to Usedom, Berlin, 10 July 1866, T. VON BERNHARDI, Aus dem Leben Theodor von Bernhardis, Vol. VII, Der Krieg 1866 gegen Österreich und seine unmittelbaren Folgen: Tagebuchblätter aus den Jahren 1866 und 1867, ed. F. von Bernhardi [Leipzig, 1897], p. 157).

[2] SYBEL, V, 243–245. During an interview with the emperor, Goltz discovered that the prospect of Prussian hegemony in Germany, the consequence of the military victory and the proposed exclusion of Austria from German affairs, created considerable apprehension in France. Goltz endeavored to alleviate Napoleon's concern relative to the Prussian federal reform project, and also emphasized the willingness of Prussia to give full consideration to French wishes. In his reports to Bismarck, the ambassador stressed the need for Prussian moderation, in order to gain French support and prevent an Austro-French combination against Prussia (Goltz to Bismarck, Paris, 11 July 1866, ONCKEN, I, 336–338; Goltz to Bismarck, Paris, 11 July 1866, ibid., 338–343; Reuss to Bismarck, Paris, 12 July 1866, ibid., 343–345).

[3] Ibid.; SYBEL, V, 243–245; RANDON, II, 146.

[4] Bismarck to Goltz, Hohenmauth, 9 July 1866, BGW, VI, 46. Cf. F. THIMME, "Wilhelm I., Bismarck und der Ursprung des Annexionsgedankens 1866," HZ, LXXIX, Heft 3 (1902), pp. 423–424. The author ascribes the decision to abandon the federal reform demand and limit such design to the creation of a North German Confederation not to a consideration of France's attitude but to the fact that Prussia planned large annexations, making it impossible for her to carry out a federal reform embracing all of Germany and, at the same time, to assimilate the annexed territory.

[5] Drouyn de Lhuys to Benedetti, Paris, 11 July 1866, FAE CP, Prusse/358, T.

Benedetti meanwhile was slowly making his way to the king's camp. After arriving in Reichenberg on 10 July, he had continued his journey by carriage, and even at times on horseb ack,arriving in Pardubitz on Wednesday, 11 July, at two o'clock in the afternoon, only to find that the king and his staff had left the previous day for Zwittau. The ambassador and the secretary remained in Pardubitz for a few hours to make preparations for continuing the journey later in the day. The trip had been particularly tiring because of the difficult terrain and transportation; moreover, Benedetti had neglected to bring ample provisions from Berlin. He and Lefèbvre de Béhaine resumed their journey at nine o'clock in the evening along the road leading to Brünn, making their way through military supply trains and convoys of wounded soldiers being moved to field hospitals in the rear. They traversed Hohenmauth, where the king had been during the day, and reached Zwittau shortly before one o'clock in the morning, 12 July.[1] Benedetti had been out of touch with the situation since late Monday afternoon. Instructed to accelerate the conclusion of an armistice and ignorant of what had taken place meanwhile, especially in regard to decisions in Paris, he was anxious to be appraised of the situation. Bismarck, who had installed himself with Heinrich Abeken and Robert von Keudell in an abandoned farmhouse,[2] was still at work and Benedetti requested an interview with him. The minister-president had had no warning of Benedetti's departure for the king's headquarters;[3] his unexpected appearance in Zwittau was especially resented by Bismarck, since he was still uninformed of the reaction in Paris to the Prussian conditions for an armistice. The presence of a French diplomat during the armistice talks at the Prussian headquarters could also have a decided disadvantage for the Prussian government.[4] Despite his misgivings, Bismarck promptly offered the

---

[1] Nothomb to Rogier, Berlin, 14 July 1866, BAE CP, Prusse/23, Pt. II, no. 259; Benedetti to Drouyn de Lhuys, Horitz, 11 July 1866, FAE CP, Prusse/358, T.; same to same, Czernahora, 12 July 1866, *ibid.*, no. 157. "Thile has come to tell me that a courier, whom it took forty-two hours from headquarters to the Görlitz railroad station, met the ambassador on the way. Considering the extreme communications difficulties, Benedetti could probably only have arrived this morning near the king at Zwittau" (Charles de Hell to Drouyn de Lhuys, [Berlin,] 12 July 1866, *ibid.*, T.).

[2] Benedetti to Drouyn de Lhuys, Czernahora, 12 July 1866, *ibid.*, no. 157.

[3] A telegram from Werther to Bismarck, announcing Benedetti's departure and the nature of his mission, arrived only after Benedetti had reached the Prussian headquarters.

[4] [Benedetti] is not quite greeted with loving eyes, but he shall not harm [our cause] nor detain us" (Abeken to his wife, Zwittau, 12 July 1866, H. ABEKEN, *Ein schlichtes Leben in bewegter Zeit* [Berlin, 1898], p. 332). "Bismarck received the unwelcome guest politely, but his discontent over his visit caused him pains in the left foot which lasted for some time" (KEUDELL, p. 296). To a telegram from Werther, announcing that military authorities had

ambassador the use of his quarters, and granted him an interview.[1]

Without delay Benedetti indicated the purpose of his journey and expressed the hope of Emperor Napoleon to mediate a speedy settlement. The minister-president did not hesitate to reveal his own views about these efforts; he felt that they could only result in an advantage for Austria which, hopelessly beaten and at Prussia's mercy, now found a supporter, if not an ally, in the French emperor. The cession of Venetia he regarded as a tactical move designed to gain time for a new concentration of Austrian forces, and he regretted an interposition by France which could jeopardize the advantages gained thus far by Prussia. Benedetti did not share this point of view and remarked that the success of the Prussian arms was guarantee enough for her legitimate claims, provided they did neither conflict with those of other powers nor with the European equilibrium. He intimated that Prussia could not continue to count upon future neutrality of those powers whose abstention from force had made the Prussian success possible. Bismarck pointed out that the king had accepted the idea of French mediation and that he agreed, provided the Italian government did not object, to the conclusion of an armistice under certain conditions – peace preliminaries which were in the process of being communicated to the emperor by Goltz and Prince Reuss. Bismarck therefore suggested that they await news about the outcome of the Paris talks. Benedetti in turn proposed that, in the meantime, the Prussian forces should remain in their present positions, to which Bismarck replied that only the king and his military staff could consider such a suggestion. Terminating the meeting at four o'clock in the morning, Bismarck promised to arrange an audience with his monarch.[2]

Benedetti was received by the king on the same morning, 12 July, at about ten o'clock. Briefed by Bismarck, William informed Benedetti that, while he accepted the idea of an armistice, such a step would depend on the concurrence of the Italian government and on a Prusso-French accord relative to peace preliminaries. Certain major considerations would also have to be kept in view. He pointed out that an armistice would permit the Austrian command to regroup its forces,

---

been instructed to assist the French ambassador in reaching the king's headquarters, Bismarck appended the comment "stupid" (*BGW*, VI, 51). Cf. A. VON WALDERSEE, *Denkwürdigkeiten*, ed. H. O. Meisner (Stuttgart, 1902), I, 37–38.

[1] "Benedetti had to share my room, while [Lefèbvre de Béhaine] shared Keudell's bed" (Abeken to his wife, Zwittau, 12 July 1866, ABEKEN, p. 331).

[2] Benedetti to Drouyn de Lhuys, Czernahora, 12 July 1866, FAE CP, Prusse/358, no. 157.

while at the same time it would restrict Prussia's advance and pursuit of the enemy. In view of the danger of a reorganization of the Austrian forces, William believed that, instead of a mere armistice, he could only agree to peace preliminaries which would guarantee Prussia a peace commensurate with her gains and sacrifices. To the ambassador's reply, that the drafting of peace preliminaries demanded time and could only be achieved during an armistice, the king remarked that he would have to consult first with his chief of staff before giving a further opinion. At the end of the interview William informed Benedetti that his headquarters would be moved to Czernahora later in the day and he invited the ambassador to accompany him there.[1] Benedetti was offered the use of Bismarck's carriage and he arrived in Czernahora at five o'clock in the afternoon.[2]

As he had intended, William immediately held a staff conference on the terrace of the castle where he had set up his headquarters. In consequence, he agreed to a three-day abstention from hostilities,[3] in order to await Italian views on an armistice and French reaction to his conditions. At Benedetti's request the minister-president drew up the terms, essentially military in character, under which the Prussian government would agree to the suspension of hostilities; the written statement would permit the French and Austrian governments to study the stipulations. The ambassador's suggestion that the time limit be extended from three to five days was refused on military grounds. While both the king and Bismarck had agreed to the suspension, Benedetti was told that the communication of the conditions for the abstention from hostilities could not be made to the Austrian command by the victorious Prussians. Benedetti resolved the momentary *impasse* by sending Lefèbvre de Béhaine to the nearest Austrian command post or, if necessary, to Vienna. The secretary left for the Austrian lines at three o'clock the following morning, 13 July.[4] The ambassador remained with the king's headquarters which were moved to Brünn later in the day.[5]

---

[1] *Ibid.*

[2] de Hell to Drouyn de Lhuys, Berlin, 14 July 1866, *ibid.*, T.; Roon to his wife, Czernahora, 13 July 1866, A. VON ROON, *Denkwürdigkeiten* (Breslau, 1892), II, 293.

[3] Benedetti to Drouyn de Lhuys, Czernahora, 12 July 1866, FAE CP, Prusse/358, no. 157. The word "abstention" rather than "armistice" was used because the Prusso-Italian alliance did not permit either party to conclude a separate armistice.

[4] *Ibid.* The secretary was guided to the Austrian lines by a Prussian officer; he took with him a report of the ambassador to Drouyn de Lhuys, which was sent from Vienna on 14 July and arrived two days later in Paris.

[5] "I followed the king to Brünn where His Majesty established his headquarters yesterday. I await the return of Lefèbvre. All the telegraph lines are down. The news and correspondence

In spite of the difficulties which Benedetti had encountered since his departure from Berlin, particularly the lack of contact with his own government, he had achieved some success in his efforts both with the king and with Bismarck. Having arrived in the early hours of 12 July at the Prussian headquarters, he had, by late evening, obtained the agreement of both William and the minister-president to a suspension of hostilities. But despite the alacrity with which the ambassador brought the emperor's influence to bear on the Austro-Prussian front, France was losing precious time through dilatory negotiations in Paris. Instead of giving the ambassador on the scene power to handle the mediation no such concentration of effort was even contemplated. The manoeuvers of Goltz and Reuss, to sound out French views on potential Prussian peace demands, meant delay when time was of the essence. While the negotiations dragged on in Paris, Benedetti was stymied in his endeavors; as long as Bismarck was awaiting results from Paris, he was unwilling to consider Benedetti's instructions further. Moreover, repeated breakdowns in the communication system rendered the ambassador's position still more difficult and the delicacy of the situation itself suggests the extend of his problems.

Discussions with Bismarck did continue while word was awaited from Goltz and from Lefèbvre de Béhaine. Reviewing these talks, Benedetti felt convinced that Prussia was determined to assure herself of gains commensurate with her military victory in the field. In order to achieve this end, it was deemed necessary by the Prussian government to arrive at an *entente* with the imperial government or to insist upon peace preliminaries which would guarantee the same end. The Prussian government was reluctant to leave the emperor a large degree of latitude in formulating the peace proposals, and the rapidity of the Prussian offensive was expected to limit Napoleon's intervention effectively. Referring to the Prussian territorial claims, Benedetti was impressed by the vigor with which Bismarck justified them. Presenting the annexation of Saxony, Electoral Hesse and Hanover as legitimate aspirations, he had told the ambassador that the acceptance of the armistice was in any case subordinate to the attainment of those objectives. In countering Bismarck's demands, Benedetti had pointed out that the days of Frederick the Great, *où ce qui*

arriving from Berlin today by courier... are three days late.... The courier with your dispatch of the 9th has only now arrived" (Benedetti to Drouyn de Lhuys, Brünn, 14 July 1866, FAE CP, Prusse/358, T.).

est bon à prendre était bon à garder, had passed and that the other powers would be justified in opposing extravagant claims. In another conversation with the ambassador, the minister-president had shifted his attention to Goltz's mission in Paris. He had remarked that the Prussian ambassador's instructions were not absolute – "their principle being to effect an accord with the government of the emperor, they authorized him to compromise by proportioning the pretensions of Prussia to the price France would put on an understanding with her, provided that certain clauses from which the government of the king was resolved not to depart would be agreed to in Paris." Moreover, Bismarck had "insisted upon the expediency for our two countries *de s'unir et de s'entendre.*" He had tried to show Benedetti that the defeat of Austria would permit France and Prussia to "modify their territorial status and to resolve... the majority of the difficulties which might threaten the peace of Europe." When the ambassador had observed that such a policy would bring a general war in Europe Bismarck had replied that he was mistaken and that "France and Prussia, united and resolved to redress their respective borders by allying in solemn engagements, would henceforth be in a position to regulate together these questions without fear of encountering armed resistance, either on the part of England or on the part of Russia." [1]

Benedetti did not fail to perceive Bismarck's intimations; it was obvious that the minister-president wished an understanding with the emperor which would assure him of mediation favorable to Prussian designs and speedy enough to forestall the intervention of the other powers. In view of this overture, Benedetti sought to gain a more precise impression of Prussian demands in a later conversation with Bismarck. To the ambassador's observation, that the realization of what Bismarck termed Prussia's legitimate claims might prolong the war and increase the threat of intervention by the other powers, the minister-president replied that these were maximum demands which the king would be willing to reduce on condition of an understanding with France. Benedetti rejected such a course as an impossible one, since the mediator could not enter into an agreement with one of the parties at war. Bismarck insisted that Prussia could hardly accept French mediation without a previous assurance of certain advantages, to be guaranteed either through a statement by the emperor or through the text of the preliminaries of peace. "A personal

---

[1] Same to same, Brünn, 15 July 1866, *ibid.,* no 158. This message was sent from Vienna on 18 July; I.A.A.b. 84.

assurance by the emperor guaranteeing him, in more or less general terms, the good intention of His Majesty on certain points, especially in regard to the contiguity of the borders of Prussia and the yet-to-be-established union of north German states, would satisfy the king." [1]

Benedetti, in accordance with his instructions, or lack thereof, did not enter into an extended discussion of the schemes of alliances and territorial compensations mentioned by Bismarck. However, he did draw the attention of Drouyn de Lhuys to them and stressed his belief that Prussia would not agree to an armistice, lest she was assured of a North German Confederation as well as territorial compensation proportionate to her sacrifices and public demand. In a conversation with Abeken, Benedetti gave a hint of his apprehension about Prussian power: "It seems that the Prussians are so superior to the other nations that they must not become their equals in number and territory." [2]

While Benedetti and Bismarck awaited further developments, Ambassador Goltz had actively endeavored to calm the growing irritation of Napoleon over the apparent ineffectiveness of his mediation efforts. War was continuing unabated, and it would seem as though Prussia was determined to dictate a peace treaty to the Austrians in Vienna. The mission of Prince Reuss had only served to heighten French suspicions and Goltz, in view of the communication problem with the king's headquarters, had been indeed hard put to allay the emperor's fears. It was not until the evening of 12 July, that he had received detailed instructions from Bismarck, drafted on 8 July in Pardubitz and partly outdated in consequence of new military and political developments. During an interview next day, Goltz cautiously developed Prussia's position. Some conditions would have to be acccepted as peace preliminaries, if Prussia were to agree to an armistice. Bismarck insisted upon the federal reform project, the payment by the defeated enemy of the costs of war, the annexation of East Friesland and Bautzen, abdication of King George of Hanover and the electoral prince of Hesse, limited annexation in Bohemia and Austrian

---

[1] Benedetti to Drouyn de Lhuys, Brünn, 15 July 1866, FAE CP, Prusse/358, no. 158. It should be noted that the material of this quote was set off by quotation marks in Benedetti's report and was linked directly to the following sentence: "*J'ai recueilli ces paroles en quelque sorte sous sa dictée.*" In his book, Benedetti attempts to treat the Brünn and subsequent Berlin conversations as one series and, in writing about the alliance proposal of late August 1866, he states: "*Je consentis à les transcrire en quelque sorte sous sa dictée*" (*MMP*, p. 193). The similarity of sentences is noteworthy, and may suggest that Benedetti, deliberately or not, confused the Brünn discussions with those in Berlin.

[2] Abeken [to his wife?, Brünn], 14 July 1866, ABEKEN, p. 333.

Silesia, a constitution for Hungary, annexation of Schleswig-Holstein and the occupied states of North Germany. Subsequent telegrams which had reached Goltz also demanded the annexation of Electoral Hesse and of the kingdom of Saxony.[1] The emperor had indicated that he would not object to the creation of a confederation of North Germany, provided that Saxony would remain outside the Prussian political system and would have the right to unite with the south German states. The emperor wanted to satisfy public opinion in France by maintaining an equilibrium in Germany; for this reason he felt that the southern states should be able to form an independent political union, with the right to make alliances and war. He likewise had demanded that the territorial integrity of Austria be maintained, and he had declared himself prepared, if King William accepted those conditions for peace, to transmit them to the Austrian government. When Goltz had alluded to territorial compensations, Napoleon had merely asked, without insisting, whether Prussia might agree to the transfer of the Saxon dynasty to the Rhineland. In conclusion he had asked Goltz to draft a document which could serve as a peace preliminary. It should be noted that during the interview Goltz did not discuss Bismarck's specific proposals for territorial annexations. On 14 July, Goltz presented his draft to the emperor who accepted it after minor textual changes. The ambassador stressed the point that his reference to the creation of the North German Confederation did not exclude the possibility of territorial annexations by Prussia. Goltz felt that he could not commit Prussia to specific territorial changes at the moment, in view of the fact that Bismarck's communications indicated that no definite decision had been reached at the king's headquarters on this most important issue.[2] Although drafted by Goltz, the document was subsequently forwarded to Vienna and Nikolsburg as an official proposal of the mediatory French government to the belligerents.[3]

The departure later in the day of Marquis Frottier de La Coste, an attaché at the Berlin embassy, enabled Drouyn de Lhuys to forward

[1] Bismarck to Goltz, Hohenmauth, 10 July 1866, SYBEL, V, 260; Goltz to Bismarck, Paris, 14 July 1866, ONCKEN, I, 351–356; Goltz to Bernstorff, Paris, 28 August [24 October] 1866, STOLBERG-WERNIGERODE, pp. 449–450; Radowitz, *Tagebuchaufzeichnung*, 25 August 1866, *ibid.*, pp. 445 ff.
[2] G. ROLOFF, "Brünn und Nikolsburg," *HZ*, CXXXVI, Heft 3 (1927), pp. 472–474. The author attributes the failure of Goltz to discuss the Prussian annexation proposals to the ambassador's opposition to Bismarck's unrestrained expansionist ambitions. Cf. Goltz to Bismarck, Paris, 14 July 1866, ONCKEN, I, 351–356.
[3] SYBEL, V, 268–269.

a copy of the text to Berlin for remittance to Benedetti in Brünn, who was still unaware of these preliminary peace conditions the emperor wished to recommend for acceptance to both powers:

The integrity of the Austrian Empire, except Venetia, will be maintained.

Austria will recognize the dissolution of the old Germanic Confederation and will not oppose a new organization of Germany of which she will not be a member.

Prussia will constitute a union of North Germany, comprising all states situated north of the Main line. She will be invested with command of the military forces of these states.

The German states situated south of the Main line shall be free to form among themselves a union of South Germany, which will have an independent international existence.

The national ties which are to be preserved between the union of the North and that of the South shall be freely regulated by a common *entente*.

The Duchies of the Elbe shall be joined to Prussia, except the districts of northern Schleswig, whose population, freely consulted, might desire to return to Denmark.

Austria and her allies should restitute to Prussia part of her war expenditures.

The foreign minister asked Benedetti to work for the acceptance of these terms in order that an armistice might be concluded and final peace negotiations begun.[1]

However, Drouyn de Lhuys' communication did not reach Benedetti in time to prevent his departure from Brünn, in the evening of 15 July, after the failure of Lefèbvre de Béhaine's mission [2] had made it obvious that nothing further could be achieved at the Prussian headquarters.[3] The conditions for the suspension of hostilities which the first secretary had presented to the Austrians had been refused, and he had returned to Brünn on 15 July with Austrian counter-proposals which King William had promptly rejected. In response to the foreign minister's wire of 11 July which had only now reached him, Benedetti decided to go to Paris to report on his mission. Since a return via Berlin would entail considerable delay he decided to go to Vienna, forward an interim report on his activities to Paris and await further instructions. Lefèbvre de Béhaine, on the other hand, was to return directly from Brünn to Berlin.[4]

Benedetti left Brünn accompanied by a Prussian officer, Joseph Maria von Radowitz, detached temporarily from the staff of the Prussian embassy in Paris. This officer had taken Lefèbvre de Béhaine

---

[1] Drouyn de Lhuys to Benedetti, Paris, 14 July 1866, FAE CP, Prusse/358, no. 71.

[2] See Gramont to Drouyn de Lhuys, Vienna, 17 July 1866, FAE MD, Autriche/67, no. 90.

[3] Benedetti told Roon that he expected to go to Paris from Vienna (Roon to his wife, Brünn, 17 July 1866, ROON, II, 296).

[4] Benedetti to Drouyn de Lhuys, Brünn, 15 July 1866, FAE CP, Prusse/358, no. 158.

to the Austrian lines on 13 July and now, together with an Austrian officer, Count Colloredo, was to conduct Benedetti through the lines. The trip was not without incident: near Nikolsburg the party ran into the fire of Prussian outposts who mistook them for Austrians, and shortly after they were fired on by Austrian troops who evidently had little respect for the white flag the party was flying from its carriage. The danger of the situation did not deter Benedetti who, in contrast to Lefèbvre de Béhaine earlier, showed no fear. To Radowitz's insistence at one time that the ambassador return to the carriage, he replied, *"Tiens*, it would be really something new, and would it not make a nice effect, if a neutral ambassador who wants to work for peace would fall under the bullets of the belligerents?" Planting himself with his binoculars in the middle of the road, exposed to the fire of the Austrians, he added, "We Corsicans, we do not hide from danger." Radowitz, however, who was responsible for Benedetti's safety was only too glad when the trip into the Austrian lines was completed and he "could deliver the spirited little man unharmed." [1]

Benedetti arrived in Vienna during the morning of 16 July and immediately telegraphed a summary of his latest impressions to the foreign minister. He felt that Prussia, wishing to eliminate any threat of being isolated in the ultimate peace negotiations, was anxious to secure the support of France through a special accord. The war would continue until such an accord was reached, in Benedetti's opinion, and for this reason an armistice was to be concluded only after the emperor had approved of the conditions which Ambassador Goltz had been charged to communicate. Benedetti emphasized Bismarck's demand relative to the contiguity of the Prussian borders and the creation of a North German Confederation.[2] Receiving this communication, Drouyn de Lhuys immediately wired Duke Agénor de Gramont, French ambassador in Vienna, to acquaint Benedetti with the draft of peace preliminaries, communicated to Vienna on 14 July. Gramont complied and also told Benedetti that Austria would accede to the terms, provided the Prussian government was ready to accept. The ambassador was requested by Drouyn de Lhuys to return without delay to the Prussian headquarters and press for the acceptance of the preliminaries and the signing of an armistice.[3]

[1] RADOWITZ, I, 106.

[2] Benedetti to Drouyn de Lhuys, Vienna, 16 July 1866, FAE CP, Autriche/492, T. Benedetti's remark regarding Bismarck's insistence on contiguous borders for Prussia contrasts sharply with Goltz's neglect to mention Prussian annexation demands to the emperor.

[3] Drouyn de Lhuys to Gramont, Paris, 16 July 1866, *ibid.*, T.

Although Benedetti had become acquainted with the text of the preliminaries, he was completely unaware that it had been drafted by Goltz and approved by the emperor.[1] Nor did he know that Goltz had ignored Bismarck's instructions regarding annexations necessary for the contiguity of Prussia's borders.[2] It was under these circumstances that Benedetti telegraphed his suggestions to Paris in the late afternoon of 16 July, after a close study of the peace preliminaries text.[3] He advised the relegation of the first paragraph regarding the territorial integrity of Austria to a place further down in the text as well as the omission of the statement that Austria would not be a member of the new organization of Germany. He feared that the failure to make a statement regarding the future of Saxony would leave it at the mercy of Prussia, and considered the mention of Prussia's military command over the north German forces as premature. In respect to the paragraph on the south German states, the inclusion of which Napoleon had insisted upon, Benedetti recommended that it either be eliminated or that a provision be added indicating the right of the envisaged South German Confederation to unite with Austria. He advised the complete suppression of the paragraph relative to the future relations between North and South Germany but proposed to maintain the entire paragraph relative to Schleswig-Holstein. In conclusion, he recommended as final paragraph the combination of the first and last sentences of the text. The ambassador reaffirmed his opinion that the Goltz text, as drafted, would not be accepted by William and Bismarck, unless a clause were added assuring Prussia territorial gains and the contiguity of her borders. Apart from these modifications, Benedetti stressed that the negotiator should be empowered to declare that in case of a rejection France would withdraw as mediator and would consult her own interests.[4]

Before returning to the Prussian headquarters,[5] Benedetti asked Drouyn de Lhuys by wire whether Goltz had been acquainted with the text, and if he, Benedetti, would be permitted to modify the terms, particularly in respect to the contiguity of the Prussian borders.

---

[1] Gramont (for Benedetti) to Drouyn de Lhuys, Vienna, 16 July 1866, *ibid.*, T. In this communication, Benedetti refers to the preliminaries as a *rédaction du département* and as *nos conditions*.

[2] See above, fts. 1, 2, p. 92.

[3] For text, see above p. 93.

[4] Gramont (for Benedetti) to Drouyn de Lhuys, Vienna, 16 July 1866, FAE CP, Autriche/492, T.

[5] The Prussian headquarters were moved on 16 July from Brünn to Nikolsburg and were set up in Castle Dietrichstein, which belonged to the wife of Count Mensdorff.

He also reminded the minister that it would be necessary to advise
the Prussian government if Italy had accepted an armistice, a development not yet confirmed. As for his own role, he was anxious to know
if, as representative of the mediatory power, he was to participate in
the agreement regulating the armistice between the belligerents.[1]
While awaiting a reply, Benedetti took the opportunity to verify
Gramont's prediction about an Austrian acceptance of the text. In
an interview with Mensdorff and Count Maurice Esterhazy he learned
that the Vienna cabinet would undoubtedly accede to the terms,
provided they were accepted by the Prussian government.[2]

In response to Benedetti's textual critique of the previous day,
Drouyn de Lhuys insisted that no change could be made. He pointed
out that Goltz had already forwarded a copy to the king's headquarters
and that Prince Reuss was to carry another copy with him on his
return journey to the Prussian camp.

> It is thus this text for which you must try to gain acceptance as a basis of the
> peace preliminaries, which ought to be negotiated and signed, not by us, but by
> the belligerents. Once this basis is accepted nothing must prevent any longer the
> conclusion of an armistice, each party, in the course of the later negotiations,
> remaining free to claim modifications of detail of composition which it judges
> necessary.[3]

The ambassador left Vienna on 18 July with the intention of doing
everything in support of an ultimate peace settlement.[4] Upon
arriving next day at the Prussian headquarters,[5] transferred meanwhile
to Nikolsburg, Benedetti was faced with the task of securing Prussian

[1] Benedetti to Drouyn de Lhuys, Vienna, 17 July 1866, FAE MD, Autriche/67, T.

[2] Gramont to Drouyn de Lhuys, Vienna, 18 July 1866, FAE CP, Autriche/492, no. 91;
"Benedetti himself returned on the 19th with the assurance that [the peace preliminaries]
had been accepted by Count Mensdorff" (KEUDELL, p. 296). Cf. the version of Benedetti's
visit given by the Belgian envoy in Vienna: "In general, Benedetti's attitude during his sojourn
here was unique. He made himself absolute master of the French embassy, established
himself there without much regard for Gramont; wrote a voluminous correspondence which
he sent off to Paris, saw Count Mensdorff only once; thirty-six hours after his arrival he
left again for the Prussian camp, taking with him, it is said, the last concession which Austria
can make to put an end to the hostilities. Since the arrival and after the departure of Benedetti, Gramont showed himself extremely reserved and seems shattered" (De Jonghe to
Rogier, Vienna, 20 July 1866, BAE CP, Autriche-Hongrie/33, no. 149.

[3] Drouyn de Lhuys to Gramont (for Benedetti,) Paris, 17 July 1866, FAE MD, Autriche/
67, T.

[4] "I leave in a few minutes for headquarters; but unless the king and Bismarck have
completely dissembled their true intentions or have reasons, of which I am ignorant, to
subscribe to our preliminaries, I cannot help but believe that all my efforts are useless. I
received your dispatch and I will conform to it" (Benedetti to Drouyn de Lhuys, Vienna,
18 July 1866, ODG, X, 99, T.).

[5] Roon to his wife, Nikolsburg, 19 July 1866, ROON, II, 297. Roon was under the mis-
apprehension that Benedetti, who left only on the 15th, had made a round trip to Paris via
Vienna.

approval of the peace preliminary text which he had examined in Vienna. The terms were already known on the 17th in Nikolsburg through a telegram from Goltz,[1] and, shortly after Benedetti's return, Prince Reuss also arrived with a copy from Paris.[2] The ambassador insisted in his first interview with Bismarck that negotiations with Austria begin as promptly as possible. However, the minister-president hesitated, and for good cause. Both the letter of the emperor and the report of Goltz, brought to Nikolsburg by Reuss, contained no definite assurances that France would agree to the contemplated annexations in North Germany. Worse, Bismarck learned that Goltz was actually the author of the peace preliminaries. It became clear that the ambassador had violated his instructions which had stressed French acceptance of Prussian expansion in North Germany. Moreover, a telegraphed report of the account of Goltz's interviews with Napoleon and Drouyn de Lhuys on the 17th strengthened Bismarck's conviction that the French foreign minister was attempting to preserve freedom of action, in order to advance French compensation demands if Prussia, after accepting the peace preliminaries of the 17th, presented territorial demands. In the instructions the minister-president had sharply criticized Goltz and urged him to obtain as quickly as possible French acquiescence in Prussian annexations in North Germany.[3]

In his conversation with Benedetti Bismarck stated that, although the king had not outright rejected the terms of the peace preliminaries, the text could not serve as a basis for the re-establishment of peace. He accused Goltz of having violated his instructions, which he read in part to Benedetti. However, the French ambassador seized the occasion to stress Austria's willingness to accept the terms. He also pointed out that Emperor Napoleon was growing insistent,

---

[1] Cf. Bismarck to Goltz, Nikolsburg, 17 July 1866, SYBEL, V, 285, in which the minister-president requested that the intended annexations be included in the peace preliminaries; cf. THIMME, *HZ*, LXXXIX, Heft 3 (1902), p. 438. This substantiates Benedetti's remarks concerning the text (Gramont [for Benedetti] to Drouyn de Lhuys, Vienna, 16 July 1866, FAE CP, Autriche/492, T.).

[2] Benedetti arrived in Nikolsburg during the very early hours of the 19th, and Reuss arrived a few hours later (Boyen to his wife, Nikolsburg, 19 July 1866, W. VON TÜMPLING, *Erinnerungen aus dem Leben des Generaladjutanten Kaiser Wilhelms I. Hermann von Boyen* [Berlin, 1898], p. 179). Prince Reuss carried also a personal reply of the emperor to King William. Napoleon urged a speedy conclusion of an armistice and peace treaty, lest public opinion in France, uncertain of Prussian objectives, trouble the relations between France and Prussia. In his letter, the emperor also alluded to the uneasiness in France created by the change in the balance of power and the prospect of Prussian military leadership of a united Germany (Napoleon III to William I, Paris, 15 July 1866, ONCKEN, I, 357-358; ft. 1, 2, *ibid.*, 357).

[3] See ft. 1. above.

in view of the embarrassment created by the apparent ineffectiveness of his role. He urged Bismarck to accept the terms, in spite of the fact that he himself, while in Vienna, had criticized the conditions as unsatisfactory from the Prussian point of view. Perhaps the extent of Prussia's demands, as revealed in the instructions Bismarck had read to him, decided him to change his point of view. He reminded the minister-president of all the advantages which were contained in the proposed terms and succeeded in gaining his admission that they were appreciable indeed. Three separate times during that day Benedetti met with Bismarck to press for acceptance of the terms; he finally insisted that he be informed of the official position of the Prussian government relative to the proposal at hand. After a council meeting held the evening of the 19th, Bismarck informed Benedetti that Prussia would consent to negotiate an armistice on the basis of the proposed terms. He emphasized, however, that the failure to include a provision relative to Prussian annexations would make it impossible for the king to go beyond an agreement for an armistice. He added that William would rather abdicate than return to Berlin without the anticipated territorial acquisitions. The decision to accept the terms at least for the conclusion of an armistice was motivated in part by the realization that Emperor Napoleon might succumb to anti-Prussian pressure in Paris and embark upon a course which could jeopardize Prussian gains. Furthermore, there was good reason to believe that the emperor would not place any serious obstacle in the path of Prussian annexations in North Germany. Under these circumstances, Bismarck gave in to Benedetti's demands and told him that Prussia stood ready to negotiate an armistice with Austria.[1] Benedetti, in his efforts to obtain the acceptance of the peace preliminaries, might have given the king and Bismarck reason to believe that the Austrian government would agree to far greater territorial annexations than were actually being considered in Vienna.[2] To be sure, Benedetti was informed that Goltz had been requested to explain to the emperor Prussian annexation wishes and Crown Prince Frederick

---

[1] See draft of report to Crown Prince Frederick, Berlin, 3 February 1867, I.A.A.b. 84; Benedetti to Drouyn de Lhuys, Nikolsburg, 19 July 1866, FAE CP, Prusse/358, no. 159; cf. L. CRUMMENERL, *Zur Geschichte der Entstehung des Friedens von Nikolsburg 1866* (Emsdetten, 1936), 91 pp.; H. WARNHOLTZ, *Bismarcks Kampf um den Vorfrieden von Nikolsburg 1866* (Hamburg, 1939), 80 pp.; GEUSS, pp. 184–187.

[2] THIMME, *HZ*, LXXXIX, Heft 3 (1902), pp. 441–442. Cf. F. K. VON HOHENZOLLERN, *Mémoires du Prince Frédéric-Charles de Prusse*, ed. W. Foerster, trans. and summarized by Corteys (Paris, n.d.), I, 371, who writes that Benedetti's remarks after returning from Vienna had given the king hope for a quick peace.

had been ordered to the king's headquarters for further conferences on the annexation issue. Yet, despite the difficulties still ahead, the ambassador had achieved a modicum of success, for he was charged to invite the belligerents to a discussion of the terms. The secretary of the French embassy at Vienna, Baron Jean E. Bourgoing, who had come to Nikolsburg with Benedetti departed late in the evening of 19 July with a note for Gramont, requesting him to invite the Austrian government to send plenipotentiaries to Nikolsburg. Benedetti himself planned to remain at the Prussian headquarters only until the arrival of the Austrians; he notified Drouyn de Lhuys that he then would leave for Vienna and await instructions there.[1]

While Benedetti waited for the Austrian delegation, expected for 22 July, Goltz had continued the efforts of the Prussian government to obtain Napoleon's assent to Prussian annexation plans, comprising a population of four million, before acceding to an armistice. The emperor agreed to it after interviews on the 17th, 18th, and 19th, stating that the extent of Prussian annexations was merely a matter of detail and should not encumber the negotiations for an armistice.[2] On the following day Benedetti was informed by Gramont that the Austrian government had agreed to the peace preliminaries as conditions for a five-day armistice.[3] Benedetti was anxiously awaiting the opening of the negotiations, hoping to be able to leave Nikolsburg at that time.[4] In anticipation of further developments on the negotiations, he passed much time at the castle where the king's headquarters were located.[5] At a dinner, to which he had been invited by William, the ambassador noted that the visit of Crown Prince Frederick had apparently exerted a conciliatory influence over the king, who was too often swayed by the advice of his military entourage.[6] The arrival of the Austrian delegates was delayed only by the technical problems of a cease-fire. The ambassador, who again spent the day of 21 July at the king's headquarters,[7] had been kept informed; that evening

---

[1] Benedetti to Drouyn de Lhuys, Nikolsburg, 19 July 1866, FAE CP, Prusse/358, no. 159.

[2] SYBEL, V, 296–297.

[3] Gramont to Drouyn de Lhuys, Vienna, 20 July 1866, FAE CP, Autriche/492, T.

[4] Benedetti to Drouyn de Lhuys, Nikolsburg, 19 July 1866, ibid., Prusse/358, no. 159.

[5] "I told [Benedetti] I did not have time [to talk to him] and continued to work, but of course he kept talking, very friendly and often very interesting stories, but nonetheless disturbing me" (Abeken to his wife, Nikolsburg, 20 July 1866, ABEKEN, p. 337).

[6] ROLOFF, HZ, CXXXVI, Heft 3 (1927), p. 490; FRIEDRICH III., p. 468.

[7] "I was interrupted here early this morning by Benedetti who however did not remain long, but long enough to keep me working late now" (Abeken to his wife, Nikolsburg, 21 July 1866, ABEKEN, p. 338).

preparations had advanced far enough to permit the cessation of hostilities for mid-day, Sunday, 22 July. Meanwhile, the Austrian government had designated its plenipotentiaries and Benedetti, who went
for a drive to Eisgrub on Sunday morning, was able to inform Crown
Prince Frederick at his headquarters that the Austrian delegates
would arrive in Nikolsburg later in the day. He told the prince that
peace was almost assured; the suspension of hostilities which went
into effect at noon along the Austro–Prussian front was to last five
days, long enough, Benedetti hoped, for agreement on a basis for
peace.[1]

During the day Benedetti was requested by Drouyn de Lhuys to
remain in Nikolsburg and to lend his efforts to a speedy and satisfactory conclusion of the armistice. The minister carefully instructed
the ambassador regarding the manner in which he was to carry out
his work and the scope of his activities:

> The role which we fulfill is that of friendly intermediaries and is limited to
> using all our influence to bring the belligerent powers upon a common terrain;
> but we are neither the arbiters imposing solutions upon the two parties, nor
> negotiators who take a direct part in the arrangements, which we desire to see
> them conclude between themselves. We do not have to sign the preliminaries;
> but, with the reserve which I indicate, we must not neglect any effort for assuring
> and speeding the adoption of the arrangements which we have proposed.[2]

The letter reached Benedetti at an opportune time, for the Prussian
minister-president had repeatedly expressed the opinion that the ambassador, in his function as a mediator, should assist at the meetings
between the plenipotentiaries. Benedetti, however, had always objected to Bismarck's interpretation of his role; now, provided with Drouyn
de Lhuys' directive, he informed Bismarck that he would not attend
the meetings which were expected to get soon under way.[3]

The Austrian delegation, consisting of Count Károlyi, General

---

[1] L. VON BLUMENTHAL, *Tagebücher aus den Jahren 1866 und 1870/71*, ed. A. von Blumenthal (Stuttgart, 1902), p. 46.

[2] Drouyn de Lhuys to Benedetti, Paris, 19 July 1866, FAE CP, Prusse/358, no. 159.

[3] Benedetti to Drouyn de Lhuys, Nikolsburg, 23 July 1866, *ibid.*, no. 162. In accordance
with his instructions, Benedetti did not attend any of the meetings but spent most of his
time at the king's headquarters in readiness to confer with any of the delegates who might
seek his help. "The French ambassador and his secretary had dinner with us, in the minister's
reception room; at the entrance of the king and the crown prince the minister went with
them to my room to confer; we finished our meal, drank our coffee, then one by one the
others all slipped away, Keudell, Bismarck-Bohlen, the French secretary, only I had no
room to go to and was left alone with the ambassador, who sat on the table with his legs
dangling down and told me Egyptian stories. The minister came in and out, advising us to
be patient; finally it occurred, happily enough, to Bene-Maledetti that he might write a letter
to his wife, and speak later to the minister [and] with that he ran off" (Abeken to his wife,
Nikolsburg, 23 July 1866, ABEKEN, p. 339).

August von Degenfeld-Schomburg and Baron Adolf Brenner-Felsach, reached Nikolsburg on Sunday afternoon, 22 July.[1] Benedetti, at a meeting next day with Bismarck, Moltke and Károlyi, reminded them that, since both sides had accepted the terms of the peace preliminaries, new political demands could only be raised at the final peace negotiations.[2] Károlyi told Benedetti that he would attempt to eliminate the demand for Austrian reparations by renouncing those still due to Austria for the campaign against Denmark. He also hoped to save the territorial integrity of Austria and Saxony[3] and prevent the Prussian army from living off the land while negotiations were being concluded. Benedetti felt that the Austrian aspirations might possibly lead to a dissolution of the armistice talks; if such a prospect threatened, he advised, Austria ought not to press her demands because he felt that Austria needed nothing more badly than a respite from the hostilities.[4] No word had as yet been received from the Italian government authorizing Barral to participate in the talks with the Austrian delegation. Bismarck had been reluctant to open the discussions under those circumstances but had finally agreed to proceed alone at Benedetti's insistence. Both the minister-president and the ambassador were hopeful that Barral would receive the necessary authorization in time to sign the armistice. Notice of the emperor's consent to Goltz's annexation demands arrived in Nikolsburg before the official opening of the negotiations, on 23 July, and the ambassador was convinced that Prussia would now readily enter into considerations for the settlement of the conflict.[5]

Benedetti learned from Károlyi, after the first meeting, that

---

[1] PRUSSIA. KRIEGSGESCHICHTLICHE ABTEILUNG DES GROSSEN GENERALSTABES, p. 713.

[2] Benedetti to Drouyn de Lhuys, Nikolsburg, 23 July 1866, FAE CP, Prusse/358, no. 162 Cf. ERNST II. (duke of Saxe-Coburg and Gotha), *Aus meinem Leben und aus meiner Zeit* (Berlin, 1892), p. 673, for his talks with Benedetti and Degenfeld in efforts to bring about a speedy armistice; see also D'HARCOURT, pp. 285–286.

[3] "The noble Emperor Francis Joseph made it a question of honor not to abandon the only German confederate who stood by his side in the hour of danger. For this reason, and only for this reason, did the Austrian plenipotentiaries in Nikolsburg designate the maintenance of the [territorial] integrity of Saxony as a *conditio sine qua non*" (VITZTHUM, p. 287). Cf. R. VON FRIESEN, *Erinnerungen aus meinem Leben* (Dresden, 1890), II, 229, whom Benedetti had told that "the demand for the mere 'existence' [of Saxony] seemed too small, and therefore he, at his own risk and responsibility, demanded instead the maintenance of the territorial integrity of Saxony and obtained the inclusion of the sentence in the treaty."

[4] Benedetti to Drouyn de Lhuys, Nikolsburg, 23 July 1866, FAE CP, Prusse/358, no. 162. Benedetti had said, "It is necessary to give Austria time to recover" (GOVONE, p. 305).

[5] Benedetti to Drouyn de Lhuys, Nikolsburg, 23 July 1866, FAE CP, Prusse/358, no. 162. Cf. ROTHFRITZ, p. 96, who believes that Goltz's handling of the Prussian demands in Paris during the pre-armistice period earned him nothing but criticism and spoiled his hope of becoming foreign minister.

the efforts to arrive at an armistice had not been productive.[1] Prussian demands for territorial and monetary compensation from Austria had met with strenuous opposition. It seemed to Benedetti that Austria was hopeful of an intervention by the great powers to restrain Prussia, while Prussia, having secured French approval of its annexation scheme, felt quite secure in its position. Progress was made next day, however, when the Austrian delegate indicated that he would not seek immunities for all of Austria's allies: Károly limited himself to a demand for the territorial integrity of Saxony and for the inclusion of Bavaria in the armistice.[2] Bismarck also wanted a settlement, indeed he expected an almost immediate signing of the peace preliminaries.[3] Yet, the negotiations met again with difficulties. Benedetti learned on 24 July that, although Italy had suspended hostilities, Barral was instructed to demand Verona, Trentino as well as the renunciation by Austria of any and all compensation for Venetia. In order to avoid trouble, because of Italian intransigence, Benedetti suggested a prolongation of the suspension of hostilities on the Austro-Italian front to 2 August.[4] King William's opposition to a mild peace was another source of anxiety for Benedetti, although Crown Prince Frederick told him at a dinner that he would endeavor to win the king's approval of the terms.[5] The situation did not improve when Baron Ludwig von Pfordten, the Bavarian plenipotentiary, arrived in Nikolsburg to discuss an armistice. As soon as Bismarck learned that he was not empowered to make territorial concessions he broke off all contact with Pfordten. The latter, ignored by Bismarck but anxious to secure an armistice for Bavaria, sought the support of Ambassador Benedetti.[6]

---

[1] Benedetti to Drouyn de Lhuys, Nikolsburg, 23 July 1866, FAE CP, Prusse/358, no. 162.

[2] Same to same, Nikolsburg, 24 July 1866, ibid., no. 166. The Austro-Bavarian treaty prohibited armistice or peace agreements by either power without the consent of the other.

[3] Ibid.

[4] Benedetti to Drouyn de Lhuys, Nikolsburg, 24 July 1866, ibid., T.; same to same, Nikolsburg, 25 July 1866, ibid., no. 167; cf. BERNHARDI, pp. 263–264.

[5] For a detailed study of the king's attitude see W. BUSCH, "Der Kampf um den Frieden in dem preussischen Hauptquartier zu Nikolsburg im Juli 1866," HZ, XCII, Heft 1 (1904), pp. 418–455; Benedetti to Drouyn de Lhuys, Nikolsburg, 24 July 1866, FAE CP, Prusse/358, no. 166; FRIEDRICH III., p. 471; Loftus to Stanley, Berlin, 11 August 1866, PRO FO 64/599, no. 138.

[6] Cf. H. POSCHINGER, Bismarck und die Diplomaten, 1852–1890 (Hamburg, 1900), p. 216, ft. 1. This note pertains to an article by A. Sckell, which appeared in the Sammler, a belles-lettres section of the Augsburger Abendzeitung, on 27 October 1868: "Pfordten's confinement lasted three days. Through some channel he managed that finally the French Ambassador Benedetti... presented his cause to the king, that Bavaria be included in the armistice negotiations. And thus Pfordten was called to Bismarck after three terrible days." Cf. F. VON BEUST, Erinnerungen zu Erinnerungen (Leipzig, 1881), p. 49, who in anticipation of such treatment had decided not to go to Nikolsburg.

The fact that Austria was obligated not to sign an armistice without Bavaria enabled Benedetti to win acceptance of a procedure which would fulfill Pfordten's hopes as well as satisfy the obligation of Austria and thus prevent a rupture of the negotiations: the Austro-Prussian armistice accord would include a stipulation inviting Austria's allies to accede to the armistice but stating that these secondary powers would later enter into separate peace negotiations with Prussia. Pfordten was to sign the armistice accord for Bavaria and the other Austrian allies.[1]

At the suggestion of Benedetti, a meeting was arranged between the king and Károlyi to clear away the obstacles inherent in the demand for Austrian monetary compensation to Prussia. A settlement was reached and the armistice talks faced nothing more than the problems of signing the accord.[2] Barral was still without authorization to accede to the armistice and again Benedetti suggested a way out. It was decided that, while Prussia, Austria and Bavaria would sign the accord, it would remain suspended until the Prussian government was in a position to declare Venetia acquired by Italy, signalling the fulfillment of the alliance which the two powers had contracted in April.[3] The Austrian and Prussian plenipotentiaries signed on Thursday, 26 July, an armistice which was to last for four weeks, as well as another act which laid down the basis for the peace negotiations.[4] The occasion was celebrated with a dinner given by

[1] Benedetti to Drouyn de Lhuys, Nikolsburg, 25 July 1866, FAE CP, Prusse/358, no. 167.

[2] *Ibid.*; "The king and Bismarck evidently had a dispute, and the excitement has not diminished. Yesterday Bismarck cried in my presence over the harsh things which His Majesty had said to him" (FRIEDRICH III., p. 473). Cf. WILHELM I., *Der alte Kaiser*, ed. K. Pagel (Leipzig, 1924), p. 287, for the following marginal comment by the king to a note from Bismarck in Nikolsburg: "After my minister-president deserts me in the face of the enemy... and because [my son] shares [his] opinion, I find myself, to my sorrow, forced to bite into this sour apple and accept this disgraceful peace after such brilliant victories of the army." As early as 17 July Bismarck had expressed the view that no Austrian territory should be demanded, a further indication that he desired a lenient peace for Austria (A. VON STOSCH, *Denkwürdigkeiten*, ed. U. von Stosch [2d ed.; Stuttgart, 1904], p. 102).

[3] Benedetti to Drouyn de Lhuys, Nikolsburg, 25 July 1866, FAE CP, Prusse/358, no. 167.

[4] Same to same, Nikolsburg, 26 July 1866, FAE MD, Autriche/67. "Hardly arrived [in Nikolsburg on 26 July] and before I got to the king, Benedetti urgently solicited an audience with me... he told me Napoleon... hoped that an armistice would be signed" (FRIEDRICH III., p. 474). For the effect of foreign intervention, real and imagined, upon Prussian disposition to conclude an armistice cf. Keudell to Duncker, Nikolsburg, 26 July 1866, M. DUNCKER, *Politischer Briefwechsel aus seinem Nachlass*, ed. J. Schultze, "Deutsche Geschichtsquellen des 19. Jahrhunderts," XII (Leipzig, 1923), p. 427; Talleyrand to Drouyn de Lhuys, St. Petersburg, 24 July 1866, FAE CP, Russie/237, no. 63; Benedetti to Drouyn de Lhuys, Nikolsburg, 29 July 1866, *ibid.*, Prusse/ 358, T.; Drouyn de Lhuys to André (for Benedetti), Vichy, 4 August 1866, FAE MD, Autriche/67, T.; K. RHEINDORF, *Die Schwarze-Meer-(Pontus-) Frage vom Pariser Frieden von 1856 bis zum Abschluss der Londoner Konferenz von 1871* (Berlin, 1925), p. 49.

the king, to which the Austrian delegation as well as Ambassador Benedetti were invited. As soon as the dinner was over, he and Abeken prepared a French draft of the documents signed earlier in the day.[1] Two days later the ratifications were exchanged.[2]

The armistice terms which had been agreed upon between Prussia and Bavaria, and the other secondary states, were signed on 28 July.[3] The minister-president planned to return to Berlin for the convocation of the chambers, and Benedetti, having accomplished his mission, planned to return with him. The adherence of the Italian government to the armistice was still awaited,[4] but on the day Benedetti departed for the Prussian capital he was able to report that the Italian government had agreed to the accord, which was to be in effect for four weeks.[5] The return journey also was difficult; the ambassador did not reach Berlin until Friday, 3 August, having been absent for twenty-five days.[6]

The achievement of the armistice arrangements in Nikolsburg marked the end of a task to which Ambassador Benedetti had been unexpectedly assigned after the sudden decision at Sadowa. His efforts give proof of a conscientious devotion to a mission during which he successfully achieved the aims of his government. As a mediator Benedetti had not been welcome at the Prussian headquarters, for his appearance had signalled the intervention of a foreign power in German affairs, a fact which the Prussian government, on the road to total victory, could only resent. His mission was particularly challenging in view of the lack of rapid communications with the

---

[1] Abeken to his wife, Nikolsburg, 26 July 1866, ABEKEN, p. 342. Benedetti, in sending the translation to Drouyn de Lhuys, termed it "a translation which has been prepared in the office of the minister-president" (Benedetti to Drouyn de Lhuys, Nikolsburg, 26 July 1866, FAE MD, Autriche/67, no. 9).

[2] According to the terms of the peace preliminaries, Prussia expected to annex outright Hanover, Electoral Hesse, that part of Grand Ducal Hesse north of the Main, Nassau and Frankfort (Lefèbvre de Béhaine to Drouyn de Lhuys, Berlin, 28 July 1866, FAE CP, Prusse/358, T.).

[3] "It was only through the benevolent intervention of Your Majesty's ambassador at the court of Berlin that my minister was able to obtain, after several days, an armistice... for three weeks, beginning 2 August" (Louis II to Napoleon III, Munich, 3 August 1866, ibid., Bavière/241).

[4] Benedetti to Drouyn de Lhuys, Nikolsburg, 28 July 1866, ibid., Prusse/358, T. Cf. same to same, Nikolsburg, 28 July 1866, FAE MD, Autriche/67. Benedetti wrote that since Prussia had obtained all she wanted from Austria, Bismarck no longer encouraged Italian opposition to an armistice. Cf. BERNHARDI, pp. 263–264.

[5] On 29 July Benedetti declared officially, and in writing, to Bismarck that the acquisition of Venetia by Italy had been secured (PRUSSIA. KRIEGSGESCHICHTLICHE ABTEILUNG DES GROSSEN GENERALSTABES, p. 717); Benedetti to Drouyn de Lhuys, Nikolsburg, 30 July 1866, ODG, XI, 298).

[6] Same to same, Berlin, 3 August 1866, FAE MD, Autriche/67, T.

government in Paris. Information or instructions were usually outdated when he did receive them, and he was thus forced to rely very
much upon his own resourcefulness and intuition. The resolute
fashion in which he carried out his task is clearly illustrated by his
perseverance on the journey to the king's headquarters and by the
promptness with which he entered into the negotiations. The fact
that Benedetti accomplished as much as he did – in restraining
the Prussian demands upon her defeated enemies – speaks well for
his powers of persuasion and logic, for he did not have the support
of a mobilized French army to back his talks with Bismarck. His
difficulties were increased by the fact that mediation negotiations
were carried on simultaneously in Paris. Information relayed to him
after considerable delay came from the foreign minister, who himself
was not a party to all of the negotiations Goltz carried on in the French
capital. Thus, Benedetti experienced once again the drawbacks of a
system which made the conduct of foreign affairs so greatly dependent
upon the views, so often veiled, of the emperor. The ambassador had
gone to Nikolsburg uncertain of the long-range intentions of Napoleon
and returned none the wiser.

Benedetti's conduct at the Prussian headquarters reveals that,
while he was willing to grant to Bismarck those demands Prussia was
determined to obtain in any case, the ambassador was definitely
opposed to exaggerated Prussian claims. His critique of the preliminary peace text drawn up by Goltz shows that he was anxious to
preserve a balance of power in Germany and that he was determined
not to concede any undue advantages to Prussia, especially in the
realm of military reorganization in Germany.

Of special interest is the attitude which the ambassador portrayed
toward Austria. Italian unification achieved, he began to view the
entire problem exclusively from the point of view of a realistic French
diplomat to whom Austria, after her defeat and ouster from Italy,
appeared in a new light. His advice to the Austrian delegation was
motivated by the desire to prevent a new outbreak of hostilities which
would make a total rout of Austria a foregone conclusion. He hoped to
see a regenerated Austria as a real check to Prussia, and for this
reason he deemed it imperative that she have a respite from war and
an opportunity to preserve and rebuild what was left of her military
power. His suggestions to Károlyi that he restrict his opposition and
his eagerness to bring the armistice into being were the consequence
of these thoughts, as were his intervention on behalf of Bavaria and

his practical advice for overcoming the technical obstacles to the signing of the armistice.

Yet, in spite of his truly remarkable conduct, Benedetti was not beyond the criticism of those concerned with the momentous events. The Prussians resented his coming to Nikolsburg and his subsequent efforts to check their claims as victors. The Austrian ambassador in Paris, Prince Richard Metternich, asserted that Benedetti had supported exclusively the exigencies of Bismarck during the negotiations, while Baron Reinhard Dalwigk, the foreign minister of Hesse-Darmstadt, complained that Benedetti's attitude in Nikolsburg was inexplicable to Prussia's foes.[1]

Benedetti must have felt pleased, however, reading the commendation of one with whom he had always differed so much on matters of foreign policy, but whose views on German affairs were to become almost his own in the near future. Drouyn de Lhuys wrote: "You understood perfectly the limits within which your action had to be confined .... I entirely approve of your steps and your language, and I note that the clauses of the Nikolsburg convention are, on the majority of points, as favorable to the interests which we have defended as we could hope for under the circumstances." [2]

---

[1] See BEYENS, II, 154; A. DUCROT, *La vie militaire du général Ducrot* (Paris, 1895), II, 279.
[2] Drouyn de Lhuys to Benedetti, Vichy, 2 August 1866, FAE CP, Prusse/359, n 80.

CHAPTER V

THE FRENCH COMPENSATION PROPOSALS

The radical change in the balance of power brought to the fore the very vital issue of compensations. The spectacular transformation of the power relationship between Prussia and the other European states was of particular interest to France; it was a foregone conclusion that the imperial government would seek to redress the disturbed equilibrium. While French neutrality at the outbreak of the war had raised speculations about a Franco-Prussian accord, the conduct of the French government during the Nikolsburg negotiations had served to heighten suspicions of collaboration between the two powers. It had given rise to fecund schemes regarding French compensation for Prussian aggrandizement.[1] Suggestions that France should demand territorial compensation were voiced of course in many quarters.[2] The question of compensation had to be faced by France, but the circumstances under which the issue was presented to Prussia were not the most favorable. From the military point of view, the golden opportunity had passed, for the entire Prussian army was no longer committed in action.[3] Nor did the possible alternatives offer France

---

[1] Baudin to Drouyn de Lhuys, The Hague, 14 July 1866, FAE CP, Hollande/665, no. 34; same to same, The Hague, 15 July 1866, *ibid.*, no. 36.

[2] R. HALT (ed.), *Papiers sauvés des Tuileries, suite à la correspondance de la famille impériale* (Paris, 1871), pp. 166–167; "I regret very much that you do not see the fatal danger of a powerful Germany and a powerful Italy. It is the *dynasty* which is threatened, and it will suffer the consequences.... Venetia having been ceded, you should have supported Austria, marched to the Rhine and imposed your conditions. To let Austria be strangled *c'est plus qu'un crime, c'est une faute*" (Queen Sophie of Holland to André, [The Hague], 18 July 1866, FRANCE. COMMISSION DES PAPIERS SAISIES AUX TUILERIES, I, 14–15). "To let Prussia.... make her own bed as she likes would mean taking in advance the engagement to dislodge her by force a little while later" (Report of Pierre Magne to the emperor, Paris, 20 July 1866, *ODG*, XI, 123–125); Pierre Magne to Drouyn de Lhuys, Château de Montaigne, 7 August 1866, DURIEUX, II, 81–82; for the reaction of French public opinion, see CASE, pp. 215 ff.; Radowitz *Tagebuchaufzeichnung*, 25 August 1866, STOLBERG-WERNIGERODE, pp. 445–448; Goltz to Bernstorff, Paris, 28 August 1866, *ibid.*, pp. 449–454.

[3] "At the time of the Bohemian campaign, there were in the Rhine provinces only two

an advantageous choice. She could either present demands now and rely on the willingness of Prussia to satisfy them or postpone the quest for compensation to a more fortuitous moment, when France might negotiate from a position of strength. The third alternative, even less attractive, was to support the Russian call for an international congress to settle the German question.[1] This alternative, of necessity, was least promising in that it would diminish the pre-eminence of French mediation and possibly emasculate a French demand for compensation.

The first alternative was taken, and on 26 July Ambassador Benedetti, while still in Nikolsburg, received instructions to search for a French equivalent to Prussian expansion in Germany. They had been drawn up on 23 July, after Napoleon had agreed to the principle of territorial annexation by Prussia but without having obtained definite Prussian assurances of compensation for France. He had merely suggested to Goltz that France receive Landau and Luxemburg so as to give her the defensive line of which she had been deprived in 1815.[2] Since the defeat of his earlier proposals, Drouyn de Lhuys had determined that the question of territorial changes in Germany should provide the occasion for redressing the balance of power.[3] He told Benedetti that the geographic re-arrangements in Germany was one of the essential problems of the negotiations for peace, and that French thoughts about an eventual settlement might now be revealed. The imperial government was not proposing to reject Prussian aspirations in a preemptory fashion; on the contrary, it was disposed to see them realized, under certain conditions and to a certain extent:

The kingdom of Saxony would have to be maintained as an independent state, the new acquisitions of Prussia would not exceed... the figure of four million souls; finally, in this case, France would obtain a rectification of borders which would restore to her her limits of 1814, [and] add [also] Luxemburg, provided compensation be arranged with the king of Holland.

This very delicate part of the negotiation, outlined first in talks between you and Bismarck, could be the object of a secret convention.

Prussian regiments which travelled incessantly back and forth by train, changing their numbers to make the appearance of a much more considerable force" (RANDON, II, 146–147).

[1] See above Chapter IV, p. 103, ft. 4.

[2] Goltz to Bismarck, Paris, 27 July 1866, ONCKEN, II, 8–11.

[3] "Each time, in my conversations with you, I initiated the question of territorial changes which will take place to the profit of Prussia, I have expressed to you the confidence that the Berlin cabinet will recognize the equity and propriety of according to France some compensations designed to increase, in a certain proportion, her defensive force" (Drouyn de Lhuys to Goltz, 3 August 1866, ibid., p. 13).

I now call your attention to this matter and invite you to let me know your opinion, while I wait before sending you later complementary instructions.[1]

Benedetti was aware of Bismarck's hope that no power, and certainly not benevolent France, would challenge the changes Prussia was about to instigate in Germany. Rather than contest the exactitude of the minister-president's presentiments, Benedetti had refrained, in view of the mediation in progress and lack of instructions, from asserting that an aggrandizement of Prussia was anything but a free gift of Europe. However, once in possession of definite instructions, Benedetti deemed it essential that Bismarck be immediately acquainted with the views of the imperial government, even at the risk of a delay in the signing of the armistice.

The ambassador's communication considerably surprised the minister-president and he retorted, with ill-concealed irritation, that this new development would necessitate the abandonment of all arrangements with Austria, and probably determine the king to resume the war.[2] Benedetti remained resolute in the face of these intimidations: "I made it a point not to let him suppose for an instant that the fear of seeing hostilities resumed would determine us to let Prussia expand all alone." [3] He recalled to Bismarck the advantages which Prussia had gained, in some measure in consequence of the attitude of the French government during the war, and stressed that concessions accorded to France would be a guarantee of the friendship of the two powers. These remarks apparently prompted Bismarck to show a more conciliatory attitude:

Taking a map and examining the importance of the territory which Prussia would have to cede to us, Bismarck assured me that on his part there would be no difficulty in establishing the frontier of 1814. He has recognized, after having pointed out to me that by the terms of the constitution the government of the king could not consent to it without the approbation of the chambers, that, in presenting unique propositions which did not contain, as would a general treaty, any modification of the changes which had been agreed to, the national representation would resign itself to acquiesce in it. The president of the council

[1] Drouyn de Lhuys to Benedetti, Paris, 23 July 1866, FAE MD, Autriche/67, no. 78bis. Cf. A. SOREL, *Histoire diplomatique de la guerre franco-allemande* (Paris, 1875), I, 22, who mistakenly assigns the receipt of these instructions to July 25, although Benedetti received them on the very day of his talk with Bismarck (Benedetti to Drouyn de Lhuys, Nikolsburg, 26 July 1866, FAE MD, Autriche/67, no. 9bis). Cf. G. PAGÈS, "L'affaire du Luxembourg," *RHM*, I, no. 1 (1926), pp. 8–9, who thinks Benedetti should have been informed of the emperor's concessions to Prussia as well as the military inability of France to impose her demands.

[2] The course of the negotiations actually shows that Bismarck, on the contrary, hastened the conclusion of a settlement with Austria.

[3] Benedetti to Drouyn de Lhuys, Nikolsburg, 26 July 1866, FAE MD, Autriche/67, no. 9bis.

could not foresee how the king of Holland could be compensated for abandoning Luxemburg.... It would therefore be better to seek another basis for the transaction, or to find in the Palatinate an equivalent for Luxemburg, either for us or for the king of Holland.[1]

After the minister-president's tactical reversal, Benedetti acceded to his request that no mention of the demand for compensation should be made to the king for the time being. Both agreed that it might unduly jeopardize the negotiations for an armistice, in view of the king's opposition to concessions in the moment of triumph. Benedetti did not insist on a definite time for resumption of the talks but left it to Bismarck to initiate further discussion.[2]

In consideration of the events which were to follow the French demands, events which culminated in the London conference of May 1867, the recommendations which Benedetti made to Drouyn de Lhuys at this time are of importance. Despite the erratic manner in which French diplomatic affairs were handled at times, the dependence upon Benedetti's views and impressions during the Nikolsburg episode is of course obvious. The ambassador stated that Bismarck alone in the Prussian government could appreciate the advantage of combining with France in an alliance at the price of territorial compensation.[3] To the king and his entourage, the abandonment of Prussian or German territory in the hour of victory would, à première vue, seem a humiliating concession. Benedetti took care to include even Crown Prince Frederick, usually wise and moderate, among those who would strongly oppose any cession of German territory. In spite of the reluctance to be expected at the king's headquarters, Benedetti advised that France should present her claims. He maintained that,

---

[1] Ibid. Cf. Nothomb to Rogier, Berlin, 26 July 1866, BAE CP, Prusse/23, Pt. II, no. 267, who considered Luxemburg a likely object of compensation for France since it was theoretically at war with Prussia, and thus disposable.

[2] Benedetti to Drouyn de Lhuys, Nikolsburg, 26 July 1866, FAE MD, Autriche/67, no. 9bis. Cf. ONCKEN, II, 5–6, fts. 1 and 2, who casts doubt on the accuracy of Benedetti's report by implying that Bismarck could not have expressed a willingness to restore the 1814 borders to France. A report of Govone of a conversation with Bismarck states that he personally "would not see any difficulty in consenting to the cession to France of all the land between the Rhine and the Moselle; Palatinate, Oldenburg and a portion of Prussian territory" (Govone to La Marmora, Berlin, 3 July 1866, GOVONE, p. 492). "I only could impede the Napoleonic policy by always letting Benedetti... presume that I was completely willing to leave the path of virtue [and agree to territorial concessions in Germany]" (Bismarck to William I, Varzin, 20 September 1873, R. FESTER, Deutsche Rundschau, CXIII, Heft 2 [November 1902], p. 229).

[3] Benedetti to Drouyn de Lhuys, Nikolsburg, 26 July 1866, FAE MD, Autriche/67, no. 9bis. On a copy of this dispatch among the Cerçay Papers, Bismarck made the marginal comment: "He honestly believed it" (see same to same, Nikolsburg, 26 July 1866, FAE PR/A).

despite a hostile attitude toward them, not one among the Prussian leaders had ever really doubted that demands for French compensation would be made:

> Our disinterest [thus far] was truly a subject for surprise. Therefore no one will be astonished to hear that France, as one has presumed, desires to cover herself against the dangers to which the advantages Prussia plans to claim expose her, and no one can maintain that our pretensions are exhorbitant. . . . Today there is no longer the same difficulty about agreeing [to an extension of France], since the Prussian monarchy . . . has risen so high among the great powers of Europe . . . . Unless one wishes to alienate France, after Austria has already been alienated by expulsion from Germany, and risk a *rapprochement* [between France and Austria] when there is every reason to prevent it, it would be best to accept favorably an arrangement which, by making us disinterested, would permit Prussia to use all her resources to secure peaceably the preponderant position which she has conquered. We must give birth to this idea and get the king and his entourage to share it, while conserving our calm and friendly attitude, but at the same time speaking a language which permits no illusion.[1]

Benedetti entertained no doubts about the Prussian government's ability to persuade the chambers to acquiesce in territorial compensation. Not only did he regard king and cabinet as all-powerful in this matter, he also felt certain that Bismarck would not attempt to shirk his responsibility toward France by pointing to such fallacious obstacles.[2] As for the nature of the territorial demands, the ambassador agreed to their justification as related to the frontiers of 1814. In respect to Luxemburg, however, he shared Bismarck's reservations regarding compensation for the Dutch king.[3] He felt this to be an "invincible" difficulty and suggested that another combination for obtaining the duchy or an equivalent possession be found. "I would

---

[1] Benedetti to Drouyn de Lhuys, Nikolsburg, 26 July 1866, FAE MD, Autriche/67, no. 9bis.

[2] *Ibid.* Cf. Bismarck to William I, Berlin, 6 August 1866, ONCKEN, II, 24, in which Bismarck states that he answered Benedetti's overture "evasively and dilatorily." As a matter of fact Bismarck had already begun a countercampaign by inspiring articles in the German press to the effect that the emperor did not expect any return for his mediation (Bismarck to the foreign office [for Count Eulenburg], Nikolsburg, 31 July 1866, *BGW*, VI, 96, T.).

[3] Since Benedetti was to overcome this reservation a short time later, it is possible that he had given little thought to the question prior to the interview and had followed Bismarck blindly into a skillfully introduced objection designed to postpone thorough discussion. All the more inexplicable is then his silence concerning possible repercussions should France seek compensation in Belgium. Cf. Bismarck to Perponcher, Nikolsburg, 31 July 1866, *ibid.*, p. 92, in which he attaches no value to the acquisition of Luxemburg by France and states that the military experts do not view the retention of the fortress as absolutely necessary. Cf. Lefèbvre de Béhaine to Drouyn de Lhuys, Berlin, 27 July 1866, FAE CP, Prusse/358, no. 173, who examines the legal basis for Prussia's garrison rights in Luxemburg. He notes that they are based essentially on the convention between Prussia and the Dutch king, signed in Frankfurt, 8 November 1816. The Germanic Confederation is mentioned only in an indirect relationship, and the convention modifies certain stipulations of the Vienna Congress. The *chargé d'affaires* concedes that Prussia has a rather good legal claim if she desires to continue her garrison rights in Luxemburg.

acquaint Your Excellency with nothing new by informing you that Bismarck is of the opinion that we should seek [compensation] in Belgium, and that he offered to come to an agreement with us about it." [1]

The speed with which Benedetti made his overture to Bismarck on 26 July is indicative of the urgency which he felt about presenting a demand for compensation. The prospect of a near settlement between Prussia and Austria, the fear of being presented with a *fait accompli* regarding Prussian annexations, decided him not to delay. The determination with which he had countered all intimidation attempts by the minister-president almost suggests that he did not realize that the French government was in no position to impose its demands; nor did he seem to know to what extent the emperor had actually acquiesced to the Prussian annexation schemes. The ambassador did not base his optimism so much upon a false assumption of Prussian readiness to agree to compensation[2] as upon mistaken ideas regarding the determination of the imperial government and the military strength of France. Indeed, Benedetti emphasized the resistance which French expansion plans would encounter in Berlin; at no time had he forecast *ipso facto* acceptance of such demands. He had assessed correctly the attitude of the king and his entourage, which, as events were to prove, did not change as long as the issue existed. When he counselled determination and firmness, Benedetti could only have done so in the expectation that his government was capable of exerting great pressure in Berlin.[3]

---

[1] Benedetti to Drouyn de Lhuys, Nikolsburg, 26 July 1866, FAE MD, Autriche/67, no. 9bis. Cf. remarks made by Bismarck in a conversation with Lefèbvre de Béhaine on 16 July in Nikolsburg: "Oh, well... your situation is quite simple: you must go find the king of the Belgians, tell him that the inevitable political and territorial aggrandizement of Prussia seems disquieting to you, that there is only one means for you to counter dangerous eventualities and to re-establish the equilibrium in reassuring conditions for Europe and you. This means is *d'unir les destinées de la Belgique aux vôtres par des liens si étroits que cette Monarchie, dont l'autonomie serait d'ailleurs respectée, devienne au Nord le véritable boulevard de la France rentrée dans l'exercise de ses droits naturels*"(Lefèbvre de Béhaine to Drouyn de Lhuys, Berlin, 25 July 1866, FAE CP, Prusse/358, no. 168); "It is established that Bismarck did not limit himself to listening to what the French said. He had conceived a whole Belgian policy.... Far from answering with an energetic *non possumus* to the attempts of the imperial diplomacy to annex [Belgium]... he welcomed the propositions of the emperor and his advisers" (L. LECLÈRE, "Bismarck et la Belgique, 1866–1867," *Académie royale de la Belgique. Bulletin de la classe des lettres et des sciences morales et politiques*, Ser. V, XIII, no. 4 [1927], pp. 172–173).

[2] OLLIVIER, VIII, 542–543.

[3] In the plan which Benedetti had offered for the simultaneous solution of the Schleswig-Holstein and Venetia questions, he had already stressed the necessity of being able to reinforce the policy chosen (see above, pp. 43–44).

The compensation issue was not further discussed in Nikols-burg, and there is no indication that Benedetti sought additional talks at the royal headquarters. However, he called the attention of the foreign minister to the preparations which Bismarck was making to execute promptly the stipulations of a final peace settle-ment. The minister-president was preoccupied with adding population figures, retracing border lines, and considering other factors as well, in an effort to prepare the annexations to Prussia, while endeavoring to stay within limits which would not offend the French emperor.[1] Benedetti stressed that Bismarck seemed undisturbed at the possible intervention of the other powers concerning the conditions imposed on the vanquished.[2] As for the compensation overture, the am-bassador reiterated his belief that the imperial demands would be successful because they were both "legitimate and moderate," but he added a warning about the devious route which Bismarck might employ to give France satisfaction, as well as about the continued antipathy of the king toward relinquishing German soil.[3]

Benedetti's report on his conversation with Bismarck reached Drouyn de Lhuys, who was in Vichy with the emperor, on 29 July, and on the same day he telegraphed the ambassador a convention proposal for submission to the minister-president. The conclusion of the armistice on the 26th, and its ratification two days later, determined him to expedite to Benedetti this draft project[4] which took into account objections raised by Bismarck to the earlier proposal:[5]

Article 1. The French Empire enters into possession of those portions of territory which, belonging today to Prussia, had been included in the delimi-tation of France in 1814.

Article 2. Prussia engages herself to obtain from the king of Bavaria, and the grand duke of Hesse, conditional upon furnishing compensation to these princes, the cession of those portions of the territory which they possess on the left bank of the Rhine, and to transfer possession of them to France.

Article 3. All dispositions attaching to the Germanic Confederation territories

---

[1] Benedetti to Drouyn de Lhuys, Nikolsburg, 28 July 1866, FAE MD, Autriche/67, no. 10bis.

[2] Cf. Drouyn de Lhuys to André [for Benedetti], Vichy, 4 August 1866, *ibid.*, T., for a new Russian proposal that the changes brought about in Germany be submitted to the powers, assembled in congress, for approval. This proposal was also rejected by France.

[3] Benedetti to Drouyn de Lhuys, Nikolsburg, 28 July 1866, *ibid.*, no. 10bis.

[4] "The emperor has expressed his regrets... that he had let himself be persuaded to make the ... compensation demands.... The day after his arrival [in Vichy, 29 July] when he was sick in bed, Drouyn de Lhuys presented to him the necessity of using the supposedly favor-able moment for extensive demands. The minister had depicted the affair as very urgent and thus obtained the emperor's agreement" (Goltz to Bismarck, Paris, 1 December 1866. *APP*, VIII, 177).

[5] PAGÈS, *RHM*, I, no. 1 (1926), pp. 11–12.

placed under the jurisdiction of the king of Holland, as well as those relating to the garrison right in the fortress of Luxemburg are to be null and void.[1]

Benedetti had left Nikolsburg before the project reached him and, in preparation for the expected compensation talks in Berlin, he had sent the following plea to the foreign minister: "It is. . . indispensable that I be perfectly informed, in all respects and for all eventualities, of the views of the emperor. I urgently ask you to let me come to confer with you, and I ask you to call me by telegraph. I will probably arrive Thursday in Berlin, and if you telegraph me on the same day I could leave the following evening." [2] Benedetti did not, in fact, arrive in Berlin until Friday, 3 August; [3] on Saturday evening he received the laconic message: "You are authorized to come to Paris as you have asked me, when you believe that the prolongation of your presence in Berlin is no longer necessary for the *conclusion* of the affair discussed in my telegraphic message of the 29th." [4]

Benedetti became concerned about the magnitude of the French demands, particularly in reference to Mainz.[5] However, the specific instructions of the minister decided him to open negotiations without further delay. Benedetti apparently felt that he ought not be a witness to Bismarck's initial reaction to the demands, and simply transmitted a copy of the project to Bismarck's office with a brief covering note:

In reply to the communication which I have transmitted from Nikolsburg to Paris, as a result of our talks on the 26th of last month, I received from Vichy the secret convention project which you will find herewith in copy. I hasten to acquaint you with it so that you may examine it at your leisure. I am, moreover, at your disposal to confer about it when you shall judge that the time has come.[6]

In order to emphasize his trepidation over the large claim, Benedetti detailed to the foreign minister his cautious approach to Bismarck:

Wanting to act prudently, I thought it suitable, in view of the temperament of the president of the council, not to witness the first impression which would

---

[1] Drouyn de Lhuys to Benedetti, Vichy, 29 July 1866, FAE MD, Autriche/67, T. This communication was sent in duplicate to Vienna, for transmission to Benedetti in Nikolsburg. When the ambassador's telegram of 30 July, announcing his impending departure from Nikolsburg, reached Vichy, another copy was sent to Berlin (Drouyn de Lhuys to Lefèbvre de Béhaine, Vichy, 29 July [actually sent, Paris, 31 July] 1866, *ibid.*).

[2] Benedetti to Drouyn de Lhuys, Nikolsburg, 30 July 1866, *ODG*, XI, 300. Cf. "I consider it indispensable to come personally to Paris to receive your orders" (same to same, Nikolsburg, 28 July 1866, FAE CP, Prusse/358, T.).

[3] "I arrived this morning. I find your telegram dated Vichy, 29 July. Article 2 is illegible. Please have it telegraphed again" (same to same, Berlin, 3 August 1866, FAE MD, Autriche/67, T.).

[4] Drouyn de Lhuys to André [for Benedetti], Vichy, 4 August 1866, *ibid.*

[5] *MMP*, pp. 178–179.

[6] Benedetti to Bismarck, Berlin, 5 August 1866, FAE MD, Autriche/67, no. 176bis.

be produced in his mind by the certitude that we claim the Rhine border up to and including the fortress of Mainz. To this end I sent him this morning a copy of your project and wrote him the private letter which you find herewith in copy.[1]

However, the course of action which he outlined showed no further trace of his own apprehension. Benedetti probably felt that his reservations needed no further emphasis:

Your Excellency can be assured that I shall neglect no effort to gain agreement for the integral dispositions, regardless of how heated the opposition may be which I am certain to encounter. Convinced that the government of the emperor shows itself moderate in limiting itself to stipulating, in the face of the aggrandizements already acquired by Prussia, the securities set out in your project, I shall be difficult about accepting, even for only referring to you, modifications of some importance. I hold that in this negotiation firmness is the best, I would say freely, the only argument which should be used. I shall show myself clearly resolved to decline any proposition which I could not accept, while taking care to show... that Prussia would misconstrue that which justice and foresight command, and that she would give us at the same time the measure of her ingratitude, if she refused to give us the guarantees which the extension of her frontiers obliges us to claim.[2]

During the day on which Benedetti had sent Bismarck a copy of the convention text, 5 August, he received word that the minister-president would receive him in the evening. Bismarck opened the conversation with remarks on the extent of the French demands and noted that they would give France a position in Germany which she had never had, except during the Revolution and Empire period. Shifting his argument, he listed all the advantages Prussia had foregone by ending the war in order to placate the French government. He also stated that the emperor, in his conversations with Goltz, had only lightly touched on the matter of compensation and had indicated that he preferred not to press claims which offered more inconveniences than advantages but, instead, to show good will toward Prussia through his disinterestedness. Benedetti refused to accept this point of view. He insisted that France had performed a signal service for Prussia, giving her the chance to harvest the fruits of military victory by forestalling the possible interference of the other powers. Pointing to the contemplated new political organization of northern Germany, he cited that as justification enough for French compensation. Bringing this large area under a united political leadership raised the possibility of a unified Germany emerging in the not too distant future. Bismarck refused to admit the contention that the political

---

[1] Benedetti to Drouyn de Lhuys, Berlin, 5 August 1866, *ibid.*
[2] *Ibid.*

reorganization in northern Germany presented a threat to French security. Moreover, he told Benedetti that it was impossible to reconcile Prussian policy with the demands France was making; to alienate German territory, especially Mainz, and to force essentially German people to become French subjects, were proposals which Prussia could not consider. Returning the discussion to the plane of the balance of power, Benedetti emphasized the fact that the new developments in Germany were of direct consequence to French security. The increase in Prussia's power, both real and potential, could not be ignored and the ambassador advised Bismarck that Prussia's interests would best be served through solidarity with France.[1]

Despite the serious differences, the interview had been friendly to the point of cordiality.[2] Before taking leave of Bismarck the ambassador briefly touched upon the possible reaction of the king, to which the minister-president replied that there was little hope of gaining the acquiescence of the monarch. Benedetti indicated that he did not share that opinion; he was certain the king could be influenced in favor of the project. He realized that Bismarck was surprised by the extent of the French claims, especially in reference to Mainz. He thought the minister-president's apprehension regarding public sentiment not without foundation in fact but did not consider it an insurmountable obstacle. He was convinced that the Prussian government would, in any case, make some effort to conciliate France but warned that such an offer might prove insignificant. Benedetti advised that the foreign ministry retain a firm stand in the matter, for Prussia would take advantage of the slightest sign of weakening. He had told Bismarck that he would insist that his government leave its propositions intact: "I expect to see Bismarck formulate counterpropositions; in my opinion, the government of the emperor must await them without fearing to appear too strongly resolved to accept only those arrangements compatible with the interests of the country." [3]

Benedetti had returned from this interview with Bismarck to

---

[1] Benedetti to Drouyn de Lhuys, Berlin, 6 August 1866, *ibid.*, no. 178bis.

[2] Cf. "I could have kicked Benedetti down the stairs at once but the consequences would have been war" (HOHENLOHE, II, 71). Cf. Bismarck's version of the interview given from the tribune of the *Reichstag*, 2 May 1871: "After the 6th of August I saw the French ambassador enter my office, waving an ultimatum in his hand, summoning us either to cede Mainz or expect an immediate declaration of war. I did not hesitate to answer, 'Well, then, we will have the war'" (GERMANY. REICHSTAG. *Verhandlungen. Stenographische Berichte* [Berlin, 1871], I, 518).

[3] Benedetti to Drouyn de Lhuys, Berlin, 6 August 1866, FAE MD, Autriche/67, no. 178bis.

find that the courier had arrived with instructions from the foreign ministry emphasizing again the necessity for the imperial government to obtain the frontiers of 1814 and Luxemburg or equivalent compensation.[1] Drouyn de Lhuys intimated that the contemplated transaction could be easily executed,[2] and made no reference to the ambassador's earlier admonition regarding the obdurate attitude in Berlin. The minister hoped that Bismarck, in order to assure the continuance of cordial relations with France, could be urged to force Bavaria into a territorial sacrifice during the peace negotiations. In addition, Drouyn de Lhuys wanted it understood by Prussia that compensation in Belgium, although not mentioned in the proposed convention, was part of the French claims. Finally, he cautioned the ambassador to conduct the negotiations in such a manner as to prevent Bismarck from arousing national sentiment against France.[3]

While Benedetti counselled his government not to deviate from its demands, Bismarck was giving vent to his irritation. He told Goltz that the king would never give his agreement to the French demands, and that he would hesitate to ask the monarch's consent as long as the claims were so exhorbitant.[4] He was particularly displeased about French insistence on Mainz and about Benedetti's hint that a refusal would lead to a deterioration of the relations between France and Prussia.[5] In respect to the fortress of Luxemburg, he intimated that Prussia might give up her garrison right since this strong point had no longer such great strategic value. It was Belgium, however, that Bismarck considered the logical area for French expansion. "I do not consider Belgium *lebensfähig*... and we can accept the increase in the power of France through [the acquisition of]

---

[1] Same to same, Berlin, 6 August 1866, *ibid.*, private letter.

[2] "If in the coming arrangements, the emperor, without drawing the sword, but by the unique effect of his moral influence, obtained what others demanded by force, that is to say, some frontier concessions, the moral effect of it would be immense; our sovereign would have put the seal to the purest of glories" (Magne to Drouyn de Lhuys, Château de Montaigne, 4 August 1866, DURIEUX, II, 78).

[3] Drouyn de Lhuys to Benedetti, Vichy, 3 August 1866, FAE MD, Autriche/67. For evidence of the reversal of German public opinion in favor of Prussia, see K. A. MÜLLER, *Bayern im Jahre 1866 und die Berufung des Fürsten Hohenlohe*, "Historische Bibliothek," XX (Munich, 1909), pp. 73–74; A. DOVE, *Grossherzog Friedrich von Baden als Landesherr und deutscher Fürst* (Heidelberg, 1902), p. 145.

[4] Cf. Bismarck to William I, Berlin, 6 August 1866, ONCKEN, II, 24, to which the king replied that Goltz might go to Vichy and remind the emperor of his national self-determination principles (see marginal comment by King William).

[5] Bismarck to Goltz, Berlin, 5 August 1866, *BGW*, VI, 101; same to same, Berlin, 5 August 1866, *ibid.*, 102. Cf. ROTHFRITZ, p. 104, who writes that Goltz thought compensation for France justified; Rouher to Conti, Cerçay, 6 August 1866, G. ROTHAN, *Les origines*, pp. 465–468.

French Belgium." [1] He emphasized that, while he did not expect a war over the Rhineland compensation issue, preparations to meet such a development should be taken.[2] To General Govone, Bismarck complained strongly about a reversal in the emperor's policy and of "impossible... inadmissable demands," which could cause Prussia to lose all the prestige she had gained in Germany, and he reiterated that Napoleon was deliberately seeking trouble with Prussia.[3]

The reaction to Benedetti's first interview had hardly crystallized in Paris, when the ambassador had his second interview in the late evening of 7 August. This time the result was even less encouraging. The secret convention text had been submitted to the king and examined by him with the crown prince and Bismarck. The French demands had been rejected lest Prussia do violence to national honor and arouse all Germany against her. When Bismarck informed the ambassador of this decision, Benedetti simply acknowledged it and stated that he would inform his government.[4] The minister-president hinted at the possibility of modifications or other combinations, and stated that Major Walther von Loë, military attaché at the Paris embassy, would take instructions to Goltz informing him of Prussia's position and requesting him to explore other areas for compensation.[5] In the absence of instructions regarding a modification of French demands, Benedetti declined to enter into discussions. Terminating the interview, Bismarck asked him not to regard his statements as a final decision. "[Bismarck] has vigorously recommended ... not to inform you that Prussia replied to our communication with a *refusal*, although he articulated this word to me, and he gave me to understand that if the government of the king could not prevent keeping Mainz for Germany, the price which he attaches to the relations maintained

---

[1] Bismarck to Goltz, Berlin, 8 August 1866, *BGW*, VI, 112.

[2] *Ibid.*, 112–113.

[3] GOVONE, p. 311.

[4] Benedetti to Drouyn de Lhuys, Berlin, 8 August 1866, FAE MD, Autriche/67, no. 179bis. Cf. OLLIVIER, VIII, 546–548; Govone to Visconti-Venosta, Paris, 12 August 1866, GOVONE, pp. 522–527.

[5] "Loë leaves this evening and carries instructions, developed at length, to Goltz to enable him to explain and submit to the emperor the considerations which do not permit Prussia to adhere to our convention project. Subsidiarily, he is supposedly authorized to seek other combinations with you, designed to satisfy us" (Benedetti to Drouyn de Lhuys, Berlin, 8 August 1866, FAE MD, Autriche/67, T.). Radowitz, leaving Berlin for Paris on 10 August, was apparently also charged with similar instructions for Goltz (RADOWITZ, I, 112). Goltz did discuss other possibilities, in particular a cession of Luxemburg with territorial and monetary compensation for the king of Holland (Rouher to Benedetti, Paris, 26 August 1866, FAE PR/A; cf. Goltz to Bernstorff, Paris, 28 August 1866, STOLBERG-WERNIGERODE, pp. 449–454).

with France would dispose him, however, to make important sacrifices in order to further strengthen [those relations]." [1]

During a meeting in the morning of 8 August, Benedetti questioned Bismarck about the sudden departure of General Manteuffel for St. Petersburg,[2] to discover if there existed a direct relationship between the general's mission and the French demands. He feared that the Prussian government might be trying to establish closer ties with Russia as a consequence of the French compensation claims. Bismarck insisted that he personally had given no information to Manteuffel touching upon the matter but added that he could not vouch for the king. Benedetti made it a point to indicate to Drouyn de Lhuys that the general had been called from his command in the field after the convention project had been submitted to the minister-president.[3]

Although his conduct during the first interview with Bismarck had received commendation in Paris,[4] Benedetti did not press as vigorously in subsequent meetings for the acceptance of the French claims. The determined opposition of the minister-president made it manifest that the demands drafted by Drouyn de Lhuys could not be satisfied short of a major crisis with Prussia.[5] Under these circumstances Benedetti deemed it imperative to go to Paris for consultation.[6] He was also concerned about possible leaks in Berlin in regard to the compensation project, realizing that they might bring additional

---

[1] Benedetti to Drouyn de Lhuys, Berlin, 8 August 1866, FAE MD, Autriche/67, no. 179bis.

[2] "I was aware that M. Benedetti... was much preoccupied with respect to the object and result of General Manteuffel's mission, and it was evident to me that he attributed to it a much greater importance than it assumed generally at the time" (Loftus to Stanley, Berlin, 6 October 1866, PRO FO 64/601A, no. 262).

[3] Benedetti to Drouyn de Lhuys, Berlin, 8 August 1866, FAE MD, Autriche/67, no. 179bis. Cf. S. GORIAINOV, Le Bosphore et les Dardanelles (Paris, 1910), pp. 146–147, who states that Manteuffel was sent to the Russian court with a personal letter from the king, in which William justified the large annexations which Prussia expected to make in northern Germany. He invited the tsar in return to discuss any issues with Manteuffel which might strengthen the ties between their states. The tsar indicated a desire to free himself of the Paris Treaty stipulation relative to the Black Sea, for when he took up the issue with William in 1870, he made reference to the conversation with Manteuffel. Cf. H. VON SCHWEINITZ, Denkwürdigkeiten (Berlin, 1927), I, 242–243, who relates that Manteuffel remained in St. Petersburg from 9–24 August and that the general explained Prussian annexation demands. VALENTIN, p. 339, sees in Manteuffel's mission also a Prussian offer of an Ausgleich for Russia with the promise to support Russian ambitions in the Black Sea area. Cf. RHEINDORF, p. 50; KOHL, I, 296.

[4] "His Majesty entirely approves of your attitude and language" (Drouyn de Lhuys to Benedetti, Paris, 8 August 1866, FAE MD, Autriche/67, T.).

[5] PAGÈS, RHM, I, no. 1 (1926), p. 15. Cf. Bismarck to Goltz, Berlin, 10 August 1866, BGW, VI, 117, who suggests the need for alliances with the south German states and even Austria, if France should make the rejection of the compensation demands a cause for war.

[6] Benedetti to Drouyn de Lhuys, Berlin, 9 August 1866, FAE CP, Prusse/359, T.

difficulties. He implied to Drouyn de Lhuys that the necessary discretion was not being observed at the royal palace. Rumors were being circulated about a misunderstanding between Berlin and Paris,[1] and during the afternoon of his departure, 9 August, Benedetti had several callers who pressed him for information. Dalwigk, who had heard of the rumors, would have welcomed a break between the two powers. He stressed the dangers of Prussian expansion to the security of France.[2] The minister from Hesse was followed by Loftus, who was anxious to verify the rumors. Benedetti, put on the spot by a direct question, admitted that he had touched on the idea of compensation for France "in the form of *une causerie sérieuse* – and not as having made a formal demand." Benedetti also told Loftus that Prussia had gone far beyond all expectations in her absorption of the smaller states and "France must claim compensation for her own security and the satisfaction of the nation. 'We can never... passively permit the formation of a German Empire, the position of the emperor would become untenable.'"[3] Subsequent to the British ambassador's call, Godefroid Nothomb, son of the Belgian ambassador and a secretary at the Belgian embassy, appeared to inquire whether Belgian territory was being mentioned in the rumored discussions with Bismarck. Benedetti denied that such territory was stipulated in the French claims but declared that Bismarck had drawn his attention to both Luxemburg and Belgium during their talks.[4] The position of the ambassador as the result of these rumors was acutely embarrassing and he was no doubt anxious to leave Berlin.

During a brief stop in Hanover, Benedetti discussed the compensation demands with Count Gustave de Reiset, the French minister there. He told him of Bismarck's determination not to yield any German territory, but he also emphasized the necessity of obtaining guarantees for the security of France. He complained that at present French policy had no direction and was being abandoned to chance achievements at a time when the Berlin cabinet was refusing everything or making unacceptable propositions.[5]

---

[1] Benedetti to Drouyn de Lhuys, Berlin, 8 August 1866, FAE MD, Autriche/67, no. 179bis. Bismarck to Goltz, Berlin, 10 August 1866, *BGW*, VI, 116. "Lord Stanley has told Count Apponyi in London that Count Bernstorff has announced that the emperor claimed from Prussia the old frontiers of 1814, the left bank of the Saar [sic] and Luxemburg" (Gramont to Drouyn de Lhuys, Vienna, 10 August 1866, FAE CP, Autriche/492, no. 111).

[2] DALWIGK, p. 246.

[3] Loftus to Stanley, Berlin, 10 August 1866, PRO FO 64/599, no 135.

[4] Rogier to Beyens, Brussels, 11 August 1866, BEYENS, II, 190.

[5] In the course of the conversation, Benedetti complained that France had made a great

Benedetti's concern that indiscretion could jeopardize the success of the compensation talks was evidently justified. The day he arrived in Paris, Friday, 10 August, revelations about the secret compensation talks between Bismarck and Benedetti appeared in the *Siècle* in Paris: "It has been confirmed ... that France, in view of the considerable aggrandizement of Prussia, is supposed to have opened talks with the Berlin cabinet regarding the Rhine frontiers. It was affirmed ...that Prussia did not believe herself able thus far to accept the French propositions." [1] Next day the newspaper carried additional information on the conversations in an article dated 8 August and signed by Joseph Vilbort:

> I have it from an authoritative source that the cabinet of the Tuileries has opened talks with the Berlin cabinet or... an exchange of views, on the subject of the frontiers of the French empire and of a considerably enlarged Prussia. Last evening the French ambassador had a meeting with Bismarck which lasted from ten o'clock until midnight. Again today, in the afternoon, he had a long interview with the minister-president. It is perhaps stretching the truth to state that the question of the frontiers of the Rhine has been officially put. But what I think I am able to confirm is that diplomatic conversations on the topic have taken place, and I can affirm that Prussia shows herself little disposed to follow France in the matter of territorial compensation. [2]

The revelations in the *Siècle* and the arrival of Benedetti in Paris opened the next phase in the compensation talks regarding the Rhine frontiers. That same day the emperor authorized Goltz to notify the minister-president that the convention project had been the result of a misunderstanding; the project should have been limited to the ideas exchanged between Bismarck and Benedetti at Nikolsburg. He expressed the view that the rejection of the French claims

---

mistake in her mediation efforts; his propositions for peace, which would have been more advantageous for France, were not accepted in Paris. He implied that Goltz's draft, received from Berlin, had instead been accepted by Drouyn de Lhuys and presented to the emperor. "It is thus that ... the peace preliminaries were arranged" (REISET, pp. 479–480). Cf. DALWIGK, p. 248, who relates that the Spanish ambassador, Don Rancés, declared to him that Benedetti had been completely fooled in Nikolsburg, and had returned triumphantly to Berlin only to learn from his distressed secretaries in what desperate straits the Prussian victory and diplomatic success had placed France, and that the French ambassador was completely ignorant about German affairs.

[1] *ODG*, XII, 70, ft. 3.

[2] *Ibid.* Vilbort had been at Bismarck's office on the evening of 7 August, when Ambassador Benedetti entered for his second compensation talk. The journalist saw the minister-president later and discussed general Prusso-French relations with him. Vilbort states that the rumors circulating in Berlin prompted him to ask Bismarck if there would be war. The next day he questioned Keudell about his smile at Bismarck's negative reply and received the entire portent of the compensation demands as well as Prussia's determination not to yield an inch of German territory. Keudell pledged Vilbort not to divulge the information until he had returned to Paris (J. VILBORT, *L'oeuvre de M. de Bismarck, 1863–1866* [Paris, 1889], pp. 522–523).

should not trouble the friendly relations between the two powers.[1] To what extent Benedetti contributed to the withdrawal of the project is difficult to say, since it is not known whether he had discussed the matter with the emperor or the foreign minister before the conversation of Napoleon and Goltz. Benedetti appears to have had an audience with the emperor on or before 12 August, as shown by the emperor's instructions to La Valette that steps be taken to refute assertions that the Rhine provinces had been refused to France.[2] After criticizing the revelations in the press, Napoleon had written: "It results from my conversation with Benedetti that for a very small gain we would have all of Germany against us.... The true interest of France is not to obtain an insignificant aggrandizement of territory but to help Germany constitute herself in a manner which would be most favorable to the interests of France and of Europe."[3] The letter intended to blame Drouyn de Lhuys for the fiasco, while remaining silent about the emperor's part in the elaboration of the project.[4] As for the view attributed to Benedetti there is substantial ground for accepting it as being valid. While Benedetti had considered the Prussian victory and the destruction of the 1815 treaties as cause and justification for French expansion, his reaction to the compensation project, pointed up by his cautious behavior, indicates that he thought the claims exaggerated or ill-directed. It seems quite logical that he would reject, at least in part, the so-called Mainz project and suggest expansion in areas where the principle of nationality would not be violated. The fact that the ambassador, in a conversation with Goltz, accepted full responsibility for his compensation

---

[1] Goltz to Bismarck, Paris, 11 August 1866, ONCKEN, II, 51; Loftus to Stanley, Berlin, 15 August 1866, PRO FO 64/599, no. 153. Cf. RADOWITZ, p. 112, who reports that Drouyn de Lhuys had assured the Prussian ambassador that the emperor had not intended to go so far, although the foreign minister himself regretted the restraint which Napoleon now imposed on the compensation question.

[2] See *Constitutionnel* article of 14 August signed by Paulin Limayrac, and obviously inspired by the emperor's letter to La Valette, which challenges the assertions of Vilbort in the *Siècle* (ODG, XII, 71, ft. 2).

[3] Napoleon to La Valette, [Paris], 12 August 1866, *MMP*, 181–182. After this letter was published in an English newspaper in 1867 and reproduced by French newspapers, Drouyn de Lhuys wrote an answer in which he noted that the emperor had read, corrected, and approved the convention project. He claimed that Benedetti had provoked the French government to demand compensation by insisting that Prussia anticipated such a demand (Drouyn de Lhuys to Napoleon III, Champvallon par Joigny [Yonne], 12 October 1867, P. PRADIER-FODÉRÉ, *Documents pour l'histoire contemporaine* [Paris, 1871], pp. 30-31). Cf. Loftus to Stanley, Berlin, 1 September 1866, PRO FO 64/600, no. 196, who claims that Benedetti on first perusal considered the letter to La Valette a fabrication but agreed later that it was authentic.

[4] See ft. 4, p. 113 above.

talks with Bismarck can be taken as an indication that he fully supported the principle, if not the specific items, of French compensation demands.[1]

The abandonment of the Mainz project decided Drouyn de Lhuys to tender his resignation on 12 August.[2] The repeated defeats which he had suffered made it clear that the Italian faction had won out over the traditionalist group and that the persuasiveness of Rouher and La Valette had exercised a telling influence on the emperor. The appointment of a member of the Italian faction to the post of foreign minister was considered inevitable. The prospect of gaining a stronghold at the *Quai d'Orsay* decided La Valette to suggest Benedetti for the post, and Rouher was more than willing to bring the ambassador's name to the emperor's attention. Benedetti's adherence to the views of the Italian group as well as his knowledge of German affairs were of course key factors. His willingness to collaborate with Prussia and Italy in foreign affairs and his support of French expansion made him a very acceptable candidate indeed. Although there is exceedingly little material available it can be established that Benedetti, during his visit in Paris, was repeatedly pressed by the emperor, as well as by Rouher and La Valette, to accept the post.[3] As late as 16 August, Rouher urged him to take on these duties; yet, neither the honor nor the pressure could persuade Benedetti to accept.[4] The reasons for his refusal are not clear; his statement that he was ill-suited to succeed Drouyn de Lhuys does not seem to be a complete explanation.[5] It is likely that Benedetti simply did not wish to shoulder the burden

---

[1] RADOWITZ, p. 112.

[2] Cf. "*Mémorandum remis à Hansen*," HANSEN, pp. 109–112. Hansen, a Danish agent, asserts that he was called to the foreign office on 11 August by Count Chaudory and asked to carry a memorandum to Berlin, proposing the establishment of a neutral state between France and Germany, with perhaps the hereditary prince of Hohenzollern-Sigmaringen as ruler, for Bismarck's examination. After days of waiting for an interview with the minister-president, his proposal was refused on the grounds that he did not have full powers to negotiate (*ibid.*, pp. 113–114). Cf. J. REINACH, "Napoléon et la paix," *RH*, CXXXVI, fasc. 2 (1921), p. 183, who claims that the emperor had seen and approved the proposal. A similar memorandum is cited in P. PRADIER-FODÉRÉ, pp. 34–35, which establishes a link between Drouyn de Lhuys and the Hansen mission. ROTHAN, *La politique française en 1866*, pp. 362–363, asserts that the failure of Hansen's mission prompted Drouyn de Lhuys to proffer his resignation on 12 August. However, the mission cannot be considered a failure until Bismarck's refusal to examine the proposal on 16 August.

[3] *ODG*, XII, 117, ft. 1. Cf. ROTHAN, *Souvenirs diplomatiques*, p. 26; Vitzthum to Könneritz, London, 3 September 1866, VITZTHUM, p. 338, who states that Rouher regretted the emperor's failure to exert greater pressure on Benedetti to accept the post. See also Goltz to Bernstorff, Paris, 28 August 1866, STOLBERG-WERNIGERODE, p. 453.

[4] Rouher to Benedetti, Paris, 16 August 1866, FAE PR/A.

[5] Benedetti to Rouher, Berlin, 23 August 1866, *ibid.*

of this high office on account of his ill health. Instead, he suggested Marquis Lionel de Moustier, the French envoy in Constantinople, who did succeed Drouyn de Lhuys.

The initial setback which France had suffered in the quest for compensation did not spell the abandonment of the claims. A new project was elaborated for presentation by Benedetti in Berlin. The extent to which the ambassador contributed to the second proposal cannot be precisely determined. His meetings with the emperor, Rouher and La Valette suggest that he was most likely a close adviser. The exclusion of all demands which might arouse German hostility and the shift of the French claim to another area – Luxemburg and Belgium – can, at least in part, be attributed to Benedetti's influence. Since the new proposal did not include *bona fide* German territory it was not expected to meet with much opposition in the Prussian capital. Had not Bismarck himself alluded to French expansion in that area, in accord with the principle of nationality? [1] The annexation of Belgium in particular was considered justified by Benedetti, in view of the racial and cultural ties existing between France and Belgium.[2] The fact that he postponed his departure on 14 August, when last minute details held up a final draft of the French demands, also suggests that he was closely connected with the formulation of the new compensation program.[3]

While in Paris, the ambassador was also acquainted with another important policy decision of the imperial government, affecting the German secondary states which had fought against Prussia. As early as 6 August, he had requested instructions to guide himself during the peace negotiations between Prussia and these states. "*A propos* the southern states, I expect to be assailed by the solicitations of their representatives as I have been in Nikolsburg. Have you any special instructions to give me? Should I lend my good offices, in what measure shall I do so, and is there any one state in which the emperor has a special interest?" [4] Only now, at an awkward time, was the ambassador instructed to plead for Prussian restraint, in order to forestall too great an extension of Prussian influence in Germany.[5]

---

[1] See ft. 1 p. 112 above.

[2] SOREL, I, 25.

[3] Drouyn de Lhuys to Lefèbvre de Bèhaine, Paris, 14 August 1866, FAE CP, Prusse/359, T. Cf. PAGÈS, *RHM*, I, no. 1 (1926), pp. 18–19.

[4] Benedetti to Drouyn de Lhuys, Berlin, 6 August 1866, FAE MD, Autriche/67, T.

[5] See ft. 5, p. 125, and ft. 1, p. 126 below.

When Benedetti arrived back in Berlin, on 16 August, he learned that the revelations about the Mainz project, as well as rumors about French expansion schemes, had quickly aroused public opinion against the demands of the imperial government, a matter about which he had warned the emperor. The cry, "Not an inch of German soil to France! Sooner war! " [1] amply revealed the mood in Germany and justified the decision to withdraw the Mainz project. In the meantime, the Prussian government had been advancing its own projects, and on 18 and 21 August it concluded offensive and defensive alliances with the north German governments.[2] At the same time pressure was exerted to bring the south German states into such an alliance system. Bismarck used the threat of a crisis with France and harsh peace treaty terms to achieve military conventions.[3] In his talks with Count Otto von Bray-Steinburg, the Bavarian plenipotentiary, the minister-president suddenly proposed an alliance. "That it was to be an alliance against France had already become unmistakably apparent from [Bismarck's] earlier comments relative to a French threat to Mainz."[4]

When Dalwigk learned on 17 August that Benedetti had returned from Paris with instructions to work on behalf of the secondary states he immediately sought an interview with the ambassador.[5] However, the Hessian plenipotentiary received little satisfaction, for Benedetti

---

[1] Lefèbvre de Béhaine to Drouyn de Lhuys, Berlin, 13 August 1866, FAE MD, Autriche/ 67, no. 184bis. See CASE, p. 220.

[2] L. HAHN, Zwei Jahre preussisch-deutscher Politik, 1866-1867 (Berlin, 1868), pp. 463-464. The ambassador had warned of this development and had forwarded a copy of an alliance proposal between Prussia and the north German states (Benedetti to Drouyn de Lhuys, Berlin, 8 August 1866, FAE CP, Prusse/359, no. 180).

[3] W. SCHÜSSLER, Bismarcks Kampf um Süddeutschland 1867 (Berlin, 1929), pp. 16 ff.; E. GÖTZ, Die Stellung Hessen-Darmstadts zur deutschen Einigungsfrage in den Jahren 1866-1871 (Darmstadt, 1914), pp. 12 ff.; J. PETRICH, "Die Friedensverhandlungen mit den Süddeutschen 1866," FbpG, Vol. 46 (1934), pp. 321 ff.; G. ROLOFF, "Bismarcks Friedensschlüsse mit den Süddeutschen im Jahre 1866," HZ, CXXXXVI, Heft 1 (1932), pp. 1-70.

[4] O. VON BRAY-STEINBURG, Denkwürdigkeiten aus seinem Leben (Leipzig, 1901), p. 103. The Bavarian prime minister, Hohenlohe, had sent Perglas to Paris to seek support for the southern states, but no commitment had been obtained (HOHENLOHE, I, 169-170). On 21 August, the Bavarian plenipotentiary wrote that Bismarck's demands had been considerably softened as a result of the agreement to ally with Prussia (BRAY, pp. 108-111). BRANDENBURG, p. 720, concludes that a very close relationship did exist between the French compensation demands and the conclusion of alliances between the south German states and Prussia.

[5] DALWIGK, p. 253. "I neglected nothing in recommending to my ambassador in Berlin the interests of Your Royal Highness and while it will be difficult for me now to intervene in the affairs of Germany, I hope that my recommendation will not be without result in safeguarding the integrity of the grand duchy [of Baden]" (Napoleon III to Grand Duke Louis, St. Cloud, 22 August 1866, ibid., p. 294). As a result of Benedetti's diversified efforts at this time, a British diplomat was prompted to remark: "Je soupçonne Benedetti d'avoir une boîte à double fond" (FRENSDORFF, PJ, XXVI, Heft 2 [1870], p. 202).

did not discuss with him the manner in which he expected to intercede.[1]
On 25 August Dalwigk was told by Lefèbvre de Béhaine that Benedetti
had discussed the peace negotiations with Bismarck and that he
had pleaded the cause of the small states.[2] Yet these efforts were
too circumspect to be effective; although the territorial integrity
of Saxony was to be respected by Prussia, Bismarck struck deeply
at its independence by demanding the surrender of its *Militärhoheit*.[3]
While the ambassador assured the Hesse and Saxon plenipotentiaries
of the support of his government, he was unable and, in view of the
compensation negotiations, reluctant to lend vigorous support. Richard
von Friesen, the Saxon representative, like Dalwigk was also unsuccessful in summoning stronger French support: "When I agreed with
Benedetti that the present demands of Prussia were unacceptable
for us... he shrugged his shoulders and broke off the conversation.
I was further convinced through this talk... that one could expect
no support from this quarter that would go beyond empty words."[4]

The unquestionable hesitancy of the French government to intercede effectively on behalf of Bavaria, Hesse, and Saxony during the
August peace negotiations was inconsistent with its other efforts to
restrict Prussian expansion and failed to prevent the strong military
links Bismarck created with South Germany.[5] In essence, Benedetti's
pleas in behalf of Prussia's former enemies were only a reminder of
France's interest in German affairs.

Apart from the discussion of the future of the secondary states,
Benedetti also took up the North Schleswig problem. Whereas the
former was based on a consideration of the balance of power, the
latter concern was related to the principle of nationality. On 14
August the French ambassador in Vienna had informed the foreign
minister that Bismarck had expressed his discontent to the Austrian

---

[1] DALWIGK, pp. 253–254. "Since his return, Benedetti limits himself... to the statement
that the emperor would regard it as a consideration extended to him personally, if the south
German princes... were not treated with too much harshness" (Roggenbach to Queen
Augusta, Berlin, 20 August 1866, BAVARIA. KÖNIGLICHE AKADEMIE DER WISSENSCHAFTEN.
HISTORISCHE KOMMISSION, *Im Ring der Gegner Bismarcks: Denkschriften und politischer
Briefwechsel Franz von Roggenbachs mit Kaiserin Augusta und Albrecht von Stosch, 1865–1896*,
ed. H. Heyderhoff, "Deutsche Geschichtsquellen des 19. Jahrhunderts," XXXV [2nd ed.;
Leipzig, 1943], p. 50.

[2] DALWIGK, pp. 256–257.

[3] *Ibid.*, p. 258.

[4] FRIESEN, II, 266.

[5] Prussian resentment of French support prompted the Saxon plenipotentiaries to break
off all contacts with the French embassy in Berlin at the end of August (*ibid.*, pp. 270–271).
Cf. Nothomb to Rogier, Berlin, 19 August 1866, BEYENS, II, 174–175.

delegate over the inclusion of a stipulation regarding North Schleswig in the Nikolsburg preliminaries. He had implied that he hoped to
exclude the provision from the final peace treaty.[1] Similar information had reached the *Quai d'Orsay* from Copenhagen shortly
after,[2] and Benedetti was instructed to take the matter up with
Bismarck. The minister-president did not deny that he had discussed
the issue with the Austrian delegates but he insisted that the suggestion
to drop the stipulation had been made by the Austrians,[3] in hopes
of a modification regarding the terms regulating the cession of
Venetia.[4] Benedetti firmly reiterated the views of his government
on the subject and obtained Bismarck's assurance that the final
peace treaty would include the text of Article III of the preliminaries,
providing for a possible retrocession of North Schleswig to Denmark.[5]

The arrival of Chauvy, a private secretary on Rouher's staff,
in Berlin on Friday, 17 August, with instructions for Benedetti set
the stage for the resumption of the French quest for compensation.[6]
While Benedetti was to state that the Mainz project be considered
non avenu,[7] he was to acquaint the minister-president with the new

---

[1] Gramont to Drouyn de Lhuys, Vienna, 14 August 1866, F. DE JESSEN, *L'intervention de la France dans la question du Sleswig du Nord* (Paris, 1919), p. 94. Cf. K. ALNOR, "Der Artikel V des Prager Friedens," *Zeitschrift der Gesellschaft für schleswig-holsteinische Geschichte*, LV (1926), pp. 547–548; cf. GERMANY. AUSWÄRTIGES AMT, *Bismarck und die nordschleswigsche Frage, 1864–1879; die diplomatischen Akten*, eds. W. Platzhoff, K. Rheindorf, J. Tiedje (Berlin, 1925), pp. 115–117.

[2] Dotézac to Drouyn de Lhuys, Copenhagen, 15 August 1866, FAE CP, Danemark/251, no. 76.

[3] F. HÄHNSEN (ed.), *Ursprung und Geschichte des Artikel V des Prager Friedens: die deutschen Akten zur Frage der Teilung Schleswigs, 1863–1879*, "Veröffentlichungen der Schleswig-Holsteinischen Universitäts Gesellschaft," XXI, no. 1–2; "Schriften der Baltischen Kommission zu Kiel," XV, no. 1–2 (Breslau, 1929), I, 273–275. Cf. M. WINCKLER, "Die Zielsetzung in Bismarcks Nordschleswig-Politik und die schleswigsche Grenzfrage," *Die Welt als Geschichte*, XVI, Heft 1 (1956), pp. 41 ff.; A. SCHARFF, "Zur Problematik der Bismarckschen Nordschleswigpolitik," *ibid.*, Heft 3–4 (1956), pp. 211–217; M. WINCKLER, "Noch einmal: Zur Zielsetzung in Bismarcks Nordschleswig-Politik," *ibid.*, XVII, Heft 3 (1957), pp. 203–210.

[4] "[Brenner] is only authorized to eliminate the whole paragraph on North Schleswig if we cooperate about Venetia" (Werther to Bismarck, Prague, 21 August 1866, GERMANY. AUSWÄRTIGES AMT, p. 117).

[5] Benedetti to Drouyn de Lhuys, Berlin, 21 August 1866, FAE CP, Prusse/359, no. 196.

[6] Chauvy was to remain in Berlin as long as Benedetti required his services; it was expected that he would return to Paris either with a treaty draft or with other confidential information. Rouher and Benedetti had decided to use a courier for all extensive dispatches, and they had arranged a special code for telegraphic messages (Rouher to Benedetti, Paris, 26 August 1866, FAE PR/A). See also W. FLETCHER, "The Benedetti Memorandum. An Episode in Franco-Prussian Diplomatic Relations," *Lock Haven Bulletin*, Series 1, Number 3 (1961), pp. 51–66; K. SCHIERENBERG, *Die deutsch-französische Auseinandersetzung und die Luxemburger Frage, dargestellt vor allem an der Luxemburger Angelegenheit des Jahres 1867*, "Publication de la Section Historique de l'Institut Grand-Ducal de Luxembourg," Vol. 65 (Marburg, 1933), 102 pp.

[7] ROTHAN, *La politique française en 1866*, p. 377.

demands. In his general observations, Rouher indicated that the project had been accepted by the emperor. He stressed that the negotiations with Bismarck should be pursued in a friendly manner and that they be kept confidential. He suggested that only the king, the emperor, Bismarck, Benedetti and he himself should have knowledge of them. Turning to the demands proper, Rouher laid down the method by which the ambassador was to state his case:

> According to the chances of success which you will encounter, your demands should move through three successive stages.
>
> In the first place, by uniting in a single thought the questions of the 1814 frontiers and the annexation of Belgium, you must claim, through a public treaty, the concession of Landau, Saarlouis, Saarbrücken, and the duchy of Luxemburg, and the option for us, through an offensive and defensive alliance treaty which would be secret, ultimately to annex Belgium.
>
> In the second place, if these bases do not seem obtainable to you, you must renounce Saarlouis and Saarbrücken, even Landau, an old poorly fortified place, whose possession would overexcite German sentiment against us, and limit our public convention to the duchy of Luxemburg, our secret convention to the reunion of Belgium to France.
>
> In the third place, if the reunion of Belgium with France, pure and simple, should provide obstacles too great, accept an article by which it would be arranged that, in order to appease the resistance of England, Antwerp could be constituted as a free city. But in no instance must you accede to the reunion of Antwerp with Holland or that of Maastricht with Prussia.[1]

As for the manner in which Bismarck should be won over, Rouher told Benedetti to stress the fact that Prussia would be assured of the powerful alliance of France, which would safeguard her recent gains. In return, Prussia would merely agree to the transfer of property which was not hers anyhow and would pledge military support to France for the contemplated annexation of Belgium – a pledge that she might never have to fulfill.[2]

In examining the instructions it became apparent to Benedetti that some of the provisions for compensation were not unlike the demands Drouyn de Lhuys had made. However, the reference to the inclusion of Landau, Saarlouis and Saarbrücken was little more than an attempt to bolster French bargaining power, and Benedetti excluded the claim to these cities already in the first draft of the proposed treaty.[3] As for the annexation of Luxemburg, Rouher expected no difficulties from either Prussia or Holland,[4] since he stipulated that the agreement be a public convention. Lastly, in respect to the

---

[1] Rouher to Benedetti, Paris, 16 August 1866, FAE PR/A.
[2] *Ibid.*
[3] Benedetti to Rouher, Berlin, 23 August 1866, *ibid.* Cf. OLLIVIER, VIII, 567–569.
[4] Cf. Mahon to Drouyn de Lhuys, Eich, 13 July 1866, FAE CC, Pays-Bas, Eich-Luxem-

annexation of Belgium, he preferred that the matter be settled and drawn up in a secret convention, which was to provide for an offensive-defensive alliance between the two powers and reserve for France the option to annex Belgium at an appropriate moment. It was clear that such an alliance was desirable in view of Britain's expected opposition to French expansion into Belgium.[1]

The talks between Bismarck and Benedetti opened in the evening of 17 August, in accordance with the instructions given to the ambassador by the emperor.[2] Benedetti at once outlined the French demands. In respect to the boundaries of 1814, Bismarck refused to consider them, stating that first the French government would have to awaken a desire for union with France among the population of Saarlouis, Saarbrücken, and Landau and prompt the people to give expression to this wish. As for Luxemburg, the minister-president acknowledged his desire to be agreeable but cautioned Benedetti that Prussia could not take the initiative in bringing about the transfer of the duchy. He suggested that perhaps the Dutch king might be brought to terms by indicating that Prussia might forego her demand to attach Limburg to the North German Confederation.[3] Considering

---

bourg/6; same to same, Eich, 6 August 1866, *ibid*. "As for the personal bonds between His Majesty and the grand duchy, they cannot be very strong. The king has rarely visited Luxemburg, and his possession, which only dates back to 1815, is for the house of Orange neither a matter of affection, tradition, nor family self-respect" (Baudin to Drouyn de Lhuys, The Hague, 14 July 1866, FAE CP, Hollande/665, no. 34).

[1] La Tour d'Auvergne to Drouyn de Lhuys, London, 29 July 1866, *ibid*., Angleterre/738, no. 158, who reports that Stanley told him England would not seriously object to French compensation as long as it did not touch upon Belgium. "If France places herself boldly upon the ground of nationality, it is important to establish as of now, that no Belgian nationality exists and to establish this point with Prussia. The Berlin cabinet seeming... disposed to make arrangements with France that France might feel appropriate to accept, there should be negotiated a secret act which would engage both parties. Without pretending that this act would be a perfectly certain guarantee, it would have the double advantage of compromising Prussia and of being a token for her of the sincerity of the policy or the intentions of the emperor. It would be well not to ignore the fact, if one knows the character of the Prussian king and that of his first minister, that the last diplomatic incidents as well as the disposition of public sentiment in France must have strengthened their conviction that we have not renounced the demand of the Rhine frontier. In order to be certain of finding in Berlin the necessary confidence for the maintenance of an intimate *entente*, we must apply ourselves to clear away apprehensions... over-excited by our last communications. This result cannot be obtained by words, an act is necessary, and it would consist of regulating the ultimate fate of Belgium in agreement with Prussia, in proving to Berlin that the emperor is decidedly seeking elsewhere than on the Rhine the expansion of France" (Note dictated by the emperor to Conti, [14–16 August 1866?], FRANCE. COMMISSION DES PAPIERS SAISIES AUX TUILERIES, I, 16–17). Cf. ONCKEN, II, 81–82, ft., who suggests that Benedetti is the author of this note, and had Rouher submit it to the emperor.

[2] Cf. Goltz to Bismarck, Paris, 20 August 1866, *ibid*., p. 90.

[3] Benedetti to Rouher, Berlin, 23 August 1866, FAE PR/A. Cf. Baudin to Drouyn de Lhuys, The Hague, 10 August 1866, FAE CP, Hollande/665, no. 40, who reports unconfirmed

the French proposal of an alliance and the option of annexing Belgium, Bismarck merely stated that he would seek to influence King William in favor of it, while pointing out the difficulty of conquering English influences on the monarch.[1] Apart from his surprise concerning the compensation demands, Bismarck was disturbed by the forceful manner of the French ambassador, whose attitude and request, that an answer be returned within the next three or four days, he resented.[2] Benedetti's impatience was indicated by his note to Bismarck of 19 August: "I am, since yesterday morning, quite prepared to talk with you and I shall wait for you to choose the opportune moment. I myself would be glad if this moment were not too far away so as not to delay too long sending back the person who has been sent to me, and to be able to give him an early notice which announces, as far as possible, the final word."[3] This message implied that the ambassador overnight was prepared to consider the points discussed in the first interview of Friday, the 17th.[4]

It would appear from the evidence that, after further talks on 22 August, agreement on a tentative draft was reached in the meeting of 23 August, before or during which Benedetti committed the terms to paper. It is quite probable that Bismarck did retain a copy of the document at this time for purposes of briefing King William, and that Benedetti forwarded the preliminary draft, along with an account of the negotiations, to Paris.[5] The ambassador pointed out in his report that he had limited his demands exclusively to Luxemburg and Belgium, convinced that a demand for the frontiers of 1814 would meet with insurmountable opposition. In respect to Belgium, Benedetti had rejected Bismarck's suggestion that Prussia receive Maastricht in return for appropriate compensation to Holland. Significantly enough, the future of Antwerp was not mentioned by the minister-

---

rumors that the Prussian government had made overtures to the Dutch government for the entry of Luxemburg into the North German Confederation.

[1] Benedetti to Rouher, Berlin, 23 August 1866, FAE PR/A

[2] Bismarck to Goltz, Berlin, 18 August 1866, *BGW*, VI, 133–134; same to same, Berlin, 19 August 1866, ONCKEN, II, 86; same to same, Berlin, 20 August 1866, *ibid.*, 87–89. The minister-president requested Goltz, to whom he revealed the French demands, to ask the emperor that he counsel moderation to Benedetti lest the ambassador jeopardize the favorable result of the talks.

[3] Benedetti to Bismarck, Berlin, 19 August 1866, *ibid.*, 86.

[4] Neither Benedetti nor Bismarck had mentioned the drafting of a treaty text nor did they give evidence of having referred to a written document during their meeting on 17 August.

[5] RADOWITZ, p. 119. Cf. ROTHAN, *La politique française en 1866*, pp.382–383, who maintains that a meeting took place on 20 August but makes no reference to the meetings of 17 and 23 August.

president, despite the fact that Benedetti had made the alliance clause as absolute as possible. In connection with the envisaged annexation of Belgium, Bismarck had sought to link this professed French ambition with one of his own, namely, the union of North and South Germany. In his opinion, the realization of the one would justify the other. Benedetti objected to this proposal: he endeavored to preserve liberty of action in regard to Belgium and to escape all attempts to make the annexation conditional. He, of course, knew that a union of Germany was inevitable and accordingly agreed to the inclusion of a provision which would remove French opposition to such a development. Benedetti had not adhered to Rouher's request that the demands be drawn up in two conventions, one public and the other secret. He was convinced that it would be impossible to give the agreement relating to Luxemburg a form suitable for publication. Furthermore, Bismarck had suggested that a provision be added to the five articles which would make the entire treaty secret. In regard to Article IV, governing the annexation of Belgium, Benedetti pointed out that, if necessary, it could be given the character and form of an additional and secret article by placing it last. He did consider this impractical, however, since Article V, providing for an alliance, should also be kept secret.[1] In addition to the discussion of the form the proposed treaty was to take, the ambassador touched upon the course of action which he deemed it best to follow. Upon imperial review of the draft, Benedetti suggested that he and Bismarck confer on whatever changes the French government deemed necessary.[2] Once a definite text was established, Bismarck was to submit it to the Prussian king, while Benedetti himself would go to Carlsbad, to escape undesirable inquiries and to take the waters.[3] The ambassador cautioned that, in examining the text of the draft, note should be taken of the difficulty of winning the approval of King William. It was advisable that the provisions of the draft be temperate, and he cited the provision respecting Luxemburg as particularly deserving of such moderation.[4]

With the dispatch of the report and the draft to Paris on 23 August,

---

[1] Benedetti to Rouher, Berlin, 23 August 1866, FAE PR/A.
[2] *Ibid.*
[3] Cf. Drouyn de Lhuys to Benedetti, Paris, 27 August 1866, FAE CP, Prusse/359, T. "Benedetti... was too much of the professional diplomat not to be the victim of those inevitable afflictions which necessitate a few weeks summering at a beneficent and political [thermal] spring" (THOUVENEL, p. 439).
[4] Benedetti to Rouher, Berlin, 23 August 1866, FAE PR/A.

the negotiations between Benedetti and Bismarck ceased for a few days. The ambassador's text essentially conformed to the ideas of both Napoleon and Rouher, and on 26 August the minister informed Benedetti that, except for a few minor suggestions, the emperor had approved the draft as submitted.[1] After having discussed the text with Rouher, Napoleon had retained the draft to formulate his final recommendations. While awaiting this communication from the emperor, Rouher had written down for Benedetti's guidance the observations which he and Napoleon had discussed in their analysis of the text. Rouher believed that greater stress should be placed upon Prussia's obligation to provide territorial compensation to Holland in return for the cession of Luxemburg to France. He deemed the monetary compensation to be made by France to the Dutch king of secondary importance. However, he stated that the article concerning Luxemburg might be approved as drafted. Referring to the question of Saarlouis and Landau, France would appreciate an official act of Prussia, ending the classification of these towns as fortresses. The ambassador's refusal to accede to Bismarck's request and relate the annexation of Belgium to German unification was sanctioned. The unification of Germany would make it imperative for France to annex Belgium but Rouher, nevertheless, preferred to reserve freedom of action. He did not object *per se* to keeping the entire treaty secret but felt that an additional public agreement between Prussia, France, and Holland should be made, indicating the cession of Luxemburg and the abrogation of Prussia's garrison right in that fortress. "It relaxes public opinion in France because of the immediate attainment of satisfaction and because of the orientation of the minds toward Belgium, which results from it." [2]

Rouher's observations did not differ essentially from those which the emperor forwarded along with the draft. Napoleon suggested that, as topics of conversation, Benedetti offer the proposal that the federal fortresses be no longer considered as belonging to the Confederation but to the states in whose respective territory they were located. Acceptance by Prussia of this proposal would ease the transfer of Luxemburg. He further stipulated that the treaty be kept secret, stressing, as had Rouher, the need for a speedy settlement of

---

[1] Rouher to Benedetti, Paris, 26 August 1866, *ibid.*; cf. Benedetti to Rouher, Berlin, 29 August 1866, *ibid.*, in which the ambassador mentions receiving a telegram with a coded message, agreed upon beforehand, signalling the emperor's approval of the draft: "*Jacques est arrivé. (Signé) Mariette.*"

[2] Rouher to Benedetti, Paris, 26 August 1866, *ibid.* Cf. CASE, p. 220.

the Luxemburg problem. "Benedetti can thus accept in principle, except for a few minor changes."[1]

In a meeting on 29 August, Benedetti informed the minister-president of Napoleon's approval of the draft. He again emphasized the French view that Prussia should convince the Dutch king to cede Luxemburg and offer him territorial compensation, stressing the secondary importance of the monetary compensation. Bismarck accepted the ambassador's statement but made it clear that he was not eager to compensate Holland with German territory. He believed that his promise to release Limburg from her ties with the Confederation would suffice to obtain the Dutch king's agreement to the cession of Luxemburg.[2] Bismarck already had acquainted William with the treaty project who had received it more favorably than expected. The minister-president stated that he had dispelled the king's fear, that France could use the provision regarding Belgium to blackmail Prussia, by pointing out that as a signatory to the treaty France would hardly be in a position to do so. He had reminded William further that Prussia, as a result of her expansion, would need the goodwill of France to protect herself against possible anti-Prussian alliances. The monarch, adamantly opposed to the French demands, had decided to delay a decision and had requested Goltz to come to Berlin for consultation.[3] In compliance with this request, Bismarck had written Goltz on 27 August, to return to the Prussian capital. In order to avoid all possible suspicions, he had advised him to return either by way of Ostend or Baden, two favorite summer resorts.[4]

Benedetti did not know what to make of the minister-president's remarks. "Was he truthful? I cannot guarantee it; he is no less Prussian than his sovereign, and you will note that the king easily thinks us capable of setting a trap for him." [5] Benedetti had his doubts and

---

[1] Napoleon III to Rouher, [Paris], 26 August 1866, *MMP*, pp. 196–197.

[2] Cf. Bismarck to Perponcher, Berlin, 31 August 1866, *BGW*, VI, 155, ft. 1, in which he instructs the envoy to indicate this view to the Dutch government.

[3] Cf. William I to Augusta, n.p., 25 August 1866, *APP*, VIII, 61, ft. 2, in which the king voiced strong disapproval of plans to annex Belgium: "Such perfidy... I will have Goltz come home so that he can breathe Prussian air, because, in his interviews with the emperor and the minister, he always comes back to the possibility of a little compensation." Cf. ROTH-FRITZ, pp. 105–106, who states that Bismarck hoped to use Goltz's influence with William to gain the king's support for the proposed alliance with France. See also Radowitz *Tage-buchaufzeichnung*, Paris, 9 September 1866, STOLBERG-WERNIGERODE, pp. 455–458. He states that the military conventions concluded with the south German states strengthened William's resistance to the French demands.

[4] Benedetti to Rouher, Berlin, 29 August 1866, FAE PR/A.

[5] *Ibid.*

also suspected the Prussian government of carrying on negotiations with Russia. Since Prussia, in Bismarck's own words, needed an alliance, Benedetti believed that a failure or termination of the Franco-Prussian negotiations would prove the existence of a Prusso-Russian alliance. In respect to his own plans, Benedetti indicated that he would begin his rest cure at Carlsbad at the end of the week. In conclusion, he wrote that he had arranged with Bismarck to call him as soon as negotiations could be resumed. In any case he expected to return to Berlin within a fortnight.[1]

Benedetti's reserve during this meeting of the 29th had been due, in part, to the fact that he had not yet received Rouher's full critique, which had been written on 26 and 27 August and which reached Berlin only on 30 August.[2] His reply to it shows concern over Rouher's insistence that Prussia both initiate the negotiations with Holland and make the territorial compensation. He emphasized the king's sensitivity to alienation of German territory and indicated that he had himself drafted the article in full consideration of William's attitude.[3] In reply to the comment regarding the absence of a time limit on the proposed alliance, the ambassador gave proof of a realistic outlook: "Our treaty... can be of no longer duration than the peace between Prussia and France, and any treaty, whatever its objective, falls... when war becomes a necessity." [4] About the proposal that the king of Saxony might be made the ruler of a buffer state on the Rhine should Saxony be annexed by Prussia, Benedetti had serious doubts. Believing that such a state would have to become a member of the North German Confederation, he noted that the proposal would thus place a vassal state of Prussia on the doorstep of France. As to the federal fortresses, he believed that Landau, Ulm, and Rastadt were no longer subject to Prussian influence and control, while Saarlouis was not a fortress in the proper sense of the term. While Mainz and Luxemburg were subject to the garrison right of Prussia, such was not the case for Landau, located in Bavarian territory. Benedetti recommended that requests for the dismantlement or declassification of these fortresses be delayed in order not to jeopardize the outcome of the treaty negotiations.[5]

---

[1] *Ibid.* To the Saxon and Hesse plenipotentiaries, Benedetti had said that he had postponed his vacation solely because of their peace negotiations (FRIESEN, II, 271).

[2] These letters have never been located.

[3] Benedetti to Rouher, Berlin, 30 August 1866, FAE PR/A.

[4] *Ibid.*

[5] *Ibid.*

Benedetti had a last meeting with the minister-president on Friday, 31 August, during which he acquainted Bismarck with Rouher's observations and with the emperor's comments on the wording of the draft text.[1] Since both had reserved the right to suggest changes after submission to their sovereigns, Benedetti endeavored to win acceptance of the modifications indicated by Napoleon. Bismarck showed himself agreeable to the suggestions put forth by the French ambassador. Thus in Article I it was agreed to suppress the clause which called for French support of the arrangements yet to be made for the organization of the North German Confederation. Benedetti was able to gain the minister-president's agreement to a rewording of Article II, in order to emphasize the fact that the French monetary compensation for Luxemburg would be merely a balance or surplus payment made after a territorial compensation by Prussia. In accord with the emperor's suggestion, Benedetti obtained a further clarification of the mutual obligations toward Holland by including the word "accessorily" in the text. Articles III and IV were accepted as drafted. The ambassador did seek to affix a time limit to the alliance, in Article V, notwithstanding his own realistic views on the matter, but agreed to the existing wording when he realized that Bismarck would not accept any further changes. In concluding the revision of the text, Benedetti made reference to the emperor's suggestion that the king of Saxony might be given a state on the left bank of the Rhine. The minister-president replied that he had already thought of such a possibility, one first mentioned at the Congress of Vienna, but that King William had shown great reluctance toward such a scheme, feeling certain that too much opposition would arise within Germany, and especially in the Rhineland. The minister-president did agree, however, to bring Napoleon's suggestion again to the attention of the king.[2]

Since the revisions, which had grown out of the conference, altered the original proposal considerably it became necessary for Bismarck to confer further with William. Anxious to bring the negotiations to speedy fruition, Benedetti had no choice but to leave the copy of the altered draft, originally put on paper by him on the 23rd, at the office of the minister-president. The unfortunate failure to reclaim the draft after the London Conference of 1867 became in time a capital blunder; it provided Bismarck with a very compromising

[1] See appendix.
[2] Benedetti to Rouher, Berlin, 1 September 1866, FAE PR/A.

document which he could and did use to good advantage in 1870. Benedetti had evidently forgotten about Bismarck's lengthy hesitation before giving a similar document to Govone in 1866. To be sure, one cannot entirely overlook certain extenuating factors in respect to Benedetti's authorship: he expected a speedy and uncomplicated conclusion of the negotiations and considered Bismarck as much involved in the formulation of the clauses as himself.

The temporary suspension of the compensation talks, while Bismarck and the king conferred with Goltz, enabled Benedetti to prepare for his vacation at Carlsbad. Chauvy left for Paris on 1 September with the other draft copy and the ambassador's report.[1] Before his own departure next day, Benedetti received notice that he had been awarded the Grand Cross of the Legion of Honor, evidently for his successful mediation at Nikolsburg.[2] Perhaps the gesture was also meant to minimize the effect of the French diplomatic fiasco of August.

Benedetti returned to Berlin for a brief stay from 14 to 30 September,[3] in anticipation of the expeditious conclusion of the alliance and compensation treaty, which Bismarck had agreed to submit to the king.[4] The illness of the minister-president prevented the resumption of the negotiations for the time being, and Benedetti was advised that nothing could be done until Bismarck's return to the foreign office.[5] Nevertheless, significant developments were beginning to shape the future course of Franco-Prussian relations. Goltz had returned to the French capital on 9 September with very prudent propositions relative to the French demands: assurances of Prussian good-will and benevolent neutrality in regard to French expansion into Belgium and Luxemburg.[6] In Paris, the caution and

---

[1] Benedetti to Rouher, Berlin, 31 August 1866, *ibid.*

[2] Benedetti to La Valette, Carlsbad, 5 September 1866, *ibid.* Cf. Goltz to William I, Biarritz, 3 October 1866, *APP*, VIII, 101, who claims that the emperor had not been able to find a successor to Benedetti and had made the award to Benedetti so that he would remain at the Berlin post.

[3] Nothomb to Rogier, Berlin, 14 September 1866, BAE CP, Prusse/23, Pt. II, no. 335.

[4] Goltz to Bismarck, Paris, 14 September 1866, ONCKEN, II, 110-111. He states that instructions for Benedetti had been sent to Berlin, authorizing him to sign an alliance treaty with or without a time limit. See also GEUSS, pp. 195 ff.

[5] Bismarck to Goltz, 14 September 1866, *BGW*, VI, 165-166, T. Bismarck had been ill since 7 September and left Berlin on 26 September for a rest at Karlsburg (FRIESEN, II, 281). See also Goltz to Thile, Paris, 16 September 1866, ONCKEN, II, 113; Benedetti to La Valette, Berlin, 19 September 1866, FAE CP, Prusse/359, no. 223. Cf. Benedetti to Moustier, Berlin, 24 December 1866, *ibid.*, Prusse/360, in which it is implied that the alliance project was discussed at this time. Thile to Goltz, Berlin, 15 September 1866, ONCKEN, II, 111.

[6] Bismarck to Goltz, Berlin, 7 September 1866, *BGW*, VI, 158-160. He states that Prus-

restraint of the Prussian government were not regarded as permanent obstacles to French aspirations, and they did not stand in the way of the famous La Valette circular of 16 September, sent to French diplomatic representatives abroad and published in the *Moniteur*.[1]

This circular, which set forth the attitude of the imperial government in respect to the developments in Germany and the expansion of Prussia, had been predicated upon Prussia's acceptance of the alliance and compensation project presented by Benedetti in Berlin. It welcomed the destruction of the 1815 system, the breakup of the coalition of the northern courts and the return of the principle of the *liberté des alliances*. In respect to Prussian expansion, the circular took note of a new trend: "An irresistible power... pushes people to unify in large agglomerations by making the secondary states disappear." The allusion to this phenomenon was a subtle hint and justification for possible French expansion in the near future into areas where similarity of language and race would do no violence to the principle of nationality. Thus, the circular endeavored to bring into accord the past support of Prussian and Italian unification with the necessity of redressing the balance of power through French acquisitions in border areas.[2]

The gratifying reaction to the circular in Berlin was reported by Ambassador Benedetti, who had learned from Thile that the Prussian ambassador in Paris would be instructed to discuss the declaration at greater length, particularly the manner in which the document related the expansion of Prussia to the interests of France.[3] Thile had not alluded, even in the smallest degree, to the pending compensation negotiations. Moreover, he had advised Goltz to avoid as much as possible a decisive discussion on the matter until the return of the minister-president.[4] The unexpected illness of Bismarck ef-

---

sia will not oppose French expansion *auf dem Boden der französischen Nationalität;* E. EYCK, II, 206; Goltz to William I, Paris, 11 September 1866, ONCKEN, II, 101–108. Cf. KEUDELL, p. 306; SOREL, I, 26; Dotézac to La Valette, Copenhagen, 21 September 1866, FAE CP, Danemark/251, no. 88, who reports a conversation between the Danish ambassador to Russia and Werther, the Prussian negotiator in Prague, in which the latter asserted that Prussia was only giving France the illusion of satisfying her demands. See also Radowitz *Tagebuchaufzeichnung*, Paris, 9 and 11 September 1866, STOLBERG-WERNIGERODE, pp. 455–458, 460.

[1] Goltz to Thile, Paris, 16 September 1866, ONCKEN, II, 112–113. See also CASE, pp. 221–226, for the effect of the circular on French public opinion.

[2] La Valette to diplomatic agents, Paris, 16 September 1866, FAE MD, France/Circulaires politiques, 1863–1869, t. 2126.

[3] Benedetti to La Valette, Berlin, 27 September 1866, FAE CP, Prusse/359, no. 229.

[4] Thile to Goltz, Berlin, 25 September 1866, *ibid.*, copy; RADOWITZ, I, 122–123.

fectively checked the ambassador's hopes and he decided therefore to resume his vacation at Carlsbad. During his brief stay in Berlin, Benedetti had become the subject of much speculation; rumors were abroad that he desired a change of post and that he had requested to succeed Moustier at Constantinople. However, by the time he left for the thermal resort it was believed that he would definitely return to Berlin.[1]

Fully cognizant of the extent to which the equilibrium of Europe had been upset by the Prussian victory, Benedetti had not hesitated to support the demand for compensation. The Nikolsburg peace preliminaries had foreshadowed a permanent transformation of Germany and had emphasized the reality of Prussian hegemony. Past anxiety that France retain her freedom of action until the appropriate moment was now followed by a fervent hope that the imperial government would take the necessary steps to assert the interests of France. Instructions to open compensation talks with Bismarck had been welcomed by Benedetti and he had complied at once with the request. During this discussion, at Nikolsburg, Benedetti had done little more than explain the views of his government on the issue and establish a justification for compensation to France. While resolute in these observations, the ambassador had not pressed too strongly since this first mention was really nothing more than an overture. Benedetti had not minimized the opposition which the demand was likely to encounter but the optimism he had shown in regard to Bismarck was unjustified. The suggestion that France present her claim without delay was well-made but it does not seem that Benedetti had been aware of the inability of the French government to back its claims with the required military power.

The formulation of the compensation program was of course a highly important step and the decision by Drouyn de Lhuys, and presumably the emperor, to forego consultation with the ambassador had been indeed a blunder. Benedetti's reaction to the demands clearly indicates that he had thought them exaggerated; yet, his instructions admitted of no critique and delay. The manner in which Benedetti had brought the compensation project to Bismarck's attention in Berlin must likewise be considered a tactical mistake. The course taken could

---

[1] Goltz to Bismarck, Paris, 15 November 1866, *APP*, VIII, 144; William I to Augusta, Berlin, 16 September 1866, *ibid.*, p. 102, ft. 6; Haymerle to Mensdorff, Berlin, 3 October 1866, HHStA, Preussen/92, no. 6D; cf. Vitzthum to Bose, London, 12 October 1866, VITZTHUM, p. 384, who claimed that Rouher and La Valette wanted Benedetti to take the post in Florence and counteract Moustier's Roman policy.

only reveal to Bismarck that the ambassador himself thought the demands exaggerated. It also had given the minister-president time to prepare a careful refutation of all the arguments Benedetti was likely to bring up in support of the demands. Benedetti, despite his able argumentation, had been unable to win Prussian approval of the project. Whether he could have done so eventually is impossible to say; the mortal blow which Bismarck had dealt the project through the newspaper revelation spelled the end of the Mainz project.

Although explicit documentation is lacking, there is reason to associate Benedetti closely with the formulation of the second French compensation project. His conversations with the emperor, Rouher and La Valette were no doubt related to the compensation issue. The fact that he had to put the demands into treaty form presupposes an intimate knowledge of the intentions of the imperial cabinet relative to the project. The new demands were very much in accord with the ambassador's views on French expansion; but he and others shared an unjustified belief that the Prussian government would be willing to help France secure adequate compensation.

The offer of the foreign ministry represents a highlight in the ambassador's career. The utter failure of the Mainz project, for which Drouyn de Lhuys had to assume the blame, necessitated a change at the *Quai d'Orsay*. While the principle of compensation was not abandoned it had become obvious that it be given a new direction. Benedetti's familiarity with German affairs, his support of compensation as well as his sympathy for the professed ideas of the emperor, made him an acceptable candidate who could also count on powerful support within the cabinet. Yet, the ambassador had decided to reject the offer and return to the Berlin post. He apparently had no desire to assume the responsibilities of high office and suffer all the drawbacks of personal government. He had dismissed the entire matter speedily and decidedly and never again was mentioned in connection with the portfolio of the foreign minister.

The negotiations which Benedetti had opened with Bismarck upon his return to Berlin in late August had permitted him to carry out his duties under almost ideal circumstances. He was fully cognizant of the views and intentions of his government and was kept fully informed by Rouher. Moreover, Benedetti had considerable authority to deal with problems likely to arise during the negotiations with Bismarck. He did show his talent and skill as a negotiator and was successful in formulating a draft which met with the approval of both Napoleon and Rouher. However, the optimism and consequent lack of caution which had prompted Benedetti to leave a copy of the draft in his own handwriting with Bismarck reveal weak points in the ambassador's ability. The consequences of Bismarck's publication of the document in 1870 were not fatal; the episode serves to illuminate, if not Benedetti's failure, Bismarck's great skill in the art of diplomacy.

CHAPTER VI

THE LUXEMBURG COMPENSATION PROJECT

Although Thile had proposed on 6 November that Goltz attempt to delay Benedetti's arrival in Berlin until Bismarck was again able to resume his duties at the end of the month,[1] Napoleon requested the ambassador, who had come from Carlsbad to Paris,[2] to return to his post. Conferring with Count Goltz prior to departing, Benedetti stated that he would not press for action on the alliance treaty for the time being, but that he would have to insist on a speedy decision once Bismarck was back. He considered his own return to the Prussian capital an indication that the imperial government firmly desired a settlement with Prussia; rather than accept another post, he had agreed to remain in Berlin and press for a definite decision on the draft treaty.[3] Benedetti was to discover that his return was not viewed with favor by the ailing minister-president, who had already resolved to render himself inaccessible and uncooperative with the plans of the imperial representative.[4]

The ambassador's arrival in Berlin on 15 November was the signal for renewed action on the part of the emperor to bring to a satis-

---

[1] Thile to Goltz, Berlin, 6 November 1866, *APP*, VIII, 133, T.; Goltz to Thile, Paris, 7 November 1866, *ibid.*, 133–134, T.

[2] During his stay in Carlsbad, Benedetti had engaged in many conversations with Sir Robert Morier, the British minister at Darmstadt, and a Cobdenite regarding ways and means to further the principle of international co-operation. The talks revolved mainly around the issue of economic interdependence, the reduction of tariffs, and the advocacy of free trade. Benedetti had asked Morier to prepare a summary of his ideas to forward to him in Berlin: both hoped that the Paris exhibition in the coming year might provide an occasion for convening an international congress to explore the means to promote the principle of international co-operation. Sir Robert did draw up such a memorandum which he sent to the ambassador on 12 December, but the congress idea was never exploited (R. MORIER, *Memoirs and Letters, 1826-1876*, ed. R. Wemyss [London, 1911], II, 92-97).

[3] Goltz to Bismarck, Paris, 15 November 1866, *APP*, VIII, 143 and ft. 1, p. 138, above.

[4] Countess Marie Bismarck to Keudell, Putbus, 19 November 1866, KEUDELL, pp. 338–339. She wrote that her father did not intend to be disturbed anymore by Benedetti, in whom he had lost confidence.

factory conclusion two questions which had been pending: the compensation in Luxemburg, and the independence of the papal state. The imminent withdrawal of French troops from Rome in accordance with the terms of the September Convention of 1864, had led Moustier [1] and La Valette to make overtures to Count Goltz on 23 and 25 October, suggesting that Prussia and France together obtain from the Italian government a guarantee of the papal possessions. Benedetti had learned during his stay in Paris that Goltz, hoping at once to diminish Austrian influence at the imperial court and win the support of the Catholics in Germany, had worked out on 29 October [2] a tentative project for King William, only to receive instructions two days later to abstain from any initiative and to declare that Prussia in principle was willing to come to a mutual accord on the matter.[3] When it appeared that the Prussian cabinet tried to procrastinate, Moustier wrote to Benedetti that Armand, *chargé d'affaires* in Rome, had reported on 12 November that King William and Tsar Alexander had offered their good offices to the pope. The ambassador viewed this step with distrust, for it pointed to an increased intimacy between Russia and Prussia and contradicted statements made by Goltz. In addition to robbing France of the initiative in supporting the Catholic cause, the reported offer by the two powers could strengthen papal resistance and render a settlement of the issue ever more difficult.[4]

The day following his arrival in Berlin, Ambassador Benedetti called at the foreign ministry to discuss with Thile affairs of interest to Prussia and France. From the references to the alliance treaty negotiations, Benedetti felt that the secretary presaged a favorable result. Thile had agreed that the uncertainty connected with the draft treaty ought to be removed [5] and that with the return of the minister-president the negotiations could be resumed. The ambassador based his optimism partly on the fact that the secretary conferred daily with the king and that he would not have spoken so encouragingly had he reason to believe that the negotiations would encounter difficulties.[6]

[1] Marquis de Moustier had assumed direction of the foreign ministry on 2 October. "He was connected by marriage to the great family of the Mérodes in Belgium, leaders of the ultramontane party" (LOFTUS, I, 141).

[2] ROTHFRITZ, pp. 109–110.

[3] ROLOFF, "Frankreich, Preussen und der Kirchenstaat im Jahre 1866," *FbpG*, LI, Pt. I, (1939), p. 111.

[4] *Ibid.*, pp. 112–113.

[5] For evidence of Prussian procrastination and evasiveness relative to the status of Luxemburg, see Lefèbvre de Béhaine to Moustier, Berlin, 2 November 1866, FAE CP, Prusse/360, no. 244; same to same, Berlin, 9 November 1866, *ibid.*, no. 245.

[6] Benedetti to Moustier, Berlin, 17 November 1866, FAE MD, Hollande/149.

Indeed, a Prussian circular of the same day, which insisted that the dissolution of the Germanic Confederation had not ended Prussia's garrison rights in Luxemburg, led Benedetti to attribute greater strength to Prussia's recommendations in The Hague, thus facilitating the transfer of the duchy to France.[1]

On Tuesday, 20 November, Ambassador Benedetti had occasion to test the impressions he had gained from Thile. Having been awarded the Prussian Order of the Black Eagle, the ambassador had requested an audience with King William to convey his gratitude for this expression of the friendly relations between Prussia and France.[2] Benedetti made fleeting allusions in the course of the conversation to the negotiations pending between the two courts, but the monarch merely seized these occasions to express, in general but cordial terms, his friendship for the emperor and gave the ambassador no opening for a discussion of the alliance problem. William's reference to a supposedly unconciliatory disposition of the Austrian cabinet and press prompted Benedetti, anxious to seek everywhere indications of the Prussian sentiments toward France, to speculate that the king's remark might convey, indirectly, a wish for an *entente* with the French government.[3]

The interview with the king had not satisfied Ambassador Benedetti. In a conversation with the new Austrian envoy in Berlin, Count Felix von Wimpffen, [4] he depicted William as a man blinded by the glory of his success and not satisfied with the gains made by Prussia in consequence of the recent war. He asserted that the monarch was not frank in his relations with others, and was unrestrained in his ambitions. Benedetti was particularly critical of the manner in which William had dealt with the king of Saxony during the peace negotiations. He remarked to Wimpffen that he suspected Prussia of seeking

---

[1] Note of Ambassador Benedetti, November 1866, *ibid.*, 150. Cf. Tornaco to Perponcher, Luxemburg, 12 October 1866, LAE, H/16, in which the Luxemburg government declared that with the dissolution of the Germanic Confederation the Prussian garrison rights in the duchy had ended. The statement rested primarily upon the view that the Prusso-Dutch accord had been concluded by the Dutch king as a member of the Confederation, the dissolution of which terminated the accord; Villestreux to Moustier, The Hague, 4 November 1866, FAE CP, Hollande/665, no. 54; same to same, The Hague, 19 November 1866, *ibid.*, no. 56.

[2] Loftus to Stanley, Berlin, 3 November 1866, PRO FO 64/601B, no. 302. Cf. Montgelas to Hohenlohe, Berlin, 13 November 1866, *APP*, VIII, 157, ft. 2, who claimed that the award was given to Benedetti for his efforts to bring the Prusso-Italian alliance to fruition.

[3] Benedetti to Moustier, Berlin, 20 November 1866, FAE CP, Prusse/360; Loftus to Stanley, Berlin, 24 November 1866, PRO FO 64/602, no. 337.

[4] On 25 September, Bylandt, the Dutch minister, had turned back the archives to the Austrian government, and Wimpffen had been accredited at the Berlin court on 5 November.

a *rapprochement* with Russia, a development which he had feared ever since the mission of Manteuffel to St. Petersburg in early August. Benedetti's conversation not only evidences his exasperation with the Prussian government but also points to a slight change in his attitude toward Austria. He spoke with great animation and warmth of Austria, expressed confidence in the political future of that empire, and suggested that more intimate relations should exist between Austria and France.[1] Certain political developments had forecast this change in the ambassador's attitude: the cession of Venetia to Italy, the destruction of the Vienna settlement, as well as the opposition or procrastination which French compensation demands had encountered in Berlin combined to produce a new appreciation of Austria. Moreover, as early as January 1866, Benedetti had contemplated the possibility of using Austria to balance the power and influence of Prussia in Germany.[2]

Despite Benedetti's interviews with both Thile and the king, the negotiations had not progressed and the ambassador was relieved to learn that the return of the minister-president was announced for the end of the month. Benedetti hoped that Bismarck's arrival would lead to a final disposition of the alliance project and, in addition, clarify the attitude the two powers would assume in the Roman question.[3] The long delay, the possibility of a disturbance in Italy, and the suspicion of increased cooperation between Prussia and Russia made a definite conclusion of the negotiations imperative. In an earlier request for instructions, Benedetti had alluded to a proposal for an additional article to the draft treaty which would obligate the two cabinets to concerted steps in Florence and Rome. Although the ambassador was prepared to take up this point with the Prussian government, he was personally reluctant to combine the Luxemburg and Roman questions in this fashion, fearing that the compensation issue, now in abeyance for nearly three months, would be unduly jeopardized.[4]

The first interview between Bismarck and Benedetti took place

---

[1] Wimpffen to Beust, Berlin, 22 November 1866, HHStA, Preussen/92, no. 9B.

[2] Benedetti to Drouyn de Lhuys, Berlin, 14 January 1866, FAE MD, Autriche/67.

[3] Benedetti to Moustier, Berlin, 24 November 1866, FAE CP, Prusse/360, no. 255. Cf. Bismarck to Thile, Putbus, 27 November 1866, *APP*, VIII, 171, in which he informed the secretary that he would participate in no measures that would disturb the relations between Prussia and the Italian government.

[4] Benedetti to Moustier, Berlin, 17 November 1866, FAE MD, Hollande/149; Pagès, *RHM*, I, no. 6 (1926), pp. 404–405. Cf. Radowitz, I, 131.

at the French embassy on 3 December.[1] The ambassador urged that a rapid agreement be reached on the questions outstanding between France and Prussia. Bismarck turned his attention first to the Roman affair; while not exactly informed, he believed that Goltz had misjudged the intentions of the Prussian government and had gone far beyond them in drawing up a convention project with Moustier for Franco-Prussian intervention in Italy.[2] He emphasized that the Berlin cabinet wished to preserve its friendly relations with the Italian government.[3] As for the alliance treaty, Benedetti thought the minister-president still favorably disposed to the project. Bismarck had stressed the necessity of gaining the king's consent and had expressed the intention of applying himself to that end, although he had added that the crown prince as well as the king were opposed to both the Roman and Luxemburg projects. Benedetti's expectation relative to his meeting with Bismarck had not been fulfilled. He suspected that the minister-president had not spoken with complete frankness; that Bismarck was uninformed as to the Goltz-Moustier project, or that he had had no opportunity to take up the alliance treaty with the king, seemed most unlikely. Benedetti had the impression that Bismarck had been somewhat embarrassed by the discussions of Luxemburg and Rome, and he concluded that further procrastination might mark negotiations relative to the duchy. In spite of the minister-president's promise to try to influence William, Benedetti was frustrated and apprehensive regarding the outcome of his efforts:

> I would be obliged if you were to send me ... instructions authorizing me to affirm that by pressing the Prussian government I conform to your recommendations. I shall act with prudence, but you will believe as I do that it is necessary to penetrate without further delay into the true intentions of the Berlin court, and that if we cannot hasten anything, neither can we continue talks destined to remain without result. [4]

Benedetti's fear that the Prussian government would seek to delay a final decision [5] seemed justified when the minister-president failed to summon him on 6 December, as had been decided during the first conversation, for a more detailed discussion of the alliance project. Determined to prevent further dilatory negotiations, Benedetti

---

[1] Benedetti to Moustier, Berlin, 3 December 1866, FAE MD, Hollande/150.
[2] Cf. Goltz to Bismarck, Compiègne, 25 November 1866, APP, VIII, 160–168; ROLOFF, FbpG, LI, Pt. I (1939), p. 121.
[3] Ibid., p. 133.
[4] Benedetti to Moustier, Berlin, 3 December 1866, FAE MD, Hollande/150.
[5] Cf. Bismarck to Goltz, Berlin, 6 December 1866, BGW, VI, 176–177.

solicited by letter an interview for the following day. Instead of being called to such a meeting, the ambassador was informed by Thile that the minister-president had nothing to communicate but would receive Benedetti if he so desired. The ambassador also learned from Thile that Goltz had been charged to communicate to the imperial government the Prussian reply regarding the Roman question. After this explanation Benedetti did not insist on a meeting, although he emphasized that he would have to inform his government of the lack of progress in the negotiations, which he supposed could be attributed to the recalcitrance of the king. This supposition was denied by the secretary, though he supplied no other explanation.[1]

Benedetti had considered his action restrained in pressing demands for bringing the alliance treaty negotiations to a conclusion. Bismarck, however, instructed Count Goltz to complain to Moustier about the ambassador's impatience in furthering the project. To be sure, Bismarck was forced to husband his strength and to limit his activities as much as possible. The foreign minister agreed to counsel moderation to Benedetti and to instruct him to seek nothing more than the abandonment of the Prussian garrison right in Luxemburg.[2] By advising his ambassador to show greater restraint, Moustier encouraged the Prussian government's game of procrastination and weakened Benedetti's position. He made it possible for Bismarck to complain whenever the French ambassador endeavored to advance the alliance project. Furthermore, by limiting the goal to be sought first, the Berlin cabinet could assume that the French demands were abating in the face of determined opposition. Indeed, Goltz in his dispatch counselled the postponement of the entire Luxemburg question until the time for the Prussian equivalent – the unification of Germany – would have matured sufficiently to warrant its implementation. The satisfaction of French compensation was no longer deemed the logical counterpart to Prussia's expansion; rather, French expansion was to permit in turn a Prussian equivalent. It seems very likely that Bismarck shared the views of Ambassador Goltz and did not wish to surrender Luxemburg to France. He no longer thought the compensation issue as vital or dangerous as in the summer months. Time had had a moderating effect upon French concern over the shift in the balance of power; moreover, the proposed minor territorial adjustment was hardly likely to silence the critics of the

---

[1] Benedetti to Moustier, Berlin, 8 December 1866, FAE CP, Prusse/360.
[2] Goltz to Bismarck, Paris, 10 December 1866, *APP*, VIII, 205–206.

emperor. Bismarck preferred to sidetrack the matter of compensation, and also escape the conclusion of an alliance with France. While he realized the advantages of harmonious ties with Napoleon, he preferred of course to maintain freedom of action in foreign affairs as much as possible.[1]

As Benedetti was to discover, the Prussian minister-president had rendered himself even more inaccesible than before. His request for an audience, made on 13 December, was answered through Thile, and Benedetti was advised that he could not be received until the following week.[2] Bismarck's avoidance of foreign representatives was contrary to all custom and Benedetti was especially disturbed by the amazing change toward himself. The minister-president used to receive him frequently and to discuss pending problems forthrightly with him and Benedetti observed the striking contrast since Bismarck's return, for which he was unable to offer a plausible explanation.[3] He was aware of course that the minister-president was giving his undivided attention to the organization of the North German Confederation.[4] Although the ambassador had attended a two-day royal hunt,[5] neither king nor minister had chosen to discuss affairs of mutual interest with him. Ironically enough, Benedetti thought Bismarck's behavior hardly that of a statesman pursuing negotiations in the hope of a successful conclusion.[6] In regard to the Italian question, increasingly important because of the evacuation of Rome on 11 and 12 December, the Prussian cabinet had declined all proposals and offered none in return. Benedetti accused the minister-president of "sending plans to Paris and maintaining silence in Berlin" – such dilatory actions could only be to the detriment of French interests.[7] In view of the rebuffs he had suffered since Bismarck's return to Berlin, the ambassador proposed to abstain from

---

[1] *Ibid.*, p. 206.

[2] Benedetti to Moustier, 15 December 1866, FAE CP, Prusse/360, Annex. Since his return to Berlin, Bismarck had received only the Austrian ambassador.

[3] Same to same, Berlin, 14 December 1866, FAE MD, Hollande/149. "Benedetti renewed his relations with the minister-president under completely different circumstances... their roles were reversed, we had nothing more to offer, but everything to ask" (ROTHAN, *Souvenirs diplomatiques*, p. 85).

[4] See HAHN, p. 481, for the 15 December opening of the conference to debate the constitution of the North German Confederation. Cf. Benedetti to Moustier, Berlin, 24 November 1866, FAE CP, Prusse/360, no. 254.

[5] LOFTUS, I, 150.

[6] Benedetti to Moustier, Berlin, 14 December 1866, FAE MD, Hollande/149.

[7] Same to same, Berlin, 14 December 1866, FAE CP, Prusse/360.

any further *démarche* until the minister-president should indicate his willingness to cooperate:

> For my part, I think that our dignity commands us henceforth a certain reserve, and I am persuaded that abstention and silence suit us better and teach us more than the new efforts which we could attempt to determine the Prussian government to show itself more explicit. Bismarck has a mind much too enlightened and a character much too enterprising not to take an exact account of things.... He knows that in Vienna an occasion to repair the reverses of the last campaign would be seized with passion, and he does not conceal from himself the dangers to which Prussia would be exposed in the case that she had to sustain a two-front war against a united Austria and France.[1]

If the French government followed this course, Benedetti predicted, Bismarck would soon rally to the proposals offered him by the imperial cabinet. Should the minister-president decide to receive him, the ambassador planned to maintain an attitude of reserve while asking Bismarck to accept the French proposals or to indicate the precise changes which he believed ought to be made.[2]

Despite the fact that Benedetti had not been received in audience since Bismarck's return to Berlin, the ambassador's impatience became the subject of additional complaints. Bismarck insisted that Benedetti's behavior jeopardized the results of the negotiations between the two powers, and he charged Goltz to have Moustier check further pressure from the ambassador.[3] Parallel to this attitude was manifested the overriding desire of the minister-president to rid himself of Benedetti, who personally represented the unfulfilled demands of the imperial government:

> I hope through this repeated emphasis on the attitude of Benedetti to bring about the conviction that his personality is the main obstacle to the wishes of the emperor.[4]

Bismarck's tenacity and the success of similar diplomatic endeavors in the past decided him not to relent in his complaints, which for the rest of the month assumed a regularity reminiscent of his tactics toward Austria earlier in the year.

A chance meeting in a street on Wednesday, 19 December, gave Benedetti an opportunity to hear from Bismarck himself how the

---

[1] Benedetti to Moustier, Berlin, 14 December 1866, FAE MD, Hollande/149.

[2] *Ibid.*

[3] Bismarck to Goltz, Berlin, 16 December 1866, *APP*, VIII, 212; Goltz to Moustier, Paris, 17 December 1866, FAE CP, Prusse/360; Goltz to Bismarck, Paris, 18 December 1866, *APP*, VIII, 217–218; cf. Goltz to Bismarck, Paris, 26 December 1866, *ibid.*, 242, in which he attributes Benedetti's impatience to his southern temperament and to the fact that he had received his diplomatic training in the consular service in the Near East!

[4] Goltz to Bismarck, Paris, 18 December 1866, *ibid.*, 222.

Prussian government envisaged the pending problems. In view of the place and the reserve he had decided to maintain, the ambassador abstained from opening a political discussion. Bismarck nevertheless used the exchange of civilities to express his regret at not having been able to receive Benedetti. Turning the conversation to the Italian problem, he explained that Prussia could not assume an obligation guaranteeing to the pope his temporal power and possessions. He stated that the use of force to maintain or, if necessary, to re-establish papal sovereignty would not be supported by the predominantly Protestant subjects of the king and would harm the cordial relations existing between Italy and Prussia. In Bismarck's view, the position of the imperial cabinet toward Italian affairs differed greatly from that of his government. Precedents as well as other considerations gave France the right as well as the duty to assist the papacy, whereas Prussia would have to limit her interference to friendly counsel. Ambassador Benedetti, who could see the careful distinction between the position of the two powers and knew that Bismarck had no desire to contribute to the solution of an issue which was part of French internal affairs, replied that the imperial government had been led to believe by Ambassador Goltz that a preparatory convention establishing the extent of such a step could be agreed upon by Prussia and France. As for the guarantee of the papal state, Benedetti depicted it as the *sine qua non* for obtaining a favorable disposition of the papacy toward the advice rendered by the two courts. The minister-president maintained his refusal of the guarantee, but he remarked that a tender of good offices could well be arranged through talks and would only require identical instructions to the representatives of the two powers in Rome and Florence. As for the language of Ambassador Goltz and his cooperation with a convention proposal, Bismarck bluntly declared that the vain satisfaction of participating in the drafting of a treaty had prompted both his actions and his words. The minister-president was determined to avoid all involvement in the Roman question. He could appreciate the emperor's dilemma, trying to reconcile his government's support of Italian nationalist aspirations relative to Rome with French Catholic opposition to the surrender of the city. Bismarck feared that, among other factors, the imperial government might try using the issue to create dissent in Germany between the Catholics of the South and the Protestants of Prussia, in order to hinder ultimate German unification.[1]

---

[1] Benedetti to Moustier, Berlin, 20 December 1866, FAE CP, Prusse/360.

Bismarck also touched upon the alliance treaty and, in accordance with Benedetti's predictions, brought up new considerations relative to the proposed stipulations. Prussia could not withdraw from Luxemburg unless new circumstances forced her to do so; the minister-president suggested that the imperial cabinet compromise itself and provoke petitions in the duchy calling for the retreat of the Prussian garrison. Benedetti pointed out that such a procedure would make it mandatory for France to be certain of the king's intentions; he reminded Bismarck of the alliance which France was proposing and emphasized the danger of a manifestation in Luxemburg which could lead to a conflict between the population and the soldiers of the king. He urged the conclusion of the alliance treaty and then concerted steps in The Hague and in the duchy. To this suggestion Bismarck replied that it had taken him four years to prepare the king for a declaration of war against Austria and that he could not, without much caution, convince William "to serve up Luxemburg to the emperor on a silver platter." [1] Noting the differences in views, Benedetti suggested a further conversation to establish the changes which the minister-president advocated in the draft treaty. Bismarck, however, passed over the ambassador's remark and instead spoke of his illness and the task of drafting the constitution of the North German Confederation. Benedetti concluded from this that he probably would not be received in the audience granted for the coming week. [2]

A few days after this conversation, Benedetti was informed by Moustier that Goltz had remarked that the French ambassador had more or less declined to negotiate the Roman question with Thile. [3] In spite of the impressions which he had gained from his chance encounter with Bismarck, and in preference to fruitless explanations, Benedetti decided to give a practical demonstration of his readiness to take up the Roman problem. On 23 December, he called on Thile to inquire whether or not the secretary was prepared to open negotiations, and he placed himself at the disposal of the Prussian government at any time to discuss the matter. The ambassador's direct approach

---

[1] Benedetti to Moustier, Berlin, 20 December 1866, FAE MD, Hollande/149. "Meanwhile the Luxemburg question remains for us a *noli me tangere*. It will be kept for eventual use for or against N[apoleon]" (Thile to Balan, Berlin, 22 December 1866, SASS, *PJ*, CCXVII, Heft 3 [September 1929], p. 268); KEUDELL, p. 355.

[2] Benedetti to Moustier, Berlin, 20 December 1866, FAE MD, Hollande/149.

[3] Same to same, Berlin, 24 December 1866, FAE CP, Prusse/360. Cf. Bismarck to Goltz, Berlin, 26 December 1866, *BGW*, VI, 213–214.

was not without effect, for the secretary brought him next day the proposals of the minister-president regarding diplomatic intervention in Italy. While reiterating Prussia's opposition to a formal convention, Bismarck was nevertheless willing to examine the utility of such a convention, provided the guarantee clause was excluded. Although the secretary discussed the steps already taken by the French representatives in Florence and Rome and the opinions of the Prussian government in respect to the draft convention, he had no authority to participate in a revision of the text with the ambassador. As Benedetti pointed out to Moustier, Thile did not have plenipotentiary powers and the ambassador was unable to enter into negotiations with him, contrary to the assertions Goltz had made in Paris.[1] From these recent experiences with Bismarck and Thile, Ambassador Benedetti concluded that the Prussian government had no intention of coming to an agreement with the imperial cabinet on the action to be taken in Italy. He thought it inadvisable to continue the present efforts; instead, he urged communication of the proposed convention on the Roman question to Bismarck along with appropriate suggestions and allow the minister-president to explain his views on the matter without pressing him.

As for the constant excuse of Bismarck's illness, Benedetti noted that the minister-president was not too ill to hunt in the snow and rain, to attend banquets, to make speeches in both chambers, and to preside over endless debates on the constitution of the North German Confederation. Only the reception of foreign representatives at the Prussian court seemed to be impossible to him. While it was admittedly difficult and time-consuming to gain the king's consent to the stipulations of the alliance treaty, Benedetti thought that in the Roman question at least Bismarck could have moved quickly to inform the imperial government of his views and propositions as soon as he had heard the proposals. Even an outright rejection would have created a better impression than the dilatory negotiations he seemed to favor.

Benedetti shared similar misgivings concerning the alliance treaty. Admitting all the difficulties of the problem, he nevertheless failed to find a reasonable explanation for Bismarck's refusal to work out a program of action with him. While recommending that France compromise herself, Bismarck was unwilling to give assurances of

---

[1] Benedetti to Moustier, Berlin, 24 December 1866, FAE CP, Prusse/360.

the attitude of the Prussian cabinet. Benedetti's suspicions had been awakened and he could not shake a feeling of distrust:

> What can be the considerations which inspire such an attitude? Could a decision have been taken in Berlin not to conclude anything with us any more, because engagements have been contracted elsewhere, or because it is possible to bring to a successful conclusion the undertaking which has been begun without having to reckon with France any longer? I can affirm nothing, but the manner in which they deal with us, the ardent haste with which they constitute the Confederation of the North and gather all the forces of which it will dispose... permit all conjectures.[1]

Benedetti was particularly disturbed over the possibility of a Prusso-Russian accord. The mission of General Manteuffel was still a mystery to him, and his apprehensions had not been dispelled. While he was not sure that an alliance had been signed, he felt that perhaps the two monarchs had assumed obligations toward each other, which would explain the apparent reluctance of the king to come to an understanding with France. Having previously been treated with great frankness and cordiality by Bismarck and having received an implicit promise of territorial annexation by way of a draft treaty to which the minister-president had contributed, the ambassador found it indeed difficult to explain the reversal of attitude toward himself and the French government.[2] Benedetti did not lose himself in speculations. He advised Moustier that the imperial government would have to be on its guard. He thought it best not to break off the discussions nor to show signs of discontent; on the contrary, he recommended patience and friendliness. But care should be taken that the demands of France should not degenerate into solicitations. Perhaps a deliberate attitude of reserve would bring the Berlin cabinet to a resumption of fruitful negotiations, provided that the Prussian government was really motivated by friendly intentions toward France.[3]

Benedetti expressed his suspicions two days later: "I cannot... affirm anything, but I have doubts which cannot be hidden from you and if I had to formulate the solution which seems most probable to me, I would say that they are resolved not to accept our treaty project."[4] Five months earlier the ambassador had first broached

---

[1] *Ibid.*

[2] *Ibid.*

[3] *Ibid.*

[4] Same to same Berlin, 26 December 1866, *ibid.* For the text of the constitution, see NORDDEUTSCHER BUND, *Bundes-Gesetzblatt des Norddeutschen Bundes, 1867, Nr. 1* (Berlin, n.d.) pp. 1–23.

the subject of compensation with Bismarck, and nothing had as yet resulted. While Benedetti saw Prussia growing more powerful each day and less and less inclined to placate France, he was forced to concede the ineffectiveness of the steps of the imperial government. The month of December in particular constituted an important time-span in the relations between the two powers: not only was the real-ization of French aspirations more uncertain, but efforts toward the organization of the North German Confederation had become more concrete – a development of major interest to France.

Meetings of the plenipotentiaries of the north German states to debate the provisions of the constitution of the Confederation had opened on 15 December, and although efforts had been made to keep the proceedings confidential, the ambassador had obtained some information about the elaboration of the constitutional project. A first draft, drawn up by Savigny, had given a far too restrictive interpretation to the sovereign attributes of the member states and had been modified at the insistence of the minister-president, who believed that Prussia only needed to retain uncontested authority and the means necessary to control all the common resources and com-munications.[1] Through a colleague who had received a copy of the federal pact, Benedetti was able to prepare an analysis of it for the imperial government. His over-all impression of the project led him to call it an attempt at undisguised subjugation: he found it difficult to imagine that the Savigny draft could have been more drastic in its limitations upon Prussia's partners. In his analysis of the proposed federal constitution, Benedetti noted that the powers of govern-ment were distributed among three branches: the federal council or *Bundesrat*, composed of representatives of the federated states, organized into permanent committees of whose forty-three votes, Prussia had seventeen; the presidency or *Präsidium*, permantly vested in the king of Prussia, whose authority admitted practically no checks and who would exercise all the prerogatives of sovereignty in the relations of the Confederation with foreign powers; and the diet or *Bundestag*, elected by direct and universal suffrage and given the right of legislative initiative. In a sense there existed also a fourth branch in that the commander of the military forces, the Prussian king, who had complete authority over all matters affecting the organization, training, and armament as well as the finances of the forces of the member states, was given certain powers for special circumstances

---

[1] Benedetti to Moustier, Berlin, 18 December 1866, FAE CP, Prusse/360, no. 277bis.

which were basically attributes of the executive. Prussian laws and regulations regarding military affairs were to take effect in the Confederation as soon as the federal pact was promulgated, and at the same time the king of Prussia would enter into his attributes as generalissimo or commander of the military forces of the Confederation. Federal legislation and authority was to prevail over the autonomous attributes of the members, and the subjects of all states were to become citizens of the Confederation. Moreover, federal legislation was to extend to all matters of common interest, and articles enumerating them included all the essential services, except the organization of local justice and police. The ambassador stressed the unity of organization and command which the Prussian constitutional project endeavored to achieve, as well as the expected centralization of the military authority in the hands of the Prussian king.[1] The emergence of a powerful force in northern Germany was not a pleasant object for contemplation for Benedetti and certainly assumed added significance in regard to the unsatisfied compensation aspirations of the imperial government. The long-range effects of the Prussian victory at mid-year were beginning to take shape; in the ambassador's mind, the project he had just analyzed conformed only too well to the expectations of Prussian hegemony in Germany.[2]

The holidays kept the political developments in abeyance for a short while, and the ambassador accepted the invitation of Count Hohenthal to Knautheim, near Leipzig, where he remained until 29 December.[3] The situation in Berlin, in particular the relationship between the minister-president and the ambassador, had undergone no change,[4] and Benedetti indicated that even Thile appeared to be completely ignorant of Bismarck's plans and could only inform him that the minister-president's illness continued to prevent confer-

---

[1] Same to same, Berlin, 20 December 1866, *ibid.*, no. 281.

[2] It may be noted that Benedetti at this time did not believe that formal military engagements existed between Prussia and the south German states (Loftus to Stanley, Berlin, 10 January 1867, PRO FO 64/617, no. 29). On the same day the ambassador made his analysis of the proposed constitution, 20 December, the Prussian lower chamber voted the annexation of Schleswig-Holstein, as well as of the territory ceded by Bavaria and Hesse. Four days later, 24 December, the decree ordering the union of the duchies with the Prussian monarchy was promulgated in Berlin (see *Allerhöchstes Patent wegen Besitznahme der Herzogthümer Schleswig und Holstein*, Berlin, 12 January 1867, HAHN, pp. 404–405. Cf. Dotézac to Moustier, Copenhagen, 3 January 1867, FAE CP, Danemark/251, no. 2, for the apprehension regarding the execution of Article V of the Prague Treaty).

[3] Bylandt to Zuylen, Berlin, 29 December 1866, RBZ, Pruisen/1866, no. 358.

[4] Bismarck soon again complained of the ambassador and referred to the threatening language of Benedetti and Moustier as well (Bismarck to Goltz, Berlin, 8 January 1867, ONCKEN, II, 167).

ences with the foreign representatives. The ambassador, too, was incapacitated and had been unable to pursue his duties with the customary regularity.[1]

The negotiations, however, were soon to receive new impetus. Moustier, prompted by the proximity of the legislative session scheduled to open in Paris in mid-February,[2] informed Benedetti that the emperor advocated a renewal of the discussions of the Luxemburg affair without delay. Rouher had already emphasized to Goltz the necessity of ascertaining the intentions of the Prussian cabinet,[3] and, while conceding Bismarck's right to reject the proffered alliance or to withdraw his offer of Luxemburg, the French ambassador was to insist on a declaration of intentions. Benedetti would be able to base himself on the minister-president's recent statement in the chamber concerning minorities which might seek annexation to another state, provided the territory was of no strategic importance. Although Bismarck had alluded to North Schleswig, the remarks might be applied to Luxemburg, whose population preferred France to Prussia. Furthermore, the minister-president's promise to facilitate the transfer suggested that the fortress was not considered necessary to the defense of the North German Confederation. In view of these factors, France would be prepared to garrison Luxemburg after the withdrawal of the Prussian troops, hold a plebiscite, and offer the Dutch king an indemnity.[4] Another alternative, to persuade the Dutch to demand that Limburg and Luxemburg be declared free of all ties with Germany, and to gain Luxemburg by way of arbitration gave less promise of success. Instead, Benedetti was to seek an immediate declaration from Bismarck, and to imply that a refusal would lead to a serious deterioration in the relations between the two powers.[5]

[1] Benedetti to Moustier, Berlin, 5 January 1867, FAE CP, Prusse/361.

[2] Just prior to the renewed interest in the treaty project, the emperor had received from Budberg, the Russian ambassador in Paris, a formal offer of an *entente* relative to the Near East, where an insurrection in Candia against the Turkish overlord had revealed the possibility of Russia applying Napoleon's principle of nationality. This proposal may have led the emperor to hope that Russian support might also be obtained to forward his own plans for Luxemburg and Belgium (PAGÈS, *RHM*, *I*, no. 6 [1926], pp. 407–408; RADOWITZ, I, 134; RHEINDORF, p. 55).

[3] Goltz to Bismarck, Paris, 3 January 1867, *APP*, VIII, 254–256, Cf. PAGÈS, *RHM*, I, no. 6 (1926), p. 408.

[4] Cf. A. MATSCHOSS, *Die Kriegsgefahr von 1867: die Luxemburg Frage* (Bunzlau, 1908), pp. 72–73, who sees the Dutch king's greed and the extravagances of his mistress, Madame Mussard, at the origin of the indemnity suggestions. Matschoss bases his opinion on the explanation offered by H. ASSER, *De Buitenlandsche Betrekkingen van Nederland, 1860–1889* (Haarlem, 1889), p. 43, ft.

[5] Moustier to Benedetti, Paris, 7 January 1867, FAE MD, Hollande/150. Cf. Goltz to Bis-

Accordingly, on 11 January, the ambassador sought out the minister-president and, emphasizing the considerations arising from French internal affairs, inquired whether the negotiations concerning the alliance treaty and the cession of Luxemburg were considered pending, postponed, or broken off. To this direct question Bismarck gave his assurance that the negotiations were pending, but he stressed again the time involved in bringing to fruition the delicate affair of winning the king's approval. He repeated his previous advice that France compromise herself, to which Benedetti answered that the imperial government could not proceed without a guarantee of Prussian intentions. The conversation revealed again the reluctance of either party to launch into the venture alone. According to the minister-president, the scruples of the king could most easily be overcome if the Luxemburg population were to manifest a symptom of its aspirations – this alone could decide William to withdraw the garrison and abandon the duchy. To Benedetti's suggestion that Bismarck, together with Moltke and Roon,[1] attempt to influence the king in favor of a spontaneous withdrawal, the minister-president countered that a negative result would cost much valuable time. He added that the question of Luxemburg would have to be regulated before the promulgation of the constitution of the North German Confederation. Yet Bismarck made no attempt to justify the dilatory course he had pursued with the ambassador. Benedetti was not encouraged by these responses and warned Moustier not to expect too much Prussian cooperation in The Hague.[2]

The French decision to accept Bismarck's suggestion to prepare manifestations in Luxemburg for the withdrawal of the Prussian garrison was taken in anticipation of a quick solution.[3] On 16 January, Moustier telegraphed this decision to Benedetti and asked him to discuss the matter in greater detail with Bismarck.[4] When on the

marck, Paris, 14 January 1867, *APP*, VIII, 303–305; Rothan, *Souvenirs diplomatiques*, pp. 112–114.

[1] The generals had supposedly been won over to Bismarck's point of view about the evacuation of the fortress (Bismarck to Goltz, Berlin, 14 January 1867, *APP*, VIII, 297–298).

[2] Benedetti to Moustier, Berlin, 11 January 1867, FAE MD, Hollande/149. Cf. *Aufzeichnung über eine Unterredung Bismarcks mit Benedetti*, Berlin, 10 [sic] January 1867, *APP*, VIII, 282–284.

[3] Already on 13 January, the French envoy in The Hague had forwarded a draft treaty which was to regulate the transfer of Luxemburg to France (Baudin to Moustier, The Hague, 13 January 1867, FAE MD, Hollande/149, Annex). Cf. Goltz to Bismarck, Paris, 17 January 1867, *APP*, VIII, 314.

[4] Moustier to Benedetti, Paris, 16 January 1867, FAE CP, Prusse/361, T. The foreign minister added that the imperial government was willing to reduce Prussia's obligations under the proposed alliance.

following day Benedetti transmitted the substance of Moustier's communication, Bismarck cautioned that the manifestations in the duchy should avoid any appearance of a demonstration hostile to Prussia or to Germany, for the susceptibility of public opinion could easily be offended and jeopardize the expected results. He added that, at his recommendation, the king had charged Roon and Moltke to examine and advise on the strategic value of the fortress to the defense of Prussia.[1]

While the negotiations were again actively pursued, the ambassador in Berlin did not receive, from 16 January to 18 February, any information or instructions from the foreign minister relative to the proceedings,[2] with the exception of one letter. In it Moustier announced that, contrary to Bismarck's expectations, General Moltke had concluded that the fortress of Luxemburg was valuable to the defense of Prussia.[3] Alarmed, Benedetti conferred at once with the minister-president who sought to make light of the difficulty by predicting either a change in the general's report before it was submitted to the king or a contrary opinion solicited from the engineering service. In view of the military objections raised, the ambassador

[1] Benedetti to Moustier, Berlin, 17 January 1867, FAE MD, Hollande/149; Bismarck to Goltz, Berlin, 18 January 1867, *APP*, VIII, 314–315.
[2] "At that moment the emperor and Moustier gave Goltz all their confidence and did not even keep Benedetti *au courant* of what was said at the Tuileries and in Compiègne.... A whole month passed in Berlin without the situation becoming clearer.... Moustier left Benedetti almost without information" (PAGÈS, *RHM*, I, no. 6 [1926], pp. 408–410). Cf. OLLIVIER, IX, 158. Meanwhile in Paris, Moustier was accepting proposals from Budberg concerning the Near East crisis, in return for Russia's neutrality *re* French aspirations in Belgium (PAGÈS, *RHM*, I, no. 6 [1926], p. 413). Moustier in turn conferred with Goltz for Prussian support in the Near East, warning however that Prussian adherence to French policy in the Near East did not constitute a ransom for his compensation plans in Luxemburg (E. DRIAULT, "Après Sadowa: la question d'Autriche et la question d'Orient, 1866–1867," *Revue des études napoléoniennes*, XXXV [September 1932], pp. 139–140). Benedetti was completely ignorant of these conversations, which however did not prevent him, at the court ball on 14 February, from strongly advising Aristarchi Bey, Turkish minister in Berlin, not to delay making the necessary concessions to appease the Christian populations. "His object... was attended with perfect success, for on returning home the same evening, Aristarchi Bey telegraphed his government that his urgent advice was to make the necessary concessions *à temps et spontanément*." (Loftus to Stanley, Berlin, 16 February 1867, PRO FO 64/618, no. 80). Cf. "Mr. Benedetti... expressed in strong terms his annoyance at receiving no communications from his government on the Eastern question being thus left in perfect ignorance of their views and acts" (Loftus to Stanley, Berlin, 23 February 1867, *ibid.*, no. 101).
[3] On 19 January Bismarck informed Goltz of Moltke's views that Luxemburg was the key railroad center between France and the Rhine (Bismarck to Goltz, Berlin, 19 January 1867, *APP*, VIII, 316–317). Goltz had related this to Moustier, who had warned him not to carry reluctance too far (Goltz to Bismarck, Paris, 25 January 1867, *ibid.*, p. 331). The private letter from Moustier to Benedetti of 22 January has not been preserved (*ODG*, XIV, 184, ft. 1).

reminded Bismarck that the dismantlement of the fortress had never been a condition for the transfer of Luxemburg to France.[1] Reporting Moustier's offer to reduce Prussia's obligation under the draft treaty, Benedetti asked Bismarck to indicate when such a revision should be made in the text. This concession prompted the minister-president to rehearse the advantages of a Franco-Prussian alliance, and he insinuated that the two governments might use the occasion of the Near Eastern crisis which preoccupied the other powers to satisfy their own aspirations. The ambassador, however, had grown wary of Bismarck's friendly overtures which all too often spelled evasiveness and delay. He also strongly opposed an inspiration of the emperor to substitute an exchange of notes for a formal treaty commitment, and he pointed to Bismarck's equivocal attitude as evidence that only a *bona fide* alliance would constitute a satisfactory guarantee of Prussian neutrality.

> Once in possession of Luxemburg, [he wrote to Moustier] we are on the road which leads to Brussels; neither public opinion nor the governments will be mistaken about it, and with the neutrality of Prussia firmly guaranteed, we would arrive there more assuredly than if she gave us only uncertain promises. Belgium can thus be united to France without unsheathing the sword.[2]

In cautioning the foreign minister not to be duped by unsupported promises of neutrality or even favorable armed mediation, Benedetti emphasized the growing might of Prussia and the significant military cooperation between the north and the south German states.[3] He reminded Moustier that the "Prussians take account of only those who are strong." [4]

Benedetti's conversation with the minister-president and his recommendations to Moustier do reveal that he was still hoping for

---

[1] Cf. Benedetti to Moustier, Berlin, 11 January 1867, FAE MD, Hollande/149; Bylandt to Zuylen, Berlin, 29 January 1867, RBZ, Pruisen/1867, no. 47, who reported that Bismarck considered the Luxemburg question completely tied to the problem of maintaining or demolishing the fortress.

[2] Benedetti to Moustier, Berlin, 26 January 1867, FAE MD, Hollande/149. Benedetti also toyed with the idea of an alliance with Austria which would permit France to regain her natural frontiers, but at the cost of war; he concluded, however, that natural frontiers were no longer a necessity: the real ones were those which were or could become national frontiers. Cf. Bismarck to Goltz, Berlin, 27 January 1867, *APP*, VIII, 334–335, in which he emphasizes Benedetti's continued support of the alliance project in contrast to Moustier's increasing indifference to it; KEUDELL, p. 355.

[3] Cf. SCHÜSSLER, p. 64, for Bismarck's plans to establish closer relations with South Germany. Benedetti thought that the Confederation was rapidly becoming "a formidable engine for war which, if it succeeded in embracing South Germany, would become the greatest danger to France" (Wimpffen to Beust, Berlin, 12 January 1867, HHStA, Preussen/95, no. 7C).

[4] Benedetti to Moustier, Berlin, 26 January 1867, FAE MD, Hollande/149.

an *entente* with Prussia. Although he advised of various methods to lead Prussia into a commitment, he failed to focus on the resolute unwillingness of Bismarck and did not suggest means of making the alliance irresistably attractive to the Berlin cabinet. The continued silence of the minister-president relative to a final military opinion on Luxemburg caused the ambassador some uneasiness.[1] Before he could meet again with Bismarck, events in Berlin increased his desire for a speedy decision on the fortress question. On 4 and 7 February, military conventions were concluded between Prussia and the member states of the Confederation,[2] and on the 8th the delegates of the north German states accepted, with minor changes, the Prussian constitutional proposal.[3]

The situation assumed an even more adverse aspect toward French interests when Bismarck told the ambassador on 12 February that the military had concluded that the Luxemburg fortress should be retained in the Prussian defense system. Benedetti was too conscious of the influence of the military upon the king and the opposition of the crown prince to the cession of Luxemburg, to receive the decision with other than great misgivings. Bismarck claimed that Moustier had proposed through Goltz to abandon the treaty project and limit the negotiations to the settlement of the annexation affair. By insinuating that, in spite of the ambassador's protestations, France did not want an alliance, he attempted to justify the hesitancy of the Prussian government to abandon the fortress. The ambassador refuted the implications and insisted that France desired an alliance as well as the acquisition of Luxemburg. When questioned about the

---

[1] On 4 February Benedetti addressed a note to Bismarck asking whether he did not have any information to relay to him (Benedetti to Bismarck, Berlin, 4 February 1867, ONCKEN, II, 196, ft. 2), to which Bismarck replied, "Taking account of your flattering predilection for autographs, I take my pen in hand to state that I have no material to furnish you today" (Bismarck to Benedetti, Berlin, 4 February 1867, *ibid.*). The same day the ambassador, frustrated in his endeavors, complained to Thile: "*Rien ne marche*, we make no progress – and we have so little time – only eleven or twelve days before the opening of the legislative session – and then comes the Yellow Book; and you know how much depends on that, even to a comma, – I tell you I am frightened" (Bismarck to Goltz, Berlin, 7 February 1867, *BGW*, VI, 258).

[2] K. LANGE, *Bismarcks Kampf um die Militär-Konvention mit Braunschweig, 1867–68,* "Quellen und Studien zur Verfassungsgeschichte des deutschen Reiches in Mittelalter und Neuzeit," VII, pt. II (Weimar, 1934), pp. 1–4. Military discussions had taken place in Stuttgart between the ministers of war of Bavaria, Baden, and Württemberg to discuss the feasibility of a military system common to all three states (R. VON MOHL, *Lebenserinnerungen, 1799–1875* [Stuttgart, 1902], II, 314–316).

[3] Benedetti to Moustier, Berlin, 8 February 1867, FAE CP, Prusse/361, T. For the constitutional developments in North Germany in 1866–1867, see PFLANZE, pp. 337 ff.; O. BECKER, *Bismarcks Ringen um Deutschlands Gestaltung* (Heidelberg, 1958), pp. 211 ff.

suggested manifestations in the duchy, Benedetti countered by inquiring how such an event would be received after the advice rendered by the military. Bismarck finally suggested the obstacles might be removed through a meeting between William and Napoleon during the coming exhibition in Paris. This interview only strengthened Benedetti's conviction that an agreement on Luxemburg and the alliance project would not be attained in the foreseeable future. He was particularly fearful that the North German parliament might concern itself with the question of the duchy.[1] That same day the election for the constituent *Bundestag* of the North German Confederation had taken place,[2] and next day King William issued a statement convoking that body for the 24th of the same month.[3]

Despite Benedetti's exertions, the imperial government had also failed to gain its objectives before the opening of the legislative session in France on 14 February. The emperor's speech was filled with platitudes and glowing remarks about the effectiveness of French mediation, and he sought to draw attention away from the fact that France had not been compensated for the expansion of Prussia.[4] The effect of the speech in Berlin was not entirely favorable, despite the general approval with which the imperial comments on the affairs of Europe had been received. At the court ball that evening the ambassador noted that the king, far from being elated by Napoleon's reference to "stopping Prussia at the gates of Vienna," treated him with a certain reserve.[5]

While the emperor had to open the legislative session without a splendid diplomatic success, hope was soon kindled that the imperial cabinet would take the necessary steps to secure Luxemburg. In a letter of 18 February, his first confidential communication since 16 January, Moustier reiterated earlier statements relative to the duchy and demonstrated the consistency of the demands of the French government since the outset of the negotiations.[6] The foreign minister

---

[1] Benedetti to Moustier, Berlin, 13 February 1867, FAE MD, Hollande/150.

[2] H. VON POSCHINGER, *Fürst Bismarck und die Parlamentarier* (Breslau, 1894–1896), I, 4–5; Benedetti to Moustier, Berlin, 15 February 1867, FAE CP, Prusse/361, no. 34.

[3] *Einberufungspatent für den Reichstag des norddeutschen Bundes*, Berlin, 13 February 1867, HAHN, pp. 496–497.

[4] See *AD*, 1867, I, 145, for the emperor's speech. For Napoleon's efforts to combat the rising tide of opposition, see CASE, pp. 227 ff.

[5] Benedetti to Moustier, Berlin, 15 February 1867, FAE CP, Prusse/361, no. 33; same to same, Berlin, 16 February 1867, *ibid.*, no. 35.

[6] Moustier to Benedetti, Paris, 18 February 1867, FAE MD, Hollande/149. The ambassador did not let the opportunity pass without reminding Moustier that instead of making important

followed up the refutation of the interpretations of Bismarck of 12 February with an announcement to Benedetti that France stood ready to sign the alliance proposed in August, with or without a time limit. As for the acquisition of Luxemburg, the imperial government was beginning *à mettre les fers au feu* in the duchy, and Baudin had returned to The Hague in order to negotiate the cession with the Dutch king.[1] In informing Benedetti of these steps, Moustier asked him to give serious thought to the consequences of a Prussian refusal to give up the fortress. War could be the result of an outright denial; if the question remained open and France became the legitimate proprietor through a treaty with the Dutch king, Prussia would have to state under what rights she proposed to maintain a garrison. France, unlike the king of Holland, could not be forced to become a member of the North German Confederation and, Moustier believed, Prussia would eventually be obliged to concede Luxemburg to France.[2]

But before Benedetti could verify Moustier's suppositions, he fixed his attention upon the opening of the constituent *Bundestag* scheduled for the 24th, believing that the king's speech would give a good indication of Prussia's course in Germany. The ambassador was conscious of the likelihood of a closer relationship between North and South and that there was much sentiment in favor of a total unification.[3] His study of the king's address forced him to conclude that it had been inspired by ideas which pushed Prussia toward the extension of her preponderance. Benedetti noted the king's reference to the necessity for regulating the ties between the North and the South and pointed out that the monarch had not mentioned that, by the terms of the Prague Treaty, Austria had a right to be

communications through Goltz, he should have made them through the Berlin embassy (Benedetti to Moustier, Berlin, 18 February 1867, FAE CP, Prusse/361).

[1] Moustier to Benedetti, Paris, 18 February 1867, FAE MD, Hollande/150. Cf. Director General of Justice to Tornaco, Luxemburg, 27 February 1867, LAE, H/28, for the arrival of a French agent, Baron Jacquinot, Under-Prefect of Verdun.

[2] Moustier to Benedetti, Paris, 18 February 1867, FAE MD, Hollande/150. The resolution to take definite steps for the acquisition of Luxemburg may have been strengthened by the declaration of Budberg that Russia would not enter any coalitions against France and would endeavor to break up such coalitions if they were formed (*ibid.*; cf. Pagès, *RHM*, I, no. 6 [1926], 413).

[3] Cf. Hohenlohe, I, 184–187, for the desire of the Bavarian government to establish closer ties with the North German Confederation; Mohl, II, 312–313; O. Lorenz, Kaiser *Wilhelm und die Begründung des Reichs, 1866–1871* (Jena, 1902), pp. 180–181, for the unification tendencies in Baden; E. Brandenburg, "Bismarck und die Reichsgründung," *Das Bismarck-Jahr; eine Würdigung Bismarcks und seiner Politik in Einzelschilderungen*, eds. M. Lenz and E. Marcks (Hamburg, 1915), p. 181; Pflanze, pp. 367 ff.

consulted on the issue.[1] The speech foretold Bismarck's plans for
establishing military relations with South Germany as soon as the
North German Confederation was in a position to conclude treaties.[2]

In view of these developments, Benedetti sought to increase the
tempo of the negotiations in Berlin. The minister-president continued
to insist that he had been unable as yet to win the king's approval
of an alliance with France. He suggested that a definite manifestation of the wishes of the Luxemburg population would be a weapon
to combat William's opposition. Agreeing that the dissolution of
the Germanic Confederation made it difficult to maintain a legitimate
claim for a Prussian garrison in the duchy, he proposed that France
provoke the Dutch king into demanding the withdrawal of the Prussian troops. Nothing could prevent a cession of Luxemburg to France
by King William of Holland, and Bismarck indicated to Benedetti
that in such an event Prussia would withdraw her troops at once,
even before the French government made such a demand.[3] The
imperial government hoped that this Prussian attitude would contribute to the success of the negotiations opened in The Hague.[4]
Moustier wrote Benedetti that Baudin had been charged to propose
a treaty of alliance to Holland and to urge the king to demand the
withdrawal of the Prussian garrison. Efforts were also being made
in Luxemburg to create a favorable climate of opinion, and he informed the ambassador that petitions were being prepared demanding
the departure of the Prussian troops. Full of optimism, the foreign
minister asked Benedetti to insinuate that King William's trip to

---

[1] For the text of the king's address, see NORDDEUTSCHER BUND, *Stenographische Berichte
über die Verhandlungen des Reichstages des Norddeutschen Bundes im Jahre 1867* (Berlin,
1867), Vol. I (24 February–17 April 1867); cf. Benedetti to Moustier, Berlin, 2 March 1867,
FAE CP, Prusse/362, no. 45, in which he notes that the ambiguous wording of Article IV
might decide the Prussian government to exclude Austria from such consultation.

[2] Same to same, Berlin, 24 February 1867, *ibid.*, no. 40. On 23 February Bismarck had
asked Crown Prince Frederick to suggest to Prince Louis that he propose that Hesse
request admission to the North German Confederation (SCHÜSSLER, p. 93). The ambassador
was still unaware that alliances had been concluded in August 1866 with the south German
states. He noted, however, that Bismarck was displaying great activity among the members
of the *Bundestag* to convert as many deputies as possible to the support of his program
(Benedetti to Moustier, Berlin, 2 March 1867, FAE MD, Hollande/150).

[3] Moustier to Benedetti, Paris, 4 March 1867, *ibid.*, 149. The ambassador's own report
of the interview with Bismarck is not extant. Moustier summarized the analysis of the
ambassador relative to Bismarck's views and asked Benedetti to verify it in a subsequent
interview with the minister-president. Cf. Olimart to Blockhausen, The Hague, 5 March
1867, LAE, H/28. In his report to Goltz of 10 March, Bismarck complained that Moustier
and Benedetti were trying to commit him to a statement, for use to overcome Dutch hesitancy, indicating that Prussia would not object at all to the transfer of Luxemburg (GEUSS,
pp. 210–211).

[4] Cf. Baudin to Moustier, The Hague, 4 March 1867, FAE MD, Hollande/149.

Paris for the exhibition might become the occasion for consolidating the expected advance.[1] In a later interview with Benedetti, the minister-president confirmed his remarks which had precipitated Moustier's optimism, though adding that they were his personal views and that the Prussian government had not yet offered an official statement.[2]

Late in the evening of 8 March the ambassador was summoned to Paris, at the request of Madame de La Valette, wife of the Marquis de La Valette who was critically ill.[3] Before his departure next day, Benedetti had an interview with the minister-president during which he learned of the secret alliances Prussia had concluded with the south German states during the summer of 1866.[4] The ambassador had suspected their existence and, in view of the situation relative to Luxemburg, had decided to gain certainty on that point.[5] In spite of his protest that such accords were in contradiction with Article IV of the Prague Treaty,[6] Bismarck admitted to him that they had been concluded and that the mutual support of the German states was a matter of national necessity.[7]

Benedetti and his wife left Berlin in the evening of 9 March [8] and remained in Paris for ten days.[9] He learned from Moustier of the negotiations being carried on in The Hague: Baudin had found the Dutch cabinet disturbed by Bismarck's refusal to reach an agreement on Limburg and Luxemburg, and the presence of large contingents of Prussian troops on the Dutch border was viewed as an attempt to intimidate the Dutch government.[10] The envoy had reported that the prince of Orange had accepted the idea of ceding Luxemburg in return for a monetary compensation and a guarantee of Holland's territorial integrity. At the instigation of his mother, Queen Sophie, he had agreed to discuss the project with the king.[11] Rumors of a

---

[1] Moustier to Benedetti, Paris, 4 March 1867, *ibid.*, Allemagne/171.

[2] Benedetti to Moustier, Berlin, 8 March 1867, *ibid.*, Hollande/149.

[3] Moustier to Benedetti, Paris, 8 March 1867, FAE CP, Prusse/362, T.

[4] "I have had an interview with [Bismarck] of which it is preferable that I give you a verbal account" (Benedetti to Moustier, Berlin, 9 March 1867, *ibid.*); Moustier to Benedetti, Paris, 19 March 1867, *ibid.*, no. 55.

[5] Bismarck to Goltz, Berlin, 15 March 1867, *APP*, VIII, 474.

[6] Same to same, Berlin, 8 March 1867, *ibid.*, p. 448.

[7] Same to same, Berlin, 15 March 1867, *ibid.*, p. 474.

[8] Benedetti to Moustier, Berlin, 9 March 1867, FAE CP, Prusse/362, T. Cf. Nothomb to Rogier, Berlin, 10 March 1867, BAE CP, Prusse/24, no. 12.

[9] Goltz to Bismarck, Paris, 20 March 1867, *APP*, VIII, 491.

[10] Baudin to Moustier, The Hague, 4 March 1867, FAE MD, Hollande/149.

[11] Same to same, The Hague, 9 March 1867, *ibid.*; same to same, The Hague, 10 March 1867, *ibid.*

transaction were already circulating in Paris and had gained added credence with the arrival of Ambassador Benedetti from Berlin.[1] His alarming revelation of the German alliances, coupled with the evasiveness of Goltz's explanations,[2] decided Moustier to speed up the negotiations[3] and he requested the French envoy to propose an immediate cession of Luxemburg in The Hague.[4] The foreign minister was rather anxious to score a diplomatic success before the existence of the alliance treaties would be revealed and create added dissatisfaction in France. He followed up his request with new exhortations: "The incorporation of the grand duchy into France... is for us one of those necessities about which there can be no reasoning."[5] The diplomatic offensive gained headway when, on the day Benedetti left Paris, the envoy in The Hague reported that the king had accepted in principle the cession of Luxemburg, with the reservation that he would inform the Prussian government of his intentions before consumating the agreement.[6]

"The final crisis began at the very moment when Benedetti regained Berlin."[7] He learned not only that the Prussian government had published the text of its alliance treaties concluded in August 1866 with Baden and Bavaria,[8] but also that the status of Luxem-

---

[1] Goltz to Bismarck, Paris, 13 March 1867, *APP*, VIII, 468–469; Lowther to Stanley, Berlin, 16 March 1867, PRO FO 64/619, no. 6.

[2] Goltz to Bismarck, Paris, 11 March 1867, *APP*, VIII, 465–467.

[3] Moustier to Baudin, Paris, 12 March 1867, FAE MD, Hollande/149, T. Cf. J. HAMSTRA, *De Luxemburgsche Kwestie, 1867* (Groningen, 1927), p. 35.

[4] The indecision of the Dutch minister, the opposition of Prince Henry, and the fear of a violent reaction from the king had prevented Baudin from pressing the government (Baudin to Moustier, The Hague, 14 March 1867, FAE MD, Hollande/149, T.; same to same, The Hague, 15 March 1867, *ibid.*; *Exposé des négociations confidentielles qui ont eu lieu entre le gouvernement français et le cabinet de Berlin au sujet de Luxembourg*, Paris, 15 June 1867, *ibid.*, 150). Baron Tornaco, president of the Luxemburg government, reported that the Dutch king would probably demand assurances of adherence of the Prussian government before making a decision (Baudin to Moustier, The Hague, 16 March 1867, *ibid.*, T.). To the French envoy, Moustier noted: "Make him understand the *absolute* political importance which we henceforth attach to the possession of Luxemburg. He can, if he says yes, obtain for himself considerable claims for our obligation, [just] as he can, by a refusal, create for us, as for himself, a very treacherous position" (Moustier to Baudin, Paris, 16 March 1867, *ibid.*).

[5] Same to same, Paris, 17 March 1867, *ibid.*

[6] Baudin to Moustier, The Hague, 19 March 1867, *ibid.*

[7] PAGÈS, *RHM*, I, no. 6 (1926), 421.

[8] Lefèbvre de Béhaine to Moustier, Berlin, 19 March 1867, FAE CP, Prusse/362, T. The text of the treaty alliance with Württemberg was published on 23 March. It was on 24 March that the ambassador had an opportunity to question Bismarck about the reasons for making the alliances and for their publication at this time. The minister-president replied that they were published at the request of Hohenlohe. Contrary to the facts, he claimed that offers had been made to him during the peace negotiations, when he thought he could no longer count on the friendly disposition of the French cabinet, implying that the alliances had arisen more or less accidentally (Cf. BRANDENBURG, *Untersuchungen*, p. 720). To Benedetti's

burg, as German territory, had been brought up in the *Bundestag*.[1] These developments were at once known in The Hague, where fear of Bismarck and war led the Dutch king to demand that the signatory powers of the London Treaty of 1839 advise on the cession of Luxemburg to France.[2] When Benedetti conferred with Bismarck on this turn of events, he was told to do everything possible to prevent such an occurrence. King William could not possibly affirm that Prussia was in accord with France on a cession of Luxemburg. Benedetti stressed to Moustier the risk involved, and advised that "all we can concede [to the Dutch king], and I myself would regret it, is that Bismarck be interrogated... and not [William]." [3] But the Dutch king remained adamant and, on 23 March, the ambassador learned that he intended to send a letter to the king of Prussia stating that the proposed cession was in the interest of the peace of Europe and requesting assurance that the transaction would not indeed disturb the peace.[4] Benedetti completely opposed such a step and warned that the letter would place the Prussian monarch before the alternative of indicating prior and written consent or opposition – the outcome of such a *démarche* would certainly be adverse to French interest.[5] Nevertheless, on 26 March, the Dutch king wrote personally to the emperor of his communication to William.[6] Two days later Bismarck informed the ambassador that a letter had indeed been received, and that the Prussian monarch had replied

inquiries about offensive as well as defensive aspects of the alliances, Bismarck intimated that the German terms gave a different effect than the French translation on which the ambassador based his observations (Benedetti to Moustier, Berlin, 24 March 1867, FAE CP, Prusse/362, no. 62). Cf. Wimpffen to Beust, Berlin, 31 March 1867, HHStA, Preussen/95, no. 41A.

[1] Lefèbvre de Béhaine to Moustier, Berlin, 19 March 1867, FAE CP, Prusse/362, no. 56. Mr. Schraps, a deputy, called the attention of the *Bundestag* to the fact that Luxemburg, German territory, was not cited in Article I of the projected constitution. Bismarck, while not renouncing the view that the duchy belonged to Germany, replied that the government did not wish to do violence to the sovereign of Luxemburg, or to add another element to those which already menaced the peace of Europe. "[The minister-president's] remarks about Luxemburg [were] *oberfaul*. I fear very much that Luxemburg will be lost for Germany" (Bennigsen to his wife, 21 March 1867, H. ONCKEN, *Rudolf von Bennigsen, ein deutscher liberaler Politiker* [Stuttgart, 1910], II, 23).

[2] Moustier to Benedetti, Paris, 21 March 1867, FAE MD, Hollande/149, T. "*Le roi a malheureusement réfléchi*" (Baudin to Moustier, The Hague, 21 March 1867, *ibid.*).

[3] Benedetti to Moustier, Berlin, 22 March 1867, *ibid.*

[4] Moustier to Benedetti, Paris, 23 March 1867, *ibid.*

[5] Benedetti to Moustier, Berlin, 24 March 1867, *ibid.*, 150, T.

[6] William III to Napoleon III, [The Hague], 26 March 1867, *ibid.*, 149; Moustier to Benedetti, Paris, 27 March 1867, *ibid.*; Benedetti to Moustier, Berlin, 27 March 1867, *ibid.* On the same day, the Prussian minister in The Hague was summoned by the king and requested to inform King William of the proposal made by the French government (Perponcher to William I, The Hague, 26 March 1867, *APP*, VIII, 512–513).

that until he could ascertain the views of the signatories of the London Treaty, he would be unable to render any advice.[1]

With the formal entry of the Prussian government into the issue, the Luxemburg affair entered a decisive phase. Although the diplomatic steps had been taken in all secrecy, enough information had leaked out to arouse wide-spread interest. Benedetti warned Moustier that should Bismarck be again questioned on Luxemburg, he would find it exceedingly difficult to be evasive.[2] Meanwhile, the Paris cabinet had been sounding out the signatories of the treaty and found that both England and Austria were disposed to support the French aspirations.[3] The foreign minister wrote that Baudin had reached an agreement in The Hague concerning the monetary compensation and was to present a letter from the emperor urging the Dutch king to sign.[4] Moustier outlined to Benedetti a superficial time schedule for the Prussian evacuation and the entrance of the French garrison into Luxemburg.[5]

The stage seemed set for the consummation of the negotiations. Yet, late on Saturday evening, a dispatch reached Moustier from Mahon that the Luxemburg government had been authorized to refute in the most formal manner all assertions that the grand duchy had been ceded to France.[6] On Sunday, 31 March, Benedetti reported that Bismarck was *fort ému* by the agitation provoked in Germany over the Luxemburg affair and that the National Liberal party had notified him of its intention to interpellate him in the Monday session.[7]

---

[1] Benedetti to Moustier, Berlin, 28 March 1867, FAE MD, Hollande/149, T.

[2] Same to same, Berlin, 26 March 1867, *ibid.*, 150, T. Cf. La Tour d'Auvergne to Moustier, London, 24 March 1867, FAE CP, Angleterre/739, no. 58; Mahon to La Valette, Eich, 25 March 1867, FAE CC, Pays-Bas, Eich-Luxemburg/6, no. 136.

[3] Moustier to Benedetti, Paris, 28 March 1867, FAE MD, Hollande/149, T., 1 p.m.; same to same, Paris, 28 March 1867, *ibid.*, 4 p.m.

[4] Napoleon III to William III, Tuileries, 30 March 1867, *ibid.*; Moustier telegraphed the *chargé d'affaires* to have Tornaco come to The Hague without delay (Moustier to Villestreux, Paris, 30 March 1867, *ibid.*).

[5] Moustier to Benedetti, Paris, 29 March 1867, *ibid.*

[6] Mahon to Moustier, Luxemburg, 30 March 1867, FAE CC, Pays-Bas, Eich-Luxemburg/6, T. The statement appeared in a government paper, *L'Union*, and was also distributed in printed hand bills. Cf. Prince Henry to Tornaco, The Hague, 30 March 1867, LAE, H/28.

[7] Benedetti to Moustier, Berlin, 31 March 1867, FAE MD, Hollande/150, T., 5 p.m.; Bismarck had suggested that the negotiations be postponed, to which Benedetti replied that it would be easier for the king to accept the union of Luxemburg and France than for the emperor to renounce it (Bismarck to Goltz, Berlin, 30 March 1867, *APP*, VIII, 532). The ambassador thought Bismarck's difficulty stemmed from the opposition of the military, the princes who supported them, and from the determination of the French government not to demolish the fortress once it gained possession (cf. Bylandt to Zuylen, Berlin, 29 January 1867, RBZ, Pruisen/1867, no. 47). Goltz suggested to Moustier that the negotiations be suspended, to which the foreign minister replied that everything was finished and nothing

Explanations were to be demanded on two points: 1. Whether or not the government had been informed of the negotiations opened between France and Holland? 2. Whether the king of Prussia was prepared to unite with his confederates to maintain, at all cost, the ties which united Luxemburg to Germany, and notably the right to a war garrison? [1] The minister-president indicated to Benedetti that he expected to reply to the first in the affirmative and, if pressed, to add that the king would consult with his allies and the other signatories of the London Treaty. The second question he planned to leave unanswered, observing that the government could not, under any circumstances, use the phrases of the interpellation. [2]

On the day of the interpellation, Monday, 1 April, the ambassador received a telegram from Moustier, stating that the Dutch king was committed to France and that the Prussian government was faced with a *fait accompli*. [3] Benedetti met Bismarck at the moment he

---

could make the French government pull back, whatever the consequences (Moustier to Benedetti, Paris, 31 March 1867, FAE MD, Hollande/149, T.; Goltz to Bismarck, Paris, 31 March 1867, *APP*, VIII, 545–546). Cf. Same to same, Paris, 30 March 1867, *ibid.*, pp. 532–533, in which Goltz states that Benedetti and Moustier had brought about the situation in order to have a war, as the sole means of saving the dynasty.

[1] The motivation for the interpellation originated in the *Nationalverein*, an association of nationalists and liberals who strongly opposed the cession of Luxemburg on grounds that the grand duchy was dominated by a German culture and was pro-German in sentiment. The *Nationalverein* had sent two observers to Luxemburg, one of whom was August Döring, later professor of philosophy at the University of Berlin. Their reports, published in the *Elberfelder Zeitung*, stressed the German aspect of the life and culture of the grand duchy (P. WENTZCKE, "Zur Luxemburger Frage von 1867," *Deutsche Rundschau*, CXCIII [December 1922], 227–229).

[2] Benedetti to Moustier, Berlin, 31 March 1867, FAE MD, Hollande/149, T., 11:49 p.m. There is conclusive evidence that Bismarck welcomed the interpellation. In a letter to his wife, Bennigsen reveals that Bismarck did not want Luxemburg to fall into French hands, a desire shared certainly by the king, the generals, and the princes. On the 30th, Bennigsen had a visit from Prince Frederick Charles, who seconded his determination to propose the interpellation. He discussed the situation on the same day with the minister-president, and his impression that Bismarck was "gladly letting himself be pushed" was confirmed in conversation with the conservatives with whom, especially Roon, he discussed his intentions on the 31st, and who agreed to support him. The crown prince as well had intimated his support, in the hope that a war might be avoided (Bennigsen to his wife, Berlin, 1 April 1867, ONCKEN, *Bennigsen*, II, 33–34). "I am certain that the National Liberals – through Bennigsen – have also conferred with Bismarck and that [he] welcomes the interpellation. Undoubtedly he wants to be able to say to Benedetti, 'You see what the situation is, what the prevailing sentiment is; I can do nothing, even if I wanted to!'" (BERNHARDI, pp. 352–353). See POSCHINGER, *Fürst Bismarck und die Parlamentarier*, II, 98, for conversations between the minister-president and the National Liberals in which he expressed the fear that French insistence on obtaining Luxemburg would lead to war.

[3] Moustier to Benedetti, Paris, 31 March 1867, FAE MD, Hollande/ 149, T., 11 p.m.; *Exposé des négociations confidentielles qui ont eu lieu entre le gouvernement français et le cabinet de Berlin au sujet de Luxembourg*, Paris, 15 June 1867, FAE MD, Hollande/150. According to the facts, Moustier had little justification to speak of a completed cession. His intent was undoubtedly to give Bismarck the opportunity to reply to the interpellation that

was leaving for the *Bundestag* building. After offering his birthday congratulations, the ambassador attempted to inform him of Moustier's communication. The minister-president told him that he was on his way to reply to the interpellation which Bennigsen intended to introduce at the opening of the session. He invited the ambassador to accompany him there and told him that, if he were forced to concede that Prussia faced a *fait accompli*, the consequences would be fatal. After arriving at the *Bundestag* building, Bismarck asked Benedetti if he wished to make a communication in view of the existing situation. The ambassador's reply was in the negative, and the two separated.[1] While it is possible that Benedetti decided, in the light of Bismarck's speculations of the consequences, not to communicate officially the foreign minister's telegram, he did write Moustier that the minister-president had declined his suggestion to state in the *Bundestag* that the cession had indeed been accomplished.[2]

The demand for explanations from the government, signed by more than seventy deputies,[3] was designed to establish the fact that no difference of opinion existed between the chamber and the government on matters of German national honor and territorial integrity. Bismarck replied immediately after Bennigsen's speech in the manner which he had previously outlined to the ambassador and in guarded language assured the *Bundestag* that no one sought to deprive Germany of her proven rights and that it would be possible to maintain the peace. "The royal government, in agreement with its allies, would watch over the interest of the nation." [4]

Although the reply implied opposition to a cession of Luxemburg, it was not at all certain that it would effect Napoleon's retreat. In a discussion with Nothomb, Benedetti rejected the Belgian am-

Prussia had not been informed in time to oppose the transaction. The foreign minister did expect the completion of the negotiations on 2 April, since Baudin foresaw no difficulties (Baudin to Moustier, The Hague, 31 March 1867, *ibid.*, 149, T., 6:20 p.m.). Moreover, Moustier stated that the cession had been considered a *fait accompli* even before the Dutch king had entered into contact with the Prussian monarch (Moustier to Benedetti, Paris, 1 April 1867, *ibid.*).

[1] Cf. KEUDELL, pp. 356–357, who implies that Benedetti did not communicate Moustier's telegram.

[2] "Bismarck has declined my suggestion to declare to the chamber that the cession was an accomplished fact, fearing that the question of war or peace would escape his control; these are his expressions" (Benedetti to Moustier, Berlin, 1 April 1867, FAE MD, Hollande/149, T., 10:42 p.m.).

[3] For the Bennigsen-Bismarck exchange, see NORDDEUTSCHER BUND, *Stenographische Berichte*, Vol. I (1 April 1867), pp. 487–489.

[4] Benedetti to Moustier, Berlin, 1 April 1867, FAE CP, Prusse/363, no. 65. Questions on the status of the grand duchy of Luxemburg were also asked in the British House of Commons on 1 and 2 April (GREAT BRITAIN, 3 Hansard, CLXXXVI [1867], 909, 981).

bassador's remark that the emperor would withdraw rather than compromise the world exposition.[1] Bismarck himself had not intended his reply as an overt threat to France, but certainly hoped that it would end French efforts to acquire the fortress.[2] Yet there were no signs pointing to a French withdrawal. In the afternoon of 1 April, Moustier telegraphed Benedetti that Baron Tornaco had been called to The Hague to sign the act ceding Luxemburg to France.[3] As for Prussian opposition, he stated that steps were being taken to assure France of Russian influence for calming military passions in Berlin.[4]

While the French government retained its attitude of determination, Ambassador Benedetti found it necessary to refute Bismarck's allegations that the imperial government had created its own difficulties. The ambassador insisted that far from advising (until the eve of the interpellation) a postponement of the impending treaty until after the sessions of the North German *Bundestag*, the minister-president had, on the contrary, constantly urged the conclusion of the negotiations and had suggested that overtures be made at The Hague. Benedetti reminded him of his request that Prussia be left out of the matter, and he pointed out that it was the Dutch king who had informed the Berlin cabinet of the pending transaction. The ambassador believed that Bismarck's concern with public opinion was but one facet of his problem: he was beset by far greater difficulty, namely, the attitude of the military circle in Prussia. "He repeated several times that it would be impossible for Prussia to lower her flag in Luxemburg at a summons from France. He had never spoken in such language to me." [5]

---

[1] Nothomb to Rogier, Berlin, 2 April 1867, BAE CP, Question du Grand-Duché de Luxembourg/1, Pt. II, no. 127.

[2] KEUDELL, p. 441; POSCHINGER, *Fürst Bismarck und die Parlamentarier*, III, 285.

[3] "King Grand-Duke requests your prompt presence here. Affair is serious, imperial reply has come" (Prince Henry to Tornaco, The Hague, 1 April 1867, LAE H/28, T.).

[4] Moustier to Benedetti, Paris, 1 April 1867, FAE MD, Hollande/150, T. Cf. E. SERVAIS, *Le Grand-Duché de Luxembourg et le traité de Londres de 11 Mai 1867* (Paris, 1879), pp. 109–110, who discusses the arrival of an agent from the French ministry of the interior to prepare the execution of the treaty of cession. Goltz, too, discovered that the emperor was reluctant to forego the acquisition of Luxemburg (Goltz to Bismarck, Paris, 2 April 1867, *APP*, VIII, 569). Cf. R. BLENNERHASSET, "The Origin of the Franco-Prussian War of 1870," *The National Review*, XL (October 1902), pp. 220–221.

[5] Benedetti to Moustier, Berlin, 2 April 1867, FAE MD, Hollande/150. Cf. ONCKEN, *Rheinpolitik*, II, 275, ft. 1. The ambassador continued to believe that Bismarck had given his advice to open negotiations with the Dutch king in good faith. "Benedetti always remained convinced, he repeated it to me to the end of his life, that Bismarck had been perfectly loyal in this Luxemburg question and that our failure was due not to his duplicity, but to the indolent slowness of Moustier and to the pusillaminous indiscretion of the king of Holland" (OLLIVIER, IX, 336). But Bismarck's conversations with the deputies imply just the

To a telegram from Moustier of 3 April, that the emperor would continue efforts to obtain Luxemburg,[1] Benedetti replied that it would be advisable to obtain the signature of the Dutch king to the treaty, in case the question were to be referred to an international congress. He made it clear that, in his opinion, Prussia would not recognize a cession and would no doubt refuse to withdraw her garrison. In view of this, he cautioned that the imperial government would have to act as though war were inevitable. "Are we ready to undertake [war] and is it expedient for us to have recourse to it, or is it preferable to look first for a pacific solution through diplomatic expedients? This is, in my opinion, the real question which is posed in this moment for the meditation of the emperor's government." [2]

Although the French government had continued to show a determined attitude, the same was not true of the Dutch cabinet. Benedetti learned that the Prussian minister in The Hague had declared that Prussia would regard the cession of Luxemburg as a "cause for war." [3] To this unequivocal statement Zuylen had replied that a cession had not yet been signed and that a threat of war left no doubt of the king's decision. He had then instructed the Dutch envoy in Berlin to tell Bismarck that the government of Holland had never considered proceeding without Prussia's adherence or concluding a convention which would threaten the peace.[4] With the victory at The Hague, Bismarck had forced the decision for war or peace on the French government, a development Benedetti had already predicted earlier in the day.[5]

---

opposite (H. V. VON UNRUH, *Erinnerungen aus dem Leben von Hans Viktor von Unruh*, ed. H. von Poschinger [Stuttgart 1895], p. 281; Bennigsen to his wife, Berlin, 10 April 1867, ONCKEN, *Bennigsen*, II, 61; ft. 2, p. 161 above).

[1] Moustier to Benedetti, Paris, 3 April 1867, FAE MD, Hollande/ 149, T.

[2] Benedetti to Moustier, Berlin, 3 April 1867, *ibid.* He added that further opposition to a cession could be expected from the North German parliament, and that the discussion on the organization of the army would probably show a solidarity of views designed to emphasize the position taken in respect to the Luxemburg affair. For the reaction of French public opinion, see CASE, pp. 231–232.

[3] Moustier to Benedetti, Paris, 3 April 1867, FAE MD, Hollande/149, T.

[4] *Ibid.*; cf. Zuylen to Bylandt, The Hague, 3 April 1867, ONCKEN, *Rheinpolitik*, II, 280 ft. 1; Baudin to Moustier, The Hague, 4 April 1867, FAE MD, Hollande/149.

[5] Benedetti to Moustier, Berlin, 3 April 1867, *ibid.*, T. Moustier's position was more difficult because of the unpredictable course of the Prussian government. On the 3rd, Goltz had remitted a letter to Napoleon from King William, proposing an adjournment of the negotiations or, if a treaty of cession had been signed, that the affair be kept secret until after the legislative session. Moustier pointed out that the declaration made at The Hague could hardly be reconciled with the royal letter. Furthermore, a report had been received from St. Petersburg indicating that Bismarck had announced there that the Dutch king had decided not to cede Luxemburg (Moustier to Benedetti, Paris, 5 April 1867, *ibid.*, 150).

Believing that Prussia would do everything to prevent France's acquisition of Luxemburg, the ambassador emphasized the necessity of leaving none of the powers in doubt that France would not yield in case Prussia threatened war.[1] In a conversation with Wimpffen on 7 April, Benedetti was still confident that the emperor would not retreat from his position; unless the Prussian government modified its stand, he remarked, war would be the most probable result.[2] As for calling an international congress to settle the issue, he believed France should attend only if she were permitted to continue arming while the deliberations were in progress. Warming perhaps to the prospect of a victorious war, and Benedetti admitted no other outcome, he told Wimpffen that France might give Austria an opportunity to redress the defeat of Sadowa. He was convinced that France could vanquish Prussia, and an armed neutrality on the part of Austria would suffice to make the outcome he predicted an absolute certainty. He conceded that in two years Germany would present a formidable military power and preferred that such a development should be forestalled.[3]

The day after his conversation with the Austrian ambassador, Benedetti regrettably learned that the imperial government had indeed been forced to retreat. Although the indication that the Dutch monarch was ready to yield to Prussian pressure had brought forth French claims that there existed a moral engagement between the emperor and the king,[4] Moustier hastened to assert that France had never expected to annex Luxemburg without the consent of its ruler and his subjects. Nor had France ever ignored the consequences the cession might have upon her relations with Prussia and upon the peace of Europe. The imperial government had always considered the acquisition of the duchy as a means to strengthen the peace and improve relations with Prussia; indeed Bismarck had spared nothing

---

[1] Benedetti to Moustier, Berlin, 6 April 1867, *ibid.*

[2] Cf. Loë to Tresckow, Paris, 5 April 1867, *APP*, VIII, 597–598.

[3] Wimpffen to Beust, Berlin, 8 April 1867, HHStA, Preussen/ 95, no. 45B. Benedetti also displayed some bitterness about his treatment at Bismarck's hands during the past year. "His exasperation with Count Bismarck and with the king and the way he believes himself to have been fooled knows no limit anymore" (*ibid.*). Cf. Benedetti to Moustier, Berlin, 6 April 1867, FAE MD, Hollande/150, in which he stressed that time would permit Prussia to weld the forces of Germany into a powerful foe, a project which was then in its infancy; cf. same to same, Berlin, 6 April 1867, FAE CP, Prusse/363, no. 72, in which Benedetti discussed the military legislation passed in the current session of the North German *Bundestag*.

[4] Moustier to Benedetti, Paris, 5 April 1867, FAE MD, Hollande/150. Cf. Goltz to Bismarck, Paris, 5 April 1867, ONCKEN, *Rheinpolitik*, II, 286.

to nourish such an illusion.[1] The attitude of moderation would be maintained by the French government and the door would be left open to all "the good inspirations" of the Berlin cabinet. Finally, Moustier expressed the pious hope that the powers would realize the importance of not leaving France unsatisfied, but he feared the issue would end simply with the dismantlement of the fortress. As for the negotiations with Holland, the minister wrote that the Dutch king's engagement toward France could only be ended by the imperial cabinet. However, no further steps at The Hague were contemplated for the present, and the entire question was to be left unresolved.[2]

Benedetti, acknowledging Moustier's excursion into hypocrisy, made no reference to his strong feeling that France should have insisted on her claims even to the possibility of war. He asserted his intention of maintaining a circumspect attitude toward the minister-president in order to forestall any additional difficulties. Although he refrained from references to the military situation in Germany,[3] he did inform Moustier that public sentiment was still much agitated and that the press continued to insist that war was preferable to a cession of Luxemburg.[4] He reported that the declaration of Moustier of 8 April in the chambers [5] had been favorably received and had been interpreted as an invitation to the powers to decide the issue.[6] Although Benedetti strictly avoided Bismarck,[7]

---

[1] "I trusted Bismarck [and] he has betrayed me," remarked Napoleon to Pierre Magne on 5 April (DURIEUX, II, 90).

[2] Moustier to Benedetti, Paris, 6 April 1867, FAE MD, Hollande/150.

[3] That he had given much thought to this was evidenced by his report of 6 April and in his conversation with Wimpffen.

[4] Benedetti to Moustier, Berlin, 9 April 1867, FAE MD, Hollande/150. Cf. ROTHAN, Souvenirs diplomatiques, pp. 273–274.

[5] Many demands for interpellations had already been deposited before the session of 8 April when Moustier presented his exposé. The minister represented the Luxemburg affair as having arisen when France and Holland entered into a general discussion on the unresolved status of Limburg and Luxemburg after the dissolution of the Germanic Confederation. No reference was made to the compensation negotiations between Benedetti and Bismarck. Prussia had entered the affair only when the Dutch king had asked for the views of the Prussian monarch, who then invoked the stipulations of the treaty of 1839. To the demands of the critics, Thiers, Favre, Garnier-Pagès, and others, to see the diplomatic correspondence, Rouher replied that no official correspondence existed since the question had not progressed beyond "a simple exchange of *pourparlers*" (FRANCE. CORPS LÉGISLATIF, *Annales*, 1867, XXI, t. 3 [8 April], pp. 237–240). A debate on the policy of the government was avoided when a number of interpellations were withdrawn and all nine bureaus of the chambers turned down the others (*ibid.*, t. 4 [10 April], p. 1). Cf. DURIEUX, II, 95–96, for the discussions between Magne, La Valette, and Rouher on 9 April, whether the government should accept the interpellations.

[6] Benedetti to Moustier, Berlin, 11 April 1867, FAE CP, Prusse/363, no. 81.

[7] Moustier to Benedetti, Paris, 11 April 1867, *ibid.*, T.; Benedetti to Moustier, Berlin, 11 April 1867, *ibid.* The official reserve of Benedetti did not prevent Bismarck's charge that

he neither hid from Wimpffen his bitterness and disappointment with the course of events, [1] nor ceased to consider that war might occur.[2]

Efforts were being made, however, to bring the Luxemburg crisis to a peaceful *dénouement*. Benedetti was informed of the various schemes proposed by the French and Russian ambassadors in London,[3] as well as propositions made by Austria for a pacific solution.[4] In reporting the various proposals to the ambassador, Moustier did not state whether the French government would prefer a neutralization of the duchy or its annexation to Belgium with compensation to France; he indicated that "our *unique* object [is] the exit of the Prussians from Luxemburg." [5] Benedetti was also able to gain considerable information of the impending solution from his colleagues. The British ambassador, Lord Loftus, had opened discussions of the problem with the minister-president [6] but Bismarck's precipitate departure

---

the ambassador was engaging in talk with other representatives which was designed to intimidate the Prussian government (Bismarck to Goltz, Berlin, 11 April 1867, ONCKEN, *Rheinpolitik*, II, 317–318). Cf. Moustier to Benedetti, Paris, 15 April 1867, FAE MD, Hollande/149, T.; Metternich to Beust, Paris, 18 April 1867, ONCKEN, *Rheinpolitik*, II, 338; Benedetti to Moustier, Berlin, 16 April 1867, FAE CP, Prusse/363, no. 87.

[1] Wimpffen to Beust, Berlin, 14 April 1867, HHStA, Preussen/95, no. 49. He wrote that Benedetti had shown such a display of vindictive temper that it was embarrassing to his friends.

[2] Benedetti to Moustier, Berlin, 13 April 1867, FAE CP, Prusse/363, no. 86; cf. same to same, Berlin, 16 April 1867, *ibid.*, no. 88, in which the ambassador reported that the Prussian government was asking the other German states what attitude they would assume in case of a war against France. "The Prussian envoy Wentzel [on 14 April] read a circular of his government to me, in which the explanation is requested,whether or not we were prepared to stand on the side of Prussia if the Luxemburg question becomes a cause for war" (DALWIGK, p. 321).

[3] Benedetti to Moustier, Berlin, 16 April 1867, FAE CP, Prusse/363, no. 87; cf. La Tour d'Auvergne to Moustier, London, 11 April 1867, *ibid.*, Angleterre/740, no. 78; *ibid.*, Annex; Moustier to La Tour d'Auvergne, Paris, 12 April 1867, FAE MD, Hollande/149, T. "The project which you have sent to me would be accepted by us if all the powers agreed to propose and recommend it to us, with the adherence of the king of Holland and the king of the Belgians. We would not want it to be thought that we invite such advice" [This was the project to unite Luxemburg to Belgium, give France territory along the Belgian border, and provide financial compensation for the Dutch king] (Moustier to La Tour d'Auvergne, Paris, 13 April 1867, FAE CP, Angleterre/740, T.).

[4] Beust to Wimpffen, Vienna, 9 April 1867, AUSTRIA. MINISTERIUM DES ÄUSSEREN, *Austrian Red Book: Diplomatic Correspondence . . . from November 1866 to 31 December 1867*, no. 1 (London, 1868), p. 47. The features of the Austrian proposals were almost identical with that outlined in London by the French and Russian ambassadors, but added another alternative: the neutralization of the duchy and the dismantlement of the fortress. Cf. *Aufzeichnung Bismarcks über eine Unterredung mit Wimpffen*, 12 April 1867, ONCKEN, *Rheinpolitik*, II, 315–317.

[5] Moustier to Benedetti, Paris, 18 April 1867, FAE CP, Prusse/363, T.

[6] Cf. Benedetti to Moustier, Berlin, 16 April 1867, *ibid.*, no. 89, in which the ambassador wrote that Loftus had found Bismarck not enthusiastic but willing to consider the idea of a congress. Same to same, Berlin, 21 April 1867, FAE MD, Hollande/150.

for the country ended them abruptly.[1] Ambassador Benedetti, in his official capacity, welcomed the efforts of the powers to solve the Luxemburg question and eliminate the threat of war which had been hanging over Europe since the early days of April. His private opinion, however, showed a distinctly bellicose tone, as revealed in remarks to Wimpffen:

> I maintain my opinion that if [Austria] were with us, we would, in six days, effect a junction in South Germany and in six weeks we would have reduced Prussia to a smaller power than she was before the last war and would dictate the peace in Berlin. They are more quickly ready than we, but I assure you we will be [ready] too and sooner than they think. To be sure, I want peace; but believe me that if war does not come in two months from now, we shall have missed a unique occasion which might never again present itself. Today one can still benefit from the state of affairs in South Germany; in a year or two Prussia will be so strong that war between us will perhaps become impossible.[2]

These views were not merely those of a diplomat who desired revenge for the way his endeavors had been frustrated time after time; they

---

[1] Benedetti to Moustier, Berlin, 22 April 1867, FAE CP, Prusse/363, no. 100. Bismarck's departure had given rise to a multitude of conjectures, among them rumors of a dispute between the king and his minister. Upon receipt of this information, Moustier immediately requested Benedetti to find out if Bismarck had perhaps gone to Pomerania for a meeting with Prince Gorchakov for the purpose of concluding an alliance with Russia (Moustier to Benedetti, Paris, 23 April 1867, *ibid.*, T.).

[2] Wimpffen to Beust, Berlin, 20 April 1867, HHStA, Preussen/95, no. 54B. But unbeknownst to the ambassador, Prussia had begun as early as 2 April to promote an Austro-Prussian-Bavarian alliance against France (Bismarck to Werthern, Berlin, 2 April 1867, HOHENLOHE, I, 222). Julius Fröbel, a south German publicist, made inquiries in Vienna on 4 April and reported Beust reserved, but not definitely opposed to the proposal (HOHENLOHE, I, 224–225). Montgelas sought to verify in Berlin Hohenlohe's opinion that a triple alliance was indeed possible (cf. Benedetti to Moustier, 11 April 1867, FAE CP, Prusse/363, no. 81, in which he concluded that Montgelas had sought to confirm rumors that the Prussian government was relenting in its intransigent attitude in the Luxemburg affair, in the hope that Bavaria might not have to carry out her alliance obligations). Count Tauffkirchen arrived in Berlin and conferred with Bismarck on 13 April concerning proposals which Hohenlohe had submitted to King Louis on 10 April, and which had been approved by the Bavarian monarch (HOHENLOHE, I, 228–229). The pact was to be applicable generally or else restricted to the Luxemburg affair; Tauffkirchen was to ascertain the obstacles to a triple *entente*, eliminate them and conclude the alliance (K. MÜLLER, "Die Tauffkirchensche Mission nach Berlin und Wien: Bayern, Deutschland, und Österreich im Frühjahr 1867," *Rietzler-Festschrift: Beiträge zur bayerischen Geschichte* [Gotha, 1913], pp. 381–435). Having met with King William and believing the discussion in Berlin very encouraging, he left for Vienna. The talks with Beust, however, spelled defeat for the Bavarian endeavors. An implacable foe of Bismarck and Prussia, Beust speculated: "Picturing to our minds France as vanquished, can we expose ourselves to the chance of having the parchment on which the Treaty of Prague is recorded thrust into our hands and being thanked for its successful defense?" (Beust to Wimpffen, Vienna, 19 April 1867, AUSTRIA. MINISTERIUM DES ÄUSSEREN, p. 89. Cf. F. BEUST, *Aus drei Viertel-jahrhunderten. Erinnerungen und Aufzeichnungen, 1809–1885* [Stuttgart, 1887], II, 119–120). Benedetti reported that the reception Beust gave Tauffkirchen did not allow him to insist on the object of his mission (Benedetti to Moustier, Berlin, 22 April 1867, FAE CP, Prusse/363, no. 101.

were those of a realist who considered a clash between France and Prussia inevitable.

While the imperial government was showing itself amenable to a settlement of the issue by the powers convoked in congress, the attitude of the Prussian cabinet was still an uncertain factor.[1] The wedding of Princess Marie of Hohenzollern-Sigmaringen to Philip, count of Flanders and son of the Belgian king, on 25 April, brought to Berlin a great number of foreign dignitaries [2] and provided the occasion for mutual assurances of good will. On the morning of the wedding, King Leopold sent Jules Devaux, a member of his entourage, to tell Benedetti that the dispositions he found in Berlin could be reconciled with those of the imperial government.[3] Meetings with members of the royal family and with Bismarck, who had returned to Berlin for the festivities, had led Leopold to believe that the issue could be resolved in a manner acceptable to both parties.[4] Loftus had communicated a personal appeal from Queen Victoria [5] to King Wil-

---

[1] Cf. Moustier to Benedetti, Paris, 18 April 1867, *ibid.*, T., no. 82; Goltz to Bismarck, Paris, 19 April 1867, ONCKEN, *Rheinpolitik*, II, 340-343; Benedetti to Moustier, Berlin, 22 April 1867, FAE CP, Prusse/363, no. 100; Moustier to Benedetti, Paris, 21 April 1867, *ibid.*, no. 84.

[2] K. ZINGLER, *Karl Anton, Fürst von Hohenzollern* (Stuttgart, 1911), p. 201. "The Belgian minister in Berlin, Baron Nothomb, having detected that there was trading about Belgium, got the idea to connect [Belgium] to the royal house of Prussia. He negotiated the marriage of a daughter of Anton of Hohenzollern... with the Count of Flanders. Queen Victoria supported the project, and King William, whose consent was indispensable, gave it with haste. It was a *noli tangere*, a prohibition to touch Belgium.... Rouher and Moustier abandoned thus the Belgian dream and dreamed only about Luxemburg" (OLLIVIER, IX, 168).

[3] Benedetti to Moustier, Berlin, 25 April 1867, FAE MD, Hollande/150, T. "I gained the conviction, through my conversation with Benedetti, that whatever the thought of his government, he personally desires war because of resentment for his diplomatic defeats. It is a real misfortune for a chief of state to be served in such fashion as that by his agent" (Jules Devaux to Beyens, Brussels, 29 April 1867, BEYENS, II, 334). King Leopold's communication had been prompted by rumors that the Luxemburg question would be discussed in the French chamber. A demand for an interpellation was made by Favre on the 25th, but was turned down by the bureaus on the 27th, after a dispatch from Rouher to Schneider on the 26th, suggesting that the question not be discussed (FRANCE. CORPS LÉGISLATIF, XXI, t. 4, [25-27 April 1867] pp. 155-156, 178).

[4] Benedetti to Moustier, Berlin, 25 April 1867, FAE CP, Prusse/363, no. 107. "Although [King Leopold of Belgium], with great prudence and judgment abstained from any direct interference in the Luxemburg question during his stay in Berlin, I have reason to think that his visit here has been at this moment of great utility... in regard to the question of peace or war" (Loftus to Stanley, Berlin, 27 April 1867, PRO FO 64/620, no. 242).

[5] Victoria to William I, [Windsor Castle,] 22 April 1867, ONCKEN, *Rheinpolitik*, II, 351, ft. 1. "My visit here has tumbled me in to the midst of the Luxemburg business, and I have had all the dispatches, and all the private letters of all the cousins submitted to me.... At present it seems that pressure should... be put upon Berlin (Disraeli to Stanley, Windsor Castle, 22 April 1867, G. BUCKLE, *The Life of Benjamin Disraeli, earl of Beaconsfield* [London, 1916-1920], IV, 470). Cf. Goltz to Bismarck, 23 April 1867, ONCKEN, *Rheinpolitik*, II, 350-351.

liam and had confided to Benedetti more precise information as a result of his conversation with Bismarck. A conference was to be called in London, at the request of the Dutch king, to settle the status of Luxemburg. No *préalable* agreements were to be made, in order that concessions might be made to Europe and not to any one of the powers.[1] Similar assurances of a peaceful outcome had been given by King William during the wedding reception.[2] Remarks by some of the princes to Benedetti, that the Prussian government sincerely desired a pacific settlement of the crisis, seemed to be borne out by the fact that on the following day, 26 April, the Prussian press showed a much more conciliatory tone.[3]

Conversations with the British and Russian ambassadors gave Benedetti an opportunity to become thoroughly acquainted with the intentions of the Prussian government. The consultations of Loftus and Oubril with Bismarck made it apparent that the Berlin cabinet would agree to the evacuation of the Luxemburg fortress. Prussia had accepted a conference and only the procedure for convoking it had not been definitely settled upon: the St. Petersburg government preferred that Austria, Britain, and Russia, rather than the Dutch king, issue the invitations to the powers.[4] This minor problem was resolved when the Russian government deferred to British wishes inviting the king of Holland, in his role of grand duke of Luxemburg,[5] to take the initia-

[1] Benedetti to Moustier, Berlin, 26 April 1867, FAE CP, Prusse/363, T.; "Prussia was disposed to accept any honorable terms of arrangement. The first thing was to find a motive for a conference, and [Bismarck] thought, therefore, that Holland should apply to the European powers in regard to the position of the Grand Duchy, and, on her invitation, a conference should be proposed.... It would be impossible for Prussia to make any concessions previous to a conference which might be viewed or interpreted as concessions to France" (Loftus to Stanley, Berlin, 27 April 1867, PRO FO 64/620, no. 238). Cf. Bismarck to Goltz, Berlin, 27 April 1867, ONCKEN, *Rheinpolitik*, II, 370–371.

[2] Loftus to Stanley, Berlin, 27 April 1867, PRO FO 64/620, no. 237. Cf. William I to Grand Duke Charles-Alexander, Berlin, 28 April 1867, WILHELM I., *Weimarer Briefe*, "Die Briefe Kaiser Wilhelms I.," ed. J. Schultze (Berlin, 1924), II, 88–89, in which he states his surprise that the king of Holland had delayed so long calling a conference of the signatory powers of the 1839 treaty, and which he believed would settle the issue. Cf. L. SCHNEIDER, *Aus dem Leben Wilhelms I., 1849–73* (Berlin, 1888), I, 306, for the peaceable attitude of the monarch.

[2] Benedetti to Moustier, Berlin, 26 April 1867, FAE CP, Prusse/363, no. 109; same to same, Berlin, 27 April 1867, *ibid.*, T. Moustier had complained about the bellicose language of the Berlin press (Moustier to Benedetti, Paris, 25 April 1867, FAE MD, Hollande/150, T.). For precautionary military measures decided upon by the Prussian government on 27 April 1867, see I.A.A.b. 27.

[4] Benedetti to Moustier, Berlin, 26 April 1867, FAE CP, Prusse/363, no. 111; same to same, Berlin, 27 April 1867, *ibid.*, T.; *ibid.*, no. 113.

[5] Ever since the beginning of the controversy, the Dutch government had carefully stated that the Dutch and the Luxemburg governments were separate and distinct organs of state (Tornaco to Prince Henry, Luxemburg, 7 April 1867, LAE, L/5).

tive in calling the conference [1] and fixing 7 May as the opening day.[2]

The prospect of a settlement of the Luxemburg question ended the reserve which Ambassador Benedetti had maintained toward the minister-president since the first days of April. The two re-established contact at a reception at the Russian legation on 30 April.[3] Bismarck had the "visible intention" of engaging Benedetti in conversation and, seizing the occasion, assured him of his satisfaction with the course the Luxemburg affair was taking. The ambassador did not reciprocate Bismarck's cordiality and merely remarked that the maintenance of peace had only depended on Prussia.[4]

The proximity of the conference did not induce the Berlin press to give up recurring demands that Prussia refuse to evacuate the fortress short of certain unspecified guarantees.[5] The fear of a last-minute development which might jeopardize the outcome of the conference created a certain amount of tension which increased as the opening day neared. Such tension did not affect the second interview between Bismarck and Benedetti on 4 May, although the conversation dealt with problems directly affecting the conference. The ambassador felt that the minister-president made every effort to display a conciliatory attitude and to show himself agreeable.[6] Bismarck was impatient with Lord Stanley's indecision concerning invitations to Belgium and Italy and the drafting of a treaty project prior to the conference; he thought such excessive caution unnecessary and ill-advised. He made it a point to assure Benedetti that the Prussian government would avoid any-

---

[1] Baudin to Moustier, The Hague, 29 April 1867, FAE MD, Hollande/150, T.; Benedetti to Moustier, Berlin, 30 April 1867, *ibid.*

[2] Baudin to Moustier, The Hague, 1 May 1867, FAE CP, Pays-Bas/666, no. 12. Cf. La Tour d'Auvergne to Moustier, London, 30 April 1867, *ibid.*, Angleterre/740, T.

[3] Benedetti to Moustier, Berlin, 30 April 1867, FAE MD, Hollande/150, T.; same to same, Berlin, 2 May 1867, FAE CP, Prusse/364, no. 120. Only a few days prior to this meeting, Bismarck had again made mention of Benedetti's reserve toward him (Bismarck to Goltz, Berlin, 26 April 1867, *APP*, VIII, 738).

[4] Benedetti to Moustier, Berlin, 2 May 1867, FAE CP, Prusse/364, no. 120. Both Bismarck and Benedetti gave their consent when Oubril suggested a toast to the success of the London conference. When the toast was drunk, Bismarck lifted his glass toward the ambassador, a gesture which led Benedetti to remark later, "*Que voulez-vous? C'était de la comédie*" (Montgelas to Louis II, Berlin, 1 May 1867, *APP*, VIII, 738, ft. 3).

[5] Benedetti to Moustier, Berlin, 2 May 1867, FAE CP, Prusse/364, no. 120. Efforts by the *Nationalverein* to organize public opinion in support of demands that the ties between Luxemburg and Germany be maintained continued up to the London conference (WENTZCKE, *Deutsche Rundschau*, CXCIII [December 1922], p. 229; cf. Leibling to Lammers, [Luxembourg,] 2 May 1867, ONCKEN, *Bennigsen*, II, 43, ft. 5).

[6] "It was clear to me already a few days ago that the minister-president wanted to approach Benedetti, when he spoke to me of his personal sympathy for the French ambassador, of his intellect and graciousness" (Wimpffen to Beust, Berlin, 4 May 1867, HHStA, Preussen/95, no. 61A).

thing which might create an obstacle to the conference or arouse French suspicions. A far more difficult problem which the two discussed was the dismantlement of the fortress. To Benedetti's question whether or not the Prussian delegate would propose dismantlement, Bismarck replied that he believed the razing of the fortifications would be the best guarantee for the neutrality of Luxemburg. A token dismantlement should be at least agreed upon in order to demonstrate that the duchy would never again become the subject of discord between France and Prussia. Benedetti did not question Bismarck further on the matter; he warned Moustier that the Prussian delegate might make an overture in that sense, but that he would not make Prussia's adherence to the treaty dependent upon it. The ambassador's observation made it appear that France preferred not to raze the fortress, in the hope that she might ultimately gain possession of it.[1]

The conference convoked in London had hardly been opened when press agitation, rumors, and mutual accusations regarding armaments seriously threatened Franco-Prussian relations. Already on 8 May Ambassador Wimpffen mentioned the possibility that the Prussian government might order mobilization and that only satisfactory news from the conference could prevent such a step within the next two days.[2] Similar apprehensions were voiced in a telegram from Moustier the same day: the ambassador was to protest the war measures of the Berlin cabinet and to insist that the imperial government was harboring no aggressive designs.[3] In his reply a few hours later, Benedetti announced that Bismarck had told both Wimpffen and Loftus that news of French armaments might force him to advise mobilization.[4] The ambassador called on Bismarck late in the evening to communicate Moustier's message and to request explanations of the Prussian military preparations. The minister-president conceded that the diplomatic situation was reassuring but that rumors about French plans to invade the Rhineland at short notice made Prussian preparations mandatory. He stated that the council of ministers would not meet until Saturday, 11 May , to take

---

[1] Benedetti to Moustier, Berlin, 4 May 1867, FAE CP, Prusse/364, no. 123.

[2] "I see that peace is still desired here and that war is basically abhorred, but that it will be precipitated the day war is considered inevitable. The official language of Benedetti is reserved but pacific. I wager, however, that he believes war inevitable and desires it" (Wimpffen to Beust, Berlin, 8 May 1867, HHStA, Preussen/95, T.).

[3] Moustier to Benedetti, [Paris,] 8 May 1867, FAE CP, Prusse/364, T.

[4] Benedetti to Moustier, Berlin, 8 May 1867, *ibid.* "To speak of a lust for war on Bismarck's part is wrong. He will firmly accept war, if it is inevitable, but he will want to avoid it if our position as a power permits it" (Stosch to Gustav Freytag, Berlin, 6 May 1867, STOSCH, p. 127).

measures arising from the situation existing at that time. Thus, the intervening meetings in London would be of decisive importance. Benedetti endeavored to prove the absurdity of Prussian apprehensions but received no assurance that the Berlin cabinet would consider his views. The ambassador believed that the Prussian government might mobilize in order to precipitate a rupture or to exert pressure on the British who were reluctant to adhere to a collective guarantee of Luxemburg neutrality.[1] Moustier did not accept Bismarck's explanations: "The allegations of which we are the object are of the most revolting absurdity .... There exists a veritable aberration of mind, if there is not an odious calculation of aggression."[2] The minister insisted that a mobilization would be considered an act of aggression in France, and he asked Benedetti so to inform Bismarck and, if necessary, King William.[3]

The tension occasioned by the armament crisis quickly reached a climax, and on 10 May the danger of war was waning. Ambassador Benedetti reported that the news from London and Paris had decided the king to countermand the council meeting scheduled for the next day. Bismarck also told him that Count Bernstorff had been authorized to sign the treaty with or without a time stipulation relative to the withdrawal of the Prussian garrison.[4] With the peaceful *dénouement* of a near-fatal development on the military level, the successful conclusion of the London conference was not in doubt. The short message *"Six heures du soir. Nous venons de signer le traité,"* [5] which reached Paris on Friday, 11 May, marked the end of a vexing diplomatic controversy.

Under the terms of the treaty King William of Holland remained ruler over Luxemburg on the basis of personal union. The duchy was declared perpetually neutral and Britain, France, Prussia, Austria and Russia agreed to respect the principle of neutrality relative to Luxemburg. The erection or maintenance of fortifications on its

---

[1] Benedetti to Moustier, Berlin, 9 May 1867, FAE CP, Prusse/364, no. 128; Bismarck to Goltz, Berlin, 9 May 1867, *BGW*, VI, 389–390. "The king received me immediately after my arrival.... He was in a very serious mood and said to me, pointing to his desk, 'You see, there lies already the mobilization order for the entire army, and I only wait, with the greatest anxiety, for the report of the ambassador in Paris'" (G. VON DIEST, *Meine Erinnerungen an Kaiser Wilhelm den Grossen* [Berlin, 1898], p. 21).

[2] Moustier to Benedetti, Paris, 9 May 1867, FAE CP, Prusse/364, T.

[3] *Ibid.* In a circular, Moustier discussed the armament question in detail. He pictured all French military preparations as defensive measures, and he rejected all accusations that France was arming for war or harbored aggressive designs (Moustier to diplomatic agents, Paris, 9 May 1867, FAE MD, France/Circulaires politiques, 1863–1869, t. 2126).

[4] Benedetti to Moustier, Berlin, 10 May 1867, FAE CP, Prusse/364, no. 131.

[5] La Tour d'Auvergne to Moustier, London, 11 May 1867, *ibid.*, Angleterre/740, T.

territory being incompatible with the new status of the duchy, the city of Luxemburg was to cease being a federal fortress and fortified town. Orders for the withdrawal of the Prussian garrison were to be given immediately after the ratification of the treaty, while the Dutch king was to make the necessary arrangements for the conversion of the fortress into an open city after the departure of the troops.[1]

For Ambassador Benedetti the conclusion of the the treaty spelled the end of French compensation hopes and inaugurated a phase in Franco-Prussian relations which precluded collaboration between the two powers. The failure of France to gain compensation for Prussian expansion could not but awaken suspicion of all of Bismarck's intentions. As an adherent to the views of the Italian faction, Benedetti had been sympathetic to the aims of the minister-president. However, he had remained enough of a realist to support the French demands for compensation. He had played a very important role in the negotiations and had done his utmost to achieve success. The defeat was destined to have a direct influence on his views and produced resentment and suspicion toward Bismarck and Prussia. He could not share the elation of the minister-president over the outcome of the episode. "In general one finds the present attitude of the ambassador of France conforming too much to the excessive coldness with which the senate and the chamber in France received the communication of the results of the London conference... which gives ample [cause] for reflecting about the future." [2] The Austrian envoy also thought that Benedetti was greatly disappointed; he was convinced that the ambassador was not reconciled to the final result and his continuation as envoy to Prussia would create uneasiness in Berlin. While Benedetti remained silent in his dispatches regarding his reaction to the treaty, he did confide his misgivings to Wimpffen:

The relations between [France and Prussia]... remain strained.... We must bring ourselves to the same military level [as Prussia].... As long as the Treaty of Prague is not executed... there will always be a cause for war. This treaty is nullified by the fact that the Main line no longer exists and I do not understand what could be put into its place.[3]

When Benedetti had returned to Berlin in the late fall of 1866 he had had every intention of bringing the compensation negotiations to a close as soon as possible after Bismarck's recovery. He had realized

---

[1] For text of the treaty see ODG, XVI, 437–439.
[2] Bylandt to Zuylen, Berlin, 17 May 1867, RBZ, Pruisen/1867, no. 181.
[3] Wimpffen to Beust, Berlin, 18 May 1867, HHStA, Preussen/96, no. 66A.

that once Prussia had consolidated her gains it might prove difficult to press the demands of the imperial government successfully. He had been optimistic about the eventual outcome of the negotiations and his expectations, strengthened by Bismarck's collaboration on the draft project, had been shared by his superiors. The belief that the minister-president, unlike the king, was most receptive to the French claims had rested upon the faulty analysis that Bismarck considered the satisfaction of such demands a *sine qua non* for his own ambitions. The minister-president, however, was reluctant to see the relative increase in Prussian power nullified by French expansion; by the time he had returned to Berlin he had decided to take a gambler's chance that delay would eventually create a situation which could effectively prevent French expansion. The risks inherent in a frustration of French compensation hopes were great; Benedetti had not expected the Prussian government to face them.

Benedetti's ambition to settle the compensation question upon Bismarck's return had not been fulfilled. Not only had the minister-president asked for more time to win royal approval of the draft treaty but he had also endeavored to give preference to the Roman question. Although Benedetti had remained for a while unsuspecting, he had been nevertheless anxious to prevent further delays. His efforts had not been supported by Moustier, whose aversion to affairs of state had rapidly become a major obstacle to successful compensation negotiations. The ambassador's task had been made even more difficult when the foreign minister, in effect, had given preference to the Roman question and accepted Prussian demands that Benedetti be restrained. He had failed to realize that these complaints about the ambassador were part of the plan of delaying tactics. He had made it virtually impossible for Benedetti to take up the compensation problem on his own initiative. A recall of the ambassador was yet another possibility Bismarck had explored to end French expansionist hopes. Incessant complaints about Benedetti had been the core of a plan which had the active support of the Prussian ambassador in Paris. Moustier's ready compliance with Bismarck's program of procrastination had made these efforts actually superfluous and they were suspended for the time being.

The dilatory negotiations during the winter months had convinced Benedetti that the Prussian government was deliberately avoiding a commitment toward France on the compensation and Roman questions. Even before he had reached this conclusion, Benedetti had made it clear in his reports that the Prussian government was procrastinating. He had warned against the apparent intention of the Berlin cabinet and had suspected, mistakenly, that the cause for Bismarck's attitude was the existence of a Russo-Prussian *entente*. It is not surprising that Benedetti had found it difficult to explain the reluctance of the minister-president: he did not think the Prussian government prepared to antagonize France and risk a conflict. Furthermore, he had never considered the likelihood that France might renounce compensation rather than go to war.

Although Benedetti had not abandoned the hope that France would gain compensation, he had begun to make determined efforts to arouse his government to the potential threat to French security of a Germany dominated by Prussia. However, he had only limited success: while the imperial government had decided to ask for a declaration of intentions it had abandoned all hope for an alliance. The entire issue, contrary to Benedetti's recommendations, had been reduced to obtaining the annexation of Luxemburg. His belief that an eventual annexation of Belgium required an alliance with Prussia was correct, but his advice had been ignored. Moustier had not even attempted to keep the ambassador informed of the course of action he was pursuing. The full extent of his failure to heed Benedetti's insistence upon a speedy settlement had become apparent when the North German parliament convened before a compensation settlement had been reached. The opposition of the National Liberals to the abandonment of Luxemburg and Bismarck's need for their support to overcome conservative opposition in the *Bundestag* had introduced a major obstacle to French expansion hopes. The interpellation in the North German parliament, the hesitation of the Dutch king and the decision of the French government not to fight for Luxemburg had been major developments in the *dénouement* which culminated in the London Treaty.

Benedetti's conduct during the Luxemburg crisis is not beyond reproach. An ardent supporter of compensation, he had surprisingly failed to take into account every last Prussian consideration of French expansion. He had neglected to view the prospect from the Prussian standpoint. His optimism had been based upon erroneous assumptions, a weakness somewhat offset by his demands for an early settlement. The ambassador's reports show that he had warned against delay, but Moustier had failed to heed the warning and act at the proper time. The foreign minister's neglect of duty had also contributed to the frustration of French compensation and the failure of Benedetti's endeavors in Berlin.

The London settlement had a definite effect upon Benedetti, for it represented the final defeat of compensation hopes. It made it clear to him that Bismarck proposed to consolidate Prussian hegemony without redressing the balance of power. France was not to be paid her due, now or later. Benedetti, who had supported Prussian ambitions because of his Italian sympathies, realized that he and his government had been duped. The realization of this fact, as well as his careful appraisal of the international situation, contributed decisively to a profound change in his views. He came to consider Prussia the main threat to French security and Austria a potential and valuable ally in the defense of French interests.

CHAPTER VII

A SEARCH FOR A *MODUS VIVENDI*

The conclusion of the London Treaty inaugurated a phase in Franco-Prussian relations characterized by a persistent undercurrent of distrust and hostility, foretelling the possibility of an irrevocable rupture. The complete failure of the French compensation demands, as well as the continued movement toward unification in Germany, brought France unequivocably to face the realization that the disturbed balance of power was not likely to be redressed. The signing of the London Treaty effected a temporary amelioration in the critical relations, but the remaining years of Benedetti's tour in Berlin were to be marked by ever-increasing tension, intermittent discords, and mutual suspicions, only infrequently relieved by periods of harmonious intercourse between the French ambassador and the Prussian minister-president. The treaty incarnated the frustration of French policy and continued the deterioration in Franco-Prussian relations which had had its origin at Sadowa.[1]

Although public opinion in Germany appeared considerably calmed, and the assurance of peace had occasioned a relaxation of tension, Benedetti warned that with the Prussian evacuation of the fortress the liberal element would accuse Prussia of a mutilation of the national territory in destroying the ties between Germany and Luxemburg.[2] The London conference had left certain problems : the evacuation of the garrison,[3] the dismantlement of the fortress, and the relationship between the grand duchy and the *Zollverein*. Benedetti reminded Moustier that Prussia, under the recent peace treaties, had the right to reconstitute the *Zollverein* to assure her preponderance and a larger

---

[1] Wimpffen to Beust, Berlin, 18 May 1867, HHStA, Preussen/96, no. 66A.

[2] Benedetti to Moustier, Berlin, 14 May 1867, FAE CP, Prusse/364, no. 135.

[3] The evacuation commenced toward the end of June and was completed on 8 September (SERVAIS, p. 186).

share of the revenue. However, the *esprit d'envahissement* in which the negotiations were being pursued, and the stipulations of the convention, could make it difficult to reconcile an independent and sovereign Luxemburg with membership therein.[1] Coupled with these issues was the thwarting of French compensation plans and the still unresolved status of North Schleswig.[2] These problems affecting Franco-Prussian relations in the spring of 1867 were indeed reason for Benedetti to endorse a personal meeting of the emperor and the king at the world exhibition in Paris. Such an occasion could form the starting point for defining more precisely French policy toward Prussia and Germany. Thus far the ambassador had received no new instructions bearing upon the developments which were slowly unifying Germany. As ambassador he was expected to report all significant information, and Moustier had done nothing more than remind him of this well-understood duty. Protocol required his presence in Paris during the royal visit, and the ambassador and Madame Benedetti therefore left Berlin on Sunday, 2 June, in order to be in the French capital for the arrival of King William three days later.[3]

Despite the warm reception given the Prussian monarch and Bismarck in Paris, Benedetti felt that relations between the two powers

---

[1] Benedetti to Moustier, Berlin, 26 May 1867, FAE CP, Prusse/364, no. 145. Moustier had indicated to Goltz that France would remain interested in the status of Luxemburg and its future relationship with the *Zollverein* (Goltz to Bismarck, Paris, 18 May 1867, *APP*, IX, 61). "[Moustier] told me that France would not tolerate that Prussia *jette en quelque sorte son grappin* over Luxemburg by way of the Zollverein" (Lightenvelt to Zuylen, Paris, 25 May 1867, RBZ, Frankrijk/1867, no. 150). Bismarck had insisted that Prussia would not make any "new concessions" to France in regard to Luxemburg (Bismarck to Goltz, Berlin, 23 May 1867, H. VON POSCHINGER [ed.], *Aktenstücke zur Wirtschaftspolitik des Fürsten Bismarck* [Berlin, 1890–1891], I, 97–98).

[2] Bismarck had accepted the inclusion of Article V of the Prague Treaty under duress, and constant prodding from the Danish and French governments still had not resolved him to hasten its execution. In February he had intimated to Benedetti that the act would first be submitted to the sanction of the North German parliament (Benedetti to Moustier, Berlin, 23 February, 1867, FAE CP, Prusse/362, no. 42). Although Benedetti had stressed the privileged position of France as mediator (same to same, 22 April 1867, *ibid.*, 363, no. 99, Annex), no attempt had been made prior to the London conference to effect the retrocession, and the Danish government had requested that the problem be placed on the conference agenda (Moustier to Benedetti, Paris, 13 May 1867, *ibid.*, 364, no. 103). The Berlin cabinet had then offered to begin talks with the Danish envoy but the introduction of the problem of minority rights of the German inhabitants and the limited territorial concession Prussia offered caused the Danish government to refuse to negotiate on Bismarck's terms (Benedetti to Moustier, Berlin, 18 May 1867, *ibid.*, no. 138). Benedetti told Wimpffen: "As long as the Treaty of Prague is not executed... there will always be a cause for war" (Wimpffen to Beust, Berlin, 18 May 1867, HHStA, Preussen/96, no. 66A). Cf. SCHARFF, *Die Welt als Geschichte*, XVI, Heft 3–4 (1956), pp. 211 ff.; WINCKLER, *"Die Zielsetzung,"* *ibid.*, Heft 1 (1956), pp. 41 ff.

[3] Benedetti to Moustier, Berlin, 30 May 1867, FAE CP, Prusse/ 364, no. 149. Cf. Bylandt to Zuylen, Berlin, 1 June 1867, RBZ, Pruisen/1867, no. 203.

had not been improved, and William had seemed popular only in contrast to the hostility shown Tsar Alexander. The minister-president had been moderate in his language, according to Benedetti,[1] who was unaware that the Paris visit had been used by Bismarck to attempt in effect the recall of the French ambassador. Although unsuccessful in insinuating this wish to the emperor,[2] the minister-president had sought out Rouher, the Duke of Persigny, and Marshal François Canrobert to tell each one how much he personally had wished that Luxemburg be ceded to France and how bungling manoeuvres of Benedetti had cost France the grand duchy. He was especially explicit to Persigny:

> Bismarck told me... that he had expected to deal with statesmen... but that he had been singularly mistaken; for in reality he was, *vis-à-vis* Benedetti, in the position of a fencing master who, believing to have to do with a serious partner, would let himself be run through by an awkward fellow.... Benedetti [he said] belongs to that school which confused intrigue with ability. Accustomed for a long time to the use of deceit with the pashas of the Near East, he imagined that he could wrest the fortress of Luxemburg from me without any kind of guarantee. In order to gratify his vanity and attribute the success to his own ability, he did not sufficiently acquaint his government with the true reason for Prussia's consent or with the difficulties of execution or with the importance of keeping it secret. Taking hold of my admission that, in the new state of Germany, one could no longer consider Luxemburg a federal fortress, he made it the core of the entire affair. With his oriental morals, he thought he could dispense with all reserve, with all consideration toward the minister who was to take the brunt of the operation.[3]

Coupled with Bismarck's reluctance to maintain relations with the imperial government through the intermediary of Benedetti – a reluctance which had evinced itself as early as the previous fall – was the ill-concealed hostility of the ambassador toward the Prussian government and its chief minister – a hostility which had mounted and become manifest in proportion to his personal frustration and bitterness over his diplomatic failures. "I would have preferred not to return," he confided to Wimpffen, "but not wanting to accept any other post, I was forced through vanity to come back to Berlin, where I have already battled and where I have suffered much unpleasantness."[4] There was no doubt that the retention of Benedetti at the Berlin embassy could not serve the best interests of France, unless perhaps Benedetti could contribute to the diplomatic isolation of Bismarck and Prussia.[5]

---

[1] Wimpffen to Beust, Berlin, 29 June 1867, HHStA, Preussen/96, no. 85B.

[2] *Ibid.*

[3] PERSIGNY, pp. 369–373; cf. G. BAPST, *Le maréchal Canrobert, souvenirs d'un siècle* (Paris, 1898–1911), IV, 102.

[4] Wimpffen to Beust, Berlin, 29 June 1867, HHStA, Preussen/96, no. 85B.

[5] "Believe me," Benedetti continued, "luck is beginning to change.... If [Emperor

Returning from Paris, Benedetti was informed by the *chargé d'affaires*, Baron Maximilian de Ring, that the negotiations for the reorganization of the customs union were progressing rapidly. The conferences of the south German foreign ministers with Bismarck, Baron August von der Heydt, minister of finance, and the king had resulted in the drafting of a convention which conformed almost completely to the proposals of the Prussian government.[1] A preliminary accord had been signed on 4 June by Baden and Württemberg and on the 7th by Hesse, to which Bavaria had adhered on the 18th by signing a separate protocol.[2] Dalwigk had kept the French embassy informed of the meetings and had termed the agreement "a large bridge over the Main" – a step toward the federal union of Germany.[3] Benedetti was of course greatly interested in this movement toward unification on the economic level.[4] In a brief interview with Thile on 30 June he took up the reorganization of the customs union in reference to the grand duchy of Luxemburg. As usual, Thile did not furnish much information, but he did tell Benedetti that the Luxemburg *chargé d'affaires*, Jean-Pierre Foehr, was expected to submit the wishes of his government to the Berlin cabinet. The ambassador cautioned Thile against any changes which would alter the political position of Luxemburg relative to Germany.[5] Benedetti, like Moustier, had hope of bringing the duchy into a closer economic relationship with France, which would make up, in part, for the failure of outright annexation.[6] The ambassador forwarded to Paris a lengthy analysis of the convention text which described the organization of the customs union. A very important addition which attracted his attention was the common institutions for legislating on economic affairs. No longer would matters affecting the commercial relations between members be negotiated through diplo-

---

Francis Joseph] wished it, we could do great things, and put in their place all the pieces of the chessboard" (*ibid.*).

[1] Benedetti to Moustier, Berlin, 26 May 1867, FAE CP, Prusse/364, no. 145.

[2] *ODG*, XVII, 165, ft. 1. For text of the convention, see *AD*, 1868, I, 13–15.

[3] Ring to Moustier, Berlin, 4 June 1867, FAE CP, Prusse/364, no. 154, no. 155. For the history of the *Zollverein* treaty negotiations, see W. SCHÜBELIN, *Das Zollparlament und die Politik von Baden, Bayern und Württemberg 1866–1870* (Berlin, 1935), pp. 18 ff.; SCHÜSSLER, pp. 231 ff,; HAHN, pp. 622–624; BECKER, pp. 572 ff.

[4] In a report of 24 June, however, Benedetti had discussed the adoption of the constitution of the confederation by the Prussian chambers, which was promulgated and was to enter into effect on 1 July (Benedetti to Moustier, Berlin, 24 June 1867, FAE CP Prusse/364, T.).

[5] *Aufzeichnung Thiles*, Berlin, 30 June 1867, *APP*, IX, 131–132.

[6] "In a letter from Foehr which relates a conversation he had had with Benedetti, I find the desire expressed by France to enter into very close commercial relations with us" (Colnet de Huart to Jonas, Luxemburg, 11 May 1867, LAE H/18). Cf. Moustier to Baudin, Paris, 3 June 1867, FAE CP, Pays–Bas/666, no. 17.

matic channels, with subsequent approval voted by the respective legislatures. Instead, an administrative council (a *Bundesrat*), composed of the appointed delegates of the member states, and a *Zollparlament*, composed of elected deputies, were to be responsible for legislation on economic affairs, which was to be obligatory for all members. He also noted that the Prussian cabinet, by virtue of its various provisions, would exercise the functions of a presidium, which it would not share with any other member state. He carefully described the function of each branch of the customs union federation, noting that the members of the North German parliament would also be members to the *Zollparlament;* the election of the delegates from the South was to be by universal suffrage, in accordance with a defined proportion between voters and delegates. The presidium, the ambassador pointed out, was to convoke the chamber and conclude, in the name of the union, commerce and navigation treaties and supervise the tax collection and the administrative machinery. In case of differences in the council, the voice of the presidium would be predominant for the maintenance of the measure or the existing institution. In all other questions, majority vote would decide the issue.[1] In appraising the new organization, Benedetti emphasized the almost absolute control which Prussia exercised. In the council the Prussian government would command forty-two of the fifty-eight votes in addition to its privileges as the presidium, while it would have nearly two-thirds of the votes in the chamber on the basis of population figures. Since all resolutions needed to be approved by both assemblies to become obligatory, Prussia obtained a tight rein over the legislative process. In contrast to the old customs union, the secondary states had now abdicated their right of initiative and control. Since the majority in council and parliament could, with Prussia's assent, legislate as it saw fit, only Prussia possessed real freedom of action. In essence the customs convention was similar to the North German constitution in that both instruments spelled the uncontested supremacy of Prussia. The ambassador felt that the Berlin cabinet had misused its power to circumvent the stipulations of the Prague Treaty, that it had used force and intimidation to compel such wholesale surrender of sovereign rights in the economic field. He was convinced that the southern states had only reluctantly made these sacrifices. The manner in which the concessions had been demanded, and in which they were designed to further Prussian hegemony should, in Benedetti's opinion, be of interest and concern to the

---

[1] Benedetti to Moustier, Berlin, 2 July 1867, *ibid.*, Prusse/ 365, no. 165.

powers. Although Bismarck had scored a major success in imposing Prussia's will upon the *Zollverein* members, the opposition expressed in the southern legislatures at the time the agreements were debated would indicate someting less than enthusiastic endorsement of his policy aimed at ultimate unification.[1]

The exodus of diplomats from Berlin was already well under way when Ambassador Benedetti left the Prussian capital for his vacation. Bismarck had gone to Varzin on 22 June, while the king was about to depart for Bad Ems. Benedetti set forth on or about 4 July, going to Corsica by way of the Brenner pass. Personal affairs required his presence there, and he stayed for the better part of the summer.[2] He arrived in Paris in early September [3] but he did not return directly to his post.[4] His prolonged absence again gave rise to speculations that he would not return to the Berlin embassy, but on 10 October Moustier informed Goltz that Benedetti would definitely return to his post.[5] Bismarck received the news with more amiability than might have been expected.[6]

On 8 November Ambassador Benedetti arrived in Berlin and resumed his duties.[7] From the *chargé d'affaires* he learned of the developments which had taken place during his absence. The signing of the customs union convention on 8 July had been followed, on 14 July, by the creation of a chancellery for the affairs of the North German Confederation and the nomination of Bismarck as chancellor.[8] On 15 August the

---

[1] *Ibid.* Moustier had discussed the *Zollverein* with Goltz and had accused the Prussian government of ignoring the Prague Treaty and of employing methods which made it impossible for the south German states to turn down the Prussian proposals (Goltz to Bismarck, Paris, 28 June 1867, ONCKEN, *Rheinpolitik*, II, 423; Metternich to Beust, Paris, 28 June 1867, *ibid.*, 421–422). See also PFLANZE, pp. 391 ff.

[2] Nothomb to Rogier, Berlin, 2 July 1867, BAE CP, Prusse/24, no. 32.

[3] ROTHAN, *Les origines*, II, 121–122; Bylandt to Zuylen, Berlin, 5 September 1867, RBZ, Pruisen/1867, no. 319; Goltz to William I, Paris, 6 September 1867, *APP*, IX, 221.

[4] Cf. Goltz to Bismarck, [Paris] 10 October 1867, *ibid.*, p. 277, ft. 9, who claimed that Benedetti had not yet returned because he was ill at ease over the language he was to use and because a reserved silence might give rise to misconceptions, but that the emperor wished to prove by the presence of the ambassador [in Berlin] that relations were good. Benedetti was not to take the initiative but was to discuss amicably whatever issue Bismarck might bring up. Relations between the two powers had been further strained in consequence of the visit of Napoleon and Eugénie with Francis Joseph in Salzburg – a visit of sympathy occasioned by the death of Emperor Maximilian of Mexico (E. VON WERTHEIMER, "Franz Joseph I. und Napoleon III. in Salzburg," *Österreichische Rundschau*, LXII [1920], p. 228).

[5] Goltz to Bismarck, [Paris,] 10 October 1867, *APP*, IX, 286, ft. 2.

[6] Bismarck to Goltz, Berlin, 14 October 1867, *BGW*, VIa, 74–75. Fundamentally, Bismarck was not opposed to Benedetti's recall from Berlin but neither was he any longer actively interested in bringing about the ambassador's departure. He preferred to work with Benedetti, whose temperament he understood, rather than chance an unknown successor.

[7] Loftus to Stanley, Berlin, 9 November 1867, PRO FO 64/624, no. 464.

[8] A. KOLLER, *Archiv des norddeutschen Bundes und des Zollvereins* (Berlin, 1868–1870), I, 871–872.

Bundesrat of the North German Confederation had begun its first session in Berlin. Of particular interest to Benedetti was the fact that the elections to the North German *Bundestag*, which had taken place on 31 August, had been favorable to Bismarck, and the National Liberals had obtained eighty-three seats to sixty-eight for the Conservatives, forty for the Free Conservatives, and thirty-one for the Progressives.[1] As for international questions of interest, Benedetti could see that the North Schleswig question had not advanced much toward a solution.[2] Moreover, a sharp dispute and press polemic had taken place when Lefèbvre de Béhaine had communicated the views of the French government to Thile on 16 July; Berlin had accused Paris of interfering in the affairs of Prussia, and the resultant tension had only disappeared gradually.[3] As for the position of Luxemburg relative to the *Zollverein*, Benedetti learned that the Luxemburg government would not ask for representation in the customs parliament, although Prussia had refused, despite French protest, to state positively that the grand duchy would not be included in the new union.[4]

Contrary to the North Schleswig and Luxemburg affairs, the Roman question had reached a very critical stage by the time Ambassador Benedetti resumed his duties. The invasion of the papal territory by Garibaldi's irregulars in October, and their defeat at Mentana on 3 and 4 November by French forces, had quickly moved the issue again into the forefront of diplomatic activities in the late fall of 1867.[5] The Italian aspirations toward Rome presented an extremely difficult problem for French diplomacy.[6] Although the sympathies of the imperial

---

[1] POSCHINGER, *Bismarck und die Parlamentarier*, I, 5.

[2] Before his departure for Corsica, Benedetti had confided to the Belgian envoy that he had no instructions in the North Schleswig issue but had insisted on the right of France to demand the retrocession: "The origin of Article 5 of the Prague Treaty cannot be contested; this stipulation imprinted upon the Nikolsburg preliminaries was sent from Paris" (Nothomb to Rogier, Berlin, 13 July 1867, BAE CP, Prusse/24, no. 39).

[3] Lefèbvre de Béhaine to Moustier, Berlin, 16 July 1867, FAE CP, Prusse/365, no. 176; Moustier to Lefèbvre de Béhaine, Paris, 11 July 1867, *ibid.*, no. 121; same to same, Paris, 20 July 1867, *ibid.*, no. 124; Lefèbvre de Béhaine to Moustier, Berlin, 18 July 1867, *ibid.*, no. 177; same to same, Berlin, 21 July 1867, *ibid.*, no. 179; same to same, Berlin, 8 August 1867, *ibid.*, no. 198; *Aufzeichnung Bismarcks*, ca. end of July 1867, *APP*, IX, 171–172; Wimpffen to Beust, Berlin, 13 August 1867, HHStA, Preussen/96, no. 98A.

[4] Moustier to Lefèbvre de Béhaine, [Paris,] 11 July 1867, FAE CP, Prusse/365, no. 122; Thile to Goltz, Berlin, 13 July 1867, *APP*, IX, 151–152; Sayve to Moustier, The Hague, 23 July 1867, FAE MD, Hollande/150, T.; Moustier to Lefèbvre de Béhaine, Paris, 29 July 1867, FAE CP, Prusse/365, no. 127.

[5] Cf. É. BOURGEOIS and É. CLERMONT, *Rome et Napoléon III 1849–1870: étude sur les origines et la chute du Second Empire* (Paris, 1907), pp. 216–217.

[6] "I had one long, good talk with the Emperor.... He was bitter against the Italian government..." (Queen Sophie to Clarendon, The Hague, 4 November 1867, H. MAXWELL, *The Life and Letters of George William Frederick, fourth earl of Clarendon* [London, 1913], II,

government for the Italian cause were never in doubt, it could ill afford to arouse the opposition of French Catholics by withdrawing its protection from the papacy. A way out of the dilemma offered itself, perhaps, in the form of an international congress which might settle the issue and free France from making unpleasant decisions. Interviews between Lefèbvre and Bismarck shortly before Benedetti's arrival from Paris had indicated that the Prussian government was extremely reserved regarding an international congress.[1] The foreign minister had therefore instructed Benedetti to make every effort to assure the support of the Berlin cabinet, and the day after his arrival he brought up the matter with Bismarck.[2]

In the first meeting with Bismarck since May, Benedetti bent all his efforts to persuade the Prussian chancellor to accept the French proposal, stressing particularly the fact that the peace of Italy concerned all the powers and that a resolute support of the congress idea would be of decisive influence on the conduct of the Italian and papal cabinets. Bismarck conceded the logic of the ambassador's views but evidently was unwilling to take a stand. He claimed that all the powers would never agree to a congress, and therefore thought it a waste of time to try to bring it about.[3] Moreover, he wished to avoid making a commitment which might adversely affect the German Catholics, especially in South Germany, and unnecessarily complicate the unification task in which he was engaged.[4] He maintained that a congress would do more harm than good and suggested that the imperial government drop the project. He felt certain that the presence of French troops in Città Vecchia would be guarantee enough for the pope and his government. The chancellor tempered his opposition with the request that the Prussian government would need to know the basis upon which France expected to bring about a solution in Italy. Benedetti had no instructions to discuss this aspect but told Bismarck that a demand for a prior agreement would postpone, if not make impossible, the conference. In concluding the interview, the chancellor told Benedetti that while he

---

339). Already in late 1866 the Italian claims had caused the emperor to remark: "[The Italians] lack only a third defeat in order to demand Paris from me" (K. von Schlözer, *Römische Briefe 1864–1869* [2nd ed.; Stuttgart, 1913], p. 208).

[1] Lefèbvre de Béhaine to Moustier, Berlin, 28 October 1867, FAE CP, Prusse/366, no. 266; same to same, Berlin, 1 November 1867, *ibid.*, 367, no. 271; Moustier to Benedetti, [Paris,] 4 November 1867, *ibid.*, no. 136.

[2] *MMP*, p. 227; Nothomb to Rogier, Berlin, 11 November 1867, BAE CP, Prusse/24, no. 68; Moustier to diplomatic agents, Paris, 9 November 1867, FAE MD, France/Circulaires politiques, 1863–1869, t. 2126.

[3] Benedetti to Moustier, Berlin, 10 November 1867, FAE CP, Prusse/367, no. 275.

[4] *BGW*, VIa, 162, note to no. 983.

personally was opposed to the congress idea a formal invitation would be duly considered. A reply would depend on the attitude of the other powers, particularly Britain.[1]

Although the ambassador had been instructed to tender a formal invitation for a conference the next day, he was unable to transmit it since king and chancellor were hunting and would not be returning until Wednesday, 15 November. Anxious to avoid delay ,Benedetti requested an audience with the king at the earliest possible moment and told Thile that he wished to tender a formal congress invitation.[2] A further complication arose over the weekend when Moustier's assertion, that the Italian government would welcome a conference, was contradicted by Benedetti's Italian colleague, Count Edoardo de Launay. After reporting this divergence in view between Launay and himself, Benedetti was assured by wire that Nigra had declared in Paris that Italy would welcome a conference but would not officially join France in calling it together.[3]

As soon as the king and Bismarck returned to Berlin, the ambassador presented the official invitation. During the interview the chancellor declared that the king deemed it indispensable to know the reaction in Rome and Florence to the French proposal before giving a reply. Furthermore, the Prussian government wished to ascertain the views of the other powers and examine the agenda. Bismarck was also interested in rumors that France had planned to invite all Catholic powers; he inquired whether any of the German secondary powers had been invited and implied that an invitation to them might make Prussia's attendance doubtful. Regarding the possibility of a prior accord, Benedetti tried to convince the chancellor that such a step might prejudice the success of the conference, but he realized that Bismarck was far from lending his support to the French proposal.[4]

Although Bismarck's attitude had been discouraging,[5] the ambassador did not feel that the conference proposal should be dropped. On the contrary, the king's speech at the opening of the Prussian

---

[1] Benedetti to Moustier, Berlin, 10 November 1867, FAE CP, Prusse/367, no. 275.

[2] Same to same, Berlin, 11 November 1867, *ibid.*, T.; Thile to Goltz, Berlin, 12 November 1867, *APP*, IX, 376.

[3] Moustier to Benedetti, Paris, 12 November 1867, FAE CP, Prusse/367, T.; Benedetti to Moustier, Berlin, 12 November 1867, *ibid.*, T.; Moustier to Benedetti, Paris, 12 November 1867, *ibid.*, T.; Nothomb to Rogier, Berlin, 11 November 1867, BAE CP, Prusse/24, no. 68; Bismarck to Bernstorff, Berlin, 13 November 1867, *APP*, IX, 381.

[4] Benedetti to Moustier, Berlin, 14 November 1867, FAE CP, Prusse/367, no. 279.

[5] Similar replies had been received from the British and the Russian governments (Talleyrand to Moustier, St. Petersburg, 14 November 1867, *ibid.*, Russie/239, T.).

legislative session on the following day, the 15th, implied that the government might make efforts to hasten the long overdue solution of the Italian question, which would satisfy the legitimate expectations of his Catholic subjects and fulfill the obligations which Prussia faced as a power.[1] As for the audience which Benedetti had requested, he was surprised by an invitation to dine at the king's table on the 16th in company with Bismarck, Eulenburg, and various officers of the royal house. He suspected that the invitation was intended to make an audience superfluous and consequently endeavored to inform William of the hopes which France placed on the proposal for a conference. The monarch showed himself willing to accept the invitation, provided that Russia and Britain as well as Italy and the papacy agreed to the proposal. The ambassador hastened to inform William that the invitations were expected to be accepted in Rome and Florence and pointed out that the decision of the Russian and English cabinets would, to some degree, depend upon the attitude of Prussia. It was obvious that the king subordinated his adherence to the conditions which Bismarck had raised earlier but that he did not think the conference condemned to failure.[2] Benedetti also profited from the occasion to discuss the pending invitations to some of the secondary powers of Germany, in particular Saxony, a member of the North German Confederation. He could plainly see that the matter had greatly irritated Bismarck and he could assume that this incident would add fuel to the chancellor's opposition.[3]

The talks thus far relative to a conference had convinced Benedetti that Bismarck was making no effort to assure Prussia's adherence to the proposal or to the convocation proper. He suspected quite rightly that the chancellor had no desire to end the difficulties which the Roman question caused the imperial government in internal politics. A solution of the Roman question might place France in a better position to combat Prussia's unification drive in Germany.[4] Nonetheless, he did not give up hope and told Wimpffen that perhaps the Prussian government eventually would make the consent of the pope the sole condition

---

[1] Benedetti to Moustier, Berlin, 15 November 1867, *ibid.*, Prusse/367, no. 280.

[2] Same to same, Berlin, 17 November 1867, *ibid.*, no. 281.

[3] *Ibid.* Bismarck told Benedetti that Saxony would simply forward the invitation to the chancellory of the North German Confederation. Cf. Moustier to Benedetti, Paris, 19 November 1867, *ibid.*, T.

[4] Benedetti to Moustier, Berlin, 19 November 1867, *ibid.*, no. 285. Cf. Bismarck to Goltz, Berlin, 28 November 1867, *BGW*, VIa, 142–143, for Bismarck's criticism of Benedetti's views. Informed of Benedetti's opinion by Moustier, La Tour d'Auvergne had mentioned it to Bernstorff, who in turn had informed Bismarck.

for its acceptance.[1] But Bismarck's determined opposition had manifestly irritated the ambassador and he indicated his displeasure to the
Austrian envoy, whom he had asked to press for Prussia's acceptance in
his next interview with the chancellor.[2] Benedetti saw Bismarck again
on 29 November and tried to overcome the distrust of French intentions.
Yet Bismarck remained adamant in his demand for a prior accord of
the powers and strongly objected to the fact that the French government had seen fit to invite states like Luxemburg, Sweden, Hesse-
Darmstadt. That they had Catholic subjects did not seem sufficient, and
he suspected, with some justification, that France was endeavoring to
assure herself of a majority in the conference.[3] Benedetti was unable to
treat with Bismarck relative to a prior accord of the powers because,
on his admission to Wimpffen, he had received no instructions from
Paris. He thought that the chancellor might use a preliminary meeting
of the powers to wreck any chance for a conference. He surmised that
the failure would only tend to emphasize the differences between the
powers, and align Prussia, Russia, and Britain against Austria and
France.[4]

The efforts of the French government to bring about the conference
continued into December with little hope of a near success. In Berlin,
the repeated attempts of Ambassador Benedetti to further the aims of
his government only resulted in a deterioration of his relations with
Bismarck. The chancellor complained that Benedetti was reserved
with communications but free with questions and criticism.[5] No doubt
the ambassador was aware of Bismarck's feelings since he made no
effort to see him unless instructed to do so. At a dinner in honor of
Queen Augusta on 6 December, Benedetti did not fail to bring up the
conference scheme when the king offered him the opportunity. He
stressed the importance of the role which Prussia might exercise, referring to Prussian influence in Florence. Although William seemed
receptive to Benedetti's arguments. he had been disturbed by the
speech of Rouher the previous day in the chamber, in which he had

[1] Wimpffen to Beust, Berlin, 22 November 1867, HHStA, Preussen/ 96, no. 140B.
[2] *Ibid.*, no. 140D.
[3] Benedetti to Moustier, Berlin, 29 November 1867, FAE CP, Prusse/367, no. 291; Bismarck to Goltz, Berlin, 29 November 1867, *APP*, IX, 457–459.
[4] Wimpffen to Beust, Berlin, 4 December 1867, HHStA, Preussen/ 96, no. 144. Cf. RHEIN-
DORF, pp. 61–62, who maintains that French failure to support Russia in the Near East
occasioned, in part, the Russian efforts toward a *rapprochement* with Prussia.
[5] Bismarck to Goltz, Berlin, 5 December 1867, *BGW*, VIa, 161; Spitzemberg to Varnbüler, Berlin, 10 December 1867, ONCKEN, *Rheinpolitik*, II, 485.

asserted that France would continue to safe-guard the pope's temporal power and possessions.[1]

Despite Benedetti's sympathies for the Italian cause,[2] his activities on behalf of the conference proposal do not indicate reluctance to further Moustier's policy. As in Nikolsburg, so now Benedetti may have been opposed to exaggerated Italian claims. Rouher's speech had indicated that the support of the Italians was subordinated to considerations of French internal affairs; the minister of state had made it clear that France supported the papacy on this issue, and it can be assumed that Benedetti was politic enough to make Rouher's views his own.[3]

The willingness of the imperial government, indicated by Moustier,[4] to accept the Prussian demand for a preliminary meeting of the great powers did effect a modification of the attitude of the Berlin cabinet, and on 12 December Bismarck was more receptive to the conference proposal. The ambassador acceded promptly to his request for a written statement of what the imperial government expected of Prussia at this time, and he gave the chancellor a copy of an extract of Moustier's dispatch of 9 December.[5] The moderation of Bismarck's attitude did not allay Benedetti's suspicions: he was convinced that the chancellor was still hopeful of creating or maintaining a situation which would prevent French interference in his own projects in Germany. The ambassador surmised that, in Bismarck's opinion, Rouher's declaration of 5 December would make it impossible for France to recover her freedom of action and re-establish her preponderant influence in Florence. Thus Prussia could well afford to consent to a conference which was already doomed to failure.[6] Although Bismarck's changed attitude [7] seemed to augur well for the convocation of the conference, the opposition of Italy, Britain and Russia made it obvious that no easy solution to the problem was at hand. Benedetti himself felt that an amicable surrender of Rome would prove the sole means to

---

[1] Benedetti to Moustier, Berlin, 7 December 1867, FAE CP, Prusse/367, no. 298; Loftus to Stanley, Berlin, 7 December 1867, PRO FO 64/625, no. 503.
[2] Benedetti felt that a prolonged dispute between France and Italy would only serve the interests of Prussia (Wimpffen to Beust, Berlin, 22 December 1867, HHStA, Preussen/96, no. 151).
[3] Moustier to Benedetti, Paris, 9 December 1867, FAE CP, Prusse/367, nos. 155, 156.
[4] Despite Benedetti's explicit statements Bismarck thought him *karg und zurückhaltend* (Bismarck to Goltz, Berlin, 15 December 1867, *APP*, IX, 538).
[5] Benedetti to Moustier, Berlin, 13 December 1867, FAE CP, Prusse/367, no. 307.
[6] Loftus to Stanley, Berlin, 14 December 1867, PRO FO 64/625, no. 517.
[7] Bismarck to Goltz, Berlin, 15 December 1867, *BGW*, VIa, 179.

a solution of the vexing problem.[1] By the time the Prussian government formally assented to the convocation of a conference, on 24 January, the failure of the French project was already a foregone conclusion.[2]

The early days of the new year actually witnessed a slight improvement in the relations between the two powers.[3] Prussia's adherence to the French conference proposal and the friendly reception in Paris of Goltz's accreditation letters as ambassador of the North German Confederation had eliminated the latest irritation.[4] Nonetheless, Ambassador Benedetti did not consider the attitude of the Prussian government sufficient guarantee against hostile designs toward France. He was convinced that assurances of friendly disposition did not preclude a Prussian attack on France. Although he did not ascribe, for the present, such designs to the Berlin cabinet,[5] he thought an attack possible if France were to come into conflict with the Italian government. The determination of Prussia to create a united Germany, while preserving its preponderant position, made it thus necessary to watch carefully for indications of changes in Prussian policy toward France.

---

[1] Loftus to Stanley, Berlin, 14 December 1867, PRO FO 64/625, no. 517.

[2] Benedetti to Moustier, Berlin, 2 January 1868, FAE CP, Prusse/368, T. Cf. Metternich to Beust, Paris, 16 January 1868, ONCKEN, *Rheinpolitik*, II, 501–502, who reports the emperor's remark upon learning that Prussia had agreed to an international conference on the Roman question: "*Nous allons joliment traiter les canailles d'Italiens.*" See also GEUSS, pp. 228–231.

[3] The personal relations between Bismarck and Benedetti were slightly marred in late December over a new protocol issue. Benedetti insisted that upon returning to his post after a prolonged absence society in Berlin was supposed to call on him first. Although this privilege, accorded to him as ranking ambassador, was not contested, his claim was thought rather absurd since the custom had almost completely disappeared from the practice of diplomacy. Bismarck thought that Benedetti raised the issue in order to complain of maltreatment in Berlin. This incident, coming at a time when France sought Bismarck's support in an important international issue, attests once again to the exaggerated attitude of Benedetti on matters of protocol (Bismarck to Goltz, Berlin, 15 December 1867, *BGW*, VIa, 182–183; same to same, Berlin, 23 December 1867, *APP*, IX, 565–566). The animosity between the chancellor and the ambassador was the subject of a discussion on 9 January between Napoleon and Goltz, during which the former allegedly expressed his doubts about Benedetti's usefulness in Berlin. He supposedly agreed with Goltz that the French ambassador was not a *homme du monde* and even raised the possibility of replacing him with Talleyrand or La Tour d'Auvergne (Goltz to Bismarck, Paris, 9 January, *ibid.*, p. 567, ft. 8). Bismarck approved of Goltz's discussion with the emperor but did not think the recall of Benedetti advisable at the time, preferring also to leave the initiative with the emperor. Bismarck considered Benedetti far more intelligent than Talleyrand and thought that a successor might actually make matters worse (Bismarck to Goltz, Berlin, 16 January 1868, *BGW*, VIa, 209–210).

[4] Benedetti to Moustier, Berlin, 5 January 1868, FAE CP, Prusse/368, no. 2. "I cannot send this... report... without repeating the opinion *that of late a change in the relations between Berlin and Paris must have occurred toward a more mild and conciliatory spirit, although it is not a rapprochement or noticeable and permanent improvement*" (Wimpffen to Beust, Berlin, 4 January 1868, HHStA, Preussen/98, no. 1C).

[5] Benedetti to Moustier, Berlin, 5 January 1868, FAE CP, Prusse/368, no. 1.

The ambassador was convinced that the Berlin cabinet feared the possibility of French interference in Germany; hence the Prussian desire to prolong situations which might distract the attention of France from German affairs. Benedetti considered Prussia's acceptance of a conference proposal merely a tactical decision, having no permanent effect upon the relations between the two powers.[1]

What is [Bismarck's] objective? What goal does he pursue? It is not to attack us, I have said and I repeat, at the risk of assuming a grave responsibility, because my deepest conviction is this: his goal is to cross the Main and to unite the South of Germany with the North under the authority of the king of Prussia. And I add that he proposes to realize it, if need be, by having recourse to arms if France were openly to oppose it.[2]

That the unification of Germany was actively pursued by Bismarck had already long been obvious ot the ambassador. The wooing of the liberal elements, the support of national tendencies in South Germany, the military alliances, the creation of the customs union parliament, and other developments were indicative of a constancy of purpose which was all too familiar to Benedetti. He thought the *Zollparlament* the major vehicle upon which Bismarck would try to achieve the unification. By enlarging its competency and giving it a role more political than economic, he was devising a system whereby the *Zollparlament* would in time eclipse the parliament of the North German Confederation and prepare the way for a single, national representative assembly for Germany. Proceedings in the *Zollparlament* therefore would bear careful watching, for Bismarck would no doubt move very rapidly with his plans when the proper moment had come for unification.[3] Aware of the implications of this in relation to French security, Benedetti thought it advisable that the imperial government decide whether or not unification threatened the position of France and whether war was the only means of avoiding the danger. If unification were not considered an adverse development, France should then make its views felt and promote harmonious relations. The ambassador was greatly concerned over the hostile sentiment in Germany which credited France with nefarious designs against the Germans. If, on the other hand, the imperial government thought it necessary to prevent the unification, then it should be fully cognizant of the consequences of its

---

[1] Benedetti told Wimpffen that Prussia would never lend a hand to bring about an accord between Paris and Florence (Wimpffen to Beust, Berlin, 19 January 1868, HHStA, Preussen/98, no. 5C.).
[2] Benedetti to Moustier, Berlin, 5 January 1868, FAE CP, Prusse/368, no. 1.
[3] *Ibid.*

decision. Particularist tendencies had not completely disappeared, and an initial defeat of Prussia might revive them. On the other hand, sentiments toward unification were by far the stronger and an initial Prussian victory in a war against France would undoubtedly sweep away all reservations and cause the masses "to impose upon themselves with passion the sacrifices demanded from them." [1] It would indeed be a formidable war, a war in which an entire people would participate against France. Thus, a decision opposing unification would make it imperative that France prepare herself at once for the task. For the time being Benedetti did not foresee any really serious deterioration, but he did expect that the next convocation of the North German parliament might accelerate the unification tendency and bring about a critical period in Franco-Prussian relations.[2] He appeared almost convinced, in a conversation with Wimpffen in mid-January, that the Main barrier would be breached regardless of opposition, external or internal; if the imperial government were unable to check such a development effectively, he preferred that France made *bonne mine* to such an event and essay to maintain friendly relations.[3]

Meanwhile, the favorable state of relations was furthered by the fact that Ambassador Benedetti was to be accredited as ambassador to the North German Confederation. The emperor had made known his intention on 25 January,[4] and in a formal audience on Sunday, 2 February, Benedetti transmitted his letters of accreditation.[5] On 26 January, Franco-Prussian commercial negotiations, freeing Mecklemburg from its treaty of commerce of 1865 with France, were terminated by an exchange of notes. Although the accord did not have any consequences of note, it had given the imperial government an occasion to demonstrate its friendly disposition.[6] The fact that the major ball at the French embassy was attended by the Prussian king and queen as well as all the members of the royal family was interpreted as an indication that relations had indeed improved.[7]

Moustier did not deem the occasion of accreditation worthy of new

---

[1] *Ibid.* Cf. OLLIVIER, X, 267–268, who remarked of Benedetti's analysis: "It was impossible [for anyone] to see and say it better." Benedetti's report had been written while the campaigns for the *Zollparlament* election began in the German states. See PFLANZE, pp. 395–399.

[2] Cf. *MMP*, p. 272.

[3] Wimpffen to Beust, Berlin, 19 January 1868, HHStA, Preussen/98, no. 5B.

[4] Napoleon III to William I, Paris, 25 January 1868, PRO FO 64/639, n.n.

[5] NORDDEUTSCHER BUND, *Bundes-Gesetzblatt*, Berlin, 5 February 1868, no. 40, p. 3; Benedetti to Moustier, Berlin, 2 February 1868, FAE CP, Prusse/368, T.

[6] Same to same, Berlin, 29 January 1868, *ibid.*, no. 14; cf. Spitzemberg to Varnbüler, Berlin, 7 January 1868, *APP*, IX, 599.

[7] Bylandt to Zuylen, Berlin, 20 [sic] February 1868, RBZ, Pruisen/1868, no. 66.

instructions to the ambassador. He merely stressed the need for friendly relations with Prussia and urged Benedetti not to become discouraged in such an endeavor. Moustier was hopeful that the Prussian government might attach greater significance to an *entente* with the French cabinet on questions affecting the peace and he asked Benedetti to further this aim by suggesting to Bismarck that they exchange views and opinions on relevant matters at frequent intervals. Yet, apart from indicating this wish he did not give Benedetti any specific instructions regarding problems at hand. He apparently thought him well enough informed and his comments on the ambassador's lengthy exposé of 5 January constitute nothing more than a polite acknowledgment. Under the circumstances Benedetti could do little more than act according to what he thought the aims of imperial diplomacy to be.[1]

The ambassador called on the chancellor in early February to inform him of Moustier's suggestion that the two powers arrive at an identity of views on problems of mutual interest in diplomatic affairs. Bismarck showed himself quite receptive, in Benedetti's opinion, and the ambassador assured him of his own wish to promote a harmony of views.[2] While the French overture thus met with a most favorable reception, Benedetti was nonetheless anxious that his government not misjudge the situation in Germany. He did not share the optimism with which Moustier reacted to the slightest encouragement, and he continued to make reference to the determination of the Prussian government to pursue actively its unification schemes. The fact that unification agitation had momentarily subsided, in consequence of the particularist gains in the *Zollparlament* elections, had not changed Benedetti's opinion about renewed efforts to further the unification cause.[3]

Before Benedetti and Bismarck were able to demonstrate their desire for closer cooperation, an event developed which placed a new strain on the relations between France and Prussia. Rumors that former Hanoverian troops had entered France from Switzerland had disturbed the chancellor and he sought verification from the ambassador. Benedetti confirmed the news on 4 February and related that

---

[1] Moustier to Benedetti, Paris, 26 January 1868, FAE CP, Prusse/368, no. 22.

[2] Benedetti to Moustier, Berlin, 4 February 1868, *ibid.*, no. 20. Although Bismarck was willing to cooperate with France, he was skeptical of the success of such an attempt. He thought Benedetti was too reserved in his communications to establish an intimate day-by-day exchange of views. "Benedetti is the most uncommunicative diplomat with whom I ever dealt. All the others tell more and ask less" (Bismarck to Solms, Berlin, 3 February 1868, *APP*, IX, 656). Bismarck rendered an almost identical judgment of Oubril shortly after (Bismarck to Reuss, Berlin, 22 March 1868, *ibid.*, pp. 799–804).

[3] Benedetti to Moustier, Berlin, 4 February 1868, FAE CP, Prusse/ 368, no 19.

the French minister of the interior had granted the soldiers hospitality in accordance with established practices.[1] They were quartered along the Loire River, and the ambassador emphasized that their presence in France should not be construed as a hostile gesture.[2] At Bismarck's request the ambassador called again the following day to discuss the matter in more detail. The chancellor insisted that the Hanoverians constituted a military contingent led by officers and that it was to be employed in a war against Prussia when an occasion presented itself. Information confirming this fact had been forwarded to him from agents who belonged to the Legion. Although he attributed no hostile intent to the imperial government, Bismarck insisted that Prussia could not tolerate that her enemies be allowed freely to make military preparations against her. The minister believed it to be in the interest of France to prevent such machinations, if an *entente* with Prussia was desirable. He insisted that an end be put to the military organization of the group, that the leaders be forced to establish themselves in separate departments – in brief: the prevention of a conspiracy backed by an organized force. Benedetti found it difficult to dissipate Bismarck's apprehensions, for he possessed no information relative to the measures the imperial government planned to take. He had been surprised by the repercussions the arrival of the Hanoverians in France had had in Berlin, and he did not doubt the possibility of Prussian retaliatory measures against King George.[3] Benedetti's indication of the views in Berlin brought a quick reply from the foreign minister, who announced the immediate evacuation of the Hanoverians from the frontier departments and their dispersal in the interior of France.[4]

---

[1] Moustier to Benedetti, Paris, 3 February 1868, *ibid.*, T.

[2] Benedetti to Bismarck, Berlin, 4 February 1868, *APP*, IX, 664, ft. 4. These troops, referred to as the Hanoverian Legion, possessed all the attributes of a military force. Efforts were made, after their arrival in France, to procure all the necessary equipment for them. Moustier did not know officially about these activities, according to Meding who acted as the Hanoverian representative in this affair and who worked closely with officers of the French army and officials of the ministry of the interior. A military staff was set up in Paris and offices were maintained in that city. Plans for military operations, in conjunction with the French army, were worked out. The Legion was disbanded in March of 1870, at the order of King George and payments to the members were suspended the following month. According to Meding, a total of 15,000 men had been maintained during the entire period (O. MEDING, *Memoiren zur Zeitgeschichte*, vol III, *Im Exil* [Leipzig, 1884], pp. 215–247, 449–500; O. MEDING, *De Sadowa à Sedan: mémoires d'un ambassadeur secret aux Tuileries* [Paris, 1885], pp. 269–270).

[3] Benedetti to Moustier, Berlin, 5 February 1868, FAE CP, Prusse/368, no. 21; Bismarck to Solms, Berlin, 7 February 1868, BGW, VIa, 242. Cf. Bismarck to Bernstorff, Berlin, 21 February 1868, *ibid.*, 271–273.

[4] Moustier to Benedetti, Paris, 7 February 1868, FAE CP, Prusse/368, T.; Bismarck to Solms, Berlin, 10 February 1868, *BGW*, VIa, 244.

This initial measure was followed by the declaration that the order had been given to intern the officers in Bourges, while the troops were to be dispersed in various localities, at least forty miles from the frontier.[1] Prussian apprehensions were calmed by the announcement and, during a soirée on the 16th, Bismarck expressed his satisfaction to the ambassador.[2] Thus the danger had been ended by the swift action of the French government. Benedetti evidently endeavored to avoid any and all recurrence of complications relative to the Hanoverian issue; the Austrian minister thought him anxious to dissociate France from Austria relative to Prussian complaints that Austria had furnished passports necessary for the troops to go to Switzerland and thence to France.[3]

The personal relations between Bismarck and Benedetti, which had gradually improved during the past two months, suffered a slight setback when the chancellor was granted an unlimited furlough after his break with the Conservatives in the Prussian parliament.[4] The fact that he remained in Berlin, retained his control over certain departments, and exchanged written communications with foreign representatives while refusing to receive them, constituted an abnormal state of affairs. Bismarck had turned the direction of the foreign office over to Thile on 26 February and had refused to receive either Loftus or Benedetti. Loftus was particularly displeased with such a procedure and called on the French ambassador to determine what step, if any, should be taken. Surprisingly, Benedetti admitted that he preferred not to register his displeasure, for fear that such a step might trouble anew the relations between France and Prussia. Not only did he refuse to participate in a formal complaint, short of instructions, but he also advised Loftus not to carry his dissatisfaction too far.[5]

In a discussion with Thile on 28 February, Ambassador Benedetti drew attention to the recent elections of the *Zollparlament*, scheduled

[1] Moustier to Benedetti, Paris, 8 February 1868, FAE CP, Prusse/368, T.
[2] Benedetti to Moustier, Berlin, 16 February 1868, *ibid.*, T.
[3] Wimpffen to Beust, Berlin, 18 February 1868, HHStA, Preussen/99, n.n.
[4] Benedetti to Moustier, Berlin, 11 February 1868, FAE CP, Prusse/368, no. 32. The break had occurred when the Conservatives had opposed a proposition by the cabinet that a large monetary fund be left to the province of Hanover, as a guarantee of its autonomy (same to same, Berlin, 7 February 1868, *ibid.*, no. 25).
[5] Same to same, Berlin, 27 February 1868, *ibid.*, no. 47; cf. Loftus to Stanley, Berlin, 29 February 1868, PRO FO 64/639, no. 126. Although Benedetti had shown great restraint in the matter, Bismarck nevertheless complained to Goltz that the two ambassadors were most unreasonable in their attitude (Bismarck to Goltz, Berlin, 14 March 1868, *BGW*, VIa, 307–310; same to same, Berlin, 21 March 1868, *ibid.*, 316–318; same to same, Berlin, 25 March 1868, *ibid.*, 328).

to meet in April. He was particularly concerned over the demands, voiced in the press, that the *Zollparlament's* powers be extended to give it the role of a national assembly. He did concede the correctness of Thile's reply, that the south German deputies would hardly tolerate such a move, but feared that Prussian denial of supporting the extension of assembly powers was not sufficient guarantee. Moreover, the fact that a Prussian general had assumed the direction of the military establishment of Baden was reason enough to question the true intentions of the Prussian government.[1] Benedetti showed a continual preoccupation with the possibility of further unification which, as he fully realized, would alter still further the balance of power in Europe.

The political scene in Berlin was animated when, on 4 March, Prince Napoleon arrived for a ten day visit,[2] of which he had previously notified Benedetti,[3] who was considered close to the prince.[4] The presence of Prince Napoleon in Berlin was marked by a number of official receptions, inspections,[5] dinner parties, and conjectures.[6] He evidently discussed those topics which his individual listeners wished to hear and departed from Berlin leaving the diplomatic colony writing lengthy reports.[7] Benedetti did not think that the visit would have a significant influence on Franco-Prussian relations; he told Wimpffen that there had been the usual protestations of good faith as well as the usual reservations about the unpredictable force of events and national spirit in Germany, which could perhaps prove stronger than the will of the king and his government.[8]

---

[1] Benedetti to Moustier, Berlin, 28 February 1868, FAE CP, Prusse/368, no. 48; cf. G. MEYER, "Die Reichsgründung und das Grossherzogtum Baden," *Festgabe zur Feier des siebzigsten Geburtstages... des Grossherzogs Friedrich von Baden, dargebracht von den Mitgliedern der juristischen Fakultät der Universität Heidelberg* (Heidelberg, 1896). p. 177.

[2] "Prince Napoleon has left Paris to make a voyage in Germany.... What is this *enfant terrible* going to do? His friendship with Benedetti and his taste for everything which touches the combined interests of Prussia and Italy seem to indicate that he will be received with open arms by the court in Berlin..." (H. IDEVILLE, *Journal d'un diplomate en Allemagne et en Grèce... 1867–68* [Paris, 1876], p. 47).

[3] Benedetti to Moustier, Berlin, 3 March 1868, FAE CP, Prusse/ 369, T.

[4] Informing Thile of Prince Napoleon's voyage, Benedetti had spoken of his close, friendly relationship with the prince (*Aufzeichnung Thiles*, Berlin, 2 March 1868, *APP*, IX, 750–751). Cf. Goltz to Bismarck, Paris, 3 April 1868, *ibid.*, p. 832: "Prince Napoleon spoke... somewhat disparagingly of Benedetti who, as he said, was nothing but a journalist.'"

[5] OLLIVIER, X, 449, claims that Bismarck and the prince discussed the possibility of annexing Belgium to France and that the former suggested such a step. Cf. Bismarck to Goltz, Berlin, 21 March 1868, *APP*, IX, 797–799.

[6] Benedetti to Moustier, Berlin, 8 March 1868, FAE CP, Prusse/ 369.

[7] Bylandt to Zuylen, Berlin, 11 March 1868, RBZ, Pruissen/1868, no. 91; Wimpffen to Beust, Berlin, 8 March 1868, HHStA, Preussen/99, n.n.; Bismarck to Goltz, Berlin, 9 April 1868, *BGW*, VIa, 337–338.

[8] Wimpffen to Beust, Berlin, 18 March 1868, HHStA, Preussen/99, n.n. OLLIVIER, X,

The temporary lull on the political scene after Prince Napoleon's departure gave Benedetti an opportunity to turn his attention to the North Schleswig question. In February he had thought that the Prussian government was beginning to show a more conciliatory attitude, but he did not anticipate a near settlement of the question.[1] The Prusso-Danish negotiations were resumed in early March, and Lothar Bucher was appointed to treat with the Danish envoy, Baron George Quaade. The fact that the Berlin cabinet had not relented in its demand for guarantees convinced Benedetti that a solution would prove extremely difficult.[2] It was not until the beginning of April that he became more optimistic, when he was told that Bismarck and Moltke, in discussing the problem with Quaade, had given indications that the Prussian government was hopeful of an imminent settlement.[3] During these negotiations Benedetti apparently made no effort to support the Danish minister; although he continued to express his sympathy for the Danish cause, he had no instructions to enter actively into the negotiations. Apparently, the implementation of Article V and the assertion of the principle of national self-determination had been subordinated to a more practical consideration – the continued improvement of the relations between France and Prussia. Perhaps the return of the chancellor to the direction of the Berlin foreign office on 18 March was the signal for avoiding all irritations which might disturb Bismarck's friendly disposition toward the imperial government.[4]

The approaching convocation of the customs parliament as well as the deliberations of the North German parliament, in session since Monday, 23 March, gave Benedetti added reason for turning his attention back to the political scene in Germany. His fear that the North German Confederation might make an effort to breach the Main Line was not realized. Benedetti had neglected to consider the effect of the elections in South Germany to the customs parliament, which had

449, states that Bismarck complained to Prince Napoleon of Benedetti's attitude: "He is intelligent but he remembers too well that he had been a consul and wants to be a proconsul...."

[1] Benedetti to Moustier, Berlin, 8 February 1868, FAE CP, Prusse/369, no. 26. Dotézac shared Benedetti's pessimism and he reported that the Prussian envoy had claimed the negotiations were carried on only *pro forma* and that both governments had no illusions as to their outcome (Dotézac to Moustier, Copenhagen, 26 February 1868, *ibid.*, Danemark/253, no. 11).

[2] Benedetti to Moustier, Berlin, 3 March 1868, *ibid.*, Prusse/369, no. 54; same to same, Berlin, 19 March 1868, *ibid.*, no. 60.

[3] Same to same, Berlin, 8 April 1868, *ibid.*, no. 73.

[4] Same to same, Berlin, 18 March 1868, *ibid.*, no. 59; Loftus to Stanley, Berlin, 21 March 1868, PRO FO 64/640, no. 166.

dealt a blow to the unification cause.[1] The adverse effects of these elections were becoming slowly apparent to observers of German affairs like Benedetti.[2] Faced with demands for national unification in North Germany and opposition to such a course in the South, the Prussian government was in a difficult position. Moustier, for one, was hopeful that Prussia would show respect for the sentiment in South Germany and not force a change.[3] Benedetti thought that Bismarck at present preferred not to complicate the situation, but he suspected that the chancellor might support certain features of the National Liberal program, perhaps even that of decentralization and self-government, in order to make unification more attractive to South Germany.[4] Although the North German parliament was displaying a rather restrained spirit, the ambassador believed indirect efforts would be made to speed unification through the *Zollparlament*.[5] He confided to Wimpffen that he expected a renewed push toward unification, which might lead to difficulties with the south German states. The Austrian envoy believed to have detected hopes of a war between France and Prussia in Benedetti's utterances, although the latter's correspondence does not indicate such an attitude.[6] The situation became somewhat strained when the press in Germany began to devote more and more space to reports of French armaments. Although Bismarck supposedly did not share such alarmist views, Thile told Benedetti on 22 April that information on French military preparations was multiplying like a *déluge d'avis sinistres*.[7] Benedetti suspected at once that the frequency of these reports constituted an attempt to influence the deputies of South Germany in the forthcoming customs parliament session, and a pretext for extending that assembly's attributes.[8] He decided on his own initiative, with the tacit encouragement of Thile, to call on the

---

[1] Benedetti to Moustier, Berlin, 3 March 1868, FAE CP, Prusse/ 396, no. 53. Cf. NORD-DEUTSCHER BUND, *Stenographische Berichte, 1868*, 2 vols.

[2] Benedetti to Moustier, Berlin, 1 April 1868, FAE CP, Prusse/ 396, no. 69, for an analysis of the reports on the elections and their significance.

[3] Moustier to Benedetti, Paris, 30 March 1868, *ibid.*, no. 64.

[4] Benedetti to Moustier, Berlin, 3 March 1868, *ibid.*, no. 53.

[5] Same to same, 15 April 1868, *ibid.*, no. 76.

[6] Wimpffen to Beust, Berlin, 15 April 1868, HHStA, Preussen/ 99, n.n.

[7] Benedetti to Moustier, Berlin, 23 April 1868, FAE CP, Prusse/369, no. 84. A report of Ambassador Lyons, supplemented by information from the British military attaché, indicates that uneasiness prevailed in Paris as to the intentions of the emperor and that military preparations were being quietly pursued to place France in an advantageous position should war break out. One may assume that similar information was being forwarded to Berlin from the Prussian embassy in Paris (Lyons to Stanley, P[aris], 31 March [18]68, ONCKEN, *Rheinpolitik*, II, 544–545).

[8] Benedetti to Moustier, Berlin, 23 April 1868, FAE CP, Prusse/369, no. 84.

chancellor and suggest that he prevent demonstrations in the *Zoll-parlament* relative to a supposed French threat.[1] During the interview, on Saturday, 25 April, the chancellor conceded the right of the French government to take whatever steps it deemed necessary for the efficacy of its *armement permanent*, as he termed it. He asserted that he had no apprehensions regarding the military preparations, but he pointed out that his views were not shared by the other members of the government. Benedetti assured the chancellor of the absence of any hostile intent in France and he reminded Bismarck of the declarations made by Rouher and Jules Baroche in this respect. Contrary to his own opinion, Benedetti maintained that the imperial government did not consider the developments which had transformed Germany as being a threat to French security. The military measures implemented in France were nothing more than a reorganization of the army on a modern basis.[2] Bismarck's emphasis that his views on French military measures were not shared by the "majority" was not lost on Benedetti. However, his efforts to explain the true intent of his government regarding military affairs were rendered more difficult by the fact that Prussia had announced plans to release about 12,000 men from military service before the completion of their three year service. Indeed, Bismarck suggested that France make a similar gesture in the interests of peace.[3] Benedetti did not think the announced release of forces an effort to reduce tension but, rather, to reduce the military budget. He pointed out to Moustier that freed from active service the men in question were still subject to four years duty in the reserve and an additional five years in the *Landwehr*.[4]

The long anticipated session of the customs parliament was opened by a royal address on Monday, 27 April.[5] The speech contained no

[1] Same to same, Berlin, 26 April 1868, *ibid.*, no. 87; Wimpffen to Beust, Berlin, 23 April 1868, HHStA, Preussen/98, no. 42. Benedetti's request for an audience was particularly noticed since both he and Loftus had avoided seeing Bismarck who, upon resuming his duties on 18 March, had asked the foreign representatives to be indulgent (Bylandt to Zuylen, Berlin, 18 April 1868, RBZ, Pruisen/ 1868, no. 142).

[2] Benedetti to Moustier, Berlin, 26 April 1868, FAE CP, Prusse/369, no. 87; Wimpffen to Beust, Berlin, 26 April 1868, HHStA, Preussen/98, no. 44. Moustier's instructions, asking that Benedetti deny all rumors of French preparations for war, reached the ambassador after he had asked for an audience (Moustier to Benedetti, Paris, 25 April 1868, FAE CP, Prusse/369, T.).

[3] Benedetti to Moustier, Berlin, 26 April 1868, *ibid.*, no. 87; cf. Bismarck to Goltz, Berlin, 27 April 1868, *BGW*, VIa, 378.

[4] Benedetti to Moustier, Berlin, 30 April 1868, FAE CP, Prusse/369, no. 93; cf. Goltz to William I, Paris, 4 May 1868, *APP*, X, 8-11, who was disappointed by the slight impression the release of Prussian troops had made in Paris.

[5] The *Zollparlament* met from 27 April until 23 May; the session of the North German

noteworthy reference to the unification question, as Bismarck had told Benedetti beforehand. During the interview of 25 April, the chancellor tried to ease French anxieties relative to the role of the *Zollparlament* and claimed that Prussia would stop any parliamentary move to force German unification upon the southern states. No doubt, Bismarck had correctly appraised the significance of the elections and was prepared to follow a cautious course, without relinquishing for a moment his aim of ultimate unification. He was aware of the fact that a major national German crisis, such as war, would sweep away the remaining obstacles. For the moment restraint seemed advisable and Bismarck bided his time. It would appear that Benedetti placed too great and permanent a meaning upon the outcome of the elections. Moreover, he was eager to think that the effect of French military reorganization had deterred the more nationalist elements in the *Zollparlament*.[1] As soon as the session commenced, he had occasion to study the disposition of the delegates. Under the guise of a proposal to reply to the king's opening speech, the National Liberals tried to provoke a debate on the ways and means to unify Germany, a move Benedetti had expected. Although the motion was defeated, largely because of Bismarck's self-imposed moderation, the ambassador was impressed by the sentiment in favor of unification. Three out of four speakers, as well as the majority of the delegates, felt that unification was a right and a necessity. He came to realize that the desire to leave unification to its natural course, and the fear of external complications, had made moderation prevail. "Our *chassepots* figured in the debate and have produced an effect there, although [Moritz von] Blankenburg, in mentioning them, did declare that Germany would have but *one soul* if they appeared on the frontier."[2] Although Bismarck had shown a very moderate attitude the ambassador was convinced that the chancellor had actually been disappointed when the assembly rejected the National Liberal motion and had passed on to the order of the day.[3] Benedetti, in contrast, regretted that the defeat of the motion had not been accompanied by more vigorous particularist demonstrations.[4] The initial failure of the attempt to promote unification through the customs parliament

Confederation parliament was prorogued during this period, since its members also sat in the *Zollparlament*.

[1] Benedetti to Moustier, Berlin, 26 April 1868, FAE CP, Prusse/369, no. 88.

[2] Same to same, Berlin, 9 May 1868, *ibid.*, no. 98; same to same, Berlin, 7 May 1868, *ibid.*, no. 97.

[3] Same to same, Berlin, 9 May 1868, *ibid.*, no. 98.

[4] Wimpffen to Beust, Berlin, 10 May 1868, HHStA, Preussen/99; cf. Moustier to Benedetti, [Paris,] 14 May 1868, FAE CP, Prusse/370, no. 79.

had not completely discouraged its supporters, although the session did not produce new debates on the issue. Ambassador Benedetti had expected further efforts,[1] but only an abortive attempt, to extend the attributes of the assembly and give it a greater political role, was made during the tax debate on 18 May. The question concerned itself with the competency of the *Zollverein vis-à-vis* the government of Hesse; its implications were highly significant and brought sharp opposition from the south German delegates. Bismarck's speech, an effort to maintain a middle course, did not surprise Benedetti. The disappointing role of the *Zollparlament* as an instrument of unification was repeated in subsequent sessions, and caused Bismarck to despair of its effectiveness.[2] The session of the *Zollparlament* ended on 23 May, and in Benedetti's opinion there had been neither victor nor vanquished on the political terrain. He feared that the success of the particularists was essentially negative, since it spelled nothing more than a temporary check of the unification drive. The nationalists, on the other hand, could still count on wide-spread popular support and could indeed expect it to increase in the future.[3] The proceedings showed that the unification movement had suffered a momentary setback, that the opposition to it was stronger than expected, and that the south German states preferred to rely on treaties with the North German Confederation rather than on common institutions. The majority report of the south German deputies called for a closer union of their states to maintain their independence and prevent their absorption by Prussia.[4] Yet, the ambassador knew that the political atmosphere offered no comfort for the imperial government.

After the *Zollparlament* had ended its sessions Ambassador and Madame Benedetti left Berlin for a short vacation in Saxony.[5] With

---

[1] Benedetti to Moustier, Berlin, 15 May 1868, *ibid.*, no. 100. The ambassador believed that the exponents of unification would in all probability shift their efforts and bring the pressure of public opinion to bear on the deputies.

[2] Same to same, Berlin, 19 May 1868, *ibid.*, no. 101. For the deliberations and issues, see DEUTSCHER ZOLLVEREIN. ZOLL-PARLAMENT, *Stenographische Berichte über die Verhandlungen des deutschen Zoll-parlaments, 1868* (Berlin, 1868); SCHÜBELIN, pp. 105 ff.; G. WINDELL, *The Catholics and German Unity 1866–1871* (Minneapolis, Minn., 1954), pp. 134 ff.; RAPP, pp. 289 ff.: BECKER, pp. 590 ff.; PFLANZE, pp. 399–403.

[3] Benedetti to Moustier, Berlin, 24 May 1868, FAE CP, Prusse/370, no. 106; *MMP*, pp. 278–280.

[4] For this report, see Benedetti to Moustier, Berlin, 26 May 1868, FAE CP, Prusse/370, no. 107.

[5] "Benedetti is here... since Saturday. This great diplomat comes to Dresden and to Saxon Switzerland to forget the torments and the vexations which his friend Bismarck causes him... I had not seen my old chief since 1865. How changed I found him, white! The death of his daughter... has caused him deep grief. The unfortunate father can not

the departure of the deputies from Berlin, the animation and suspense occasioned by the *Zollparlament* session gave way to a more relaxed and quiet atmosphere. The North German parliament continued to meet until 20 June, but its debates did not point to any important decision. The calm which had befallen the Prussian capital was not expected to be disturbed, and already on 16 June Bismarck departed for his estate at Varzin.[1] Benedetti left five days later for Carlsbad where he planned to take the waters. He did not begin his official leave until 11 August, which he spent at Bad Gastein.[2]

When the ambassador returned to his post on 18 November,[3] he first preoccupied himself with the negotiations carried on between Bavaria, Württemberg and Baden relative to mutual military problems.[4] During the session of the *Zollparlament* the delegates of Bavaria and Württemberg had begun conversations which, at that time, had dealt mainly with the future of the south German federal fortresses Ulm, Rastatt, and Landau. On 23 May, Varnbüler and Hohenlohe had signed a preliminary accord regulating the occupation of the fortress at Ulm.[5] Negotiations had continued throughout the summer months and had been marked by the reluctance of Baden, perhaps at Prussian instigation, to enter into a military convention with Bavaria and Württemberg.[6] In late September military conferences between representatives of the three states had opened in Munich, and on 10 October they had signed an accord establishing a permanent *Festungskommission* (actually constituted on 26 August 1869), charged with the administration of the fortresses, their facilities, and the general defense preparations of the south German fortress system.[7] The accord was far from consti-

---

console himself..." (IDEVILLE, p. 82); cf. R. BALDICK, ed., *Pages from the Goncourt Journal* (London, 1962), pp. 242–243.

[1] Bismarck to William I, Berlin, 13 June 1868, *BGW*, VIa, 400–401.

[2] Moustier to Benedetti, Paris, 21 June 1868, FAE CP, Prusse/370, T. Benedetti returned from Carlsbad on 6 August and remained in Berlin over the weekend. He left for Gastein on the 11th, expecting to remain there for a prolonged cure. Just prior to his first vacation there had been rumors. totally unfounded, that he would be transferred to the Florence post (Bylandt to Zuylen, Berlin, 15 June 1868, RBZ, Pruisen/1868, no. 228; same to same, Berlin, 7 August 1868, *ibid.*, no. 301; same to same, Berlin, 21 September 1868, *ibid.*, no. 371).

[3] Same to same, Berlin, 23 November 1868, *ibid.*, no. 449.

[4] In conversations with Gramont at Carlsbad, Benedetti had repeated his view that the Prussian government would not rest until it had brought about the union of North and South Germany (Gramont to Moustier, Vienna, 23 July 1868, FAE CP, Autriche/498, n.n.).

[5] Rothan to Moustier, Frankfort, 3 July 1868, *ibid.*, Francfort/ 5, no. 211. According to Rothan, the agreement between Bavaria and Württemberg was not viewed with favor in Berlin, because it was felt that military cooperation between the south German states would make the unification of Germay still more difficult to achieve.

[6] Lefèbvre de Béhaine to Moustier, Berlin, 23 July 1868, *ibid.*, Prusse/371, no. 136.

[7] KOLLER, II, 854–855; Châteaurenard to Moustier, Stuttgart, 5 October 1868, FAE CP,

tuting a south German military alliance, and it expressly made reference to the alliances with Prussia and the common military interests of both areas.[1] In an audience on 28 November, during which he was shown great cordiality, Benedetti conversed at length with William on the military problems which seemed to occupy the attention of a number of German cabinets. The monarch did not think that reorganization efforts in that field need arouse any apprehension. Although the discussion of the state of affairs in Europe was quite general, the ambassador came away feeling that William desired to avoid any dissention between Prussia and France.[2] Bismarck's return to the capital on 2 December found the ambassador incapacitated and unable to receive the chancellor who called on the chiefs of the principal missions. The main question of interest to Benedetti was the reply which the Prussian cabinet was going to make to a Bavarian proposal that the *Liquidationskommission*, composed of Prussia, Bavaria, Baden, Hesse, and Württemberg and charged with the liquidation of the war matériel in the federal fortresses, be convoked.[3] He suspected that a further

Württemberg/88, no. 65; Astorg to Moustier, Darmstadt, 10 October 1868, *ibid.*, Hesse-Darmstadt/30, no. 48; HOHENLOHE, I, 336; MOHL, II, 314; see also H. VON POSCHINGER, "Eigenhändige Aufzeichnungen des Präsidenten des badischen Ministeriums des Auswärtigen Rudolf von Freydorf über die militärischen Einigungsversuche der süddeutschen Staaten," *Annalen des deutschen Reichs*, XXXVIII, no. 1 (1905), pp. 1-30.

[1] KOLLER, II, 854-855.

[2] Benedetti to Moustier, Berlin, 29 November 1868, FAE CP, Prusse/372, no. 209. The question of control of the federal fortresses in South Germany was but one of the avenues Bismarck explored to achieve a high degree of coordination and integration in German military affairs. The military alliances which had been concluded in 1866 assured Prussia of supreme command in case of war. However, in order to render the military power of the south German allies effective, a complete reorganization was imperative. The spectacular success of the Prussians in 1866 evoked a desire among the south German states to initiate reforms along the lines of the Prussian military establishment. Under Hohenlohe's leadership efforts were made to coordinate the reform programs, leading to an accord signed in Stuttgart in February 1867. Although the southern states agreed upon guiding principles, very considerable divergence of views relative to specific aspects of the program manifested itself. While the Luxemburg crisis offered a possibility of speeding up the reform program, the threat of war passed too swiftly to have great effect. Moreover, during the parliamentary debates in the southern legislatures, the threat of a Prussianization of the southern armies generated considerable opposition. Yet, once the necessary acts had been passed the process of assimilation and integration ran its inevitable course. The appearance of Prussian military missions in South Germany, the exchange of personnel, the joint planning in the field of training, equipment and organization produced the results expected in Berlin. By the close of 1869, a high level of coordination had been achieved, culminating in closely related plans for mobilization and military operations (M. LEYH, *Die bayerische Heeresreform unter König Ludwig II., 1866-1870*, "Darstellungen aus der bayerischen Kriegs- und Heeresgeschichte," Vol. 23 [Munich, 1923], pp. 32 ff.; HOHENLOHE, I, 194-195, 320 ff.; H. BAUMGARTEN, *Staatsminister Jolly* [Tübingen, 1897], pp. 83 ff.; BECKER, pp. 597 ff.; RAPP, pp. 333 ff.; PFLANZE, pp. 406-411).

[3] Benedetti to Moustier, Berlin, 5 December 1868, FAE CP, Prusse/372, no. 214. The commission had been created after the war of 1866 and had met in Frankfort from October 1866 until July 1867, when it adjourned without having completed its work (MOHL, II, 278 ff.;

consolidation of the military ties between the North and the South might result from such a meeting; he also thought Prussia rather anxious to assert her rights as co-proprietor of this matériel and attributed Bismarck's hesitation to this factor.[1] A week later Benedetti had gathered more definite indications of the chancellor's plans: Bismarck expected to propose the convocation of the *Liquidationskommission*, which would be enlarged to include representatives from all the German states. Benedetti was convinced that such a commission would, in due time, assume a very large role in German military affairs and permit Prussia, through her preponderance, to integrate and control the military forces of the various states.[2]

Meanwhile, after the resignation of Moustier and his replacement by La Valette on 18 December [3] the powers were confronted with dangerous complications in the Turkish-Greek controversy. As a result of Greek support of an uprising on Crete against the Turkish authorities, the latter had broken off diplomatic relations with Greece and threatened the expulsion of all Greek subjects from Turkish soil. The possibility of armed conflict in the Near East greatly troubled Bismarck, who saw the hand of Beust behind efforts to create trouble. Anxious to forestall a conflict and to isolate the anti-Prussian element in Vienna and Paris, Bismarck appealed to the vanity of Emperor Napoleon. The Prussian government proposed that the signatory powers to the Paris Treaty of 1856 meet to mediate the conflict between Turkey and Greece. Napoleon showed himself more than willing to preside over such an international meeting and was also encouraged by La Valette.[4]

HOHENLOHE, I, 310, note). The meetings were finally resumed in April 1869 (MOHL, II, 314 ff.).

[1] Benedetti to Moustier, Berlin, 5 December 1868, FAE CP, Prusse/372, no. 214; cf. Perglas to Louis II, Berlin, 9 December 1868, *APP*, X, 332–334, who believed that Bismarck's reluctance to make his views known was occasioned by caution *vis-à-vis* France.

[2] Benedetti to Moustier, Berlin, 12 December 1868, FAE CP, Prusse/372, no. 221.

[3] Moustier "was clever, sagacious, a good speaker, but naturally indolent and a man of pleasure. When minister for foreign affairs in Paris, he was rarely to be found, and acquired the sobriquet of '*le ministre introuvable*'"(LOFTUS, I, 140–141). "In regard to Moustier, I see his retirement with regret. The fact that he was seldom found in his office and disliked affairs made him actually less obnoxious than diplomats who always wanted to make arrangements with Prussia. Moustier desired peace and as few as possible negotiations. In the ministry of foreign affairs, the employees are happy over his departure because he had been away from office at times for days, seldom put his signature to documents which should have been dispatched without delay; time and again the couriers were held up because the minister had gone out. All this is connected with his relationship with Mme Durand whom he had known in Constantinople and whose husband did not object to this liaison which permitted him lucrative business affairs. All this contributed markedly to Moustier's fall" (Solms to Bismarck, Paris, 18 December 1868, *APP*, X, 366–367).

[4] La Valette to Benedetti, [Paris,] 23 December 1868, FAE CP, Prusse/372, no. 109. Bismarck, in taking the initiative for calling a conference, wanted to check the bellicose

Ambassador Benedetti also had a great interest in the Near East crisis, in part due to his previous service in the area and his role as secretary of the Paris congress of 1856. Favoring immediate steps to check the crisis, he suggested that, in order to convoke a conference, guarantees be offered to both Turkey and Greece to permit them to abandon all measures likely to increase the tension. He also thought it advisable that the object and the bases for the deliberations be laid down at once. This double condition could be fulfilled by an appropriate declaration of the powers. The ambassador, like La Valette, felt that the Turkish government had a legitimate complaint, and he believed that the powers should take cognizance of it by assuring Turkey of a just consideration.[1] Plans for an international conference made rapid progress, and at a royal dinner, to which Benedetti and Loftus were invited on 22 December, King William expressed the wish that the threatening crisis be dealt with as quickly as possible.[2] The initiative of Prussia was given further impetus when, in the evening of 23 December, Bismarck asked the French ambassador to his residence to discuss the scope of the conference, apparently in consequence of British insistence.[3] Instructed not to assume the initiative in the preparatory work, Benedetti merely acquainted himself with Bismarck's wish that the conference limit itself to the examination of Turkey's demands and make appropriate recommendations.[4] Already on Thursday, 24 December, La Valette had drawn up the formula for the conference invitation and requested Benedetti to submit it to Bismarck for approval.[5] The ambassador called Thursday evening to acquaint the chancellor, semi-officially, with the tenor of the French invitation.[6] The fact that Bismarck voiced no objection, and no

---

attitude of Beust and bring about a *détente* between France and Austria. He also hoped to loosen any *rapprochement* between Britain and France, expecting, in the final analysis, to isolate all the powers to a degree (ROTHFRITZ, p. 316; H. MICHAEL, *Bismarck und Europa von 1866–1870. Eine Studie zur Geschichte Bismarcks und der Reichsgründung* [Munich, 1929], p. 23). Benedetti evidently tried to prevent a *détente* between Austria and France and made efforts to reassure the Austrian envoy (Wimpffen to Beust, Berlin, 9 December 1868, HHStA, Preussen/98, no. 102; same to same, Berlin, 26 December 1868, *ibid.*, no. 110). See GEUSS, pp. 236–238.

[1] Benedetti to La Valette, Berlin, 22 December 1868, FAE CP, Prusse/372, T.; Wimpffen to Beust, Berlin, 23 December 1868, HHStA, Preussen/98, no. 85.

[2] Benedetti to La Valette, Berlin, 23 December 1868, FAE CP, Prusse/372, no. 227; Loftus to Clarendon, Berlin, 24 December 1868, PRO FO 64/645, no. 24.

[3] Thile to Benedetti, Berlin, 23 December 1868, FAE CP, Prusse/372, n.n.; Benedetti to La Valette, Berlin, 24 December 1868, *ibid.*, no. 228; Bylandt to Roest van Limburg, Berlin, 26 December 1868, RBZ, Pruisen/1868, no. 485.

[4] Benedetti to La Valette, Berlin, 24 December 1868, FAE CP, Prusse/372, no. 228.

[5] La Valette to Benedetti, Paris, 24 December 1868, *ibid.*, T.

[6] Thile to Solms, Berlin, 25 December 1868, *APP*, X, 394, T.; Bismarck to Solms, Berlin, 25 December 1868, *ibid.*, 394–395.

difficulties were expected on the part of the other powers, prompted Benedetti, although lacking specific instructions, to present the official invitation of the French government on Friday.[1] His haste created a problem when the Russian government demanded that a Greek delegate be admitted to the conference. Bismarck, acting on Benedetti's assurance that invitations had been sent to the other powers, informed Prussian representatives abroad that the French invitation had arrived. It was only when Reuss telegraphed Russia's new demand that the chancellor realized Benedetti's mistake. Although he had not compromised his position by announcing Prussia's acceptance, he was nevertheless very much displeased with Benedetti who, in contrast, took a rather nonchalant view of the matter.[2] The final arrangements were made without further difficulty and on 30 December the ambassador received notice that the powers had agreed to both principle and object of the conference.[3]

By the time the Paris conference opened, on 9 January, Ambassador Benedetti had become seriously concerned over a Prussian press polemic against Austria; he felt that it was directed in particular against Beust, whose bellicose attitude during the Greco-Turkish controversy had strengthened Bismarck's determination to see him toppled from his post.[4] Benedetti considered the campaign laden with danger and he repeatedly cautioned Wimpffen against a counter-attack by the Austrian press. The close friendship between Benedetti and La Valette gave Wimpffen hope that the imperial government would be kept informed of the true situation.[5] The press campaign did come to an end by mid-January, when Austrian silence proved too strong an opponent.[6] Moreover, the resolutions adopted by the Paris conference, which concluded its meetings on 20 January, also contributed to the lessening of tension in Europe, since they seemed to point up a certain solidarity between the great powers on issues threatening the peace.[7]

---

[1] Benedetti to La Valette, Berlin, 25 December 1868, FAE CP, Prusse/372, T.

[2] La Valette to Benedetti, Paris, 25 December 1868, *ibid.*, T.; Bismarck to Solms, Berlin, 28 December 1868, *BGW*, VIa, 491–492.

[3] La Valette to Benedetti, [Paris,] 30 December 1868, FAE CP, Prusse/372, no. 117.

[4] Benedetti to La Valette, Berlin, 14 January 1869, *ibid.*, 373, no. 9; Wimpffen to Beust, Berlin, 2 January 1869, HHStA, Preussen/ 101, n.n.; Gagern to Dalwigk, Berlin, 13 January 1869, *APP*, X, 448, ft. 1.

[5] Wimpffen to Beust, Berlin, 2 January 1869, HHStA, Preussen/ 101, no. 1B; same to same, Berlin, 10 January 1869, *ibid.*, no. 4.

[6] Same to same, Berlin, 16 January 1869, *ibid.*, no. 6A; cf. Bernstorff to Bismarck, London, 13 January 1869, *APP*, X, 456; Loftus to Clarendon, Berlin, 15 January 1869, *ibid.*, 456, ft. 2 to no. 434.

[7] Benedetti to La Valette, Berlin, 22 January 1869, FAE CP, Prusse/373, no. 13. Prussia's

The momentary relaxation of tension did not distract Benedetti from the observation of German affairs. Rumors that an agreement, being worked out between the North German Confederation and Baden and providing a reciprocal basis for the training of recruits liable for military service in one but residing in the other state,[1] would be extended to Bavaria and Württemberg prompted the ambassador to seek further information. Although he learned that such was not the case, he was disturbed by the fact that the Bavarian envoy in Berlin could no longer be regarded as possessing Hohenlohe's confidence, a fact which made it difficult to follow Prusso-Bavarian relations with accuracy.[2] Relations between these two governments were indeed an enigma to Benedetti.[3] French concern with German affairs was also highlighted when debates in the Prussian chambers relative to the sequestration of the domains of King George of Hanover and the elector of Hesse occasioned French press attacks against the measures contemplated by the Prussian government.[4] The replies in the German papers decided Benedetti to protest, a step which the foreign minister seconded in talks with Solms in Paris.[5] The press attacks subsided almost at once and the friendly relations between the two powers did not suffer from the short campaign of vituperation.[6] Considering future developments in Germany, Ambassador Benedetti did not expect a radical attempt to establish a unified Germany: he did not think Bismarck prepared to risk a major disturbance which such a step might produce. He believed that the chancellor would probably further his plans through efforts which were unlikely to cause conflict with other powers.[7] Among such moves Benedetti considered the establishment of a responsible ministry for the North German Confederation[8] as well as

---

satisfaction with the settlement of the Greco–Turkish dispute is evident in King William's speech opening the session of the North German parliament (NORDDEUTSCHER BUND, *Stenographische Berichte, 1869*, I, 1–2).

[1] Benedetti to La Valette, Berlin, 22 January 1869, FAE CP, Prusse/373, no. 13.

[2] Same to same, Berlin, 29 January 1869, *ibid.*, no. 19.

[3] *Ibid.* Cf. Solms to Bismarck, Paris, 9 February 1869, *APP*, X, 536–538, for La Valette's interest in Prussia's relations with Baden.

[4] Benedetti to La Valette, Berlin, 29 January 1869, FAE CP, Prusse/373, no. 19.

[5] Same to same, Berlin, 13 February 1869, *ibid.*, no. 30. Cf. Perglas to Louis II, Berlin, 12 February 1869, *APP*, X, 542, who believed that Bismarck might use the press feud to cause anxiety in South Germany about French intentions and thus obtain greater concessions from those states relative to their military agreements with Prussia.

[6] "Benedetti himself came to tell me that after Bismarck's friendly speech... [he] considered the polemic against France as having ended" (Wimpffen to Beust, Berlin, 15 February 1869, HHStA, Preussen/101, T).

[7] Benedetti to La Valette, Berlin, 13 February 1869, FAE CP, Prusse/373, no. 29.

[8] The *Bundesrat* was presented with the respective proposals by the presidium on 20

the convocation of the *Liquidationskommission*. The possibility that Prussia, with the aid of Baden, might establish her right to participate in decisions affecting the fortresses in the South was raised by the ambassador. In his opinion such a development would contribute further to the ineffectiveness of Article IV of the Prague Treaty, upon the inclusion of which the imperial government had once so strongly insisted. He deemed it most unlikely that Bismarck would agree to any other decision, despite the opposition which Bavaria and Württemberg might furnish.[1] The opening of the *Bundestag* on 4 March by King William was attended by the ambassador, and he noted that the agenda did not include propositions touching on constitutional or international affairs. Although some members did wish to replace the Confederation with a German kingdom, Benedetti did not predict any such attempt by the North German parliament.[2]

However, the somewhat reassuring outlook regarding German affairs was not paralleled in international affairs. In March the Franco-Belgian railroad controversy, arising from the Belgian government's opposition to the convention between the French government-supported *Compagnie de l'Est* and the Belgian *Grand-Luxembourg* railroad companies signed on 31 January 1869, had begun to reach a critical stage.[3] The promulgation of a Belgian law on 23 February, prohibiting the sale of the *Grand-Luxembourg* or any other Belgian railroad to a foreign company, had aroused the ire of the imperial cabinet as well as its determination to see the convention implemented.[4] Ambassador Be-

---

February (Benedetti to La Valette, Berlin, 25 February 1869, *ibid.*, no. 41; Stosch to Crown Prince Frederick, Berlin, 5 February 1869, STOSCH, p. 149).

[1] Benedetti to La Valette, Berlin, 26 February 1869, FAE CP, Prusse/373, no. 42. NORD-DEUTSCHER BUND, *Stenographische Berichte, 1869*, I, 1–2.

[2] Benedetti to La Valette, Berlin, 4 March 1869, FAE CP, Prusse/373, no. 48.

[3] The controversy had originated when the directors of the *Grand-Luxembourg* railroad, anxious for financial relief, had signed a provisional purchase agreement with the *Compagnie de l'Est*, which in turn was closely connected with the *Comité des Forges*, on 8 December 1868. Already on the 17th, Jamar had declared that the Belgian government would not agree to the proposed transaction. Yet, the stockholders of the Belgian company had agreed to the provisional accord and, on 31 January 1869, the two companies had signed the final agreement. The reaction of the Belgian government had been quick; a bill prohibiting the sale of Belgian railroads to foreign companies and making the participation of foreign capital dependent upon the consent of the government had been introduced on 6 February by Frère-Orban and had been promulgated on 23 February. The imperial government, supporting the case of the *Compagnie de l'Est*, insisted that the new law could not apply to the sale of the *Grand-Luxembourg* on grounds that the agreement had been signed before the law had been promulgated (K. RHEINDORF, "Der belgisch-französische Eisenbahnkonflikt," *Deutsche Rundschau*, CXCV [May 1923], pp. 114–124; M. BLANCHARD, "D'une version de l'affaire des 'chemins de fer belges,'" *RH* [1940], pp. 222–226; G. CRAIG, "Great Britain and the Belgian Railways Dispute of 1869," *AHR*, L [July 1945], pp. 743–748).

[4] La Valette to La Gueronnière, Paris, 17 February 1869, FAE CP, Belgique/247, no.2.

nedetti had been aware of the dispute, generated by fears of French economic penetration of Belgium, but had not been officially informed by La Valette until 1 March, when he was acquainted with the instructions issued to the French envoy in Brussels.[1] The foreign minister made no mention of the suspicion entertained in French government circles that the hand of Bismarck was behind the remarkably determined opposition of the Belgian government.[2] Benedetti was uninformed about these suspicions entertained in Paris, and in a conversation with Nothomb he readily conceded that the Belgian government had received no encouragement in Berlin.[3] Agitation in Berlin relative to the Belgian affair had been restrained, and only belatedly had the incident been thought very serious. As for the position of the Prussian government, the ambassador had no information to relay to Paris. He was unaware of Bismarck's willingness to cooperate with England in bringing pressure to bear on France, provided the British government would clearly commit itself to such a course.[4] The news that the Belgian government had agreed, on 15 March, to a French proposal that a mixed commission examine the entire problem, seemed to justify the little concern which the ambassador had shown.[5]

[1] La Valette to Benedetti, Paris, 1 March 1869, *ibid.*, Prusse/373, no. 33.

[2] "The Belgian government shows publicly its ill will toward France, and public opinion is persuaded, rightly or wrongly, that Belgium is only arrogant because she has Prussia behind her. To show oneself accommodating in these circumstances, or to retreat in the face of a conduct which offends us, would mean to abdicate before Europe all legitimate influence. Will war be the result of this conflict? I do not know but one must act as though [war] will result from it. In this supposition, what do we have to fear? Before envisaging this hypothesis, it is necessary first to examine coldly our situation in Europe. France feels herself diminished since the successes of Prussia; she would like to find the occasion to establish her influence in the best possible conditions and without arousing all the passions in Germany by unfurling a flag hostile to the German nationality.... If, in the present case, a war with Belgium were to take place, Germany would have no right to mix into it, and if she did intervene, she would be the *provocateur...*" (Napoleon III to Niel, Paris, 19 February 1869, OLLIVIER, XI, 375–376). Cf. Lyons to Clarendon, Paris, 16 February 1869, T. NEWTON, *Lord Lyons, a Record of British Diplomacy* (London, 1913), I, 213–214, who reports that La Valette emphasized the emperor's displeasure with the Belgian government.

[3] "Benedetti is convinced and assures me that in Paris one is certain that we have received neither encouragement nor impulsion from Berlin" (Nothomb to van der Stichelen, Berlin, 12 March 1869, BAE CP, Incident Franco-Belge [1869–1870], no. 60).

[4] Benedetti to La Valette, Berlin, 11 March 1869, FAE CP, Prusse/373, no. 50. "Bismarck is biding his time quietly. If France annexes Belgium and we take no part he will be delighted, since France could no longer complain of Prussian aggrandizement. If we do take part, he would be equally delighted at the rupture between England and France, and would come to our assistance. Either way he thinks Prussia would gain. Why should Napoleon and La Valette assist him? A quarrel between France and England or even a coolness is the great German desideratum" (Clarendon to Lyons, London, ca. 12–15 March 1869, NEWTON, I, 214–215). "I believe therefore: if England wants to be serious, we will go along, if not, we will not [go against France]. *Why pull the chestnuts out of the fire for John Bull?*" (Thile to Balan, Berlin, 10 March 1869, SASS, *PJ*, CCXVII, Heft 3 [September 1929], p. 271).

[5] La Valette to Benedetti, [Paris,] 15 March 1869, FAE CP, Prusse/373, no. 53; La Gueronnière to La Valette, Brussels, 15 March 1869, *ibid.*, Belgique/ 247, T.

News that the *Liquidationskommission* would meet 4 April in Munich caused Ambassador Benedetti to turn his attention fully to the affairs in Germany. He felt qualified to predict that the participating governments would agree not to divide the matériel nor to dispose of it. They would continue to leave it in communal possession and thus the only problem would be that of custodianship and upkeep.[1] As for the other tendencies toward unification, Benedetti believed that agitation in the matter had noticeably subsided. Moreover, at the king's birthday reception, he had gained the impression from talks with William and Bismarck that no change in the relationship between the Confederation and the south German states was likely. To be sure, Benedetti cautioned that Bismarck would always endeavor to further the scheme of unification.[2] By contrast, the manner in which La Valette viewed the developments in Germany, expressed in a speech in the chamber on 10 April, seemed to show less concern over Prussian designs toward unification:

> Germany traverses one of those periods of transition, and it is a motive for us to avoid any *démarche* which could be interpreted as an interference in questions which do not interest us directly. We made it our duty not to awaken susceptibilities, and only legitimate interests could engage us to depart from this attitude of abstention. But nothing is of a nature to cause us to foresee such eventualities; the Confederation of North Germany is concluding its organization; the states of the South have associated themselves with this movement within the limit of their national aspirations and their general interests; they are separated from it by their autonomous sentiments and by their particular needs; we have no claim for interfering in the double movement which develops freely and spontaneously on the other side of the Rhine. We have not done it, we did not have to do it. It would only be in the case where this movement, in going beyond its legitimate boundaries, would threaten our rights that our situation in this respect would change.[3]

The favorable attitude of the imperial government, designed to forestall Prussian opposition relative to the Franco-Belgian incident,[4] might well have strengthened Bismarck's determination to ignore demands for the creation of a ministry responsible to the North German Con-

---

[1] Benedetti to La Valette, Berlin, 13 March 1869, *ibid.*, Prusse/373, no. 53.

[2] Same to same, Berlin, 18 March 1869, *ibid.*, no. 59; same to same, Berlin, 21 March 1869, *ibid.*, no. 62; same to same, Berlin, 25 March 1869, *ibid.*, no. 63; Loftus to Clarendon, Berlin, 27 March 1869, PRO FO 64/661, no. 158; cf. Bismarck to Rosenberg, Berlin, 25 March 1869, *BGW*, VIb, 35–36, who felt that the best way to further the unification was to display, at present, an attitude of watchful waiting and to show no "*Eifer und Beflissenheit.*"

[3] OLLIVIER, XI, 457–458.

[4] Cf. Benedetti to La Valette, Berlin, 13 April 1869, FAE CP, Prusse/374, no. 76; same to same, Berlin, 15 April 1869, *ibid.*, no. 77.

federation. Benedetti believed this opposition was motivated, in small part, by a desire to reassure particularists in South Germany.[1]

On 26 April Ambassador Benedetti left for a short visit to Paris, having previously called on the chancellor to inform him that his departure was necessitated by private affairs.[2] During his stay in the French capital he was probably acquainted with the Franco-Belgian talks. On 27 April a joint protocol was issued, in consequence of the negotiations carried on with Frère-Orban, that a mixed commission composed of six members would meet to consider a new treaty which was to be strictly commercial in nature.[3] The decision could not be considered a victory for France. It is ironical that Benedetti was created a count at this time, when yet another ambitious imperial aspiration was consigned to the graveyard of shattered schemes.[4]

Although Ambassador Benedetti was "full of peace" on arriving in Berlin on 6 May and expressed himself in the most pacific terms, he did not fail to tell Bismarck that the imperial government might be forced to change its attitude toward Belgium, should that state continue to act without regard for the interests of France. He made no reference at all to the role which Prussia was suspected of having played. Indeed, the ambassador considered the Belgian issue almost settled, and he devoted his attention to the affairs in Germany.[5] The meeting of the

---

[1] same to same Valette, Berlin, 16 April 1869, *ibid.*, no. 78; same to same, Berlin, 21 April 1869, *ibid.*, no. 80.

[2] Cf. Loftus to Clarendon, Berlin, 1 May 1869, PRO FO 64/663, no. 222; same to same, Berlin, 8 May 1869, *ibid.*, no. 235, who writes that Bismarck expected Benedetti to ask for a change of post on account of the health of Madame Benedetti. The private nature of the ambassador's voyage to Paris is indicated by the text of La Valette's telegram: "You can come the day it suits you. I place no limit beforehand on the stay which you will make in Paris.... If you come alone, come down to the *Affaires étrangères*" (La Valette to Benedetti, Paris, 21 April 1869, FAE CP, Prusse/374, T.).

[3] The accord between France and Belgium of 27 April 1869 had no doubt been speeded along after Clarendon had made it clear in Paris that he could obtain almost immediately an alliance with Prussia to safeguard Belgium. Bismarck was far from pleased with Clarendon's claim and believed that the British government was rattling Prussia's saber in Paris. Bismarck was worried that a Prusso-British accord might prompt France to seek closer ties with Russia, and that such a *rapprochement* might outweigh the advantages of Prussian collaboration with Britain. "We might tomorrow, if we pleased, enter into a coalition with Prussia against France for the protection of Belgian independence which is a European and not exclusively French question" (Clarendon to Lyons, London, 19 April 1869, NEWTON, I, 218). Cf. RHEINDORF, *Deutsche Rundschau*, CXCV (May 1923), pp. 121–123; CRAIG, AHR, L (July 1945), p. 759; Jules Devaux to Frère-Orban, Brussels, 26 April 1869, P. HYMANS, *Frère-Orban* (Brussels, 1905), II, 277.

[4] It will be recalled that Benedetti had received the *grand-croix* of the Legion of Honor after Prussia had rejected French compensation demands of August 1866.

[5] Loftus to Clarendon, Berlin, 15 May 1869, PRO FO 64/663, no. 253; cf. Bismarck to Solms, Berlin, n.n., May 1869, BGW, VIb, 82; Nothomb to van der Stichelen, Berlin, 25 May 1869, BAE CP, Incident Franco-Belge/3 (1869–1870), no. 151.

Liquidationskommission was in full progress, and he sought to obtain information on the decisions that were being taken. A stalemate which had developed when a proposal by the Baden delegation, to give Prussia an analogous position to that of the south German governments, had been rejected by Bavaria and Württemberg. An appeal by Hohenlohe to Bismarck had resolved the difficulty and had opened the way for a consideration of the functions of the inspectors.[1] During the first week in June, the ambassador was able to verify indications that a Prussian and a Bavarian officer had worked out a plan for the inspection of the south German fortresses as well as Mainz. Accordingly there were to be annual inspections of the matériel in common ownership. The officers charged with this duty were to be selected by Prussia and by the south German *Festungskommission*. Thus, Prussia had succeeded in her effort to prevent a division of the matériel; yet the inspection right she had acquired was an unsatisfactory substitute for her ambition to establish a commission deciding defensive measures of a much wider scope.[2] The Prussian government did gain a significant success in that the *Bundesrat* had given its approval to the military convention with Baden, which permitted recruits of one state to absolve their military obligation in the other, if they resided there.[3]

While a decision had finally been reached regarding the federal fortresses, there was no indication of renewed agitation for unification. Not even the convocation of the *Zollparlament* stimulated much sentiment. The ambassador could not fail to notice the relative quiet which reigned in Berlin. The tenor of the debates in the North German parliament, a valid gauge for the sentiment which would prevail in the *Zollparlament*, had been quite restrained; Benedetti thought the delegates far more anxious to obtain parliamentary concessions than to expostulate upon the virtues of nationalism and unification.[4] The relaxed note which marked the political scene in Berlin permitted the ambassador to prepare for his annual leave and he departed early on 6 July.[5]

---

[1] Benedetti to Rouher, Berlin, 11 May 1869, FAE CP, Prusse/ 374, no. 90; cf. Wimpffen to Beust, Berlin, 8 May 1869, HHStA, Preussen/101, n.n., to whom Benedetti had said: "It is true that [the imperial government] is pacific but, on the other hand, it is more attentive and vigilant than ever and it will not tolerate the slightest *écart* on the part of Prussia."

[2] Benedetti to La Valette, Berlin, 18 June 1869, FAE CP, Prusse/ 374, no. 123. The final agreement was signed on 6 July 1869, and ratifications were exchanged on 14 August 1869 (KOHL, II, 849–851; MOHL, II, 316, ft. 1).

[3] Benedetti to La Valette, Berlin, 3 June 1869, FAE CP, Prusse/ 374, no. 111.

[4] Same to same, Berlin, 18 June 1869, *ibid.*, no. 125.

[5] Same to same, Berlin, 6 July 1869, *ibid.*, T.; La Valette to Benedetti, Paris, 6 July 1869, *ibid.*, T.

In reviewing Benedetti's activities since May 1867, it becomes clear that the compensation fiasco had affected him deeply. It had left him with a feeling of distrust and bitterness toward Bismarck and the Prussian government. The suspicions which he had harbored since the fall of 1866, regarding the chancellor's sincerity in the compensation negotiations, had been amply justified. The ambassador had been duped, and one may assume that he wished to avoid a recurrence at all cost. He was convinced that Bismarck would upset the balance of power even further, if permitted to do so, and achieve the unification of Germany. His reports show a definite consistency in this view and make proper allowances for the tactical considerations which prompted Bismarck to press or to relent his efforts to attain that goal. Benedetti believed that the imperial government was faced with a fundamental decision: accept the unification of Germany or oppose all schemes designed to bring it about. He realized the consequences either decision involved for France, and he had not neglected to point out that a timely decision was essential. Yet, time went on and the imperial government had been reluctant to come to a decision. Instead, it had hoped to find a *modus vivendi* for the time being. Rather than suggest a course, Benedetti had endeavored to acquaint his government with all the facts bearing on the situation in Germany. The accuracy of these reports leaves little to be desired, although they no longer reflected the close association between the ambassador and Bismarck of earlier times. Benedetti did not err regarding the aims of Prussian policy in Germany. To be sure, his insight was not exceptional in this matter and his colleagues expressed very similar views.

Although he had taken no active part in the negotiations with Belgium one can assume, on the basis of earlier expressed opinions, that Benedetti had not opposed French economic expansion, in *lieu* of annexation. French control of the Belgian railroad system was expected to benefit the French steel industry in particular. However, equally important was such control for strategic considerations based on the possibility of war with Prussia. Benedetti had not shared the belief, initially held in Paris, that Bismarck had been responsible for the determined opposition of the Belgian government. His correspondence does not show that he had suspected the chancellor of such an effort but neither had he known of the British-inspired attempts to obtain Prussia's support for Belgium. Benedetti's sympathy for the Turkish cause had been motivated essentially by the desire to prevent the expansion of Russia's influence, through her support of Greece, in the eastern Mediterranean. His concern with the issue had been rather indirect and limited and his haste had revealed essentially a wish to see a threat of war checked.

The appointment of La Valette as foreign minister proved a mixed blessing for Benedetti. The long and intimate friendship between the two men, as well as their adherence to the views of the Italian faction, had established a closer and more regular link between the ministry and the embassy. One can assume, moreover, that the minister paid greater attention to the ambassador's views and suggestions than had his predecessors. Yet, a definite difference of opinion separated them in their attitude toward German affairs. Whereas Benedetti considered every advance of Bismarck's unification scheme an increase in the potential threat to the security of France, La Valette did not show such concern and, while in office, did not share the degree of alarm which Benedetti lent to his reports.

The ambassador's restrained relationship with Bismarck did not ease his task. The intimate friendship of the pre-Nikolsburg era was definitely a thing of the past, and the disappointing compensation negotiations had served to emphasize that fact. The usefulness of the ambassador in Berlin was greatly handicapped, and it appears that Bismarck's reluctance to take the initiative for a recall was the primary reason for his continued assignment in Berlin. Benedetti himself seemed to have been of two minds about remaining in the Prussian capital. The hope of ultimately scoring a diplomatic victory over Bismarck had prompted him to stay on, while repeated disappointments and defeats counselled him to leave. It is regrettable, and damaging to Benedetti's reputation as a diplomat, that he made no real effort to improve his own relations with the chancellor. Whether such was possible, in view of the conflicting interests which they represented, is difficult to say; the fact remains that Benedetti did not really try. He let personal vanity interfere with his duties, a fact which hampered him in a task for which he was otherwise adequately prepared.

CHAPTER VIII

THE HOHENZOLLERN CANDIDACY

Ambassador Benedetti returned to the Prussian capital on 10 November 1869 and found that "no affair of an international character seemed to keep... the Berlin cabinet vigilant."[1] However, the imperial government had taken a renewed interest in the implementation of Article V of the Prague Treaty. Benedetti learned from Lefèbvre de Béhaine that a Prussian press polemic against Denmark in July had not been followed by new developments. The Danish minister had confided to the *chargé d'affaires* that the Prussian cabinet had given no indication that the negotiations would be resumed.[2] Indeed, nothing had happened since March 1868 when the talks had been suspended. In the words of the French minister to Denmark, the North Schleswig question was "sleeping a profound sleep."[3] French interest had revived after a large number of North Schleswig inhabitants had petitioned William for the execution of Article V. He had refused to receive a delegation carrying the petition on grounds that the matter in question was a purely administrative one.[4] The question had been taken up with Tsar Alexander and Gorchakov by General Fleury, the new French ambassador to Russia, upon his arrival in St. Petersburg. The assurances given to Fleury, that the Russian government would recommend in Berlin the implementation of Article V, had prompted La Tour d'Auvergne to ask Benedetti to watch carefully the reaction of the Prussian government. The ambassador himself was to maintain an attitude of reserve in the matter.[5] But even before Benedetti was

[1] Benedetti to La Tour d'Auvergne, Berlin, 18 November 1869, FAE CP, Prusse/376, no. 206. The new foreign minister had assumed his duties on 19 July 1869 (La Tour d'Auvergne to Benedetti, Paris, 19 July 1869, *ibid.*, 375, T.).

[2] Lefèbvre de Béhaine to La Tour d'Auvergne, Berlin, 29 July 1869, *ibid.*, no. 140.

[3] Dotézac to La Valette, Copenhagen, 17 April 1869, *ibid.*, Danemark/254, no. 19.

[4] Benedetti to La Tour d'Auvergne, Berlin, 21 November 1869, *ibid.*, Prusse/376, no. 219.

[5] La Tour d'Auvergne to Benedetti, [Paris,] 22 November 1869, *ibid.*, no. 115.

able to act upon the minister's request, La Tour d'Auvergne had already minimized the significance of Fleury's step in talks with Ambassador Werther, who had told the French foreign minister that any pressure would make a satisfactory solution wellnigh impossible. "[Fleury], in speaking to Emperor Alexander about North Schleswig, could have only envisaged this question as being but one of the elements of the general situation, and his language on this point... did not have any other significance." [1] As for the success of a Russian intervention in Berlin, Ambassador Benedetti did not seem particularly optimistic. The long resistance of the Prussian king to retrocession was not likely to cease because of a Russian suggestion. Even the Danish government, in view of William's opposition, had decided to exclude Alsen and Düppel from the territory it wished returned to Denmark. Only a very firm stand could possibly decide the Prussian monarch to give in and hasten a retrocession. Benedetti expected Prussia to evade such a step by pleading "good and pacific intentions" and by advising that a more propitious time be chosen to settle the matter.[2] Although Fleury's remarks had caused concern in Berlin,[3] the agitation relative to North Schleswig was, as Benedetti had predicted, short-lived; the retreat of the French government as well as the reply of King William to the letter of the tsar once again consigned the matter to oblivion.

It was not until the spring of 1870 that the North Schleswig question became again a matter of concern to Benedetti. In April the *Allgemeine Norddeutsche Zeitung* unleashed a new polemic against Denmark, blaming the attitude of the Danish cabinet for the stalemate in the North Schleswig question. The version of the negotiations, as printed in the newspaper, appeared singularly misleading to Benedetti who blamed the Prussian government for the repeated failures of the talks. Prussia subordinated any agreement on retrocession to the guarantees

---

[1] La Tour d'Auvergne to Benedetti, Paris, 29 November 1869, *ibid.*, n.n.; Werther to Bismarck, Paris, 29 November 1869, GERMANY. AUSWÄRTIGES AMT, *Bismarck und die nordschleswigsche Frage*, p. 338.

[2] Benedetti to La Tour d'Auvergne, Berlin, 30 November 1869, FAE CP, Prusse/376, no. 221; cf. La Tour d'Auvergne to Benedetti, Paris, 7 December 1869, *ibid.*, no. 119, in which the French foreign minister more or less disavowed Fleury's representations. Nevertheless, the tsar did write a letter to King William on 23 November, suggesting that North Schleswig be retroceded. Bismarck, anxious to avoid difficulties with Russia, advised that the king agree at least to a limited retrocession. William refused to go beyond an assurance of his good intentions: "I am... far from refusing the execution of Article V of the Peace of Prague, and I have not at all the intention of evading it" (A. zu STOLBERG–WERNIGERODE, *Bismarck und die schleswig-holsteinische Frage* [Kiel, 1928], p. 97).

[3] A discussion between Schweinitz and Moltke on 12 December, in reference to the implementation of Article V, revealed that the latter was considering the possibility of a war with France on this question (SCHWEINITZ, I, 249).

which Denmark was prepared to give in regard to the German minority living in the area which was to be returned to Denmark. It was of course feared in Copenhagen that the Prussian government might use such guarantees to intervene in internal Danish affairs and control administrative acts of the Danish government. The fact that the paper in question was considered an organ of the Prussian government decided Ambassador Benedetti to discuss this new dispute with Thile. The latter assured the ambassador that the statements in the paper did in no way reflect the attitude of the Prussian government.[1] Through Quaade, the Danish minister in Berlin, Benedetti learned that Bismarck was planning to determine, in accord with Austria – party to the Vienna and Prague treaties – the new delimitations of the Prussian possessions in Schleswig and, consequently, that portion which was to be returned to Denmark. According to Quaade, the Danish government would be asked to agree to the division without any further negotiations. In case Denmark should decline, the Prussian government would consider its obligations under the Prague Treaty as terminated. Benedetti learned further that while Prussia would definitely retain Alsen and Düppel she would, in order to obtain Austria's consent, abandon the guarantee demands.[2] The fact that Bismarck was still incapacitated made it impossible for the ambassador to seek confirmation of Quaade's assertion from the chancellor. Benedetti did discuss the matter with Wimpffen who told him that the Austrian government had received no communication relative to North Schleswig. He strongly doubted the plans related to Benedetti by Quaade were being pursued in Berlin.[3] The course which Quaade had predicted seemed to be an unlikely development to Benedetti and his talk with Wimpffen had served to strengthen that opinion. Indeed, his reports on this brief reference to the North Schleswig question discounted the possibility of a near solution.[4]

---

[1] Benedetti to Daru, Berlin, 7 April 1870, FAE CP, Prusse/378, no. 47; same to same, Berlin, 11 April 1870, *ibid.*, no. 51. Daru informed Benedetti that the Danish cabinet expected to make a new *démarche* in Berlin in November when, in accordance with the Treaty of Vienna, the delay for voting in favor of Prussia or Denmark granted to the Danish population of Schleswig was due to expire (Daru to Benedetti, Paris, 11 April 1870, *ibid.*, no. 34).

[2] Benedetti to Ollivier, Berlin, 18 April 1870, *ibid.*, no. 54.

[3] Same to same, Berlin, 20 April 1870, *ibid.*, no. 56; same to same, Berlin, 21 April 1870, *ibid.*, no. 57.

[4] Same to same, Berlin, 22 April 1870, *ibid.*, no. 59. In April 1878, Bismarck finally achieved the cancellation of Article V of the Prague Treaty by secret agreement with Austria. On 4 February 1879, a public announcement to this effect was made (M. WINCKLER, "Die Aufhebung des Artikels V des Prager Friedens und Bismarcks Weg zum Zweibund," *HZ*, CLXXIX, Heft 3 [1955], pp. 471–472; SCHARFF, *Die Welt als Geschichte*, XVI, Heft 3–4

The inclusion of the Prussian ministry for foreign affairs in the presidium of the North German Confederation, effective 1 January 1870, did not disturb Benedetti. Such a step had been expected and was considered a part of the organizational process which the governmental structure of North Germany was destined to undergo until a final system had evolved. The chancellory of the Confederation was divided into two sections, one for internal affairs under Delbrück and one for external affairs under Thile, both supervised by Bismarck as minister of the Confederation. Benedetti had been told by Bismarck that, in accord with these changes, the foreign missions of the member-states would soon be ended and that envoys of the Confederation would represent the member-states, both collectively and individually, in their relations with the foreign powers.[1] The ambassador showed considerable interest in recurring rumors that Baden was endeavoring to gain admittance to the North German Confederation. He was aware that there was much sentiment favoring such a step, both in Berlin and in Karlsruhe. In October, Lefèbvre de Béhaine had heard that Baron von Althaus, the *chargé d'affaires* of Baden in Berlin, had spoken of Baden's entry into the Confederation to Balan, the Prussian envoy to Belgium.[2] Keudell, of whom the French *chargé d'affaires* had inquired shortly afterwards about such an extension of the Confederation had told him that there was no Baden question. He had insisted that the Prussian government could not and would not agree to a discussion of Baden's admittance.[3] Benedetti, after appraising the situation himself, estimated that Baden would not be admitted in the near future. Confirming Lefèbvre de Béhaine's report that *pourparlers* had taken place, the ambassador added that they had revealed a great divergence in views and pretensions, making it highly unlikely that Baden's admission would be supported by the Prussian government at this time. Indeed, he felt certain the Prussian cabinet was anxious to avoid anything and everything, regarding the organization of Germany, which might awaken French susceptibilities.[4]

[1956], pp. 211 ff.; HÄHNSEN, pp. 273 ff.; WINCKLER, "Die Zielsetzung," *Die Welt als Geschichte*, XVI, Heft 1 [1956], pp. 41 ff.).

[1] Benedetti to Daru, Berlin, 14 January 1870, FAE CP, Prusse/ 377, no. 4.

[2] Lefèbvre de Béhaine to La Tour d'Auvergne, Berlin, 2 October 1869, *ibid.*, 375, no. 176.

[3] Same to same, Berlin, 8 October 1869, *ibid.*, T.

[4] Benedetti to Daru, Berlin, 27 January 1870, *ibid.*, 377, no. 9. Interestingly enough, in February 1870 a motion by Lasker in the North German parliament to bring Baden into the Confederation met with sincere opposition on the part of Bismarck. The chancellor was trying to promote the renewal of the imperial dignity, to be bestowed upon William, and hence wished to avoid particularist antagonism the Lasker motion might generate (PFLANZE, pp. 415 ff.; NORDDEUTSCHER BUND, *Stenographische Berichte*, 1870, I, 58–77).

Tendencies toward unification had certainly revived in the fall of 1869, and the agitation relative to Baden had indicated as much. It was obvious to Benedetti that the process of change in Germany, initiated by the Prussian victory at Sadowa, had not yet come to a final conclusion. Talk of unification and of national sovereignty had already awakened the apprehensions of Lefèbvre de Béhaine in October 1869, and he had been quite disturbed by the *mollesse des résistances* to the unification movement in Berlin.[1] Benedetti, on the other hand, felt easily reassured by the official assertions relative to Baden. He of course distinguished between the demands and aspirations of German public opinion and the plans which Bismarck thought possible of implementation. Benedetti did not expect him to support schemes which might bring a conflict with France. Instead, he thought that Daru, the new foreign minister, could expect full reciprocation of his peace policy at present.[2] As for efforts to lessen the threat of war through mutual disarmament, Benedetti thought them *a priori* condemned to failure. He heard in March 1870 that the British ambassador had discussed the possibility of such a step with Bismarck and, as Benedetti had expected, the chancellor had left Loftus in no doubt about the futility of such negotiations. Benedetti did not believe that the king would support considerations which might reduce the armed forces of North Germany. Indeed, he knew that William thought disarmament as difficult a matter as the transformation of social and political institutions.[3] The ambassador was not overly concerned over Prussian opposition to disarmament; he considered Prussia's military preparedness an inescapable fact, which the imperial government was countering with appropriate military reforms. Neither the ambassador

---

[1] Lefèbvre de Béhaine to La Tour d'Auvergne, Berlin, 6 October 1869, FAE CP, Prusse/375, no. 179.

[2] Benedetti to Daru, Berlin, 27 January 1870, *ibid.*, 377, no. 9.

[3] Same to same, Berlin, 8 March 1870, *MMP*, pp. 294–295. Cf. E. STOFFEL, *Rapports militaires écrits de Berlin, 1866–1870* (Paris, 1871), pp. 383–411. Disarmament talks had been going on since late January, when La Valette had asked Clarendon to sound out Bismarck regarding the possibility of mutual disarmament. On 30 January, Ollivier also had approached Ambassador Lyons on the matter and on 2 February Loftus was instructed to ascertain the chancellor's views. The report of the British ambassador of 8 February was rather discouraging and on 22 February Daru was acquainted with its contents. Daru asked that Bismarck be approached once more and, four days after Benedetti's report, Loftus met once again with Bismarck to discuss disarmament. The impression which Loftus gained from this interview caused him to doubt the usefulness of further efforts. Thus, disarmament talks never progressed beyond these preliminary feelers (M. RAOUL-DUVAL, "Projects de désarmement franco-prussien en 1870," *Revue de Paris*, XXI, no. 4 [15 February 1914], pp. 727–739; G. ROLOFF, "Abrüstung und Kaiserplan vor dem Kriege von 1870," *PJ*, CCXIV [November 1928], pp. 195–197; A. PINGAUD, "Un projet de désarmement en 1870," *Revue des deux-mondes*, CII, t. VII [15 February 1932], pp. 905–914).

nor his government were in doubt about Bismarck's future aims and about the likelihood that the relations between the two powers might undergo sudden and fundamental changes.[1]

In his observations on unification tendencies, Benedetti had mentioned to Daru in January rumors circulated in Berlin that the confederation might be converted into a sort of empire of North Germany; he had been assured "that the word... had been pronounced and that the king supposedly heard it with favor." [2] Benedetti had not rejected the possibility of such a development but thought it imperative that Bismarck first receive the support of the National Liberals, in order to carry out such a scheme in peacetime.[3] At the time he had not thought that Bismarck was seriously considering such a plan.[4] However, during the latter part of April rumors circulated again in Berlin to the effect that the Prussian king was to be given the title of emperor. Bismarck had not dismissed the scheme from his mind and the presence of the *Zollparlament* delegates in Berlin had given rise to such speculation and conjecture on the subject.[5] This renewed preoccupation with the *Kaiserplan* did not escape Benedetti's attention and he called on Thile to obtain an official statement on the matter. The secretary informed him that the rumors were without foundation in fact and that the Prussian government had not opened any negoti-

---

[1] Benedetti to Daru, Berlin, 10 March 1870, FAE CP, Prusse/ 377, no. 32; same to same, Berlin, 25 March 1870, *ibid.*, n.n.

[2] Same to same, Berlin, 27 January 1870, *ibid.*, no. 9.

[3] *Ibid.; MMP*, pp. 285–286. Actually there existed some support in the South for the revival of the imperial dignity. Quite apart from the expected sympathy in Baden, leaders of the Bavarian Patriot Party, ignorant of Bismarck's plans, were proposing to elevate William of Prussia to the imperial purple. They did expect of course to pose certain conditions, including the admission of Austria into the proposed empire (PFLANZE, p. 417; *BGW*, VIb, 260, 279).

[4] It would appear that Bismarck's preoccupation with the *Kaiserplan* was revealed to Ambassador Loftus through an indiscretion by Max Duncker. Although Clarendon indicated his support of the idea, he did tell Bernstorff finally that he feared a new crisis would result because of French apprehensions. The warning was not lost on Bismarck and for the next two months he did not push his plan (PFLANZE, pp. 417–418; VALENTIN, pp. 404–405; ROLOFF, "Abrüstung und Kaiserplan," *PJ*, CCXVI [November 1928], pp. 188–197; W. PLATZHOFF, "England und der Kaiserplan vom Frühjahr 1870," *HZ*, CXXVII [1923], pp. 454–467; *BGW*, VIb, 212–214, note).

[5] For Bismarck's abortive efforts to gain acceptance of his scheme in Württemberg and Bavaria, see PFLANZE, p. 418; *BGW*, VIb, 279–281; J. FRÖBEL, *Ein Lebenslauf* (Stuttgart, 1890–1891), II, 546–547; M.DOEBERL, *Bayern und die Bismarckische Reichsgründung* (Munich, 1925), pp. 301–302; E. BRANDENBURG, "Die Verhandlungen über die Gründung des deutschen Reiches 1870," *HVj*, IX (1912), pp. 504–506; FRIESEN, III, 108 ff.; HOHENLOHE, II, 5 ff.; VALENTIN, pp. 410–413; "I learn on exceptional authority [Crown Prince Frederick] that Bismarck is occupying himself with the thought of proclaiming the German Empire, and investing his Royal Master with the Imperial diadem, and that confidential pourparlers have been exchanged on the subject within the last fortnight" (Morier to Clarendon, Carlsbad, 25 April 1870, MORIER, II, 150).

ations for the purpose of securing the imperial title for King William.[1] As on the previous occasion, the matter did not progress beyond the conjectural stage and the ambassador made no further reference to it.

Recent developments in Bavaria also convinced Benedetti that the unification movement appeared to be losing momentum. The Hohenlohe cabinet was confronted with the opposition of particularists who wanted to check the unification tendencies of the government. They were especially concerned about military obligations arising out of the alliance with Prussia. The lack of a clear-cut definition of the *casus foederis* made it difficult to decide the exact nature of Bavaria's commitments and had aroused the suspicions of Hohenlohe's opponents. While Prussia had reminded her allies of their obligations during the Luxemburg crisis, nothing had been done at that time to determine the precise duties of each party to the alliance. Ambassador Benedetti was fully aware of the fact that the deliberations in Munich had not been to Bismarck's liking; he suspected that press articles, denying either party the right to discuss the *casus foederis* and emphasizing the view that the alliance was subject to neither reserve nor time limit, had been written under the supervision of the foreign office in Berlin.[2] Although Daru reminded Benedetti of the reserved attitude of the imperial government, he welcomed his close observations and shared his views regarding the political situation in Germany.[3] Benedetti did not expect the particularist views, expressed in Munich, to go unchallenged and in his speech to the North German parliament, the king had stated that "the *entente* to be established relative to the national ties between the North German Confederation and the south German states was the object of [his] constant attention."[4] The tenor of the royal address, as well as the omission of remarks noting the independent status of those states, reaffirmed the ambassador's conviction that the establishment of a closer relationship with the South was, despite the temporary lull, a primary objective. He felt that the international status of the southern states had already been greatly curtailed, and he was disturbed over the subtle threat which the king's

---

[1] Benedetti to Ollivier, Berlin, 1 May 1870, FAE CP, Prusse/378, T. "Since writing the above [letter of 25 April], I have again seen my informant who tells me that Bismarck has for the moment given up ventilating the idea of the empire. I, nevertheless, send what I have written as it is always useful to be acquainted with even the temporary tenants of so important a brain as Bismarck's" (Morier to Clarendon, Carlsbad, 27 April 1870, MORIER, II, 151).

[2] Benedetti to Daru, Berlin, 12 February 1870, FAE CP, Prusse/ 377, no. 15.

[3] Daru to Benedetti, Paris, 15 February 1870, *ibid.*, no. 11.

[4] Benedetti to Daru, Berlin, 15 February 1870, *ibid.*, no. 18.

speech directed at the opponents of unification. He rightly wondered whether or not the French government could remain indifferent to the situation much longer. Although he apparently favored eventual intervention he did not advise such a step at the present.[1] Daru's reply revealed that the minister fully shared these apprehensions and that he had discussed the situation with the Prussian ambassador. For the benefit of Benedetti, Daru stated the attitude of the *cabinet du 2 janvier* relative to affairs in Germany. France accepted the *status quo* as is [*tel qu'il est*] in Germany and had no intention of opposing the results of the accomplished events. Daru emphasized the determination of the government to avoid recrimination and untimely interference in the affairs of others "but we must attentively watch so that the actual state of things does not become aggravated to the prejudice of the European equilibrium and [France's] own detriment." [2] The independence of the south German states was, in his opinion, guaranteed at present by the balance of power and the harmonious relations between the powers. Any attempt to alter, directly or indirectly, the conditions of the international existence of the southern states would have as its consequence a general upheaval.[3] The portent of the last remark was clearly understood by the ambassador, and he well knew that France would not tolerate a further disturbance of the power equilibrium.

The fact that the relations between Prussia and France were relatively friendly did not exclude the possibility that the chancellor might cross the Main and bring about the unification.[4] If Bismarck could do it without running the risk of war with France, Benedetti was certain that that step would be taken without delay. The ambassador was not likely to forget a remark which the chancellor had recently made to him about unification: "*Le courant de notre eau nous y porte fatalement.*"[5] Despite the fact that Bismarck had rejected a motion for the admittance of Baden into the North German Confederation, the ambassador maintained his views relative to Bismarck's ultimate goal. His remarks against the motion pointed up the fact that only the fear of a war with France restrained Prussia's ambitions.[6]

---

[1] *Ibid.*

[2] Daru to Benedetti, Paris, 23 February 1870, *ibid.*, no. 13.

[3] *Ibid.*

[4] Cf. WALDERSEE, I, 49, to whom Bismarck had remarked, on 6 February, that the international situation was one of idyllic peace but that no one could predict how long it would last.

[5] Benedetti to Daru, Berlin, 25 February 1870, FAE CP, Prusse/377, n.n.

[6] *Ibid.*, T.

Late in April Benedetti heard from an unidentified source further confirmation of his suspicions. He learned that the chancellor had tried to get the south German states to solicit, on their own initiative, entry into the North German Confederation. Bismarck supposedly stood ready to guarantee the sovereignty and territorial integrity of each of them through the exact definition of the attributes of federal authority. The price for such an arrangement would be the imperial purple for the Hohenzollern dynasty. Apparently Bismarck hoped to prevent French interference in the unification process by placing the initiative with the southern states. Benedetti was of course not surprised to learn that such overtures had supposedly been received with enthusiasm in Karlsruhe and with progressively less favor in Darmstadt, Stuttgart and Munich; indeed, the Bavarian cabinet was now considered as being opposed to any change in the *status quo*. The Bavarian opposition was expected to stiffen the resistance of Württemberg, and it was predicted that, for the time being, Bismarck would limit his efforts to Hesse and Baden. Benedetti did not expect Bismarck to *brusquer les choses* and he anticipated a continuation of the cautious unification policy thus far pursued by the Berlin cabinet. As for the long-range ambitions of the chancellor, Benedetti did not tire of emphasizing ,as he had on so many occasions, the transformation which was bound to come in Germany:

But from all this there emerges one lesson of which we must not lose sight, that in Berlin they are resolved and ready to ignore the stipulations of the Treaty of Prague, as far as Germany is concerned, as soon as they think they are able to try it with impunity; they are not only pushed by ambitious calculations and by interior necessity, but further excited by the solicitations of the secondary states of the North, which imagine that it will be less difficult for them to safeguard what little of their independence is left to them when the states of the South shall be... a part of the Confederation and that it will be possible for them to unite their efforts in a common interest. If we can thus presume that the Prussian government, as it guarantees us, does not think today about creating complications which could threaten our security and the peace of Europe, the incident of which I just gave you an account merits nevertheless to awaken the solicitude and the meditations of the government of the emperor.[1]

---

[1] Benedetti to Ollivier, Berlin, 1 May 1870, FAE CP, Prusse/378, no. 66; "These reports [in the press about Baden and Hesse] could scarcely fail to attract the vigilant attention of the French ambassador. Count Benedetti accordingly took an opportunity of referring to them in a conversation with Baron Thile, and without addressing an official interpellation to His Excellency, inquired whether there was any foundation for these reports. [Thile said that they were groundless but inquired of the king] and subsequently informed Count Benedetti on the authority of His Majesty that the reports in question were entirely without foundation. This clear and positive refutation... has given satisfaction to Count Benedetti and this enabled him to assure his government of the maintenance of the 'status quo' in Germany" (Loftus to Clarendon, Berlin, 1 May 1870, PRO FO 64/687, no. 221). "I have had

The assurances given to Benedetti by Thile and the relative quiet on the Berlin political scene probably decided Benedetti to make use of an authorization, issued in April by Daru,[1] to go to Paris on 22 May in order to attend to some family affairs.[2] During his stay in Paris, he met the new foreign minister, the duke of Gramont, who had succeeded Daru on 15 May at the *Quai d'Orsay*, and with whom he discussed the general political situation in Germany.[3] The ambassador also reviewed the affairs in Germany with the British ambassador in Paris, Lord Lyons, whom he told that "he did not apprehend any danger to the peace, unless circumstances were too strong for [William and Bismarck], and this he thought impossible." [4] Returning to Berlin on 11 June, Benedetti did not expect any developments which might delay his departure for Wildbad on 1 July. Already many of the foremost members of the diplomatic colony had left the Prussian capital. Bismarck, who had come to Berlin on 21 May and had gone to Ems to be present at the meeting of William and Tsar Alexander, had returned to Varzin on 7 June. It was a *sauve qui peut* in view of the lack of affairs. "A complete calm results... which is the despair of all the young *chargés d'affaires par interim,* full of zeal and finding not the slightest subject for a dispatch! A general weariness seems to have overcome the minds, the affairs, and those who direct them."[5] Benedetti left Berlin on 1 July, fully assuming that nothing would disturb his vacation at Wildbad. He interrupted his journey in Wiesbaden next day, where he spent the evening in the company of Baron Nothomb. Benedetti was preoccupied with his health and his talks with Nothomb indicate that he did not expect any significant political

the opportunity of ratifying the information I sent you in regard to Bismarck's intended Caesarian operations, and thus corrected, it is in perfect harmony with the declaration made to Benedetti by the king, which you inform me of" (Morier to Clarendon, n.p., May 1870, MORIER, II, 151).

[1] Nothomb to van der Stichelen, Berlin, 23 April 1870, BAE CP, Prusse/25, no. 57.

[2] Bylandt to Roest van Limburg, Berlin, 23 May 1870, RBZ, Pruisen/1870, no. 187; Loftus to Clarendon, Berlin, 28 May 1870, PRO FO 64/687, no. 287.

[3] Wimpffen to Beust, Berlin, 11 June 1870, HHStA, Preussen/101, no. 61. "...as guarantee of the dispositions which the emperor has shown to him, [Gramont] demanded the retirement of the two ambassadors of France in Berlin and in London, Benedetti and La Valette. The emperor consented, at once, to the recall of Benedetti but he demanded a delay to decide the situation of La Valette, who was very much in favor with the empress; since the two ambassadors were to be recalled at the same time, they both remained provisionally at their posts" (HANSEN, p. 213).

[4] NEWTON, I, 293. Benedetti did tell Wimpffen, upon his return, that it would be impossible for France not to intervene in case of new Prussian trespasses (Wimpffen to Beust, Berlin, 11 June 1870, HHStA, Preussen/101, no. 61).

[5] Bylandt to Roest van Limburg, Berlin, 13 June 1870, RBZ, Pruisen /1870, no. 212; same to same, Berlin, 4 July 1870, *ibid.*, no. 252.

developments.[1] The ambassador continued his journey on the following day to Coblenz, where he planned to call on Queen Augusta and pay his respects. Arriving in that city in the morning of 4 July, he went first to the hotel *Zum Riesen* and then had himself announced at the royal residence. He was received by Queen Augusta later in the day and was invited to dine with her and her guests. Unable to devote herself to the ambassador, in view of the overnight stay of the grand-duke and the grand-duchess of Baden, Queen Augusta asked Benedetti to prolong his stay in Coblenz. Conforming to the wishes of the queen, he remained in Coblenz and was again received the following day.[2]

During the second visit at the queen's residence Benedetti most likely learned about the candidacy of Prince Leopold of Hohenzollern-Sigmaringen for the Spanish throne, vacant since the flight of Queen Isabella. This sudden revelation had originated in Madrid,[3] and already on 2 July the *Gazette de France* had published the news.[4] It was confirmed by *Havas* on Sunday, 3 July.[5] Benedetti probably had heard of the acceptance during his stay in Coblenz, yet he continued his journey to Wildbad, arriving on 6 July. It appears that the news did

---

[1] LeSourd to Gramont, Berlin, 3 July 1870, FAE CP, Prusse/379, T.; Nothomb to Anethan, Berlin, 24 July 1870, BAE CP, Prusse/25, no. 80.

[2] Prince Anton von Radziwill to wife, Ems, 5 July 1870, PRINCESS A. RADZIWILL, *Souvenirs, 1840–1873*, eds. E. and H. Potocka (Paris, 1931), pp. 156–157; R. FESTER, *Die Genesis der Emser Depesche* (Berlin, 1915), p. 68; C. SAUREL, *Juillet 1870. Le drame de la dépêche d'Ems* (Paris, 1930), p. 134.

[3] The plans of the Spanish government to proceed speedily with the election of Leopold in a secret session of the Cortes, once the prince had posed his candidacy, were negated when the Cortes was adjourned prematurely. A message from Don Eusebio de Salazar y Mazarredo, the principal Spanish agent, communicated from Sigmaringen via Berlin, indicated that he would return to Madrid before 1 July. Accordingly, the Cortes was to be kept in session for the purpose of electing Leopold. Faulty decoding of the message gave the date of Salazar's return as 9 July. Under the circumstances, Ruiz Zorilla, president of the Cortes, adjourned the session of that body on 23 June. By the time Salazar reached Madrid, 28 June, the deputies had departed from the capital. Rumors about Leopold's active candidacy began to circulate in Madrid, and when Prim arrived on 1 July he learned to his amazement that the secret about the Hohenzollern candidate was widely known. He of course realized the possible international repercussions the candidacy might have and seemed to be especially apprehensive about reaction in Paris (L. STEEFEL, *Bismarck, the Hohenzollern Candidacy, and the Origins of the Franco-German War of 1870* [Cambridge, 1962], pp. 99–101; I.A.B.o. [Spanien] 32 secreta, nos. 220, 221, 222, 225, 227, 229, 230, 231, 232, 235, 247, 254, 287).

[4] The news of Leopold's candidacy was first published in *Epoca*, the director of which, Ignacio Escobar, had close ties with Zorilla. It became known in Paris in the forenoon of 2 July, through information received by Viscount Walsh and transmitted by him to Gramont as well as to the editor of the *Gazette de France* (OLLIVIER, XIV, 20–21; R. FESTER, *Briefe, Aktenstücke und Regesten zur Geschichte der hohenzollernschen Thronkandidatur in Spanien* [Leipzig, 1911], I, no. 250; ODG, XXVIII, p. 19, ft. 2; Mercier de Lostende to Gramont, Madrid ,3 July 1870, FAE CP, Espagne/876, T.; STEEFEL, *Bismarck*, pp. 102–103; *The Times* [London], 4 July 1870, p. 9).

[5] ODG, XXVIII, p. 19, ft. 2.

not prompt the ambassador to notify the foreign ministry or the embassy in Berlin.[1]

Rumors about a Hohenzollern candidacy for the Spanish crown had repeatedly circulated in European capitals and had of course come to the attention of the ambassador some time before. Among the names put forth as likely candidates had been that of Leopold of Hohenzollern-Sigmaringen, eldest son of Prince Charles Anton and brother of King Charles of Rumania.[2] Of the Catholic faith,married to the sister of King Pedro V of Portugal, distantly related to Napoleon III through the Murat and Beauharnais families, the supporters of his candidacy expected Leopold to meet with the approval of France as well as with that of the advocates of an Iberian union.[3] Although mention of Leopold's name occurred repeatedly, Ambassador Benedetti had not been requested by the foreign office to inquire into the veracity of the rumors.[4] Indeed, it was Benedetti himself who had alluded to such a possibility in his official correspondence. The presence in Berlin of the former Spanish envoy to the Prussian court had arroused the interest of Benedetti when he had learned that, apart from his audience with the king, Manuel Rancès y Villanueva had also met twice Count Bismarck. Writing to La Valette, 27 March 1869, Benedetti had

---

[1] Queen Augusta had received word of Leopold's candidacy in a letter from Charles Anton (Charles Anton to Queen Augusta, Sigmaringen, 26 June 1870, J. DITTRICH, Bismarck, Frankreich und die spanische Thronkandidatur der Hohenzollern. Die "Kriegsschuldfrage" von 1870. Im Anhang Briefe und Aktenstücke aus dem Fürstlich Hohenzollernschen Hausarchiv [Munich, 1962], pp. 401–402; Benedetti to Gramont, Wildbad, 7 July 1870, FAE CP, Prusse/379, T.; FESTER, Die Genesis, p. 68).

[2] Press references to Leopold as a possible candidate for the Spanish throne had appeared as early as 9 October 1868 in Süddeutsche Zeitung and The Times, 11 October in Augsburger Allgemeine Zeitung, 12 October in Correspondance Havas, 13 November in Indépendance belge and Journal des débats (R. FESTER, "Neue Beiträge zur Geschichte der hohenzollernschen Thronkandidatur in Spanien," HVj, XV, Heft 2 [1912], pp. 222 ff.; STEEFEL, Bismarck, pp. 25–28; G. BONNIN, ed., Bismarck and the Hohenzollern Candidature for the Spanish Throne. The Documents in the German Diplomatic Archives, tr. I. M. Massey [London, 1957], p. 288; H. SALOMON, L'incident Hohenzollern [2nd ed., Paris, 1922], p. 24; P. LEHAUTCOURT, La candidature Hohenzollern [Paris, 1912], p. 17; R. FESTER, "Bismarck und die hohenzollernsche Thronkandidatur in Spanien," Deutsche Rundschau, CXL, Heft 10 [1909], p. 26).

[3] Cf. F. FRAHM, "Frankreich und die Hohenzollernkandidatur bis zum Frühjahr 1869," HVj, XXIX, Heft 2 (1934), pp. 342–370, for the meaning of Leopold's candidacy in terms of Iberian union schemes.

[4] Steefel's very thorough study of the evidence bearing on Spain's search for a king has led him to conclude that Bismarck did not further the candidacy of Leopold before February 1870. To be sure, Bismarck was aware of the press references to the prince, but he also was informed of the fact that the Hohenzollern-Sigmaringen family had rejected the candidacy in April 1869. Steefel has not only studied the archival materials bearing on Leopold's candidacy but has also reviewed critically the large body of historical literature relative to the genesis of the Hohenzollern candidacy (STEEFEL, Bismarck, pp. 11–46; cf. DITTRICH, pp. 37–82; GEUSS, pp. 252–267).

mentioned the possibility that the Hohenzollern candidacy had progressed beyond the speculative stage:

In presence of the difficulties which the choice of the new sovereign causes in Madrid could one have thought there of the prince of Hohenzollern, and did Rancès receive the order to confer about it with Bismarck; or else did this arise in Berlin itself or in Düsseldorf, and was Rancès aware thereof and decided to make the voyage after having received the orders of his government: I do not know but it has seemed expedient to me not to let you ignore these suppositions which will help you control any other information which would lead to believe that negotiations on this subject do exist.[1]

Benedetti's remarks had not been lost upon the foreign minister who directed the ambassador to ascertain whether the Hohenzollern candidacy was being seriously considered.[2] Already on 31 March 1869, the ambassador had called upon Thile, charged with the conduct of the Prussian foreign office during Bismarck's absence, and had asked if he should attach some importance to the rumors about Prince Leopold and the Spanish throne. He had told Thile that such a possibility would directly interest the imperial government – if there were reasons to believe that it might be realized. Thile had given the ambassador the most formal assurance that at no time had he had any indication which would permit such conjectures and he maintained that Rancès' talks with the chancellor had not touched upon a Hohenzollern candidacy.[3] Although he had not doubted the secretary's assurance, Benedetti had not seemed completely convinced and he had reminded La Valette that Thile was not always informed of Bismarck's plans.[4]

[1] Benedetti to La Valette, Berlin, 27 March 1869, FAE CP, Prusse/373, no. 68. Although Rancès probably discussed the political situation in Spain, it is unlikely that he brought up a Hohenzollern candidacy since he was known as a supporter of the candidacy of the duke of Montpensier (A. PIRALA, *Historia contemporanea* [Madrid, 1875–1879], III, 730; H. LEONARDON, "Prim et la candidature Hohenzollern," *RH*, LXXIV [November/December 1900], pp. 289–290).

[2] "Find out if the candidature of the prince of Hohenzollern in Spain is serious. I need not tell you that we would not be favorable toward it, and I can leave it to you to appreciate the extent to which you will judge it useful to let it be known. The example of Rumania is made to enlighten us" (La Valette to Benedetti, Paris, 30 March 1869, FAE CP, Prusse/373, T.).

[3] In his discussions with Rancès, Bismarck had actually spoken of the duke de Montpensier as the most obvious candidate worth considering (Rancès y Villanueva to Sagasta, 24 July 1870, in CONDE DE ROMANONES, *Amadeo de Saboya. El rey efímero. España y los orígenes de la guerra franco-prusiano de 1870* [Madrid, 1935], pp. 244 ff.).

[4] Benedetti to La Valette, Berlin, 31 March 1869, FAE CP, Prusse/373, no. 71; Münch to Beust, Berlin, 1 April 1869, HHStA, Preussen/100, no. 29. Shortly after the interview between Benedetti and Thile, Theodor von Bernhardi, an *homme de confiance* of Bismarck, was sent to Spain as a military observer. The secrecy which surrounded Bernhardi's mission has been the subject of much conjecture, even to the extent of crediting him with efforts to buy the Cortes votes for the election of Leopold. Steefel's research would indicate that his role was

Benedetti had again become concerned with the candidacy of Leopold during his sojourn in Paris between 27 April and 5 May 1869. At that time Benedetti had discussed the possibility of a Hohenzollern candidacy with the emperor, who unequivocably had stated his opposition to it: "The candidacy of the Prince of Hohenzollern is essentially anti-national; the country will not tolerate it, and it must be prevented."[1] At the suggestion of Rouher, Benedetti had questioned the chancellor upon his return to Berlin. Bismarck, in reply to the ambassador's direct query, had acknowledged that the candidacy had been discussed. Benedetti, who apparently had hoped for a statement that the king, as head of the Hohenzollern family, would forbid Leopold to accept an offer of the crown, had been disappointed. The chancellor had made no such declaration; instead, he had simply discussed the difficulties which the prince would encounter in Spain and had expressed the belief that both William and Prince Charles-Anton would advise against acceptance. Not satisfied with Bismarck's evasive talk, Benedetti had asked him pointedly if the king's consent would not be a necessary prerequisite to an acceptance. Bismarck had agreed that it was, and Benedetti had preferred not to press the issue any further at the time. Short of a proper authorization, to which he alluded in his reports, he had not thought it advisable to insist.[2] Rouher, who had charge of the foreign ministry during La Valette's leave, had in fact decided against further steps for the moment. "This candidacy so far does not seem to have found support in Spain, and it is only in case that it should take on consistency... that we will have to preoccupy ourselves with the real intentions of Prussia." He had suggested that the ambassador keep a sharp lookout for any information which could shed light upon the affair as well as upon Bismarck's intentions.[3]

Although Benedetti had learned on returning to Berlin in the late fall 1869, that Rascòn, Spanish envoy to the Prussian court, had been

---

that of a military and political observer (STEEFEL, *Bismarck*, pp. 18–21; cf. J. ACTON, *Historical Essays and Studies*, eds. Figgis and Laurence [London, 1908], p. 213; H. TEMPERLEY, "Lord Acton on the Origins of the War of 1870, with some unpublished letters from the British and Vienna archives," *Cambridge Historical Journal*, II, no. 1 [1926], pp. 69–70; W. SÄLTER, *Theodor von Bernhardi als Politiker* [Hagen/Westfalen, n.d.], pp. 126–128; FESTER, "Bismarck," *Deutsche Rundschau*, CXL, Heft 10 [1907], p. 29).

[1] *MMP*, p. 307. The imperial ambassador to Spain was also in Paris at this time and was probably consulted regarding the Spanish dynastic problem.

[2] Benedetti to Rouher, Berlin, 11 May 1869, FAE CP, Prusse/374, no. 92; Bismarck to Solms, Berlin, May 1869, *BGW*, VIb, 82; "Benedetti... who had been instructed to be particularly cautious in his behavior in [the Hohenzollern] affair had not mentioned the emperor's remarks to Bismarck" (KEUDELL, p. 439).

[3] Rouher to Benedetti, Paris, 19 May 1869, FAE CP, Prusse/374, no. 68.

in Varzin for two days during September, he had not obtained any
information pointing to a new development regarding Leopold's
candidacy.[1] The ambassador himself had called on Leopold's brother,
King Charles of Rumania, during the latter's visit in Paris when
Benedetti was there and had had a meeting with him at the Bristol
Hotel on 11 October. Although no record of this conversation exists,
it is doubtful that Benedetti touched upon the candidacy during the
conversation.[2] Moreover, the recent passage of General Prim in Paris

---

[1] Lefèbvre de Béhaine to La Tour d'Auvergne, Berlin, 31 July 1869, *ibid.*, 375, no. 44;
same to same, Berlin, 27 October 1869, *ibid.*, no. 198. Unknown to either Benedetti or Lefèbvre de Béhaine, Salazar, after having conferred with Prim in Vichy, came to Germany
to approach the Hohenzollern-Sigmaringen family relative to the throne vacancy. Salazar
arrived in Munich on 15 September and contacted the Prussian envoy, Georg von Werthern,
who had mentioned Leopold to him as a possible candidate at a party given in Biarritz in
1866 by a Mrs. O'Shea. Salazar asked for Werthern's help in securing an introduction to the
Sigmaringen family at Weinburg. That same day, Werthern met Salazar as well as King
Charles of Rumania, who was in Munich and who left next day for the family residence. It
is conceivable that Werthern told him of Salazar's mission, although there is no evidence
to support this conjecture. Werthern and Salazar travelled to Weinburg on 17 September
and, after Werthern had been received by Charles Anton and explained the purpose of the
call, the prince received Salazar. In a lengthy interview, the latter discussed the dynastic
problem of Spain and found an interested listener in Charles Anton. Salazar was ultimately
introduced to Leopold and then withdrew to his hotel in Rheineck. Werthern remained at
the castle as a guest of Prince Charles Anton and endeavored in the course of the evening
to arouse the interest of Princess Antonia in the Spanish crown. He found her reluctant to
consider the possibility of reigning over Spain, a reaction much like that shown by Prince
Leopold. Werthern returned next day to Munich, while Salazar remainèd in Rheineck. The
following day, 19 September, Prince Charles Anton and King Charles had a morning interview with Salazar, in the course of which the Spaniard suggested that perhaps Charles would
consider posing his candidacy for the Spanish throne. He was politely turned down but had
an opportunity to make a new proposal to Leopold and Antonia in an afternoon meeting.
Both showed a decided lack of interest, although Leopold did not reject the offer out of hand.
He made it clear to Salazar that he would not compete with others for the honor, and that
he would not wish his candidacy to create political difficulties with Portugal. Neither
Charles Anton nor Leopold committed themselves, and supposedly told Salazar that it
would be necessary to enlist the aid and support of Emperor Napoleon and King William
in the matter. Salazar was relatively satisfied with the outcome of the interviews. Although
he had some reservations about Leopold's attitude relative to the prospect of ruling Spain,
he had every intention of furthering the candidacy. Salazar expected the Spanish government
to secure French approval, while Werthern would seek William's support. Although Werthern did travel to Baden and was received in audience by the king, there is no indication that
they discussed a Hohenzollern candidacy. In Spain, Salazar's efforts were not followed up.
Instead, a commission voted to secure the young duke of Savoy as the next monarch. In
December 1869, this plan ended in failure when King Victor Emmanuel, in view of the
political dissention in Spain and the reluctance of the duke's mother, withdrew his support
of the candidacy (DITTRICH, pp. 351–355; FESTER, "Neue Beiträge," *HVj*, XV, Heft 2
[1912], pp. 227–236; BONNIN, pp. 63–65; [CHARLES I], *Chroniques, actes, documents*, ed. D.
Sturdza [Bucarest, 1899], I, 525–526; KARL I., *Aus dem Leben König Karls von Rumänien*
[Stuttgart, 1894–1900], II, 5–6; ZINGELER, p. 234; STEEFEL, *Bismarck*, pp. 41–46).

[2] KARL I., *Aus dem Leben*, II, 16. An aide-de-camp of the emperor left this statement relative
to the visit of Charles in Paris: "We learned that Prince [Anton] of Hohenzollern, who had
been approached on the matter [of the Spanish throne] would give no positive answer, and
it was believed that the conditions stated by Prince Leopold were equivalent to a refusal
of the proffered offer (M. FLEURY, *Memoirs of the Empress Eugénie* [London, 1920], II, 204).

had apparently also failed to offer any new clues as to Leopold's prospects.[1] Rumors had not abated during the winter season in Berlin and in diplomatic circles the Hohenzollern candidacy had been rather frequently the topic of discussion, even in Benedetti's own salon.[2] Yet, he had made no attempt to seek any information from the Spanish envoy whom he had encountered frequently at social events. Benedetti's reserve toward Rascòn had appeared almost deliberate and was a source of mystification to his colleagues.[3] He evidently had not attributed great significance to the rumors, despite the fact that he had suspected Bismarck of wanting to keep all avenues open relative to the affairs of Spain. Nonetheless, Benedetti had shown no apparent inclination to find out the exact status of Leopold's candidacy.

The presence in Berlin of Charles Anton and Leopold during mid-March 1870 had marked an important stage in the development of the Hohenzollern candidacy. They had come to Berlin, at Bismarck's request, to participate in a crown council meeting on a formal Spanish throne offer to Leopold.[4] Ambassador Benedetti had noted the arrival

Cf. Mercier de Lostende to La Tour d'Auvergne, Madrid, 8 October 1869, FAE CP, Espagne/ 874, no. 147, who thought it unnecessary to preoccuppy oneself with a Hohenzollern candidacy at this time.

[1] Prim had come to France for a vacation. He had arrived in Paris 27 August and had gone on to Vichy a few days later, remaining there for about two weeks. On his return to Spain, he had passed through Paris and had been received in audience by the emperor on 14 September and had left for Spain four days later. In the interview between the emperor and Prim no reference to the Hohenzollern candidacy was made, although Randon claims that Napoleon himself had suggested Leopold to Prim (OLLIVIER, XII, 64; RANDON, I, 306; ODG, XXV, 253, ft. 1).

[2] After the refusal of the duke of Genoa, received in Madrid on 2 January 1870, the search for a prospective ruler was temporarily held in abeyance. Although there were a number of candidates, few of them could expect to be considered very seriously. Under the circumstances, the name of Leopold was again mentioned quite frequently. Salazar was most optimistic about Leopold's chances in a letter to Werthern of 6 February 1870, and seemed anxious to resume his efforts to win over the Hohenzollern-Sigmaringen family (FESTER, "Neue Beiträge," HVj, XV, Heft 2 [1912], pp. 240–242; cf. Werthern to Charles Anton, 12 February 1870, DITTRICH, pp. 353–355; FESTER, Briefe, I, 52–54; STEEFEL, Bismarck, pp. 47–50).

[3] Nothomb to Anethan, Berlin, 10 July 1870, BAE CP, Prusse/25, no. 62. "If there was one thing which has always surprised me, it is the silence and indifference of the [French] ambassador during this winter on the subject of the candidacy of Prince Leopold of which everyone spoke and about which one even jested.... Count Benedetti never spoke to me about the candidacy..." (Nothomb to Anethan, Berlin, 24 July 1870, ibid., no. 80).

[4] In early February 1870, apparently in consequence of conferences held in Madrid in January, Prim decided to renew Spanish efforts to win Leopold over as a candidate. Accordingly, Salazar left Madrid on 17 February, carrying letters from Prim to King William, Bismarck and Prince Leopold. Although the letters differed as to content, they all indicated the serious efforts of the Spanish government to win Leopold's consent to pose his candidacy (Prim to William, Madrid, 17 February 1870, I.A.B.o. [Spanien], 32 secreta; Prim to Bismarck, Madrid, 17 February 1870, ibid.; Prim to Leopold, Madrid, 17 February 1870, DITTRICH, pp. 356–357). Salazar was received by Charles Anton in Düsseldorf upon his arrival on 24 February. In the absence of Leopold, who was in Berlin, he told the prince that he was

of Charles Anton in Berlin but had fallen victim to a ruse designed to hide the real reason for the prince's presence. He had been told by various officials, in a round-about fashion, that Charles Anton's visit was connected with the possible entrance of Hesse and Baden into the North German Confederation. The ambassador had been satisfied with that explanation for his correspondence makes no mention of

authorized by the Spanish government to negotiate for the candidacy of Leopold. It would appear that Charles Anton was less hesitant about giving consideration to the Spanish proposal, although he favored acceptance only if the interests of Prussia demanded it (Charles Anton to William, Düsseldorf, 25 February 1870, BONNIN, p. 62; cf. ZINGELER, pp. 235–237; Charles Anton to Leopold, Düsseldorf, 24 February 1870, DITTRICH, p. 358; Charles Anton to Leopold, Düsseldorf, 25 February 1870, ibid., pp. 358–359; Charles Anton to Bismarck, Düsseldorf, 25 February 1870, BONNIN, pp. 63–65). After his interview with Charles Anton, Salazar continued on to Berlin. He was received by Leopold in the evening of 25 February, and discovered that the prince was still inclined against acceptance. However, he did make it clear that he would abide by the wishes of the king and subordinate his own interests to those of Prussia. Leopold subsequently helped Salazar obtain an interview with Bismarck, which took place on the 27th (Leopold to Charles Anton, Berlin, 26 February 1870, DITTRICH, pp. 359–360; same to same, Berlin, 27 February 1870, ibid., pp. 361–362; Keudell to Leopold, Berlin, 27 February 1870, ibid., p. 364; Aufzeichnungen Leopolds, Berlin, 1 March 1870, ibid., pp. 363–364; Leopold to William, Berlin, 2 March 1870, BONNIN, pp. 66–67). In a conversation between Bismarck and Leopold, at a ball given by Ambassador Loftus on the 28th, the chancellor presented the reasons for accepting the Spanish offer. Bismarck claimed that the creation of a monarchical government in Spain would contribute to the peace of Europe, that it would add luster to the Hohenzollern house, and that a Hohenzollern prince would also offset the ambitions of the ultra-montane faction. Prince Leopold also learned that, on the basis of Bismarck's general report to William on either the 27th or 28th, the king would not force him to accept the offer. However, Bismarck was not prepared to abandon the project and hoped that Prince Charles Anton might come to Berlin to help persuade William to support the Hohenzollern candidacy (Leopold to Charles Anton, Berlin, 1 March 1870, DITTRICH, p. 362; same to same, Berlin, 2 March 1870, ibid., p. 364). A consequence of Salazar's soundings in Düsseldorf and Berlin was the Immediatbericht of 9 March, in which Bismarck outlined in considerable detail the advantages which would be derived if a Prussian prince ruled in Spain. William, despite his own misgivings, decided to summon a crown council, in order to give very thorough consideration to the matter (Bismarck to William, Berlin, 9 March 1870, I.A.B.o. [Spanien] 32 secreta; cf. BGW, VIb, 266–274; circular to Moltke, Schleinitz, Roon, Delbrück, Thile, Berlin, 15 March 1870, Wilhelm I., Kaiser Wilhelms des Grossen Briefe, Reden und Schriften, ed. E. Berner [Berlin, 1906], II, 197; E. VON WERTHEIMER, "Kronprinz Friedrich Wilhelm und die spanische Hohenzollern-Thronkandidatur [1868–1870]. Mit Benutzung ungedruckter Quellen," PJ, CCV, Heft 3 [1926], pp. 276–277).
  The crown council took place on 15 March, disguised as a dinner party given by Charles Anton. The discussion lasted over two hours and all officials advised acceptance of the Spanish offer. William, however, refused to order Leopold to accept and the latter refused to do so short of the king's command. The impasse continued, for the next evening, in a meeting with the king, Leopold again stated that he was prepared to pose his candidacy only if the king so ordered. William of course refused to issue such an order but agreed to the proposal of Charles Anton to put forth Leopold's younger brother Frederick (Aufzeichnung Karl Antons über das 'Diner' am 15. März im königl. Schlosse, Berlin, 16 March 1870, DITTRICH, pp. 366–368; Charles Anton to William, Berlin, 17 March 1870, BONNIN, pp. 80–82; William to Bismarck, Berlin, 17 March 1870, ibid., pp. 82–83; Bismarck to Charles Anton, Berlin, 17 March 1870, ibid., p. 83; Notiz Leopolds, Berlin, 17 March 1870, DITTRICH, p. 369; Charles Anton to his wife, Berlin, 17 March 1870, K. ZINGELER, "Briefe Karl Anton von Hohenzollern an seine Gemahlin Josephine, geborene Prinzessin von Baden," Deutsche Revue, XXIX, Heft 2–3 [1914], p. 113).

efforts to check the information. Indeed, Benedetti had hoped to gather further information about the very scheme which had been used to dupe him.[1]

Benedetti evidently had learned nothing new about the throne candidacy during his visit in Paris from 22 May to 11 June, for one does not discern, upon his return, any evidence of efforts designed to clarify the matter through new and persistent inquiries. The very fact that he had left for a prolonged vacation shortly after is indicative of a regrettable lack of concern about the rumors which circulated in Berlin and elsewhere. Despite the fact that Benedetti had failed to discover any real clues, however small, it would be unfair to hold him primarily responsible for the ignorance in Paris about the negotiations carried on between Prim, Leopold and Bismarck.[2] It must be noted that these

---

Although Bismarck was quite responsive to the proposed candidacy of Prince Frederick, not much came of the matter. While Charles Anton had some reservations about the ability of his son to succeed in the proposed role, Frederick himself was as reluctant as his brother Leopold to accept the Spanish offer. Nonetheless, Charles Anton was apparently prepared to continue with his efforts and indicated that, if William made it clear that he wanted a Hohenzollern prince in Spain, he could exert more effective parental influence upon his son. In an interview on 3 April, the reluctance of Prince Frederick was all too obvious and William of course refused to order the prince to pose his candidacy. Charles Anton, preferring a temporary postponement of any final decision, endeavored next to seek certain positive assurances relative to the election of a Hohenzollern prince and the viability of such a régime in Spain. It was decided to send Bucher as well as a competent general staff officer to Spain to seek the desired assurances and to gain a clear picture relative to the Spanish army (William to Bismarck, Berlin, 2 April 1870, BONNIN, pp. 105–106; same to same, Berlin, 3 April 1870, *ibid.*, p. 106; Crown Prince Frederick to Bismarck, Berlin, 3 April 1870, *ibid.*; Charles Anton to Bismarck, Berlin, 4 April 1870, *ibid.*, p. 107; Crown Prince Frederick, to Bismarck Berlin, 4 April 1870, *ibid.*, pp. 107–108; *Aktennotizen Karl Antons, aufgezeichnet in Dessau*, 5 April 1870, DITTRICH, pp. 372–373; STEEFEL, *Bismarck*, pp. 65 ff.).

[1] Benedetti to Daru, Berlin, 25 March 1870, FAE CP, Prusse/377, no. 40. Despite the cloak of secrecy surrounding the meeting of 15 March, rumors about the real reason for the presence of Charles Anton and Leopold in Berlin did leak out; however, they did not reach Ambassador Benedetti (Charles Anton to his wife, Berlin, 10 March 1870, ZINGELER, "Briefe," *Deutsche Revue*, XXIX, Heft 2–3 [1914], p. 345; Charles Anton to Charles, n.p., 14 April 1870, CHARLES I, *Chroniques*, I, 576–577).

[2] In spite of the adverse March developments relative to a Hohenzollern candidacy, the issue remained very much alive. On 9 April, Bucher left Berlin for Madrid, conferring on the way with Charles Anton in Düsseldorf about the assurances he was to seek in Spain. Upon his arrival in Madrid on 13 April, Bucher met with Salazar and subsequently with Prim. It was obvious to him that speed was of the essence if a Hohenzollern prince were to secure the Spanish crown. The provisional state of affairs could not be prolonged indefinitely. The Cortes was scheduled to meet on 19 April and it was stressed to Bucher that acceptance by the Hohenzollern candidate should be secured by that date. Prim and Salazar left no doubt about their preference for Leopold over his brother Frederick. They felt relatively certain that the election of Leopold in a secret session of the Cortes would place France before a *fait accompli*, involving henceforth the interests of Spain rather than of Prussia (Bucher to Bismarck, Madrid, 14 April 1870, I.A.B.o. [Spanien] 32 secreta; Salazar to Charles Anton, Madrid, 14 April 1870, *ibid.*; Salazar to Bismarck, Madrid, 14 April 1870, *ibid.*). Major von Versen arrived in Madrid on 18 April, bringing Bismarck's letter of the 11th. The chancellor took great pains to explain to Prim the difficulties of the issue but assured him that in time the plan would be successful (Bismarck to Prim, Berlin, 11 April 1870, *ibid.*).

The expectation of the Spanish government, implied in messages from Madrid, that Leopold would agree to become a candidate troubled Charles Anton who regarded his son's refusal as definite. He was of course still willing to support the candidacy of Frederick and evidently believed that the assurances sought in Madrid by Bucher could be counted upon (Charles Anton to Bismarck, Düsseldorf, 17 April 1870, DITTRICH, pp. 376–377). However, by 22 April it appeared as though the likelihood of a Prussian prince ruling in Spain would not be realized. Charles Anton had arrived in Berlin on the 21st, and in subsequent audiences both he and his son Frederick discussed the Spanish issue with William. Frederick's reluctance to become a candidate and William's refusal to order him decided Charles Anton to have the adverse development communicated to Madrid. In view of Bismarck's illness at Varzin, Thile communicated to Ambassador Canitz the abandonment of the Hohenzollern candidacy. He also instructed Bucher to return to Berlin (*Aufzeichnung Karl Antons*, Berlin, 21 April 1870, *ibid.*, p. 377; *Aufzeichnung Karl Antons*, Berlin, 22 April 1870, *ibid.*; Thile to Canitz, Berlin, 20 April 1870, BONNIN, p. 135).

In spite of the disappointing communication from Berlin, the Spanish government did not give up hope. At the recommendation of Bucher, Salazar in effect ignored for the moment the Hohenzollern refusal, and Prim's letter to Bismarck, of 24 April, urged a speedy decision in Berlin. The intent was to gain a reconsideration of the Hohenzollern candidacy in Berlin. Upon his arrival Bucher, as well as Abeken, did confer with William on the issue but the monarch remained firm in his decision not to order or pressure the Hohenzollern princes. Consequently, in a cryptic message of 4 May, the Spanish government learned once again that the Hohenzollern candidacy seemed lost (Prim to Bismarck, Madrid, 24 April 1870, I.A.B.o. [Spanien] 32 secreta; Bucher to Bismarck, Madrid, 24 April 1870, *ibid.*; Bucher to Bismarck, Berlin, 27 May 1870, *ibid.*; same to same, Berlin, 2 May 1870, *ibid.*; Thile to Canitz, Berlin, 4 May 1870, *ibid.*).

While the Spanish government was again sounding out other candidates, the Hohenzollern candidacy was revived once more in Germany. King William received on 11 May the interesting and rather optimistic reports of Major Versen. Although the king had no desire to see the matter revived, he nevertheless gave Versen permission to travel to Varzin and report to the chancellor. Surprisingly enough, Bismarck was not very eager to concern himself with the matter. Versen, on the other hand, called upon Crown Prince Frederick in an effort to rekindle interest in the candidacy. Apparently the officer succeeded to a degree, for Frederick agreed to arrange for Versen to travel to Düsseldorf and discuss his views with Charles Anton and Leopold. It was not without difficulty that Versen was able to contact both; he had but a very brief opportunity to confer with Leopold and his wife. Versen met Charles Anton actually at Bad Nauheim and was there from 21 to 23 May. Charles Anton was rather impressed by Versen's reports. In a letter to Crown Prince Frederick, the prince indicated that Leopold might be willing to reconsider the candidacy, if both the crown prince and Bismarck thought it desirable. Charles Anton suggested that Crown Prince Frederick could serve as intermediary with the king. A similar view was expressed in a letter to Prince Leopold, but Charles Anton indicated that the initiative could not come from Leopold. Versen endeavored to secure Moltke's support by asking him, in a letter of 22 May, to get Bismarck to write to Charles Anton that a Hohenzollern candidacy was indeed in the interests of the Prussian state. Moltke summoned Versen back to Berlin on the 23rd, and the very next day took him to meet the chancellor. Bismarck did not appear very optimistic but did appreciate the spark of interest which Charles Anton, Leopold and Crown Prince Frederick had shown in their talks with Versen. Versen again met with the crown prince that very afternoon, bringing him the letter from Charles Anton and discussing with him the resumption of the negotiations with the Spanish government. On the 29th, Crown Prince Frederick announced the new developments to King William, who did not conceal the unpleasant effect the news had in his view. Nonetheless, the fact that Prince Leopold had shown renewed interest decided William to confer at least on the matter with Bismarck. The chancellor had not remained idle; on the 28th he had sent Bucher to Bad Nauheim with a letter to Charles Anton, stressing the fact that Prussia's interests would indeed benefit from the founding of a Hohenzollern dynasty in Spain. As expected, Bismarck struck a responsive cord in Charles Anton, who indicated in his reply that Leopold would probably be willing to make the expected sacrifice. He even suggested that the Spanish government be appraised of a probable reversal. Writing to Leopold on 1 June, Charles Anton indicated that it was necessary to yield to the higher interests of state. Leopold himself rejoined his father at Bad Nauheim and concurred with him. Both were in agreement that the initiative could not come

negotiations were not centered in the Prussian capital.[1] Not even the imperial ambassador in Madrid, the hub of the negotiations, had known definitely of Leopold's acceptance until the evening of 2 July, when

from them. On 2 June, a courier carried Bismarck's reply to Prim's letter of 24 April to Madrid, in which Leopold's willingness to pose his candidacy and accept if elected was indicated, subject to satisfactory constitutional safeguards and political and financial agreements. The courier also carried instructions for Canitz which, as Steefel shows, had been wrongly identified by Pirala as instructions for Bucher. After a meeting in Giessen between William, Charles Anton and Bismarck, during the return from Bad Ems where the king had called on Tsar Alexander, the die was cast indeed (William to Charles Anton, Berlin, 12 May 1870, ZINGELER, Karl Anton, p. 243; FESTER, Briefe, I, n. 162; G. VON WERTHERN, General von Versen. Ein militärisches Zeit-und Lebensbild. Aus hinterlassenen Briefen und Aufzeichnungen [Berlin, 1898], pp. 81–82; Thile to William, Berlin, 11 May 1870, BONNIN, p. 156; Thile to Eichmann, Berlin, 16 May 1870, ibid.; Frederick William to Charles Anton, Berlin, 12 May 1870, FESTER, Briefe, I, nos. 162, 176; Versen diary, 19, 20, 21 May, I.A. [Deutschland] 158 secreta; Leopold to Frederick William, Benrath, 21 May 1870, DITTRICH, pp. 385–386; Aktennotiz Karl Antons, Nauheim, 21 May 1870, ibid., p. 386; Charles Anton to Frederick William, Nauheim, 23 May 1870, ibid., pp. 386–387; Charles Anton to Leopold, Nauheim, 27 May 1870, ibid., pp. 387–388; SCHWEINITZ, I, p. 258; Versen diary, 23 ,24, 25 May 1870, I.A. [Deutschland] 158 secreta; Frederick William to Bismarck, Postdam, 30 May 1870, FESTER, Briefe, I, no. 189; Bismarck to Charles Anton, Berlin, 28 May 1870, BGW, VIb, no. 1557; Charles Anton to Bismarck, Nauheim, 31 May 1870, BONNIN, pp. 162–163; Bismarck to Prim, Berlin, 1 June 1870, ibid., pp. 163–164; Bismarck to Canitz, Berlin, 1 June 1870, ibid., 165–166; Leopold to Crown Prince Frederick, Benrath, 4 June 1870, ibid., pp. 169–170; Bismarck to Canitz, Berlin, 5 June 1870, ibid., p. 170; cf. L. D. STEEFEL, "Bismarck and Bucher. The Letter of Instructions," Studies in Diplomatic History and Historiography in Honor of G. P. Gooch, C. H., ed. A. O. Sarkissian [New York, 1962], pp. 217–224; STEEFEL, Bismarck, pp. 76 ff.).

[1] On 7 June, the Cortes had approved the law regulating the election of a king. The provision requiring an absolute majority of the deputies, i.e., a minimum of 176 votes, was interpreted as an insurmountable obstacle for the duke of Montpensier. Salazar felt that the moment for decision was rapidly drawing near. When Bucher arrived in the morning of 9 June, the Spanish government was ready to enter into formal negotiations with the Prussian government. Bismarck was determined to keep Prussia officially out of the issue and, rather than dispatch the required instructions, let it be known in Madrid that direct negotiations with Leopold should be opened. Prim had good reason to feel concerned over the prospect of lengthy negotiations and would have been satisfied with an official communication from Berlin authorizing the candidacy. But Bismarck was determined not to enter into official contact and merely repeated his advice to negotiate directly with Leopold. Although the Cortes fully expected Prim to report before the 9th of June on his efforts to find a Spanish king, he was able to delay until the 11th. His report stressed the problems of the search, touched upon the negotiations with some of the candidates, but did not identify Leopold as a candidate with whom negotiations had been conducted. In view of the fact that no formal talks had begun with Leopold, Prim could only state that his government at the moment did not have a candidate. Although partisans of Montpensier tried to seize upon Prim's difficulty to force the election of the duke, the danger passed and the Cortes turned its attention to less momentous issues (ibid., pp. 88–94).

Bucher and Salazar left Madrid on 14 June, for the purpose of beginning direct negotiations with Leopold at Reichenhall. Versen arrived there from Berlin on the 14th, and Leopold met him there next day. The officer, carrying copies of Salazar's requests to Bismarck that the candidacy be endorsed officially, asked Leopold to agree to such a step and write a letter to William for approval of his candidacy. Leopold refused to accede to Versen's demand, wishing to see the election in Spain postponed until all formal conditions had been met. He did consent to travel with Versen to Sigmaringen for consultation with Charles Anton. The three met on the 17th, and were joined two days later by Bucher and Salazar, who discussed the political situation in Spain and urged speedy negotiations. The Cortes was expected to adjourn in the very near future, and an immediate decision by Leopold was

Prim had acquainted him with the situation.[1] Until that time, Mercier de Lostende had been unable to relay to his government anything more than rumors and conjectures.[2] The well-kept secret of the negotiations had prevented the French government from obtaining accurate information and it was only the blunders in Madrid which prematurely rent the veil of secrecy and revealed the scheme of the Hohenzollern candidacy to the world and to French diplomacy.

Even after his arrival in Wildbad, Wednesday, 6 July, Ambassador Benedetti seemed not particularly anxious to get in touch with the *Quai d'Orsay*. Only on the following afternoon did he inform Gramont of his arrival, giving no account of the stop-over in Coblenz. By that time Benedetti was aware of the gravity of the situation, for he indicated his readiness to comply with whatever orders he might be given.[3]

deemed imperative. Salazar did inform the president of the Cortes that Leopold was willing to accept and that only the king's formal approval was required. While Versen left on the 19th with a letter from Charles Anton to Bismarck, Bucher departed for Bad Ems to secure royal approval of the candidacy. Salazar remained at Sigmaringen, to await news of the king's decision and to take a letter of acceptance from Leopold to Madrid (Versen diary, I.A. [Deutschland] 158 secreta; *Aktennotiz Karl Antons*, Sigmaringen, 17 June 1870, DITTRICH, pp. 395–396; *Notiz Leopolds, ibid.*, p. 396; Charles Anton to William, Sigmaringen, 19 June 1870, K. ZINGELER, "Das fürstliche Haus Hohenzollern und die spanische Thronkandidatur. Unter Benutzung bisher ungedruckter Schriftstücke," *Deutsche Revue*, XXXVII, Heft 1 [1912], p. 66; Leopold to William, Sigmaringen, 19 June 1870, ZINGELER, *Karl Anton*, pp. 245–246; Charles Anton to Bismarck, Sigmaringen, 19 June 1870, BONNIN, p. 193; Versen to Bismarck, Sigmaringen, 19 June 1870, *ibid.*, pp. 191–192).

It was only after a lengthy discussion that Bucher was finally able to win the king's approval and that he was able to send the news to the princes and Salazar at Sigmaringen. William had only recently learned from Crown Prince Frederick the details of the Hohenzollern candidacy revival. He did not wish to stand in Leopold's way but certainly was not enthusiastic about the candidacy. However, he did insist on being informed about all matters pertaining to the negotiations, and his request caused Bismarck and Thile some anxious moments (*Aktennotiz Karl Antons*, Sigmaringen, 23 June 1870, DITTRICH, pp. 397–398; William to Leopold, Ems, 21 June 1870, BONNIN, pp. 197–198; William to Charles Anton, Ems, 21 June 1870, *ibid.*, pp. 198–199; Bucher to Charles Anton, Ems, 22 June 1870, DITTRICH, pp. 399–400; same to same, Berlin, 23 June 1870, *ibid.*, pp. 400–401; Charles Anton to Queen Augusta, Sigmaringen, 26 June 1870, *ibid.*, pp. 401–402; Leopold to Crown Prince Frederick, late June 1870, *ibid.*, p. 402; Thile to Bismarck, Berlin, 19 June 1870, BONNIN, pp. 190–191; Abeken to Bismarck, Ems, 24 June 1870, *ibid.*, pp. 204–206).

As soon as King William's approval had been secured, Salazar was in a position to telegraph the news to Madrid. Three telegrams, brought to Berlin by Versen, were transmitted for this purpose by Thile to Canitz. All messages were dated from Sigmaringen and were destined for Prim, Zorilla, president of the Cortes, and to Salazar's family. It was the faulty decoding of the message to Zorilla which prompted the premature end to the Cortes session and thus destroyed all hopes for a secret, speedy election of Leopold (Thile to Canitz, Berlin, 21 June 1870, *ibid.*, pp. 195–196; Leopold to Prim [draft], Sigmaringen, – June 1870, *ibid.*, p. 194; Bismarck to Prim [draft], Varzin, – June 1870, *ibid.*, pp. 194–195; Bucher to Bismarck, Berlin, 22 June 1870, *ibid.*, p. 201; Charles Anton to Bismarck, Sigmaringen, 23 June 1870, *ibid.*, pp. 203–204).

[1] Mercier de Lostende to Gramont, Madrid, 3 June 1870, FAE CP, Espagne/876, T.

[2] Ollivier had stated as late as 30 June that the maintenance of peace had never looked so hopeful and that no irritable problems were in the offing (SALOMON, p. 37).

[3] Benedetti to Gramont, Wildbad, 7 July 1870, FAE CP, Prusse/379, T. Although the

Almost as soon as his communication had been received, Benedetti was ordered to leave for Ems, where King William was in summer residence.[1] A courier was to meet him there with instructions for his mission.[2] Shortly after Gramont's telegram had arrived in Wildbad, early on Friday, the 8th, Benedetti started his fateful journey to Ems, not expecting the quick and devastating *dénouement* yet to come.[3] He decided to travel by way of Coblenz, expecting to meet there the courier coming from Paris and, if possible, to call again on Queen Augusta. He probably was hopeful of enlisting her support in his efforts to obtain Leopold's renunciation. The queen's influence might make William more amenable to the considerations of the French government and thus ease the ambassador's task.[4] While waiting for the Paris train, Benedetti sought and obtained an audience, during which the queen agreed to make the monarch receptive to the ambassador's proposals. The audience was short but apparently satis-

editors of the *ODG* credit the ambassador with the initiative for the trip to Ems, there is no real proof that Benedetti suggested it. The fact that Gramont thanks the ambassador for offering to go is not sufficient evidence; it is more likely that he thanked Benedetti for the latter's offer to comply with whatever orders his government might send him (Gramont to Benedetti, Paris, 7 July 1870, *ibid.*, T.). There is evidence to support the view that Benedetti was ordered to Ems (Gramont to Cadore, Paris, 14 July 1870, ONCKEN, *Rheinpolitik*, III, 438–439; FLEURY, II, 228; CHAPPUIS, p. 72)..

[1] Gramont to Benedetti, Paris, 7 July 1870, 11:45 PM, FAE CP, Prusse/379, T.

[2] Same to same, Paris, 7 July 1870, *ibid.*, n.n. The decision to send Benedetti to Ems was taken in conformity with the belief in Paris that inquiries directed at the Prussian, rather than the Spanish, government were more likely to bring clarification. After consulting with the emperor, and in the absence of Ollivier, Gramont instructed LeSourd in Berlin on 3 July to ask formally in Berlin whether or not the Prussian government was aware of the Spanish throne offer to Leopold. Thile was evasive in his reply of the 4th, thus strengthening Gramont's suspicions. On that same day, both he and Ollivier also discussed the matter with Ambassador Werther in Paris, who was about to leave for Ems. They left no doubt about the deep resentment felt in Paris over the prospect of a Prussian dynasty in Spain. Although they had no proof that the Prussian government was involved in the matter, they stated that the secrecy of the affair might well prompt such a conclusion by Frenchmen. They impressed upon Werther their hope that King William would oppose a Hohenzollern candidacy for the Spanish throne, for Napoleon could not accept such a solution of the dynastic problem of Spain (Gramont to LeSourd, Paris, 3 July 1870, *ibid.*, T.; LeSourd to Gramont, Berlin, 4 July 1870, *ibid.*, T.; Werther to William, Paris, 5 July 1870, FESTER, *Briefe*, I, no. 265).

Tension was heightened on 6 July, when Gramont stated in the chamber that France would never tolerate a Prussian prince on the throne of Spain. Yet, thus far the French government had not obtained a full explanation in Berlin. With William in Ems and Bismarck in Varzin, there was little hope of penetrating the secrecy surrounding the candidacy. It was only logical therefore to send Benedetti to Ems (OLLIVIER, XIV, 96–108; A. GRAMONT, *La France et la Prusse avant la guerre* [Paris, 1872], p. 57).

[3] Benedetti to Gramont, Wildbad, 8 July 1870, 11:50 AM, FAE CP, Prusse/379,T.

[4] SAUREL, p. 156. "Count Benedetti, whose life has been spent in diplomacy and who had seen with his own eyes the gradual development of the military strength of Germany, keenly felt all the difficulties of the part he was about to play. He was to try to soften down the rather arrogant speeches and dispatches of the Duc de Gramont and to do his best to get his country out of an awkward position" (FLEURY, II, 230).

factory from Benedetti's point of view, for the queen herself hastened to Ems later in the day, hopeful of contributing to the peaceful settlement of an issue which was rapidly becoming charged with tension.[1] The ambassador continued his journey late in the evening with Baron Bourqueney, the courier, acquainting himself with his instructions before the train arrived at Bad Ems.

In order for Benedetti to appreciate the situation accurately and understand his instructions, Gramont had included dispatches to and from LeSourd and Mercier de Lostende, as well as a copy of the declaration made to the *corps législatif* on 6 July. In the dispatch to Benedetti, the minister expressed the hope that King William would intervene to eliminate the candidacy of Leopold and thus rid the world of a dangerous project. Gramont asked Benedetti to try and obtain that "His Majesty advise [*conseille*] the prince of Hohenzollern to reverse his acceptance."[2] In a private letter of 7 July, written after the official dispatch but carried by the courier to the ambassador, Gramont was more explicit and forceful when he asked that the Prussian government give Leopold the order to withdraw. Gramont cautioned Benedetti against a statement by the king that he was indifferent to Leopold's negotiations with the Spanish government. "We could not accept such an answer as being satisfactory, because the government of the king can not disinterest itself today through simple words about a situation to the creation of which it has contributed. It is necessary that it modify it, that it redress it before we accept the assurance of its disinterest."[3] Although there existed a marked difference in emphasis between the official dispatch and the letter, the intentions were nevertheless the same: that the king persuade Leopold to withdraw his candidacy.[4] Benedetti of course realized the danger of the adopted course; should the king refuse to comply with the French request, the

---

[1] Cf. L. RIESS, "Eine noch unveröffentlichte Emser Depesche König Wilhelms I .vom 11. Juli 1870," *FbpG*, XXVI, Pt. 1 (1913), p. 193, for Queen Augusta's efforts to bring about Leopold's renunciation; H. BOSBACH, *Fürst Bismarck und die Kaiserin Augusta* (Cologne, 1936), pp. 43–44.

[2] Gramont to Benedetti, Paris, 7 July 1870, FAE CP, Prusse/379, n.n. For a fine summary of the events surrounding the interpellation of Cochéry, the fateful meeting of the council of ministers, and the Gramont declaration, see STEEFEL, *Bismarck*, pp. 112–119.

[3] Gramont to Benedetti, Paris, 7 July 1870, FAE CP, Prusse/379.

[4] *Ibid.* Gramont's stronger language in the private letter might have been occasioned by a report he had received from Madrid just before he wrote the letter, in which Mercier de Lostende announced that Prim was prepared to release Leopold from his acceptance if such a demand were made. Perhaps Gramont hoped to bring this about by making a more determined request that Leopold's candidacy be withdrawn (Mercier de Lostende to Gramont, Madrid, 7 July 1870, 4:20 PM, *ibid.*, Espagne/876, T.).

consequences would spell a French diplomatic defeat or war between the two powers. Gramont's anti-Prussian sentiments were no secret to Benedetti, and he had every reason to feel apprehensive about his mission. He had had also opportunity to judge the effect the declaration in the *corps législatif*, on 6 July, had in Germany. It is perhaps not surprising that Benedetti came *"händeringend"* to Ems.[1]

The ambassador's arrival on 8 July had been expected and, upon leaving the train, he was met by the king's aide-de-camp, Prince Anton von Radziwill. Benedetti made an immediate request for an audience and then retired to his hotel, *La Ville de Bruxelles*.[2] Already at an early hour next morning he was informed that the king would receive him in audience at three o'clock in the afternoon.[3] Shortly after, Ambassador Werther called on Benedetti, presumably to find out about the nature of his mission and to invite him for dinner at the king's table that evening. Anxious for a solution of the crisis, Benedetti explained in detail to Werther the views of the imperial government and indicated its expectations as well. He hoped to prepare the ground for the audience with the king and thus speed the solution. Werther's remarks about royal reluctance to advise a renunciation raised doubts in the ambassador's mind as to the success, at least a quick success, of his mission.[4]

---

[1] Cf. FRANCE. ASSEMBLÉE NATIONALE, *Enquête parlementaire sur les actes du gouvernement de la défense nationale. Dépositions de témoins* (Versailles, 1872), I, 86, in which Benedetti declared: "I had been sent to Ems to arrange a delicate and difficult affair, even to investigate it, because we were not exactly informed about the relations which had been established between the prince of Hohenzollern and the king of Prussia on the one hand and Marshal Prim on the other. I had to proceed therefore with an extreme moderation in order not to aggravate the situation which was already very difficult and very dangerous. I had to act with equal circumspection in obtaining information which we lacked [in order] to enlighten us as to the intentions which [the Prussian government] had in concerting itself with Marshal Prim"; Albedyll to his wife, Ems, 9 July 1870, J. ALBEDYLL-ALTEN, *Aus Hannover und Preussen. Lebenserinnerungen aus einem halben Jahrhundert*, ed. R. Boschan (Postdam, 1914), p. 82.

[2] Benedetti to Gramont, Ems, 9 July 1870, 7 AM, FAE CP, Prusse/ 379, T.; Abeken to Bismarck, Ems, 8 July 1870, 7:45 PM, R. LORD, *The Origins of the War of 1870; new documents from the German archives*, "Harvard Historical Studies," XXVIII (Cambridge, 1924), p. 154; FESTER, *Die Genesis*, pp. 68–69.

[3] Benedetti to Gramont, Ems, 9 July 1870, 10:30 AM, FAE CP, Prusse/379, T.; Radziwill to his wife, Ems, 9 July 1870, RADZIWILL, pp. 158–159.

[4] Benedetti to Gramont, 9 July 1870, FAE CP, Prusse/379, no. 1. Benedetti's message was badly garbled, apparently in consequence of an electrical storm. Gramont gained the impression from the message that William was strongly opposed to a renunciation, while in actuality the king simply refused to take the initiative in bringing about Leopold's withdrawal (Gramont to Benedetti, Paris, 10 July 1870, *ibid.*, T.). Interestingly enough, Werther's reports on the reaction in Paris to Leopold's candidacy disturbed Bismarck, Thile and Abeken. It was felt that he should have refused to discuss the matter with Gramont and Ollivier and simply referred them to Madrid and Reichenhall. Bismarck and Thile stressed to Abeken the necessity to convince Werther that the Prussian government could not, and would

At three o'clock Benedetti was summoned to the royal residence, where he was received at once by King William. He acquainted the monarch with the reason for his audience and then explained the attitude of the imperial government relative to Leopold's candidacy. He asked the king to counsel the prince to withdraw. William replied that the affair concerned him solely as the head of the Hohenzollern family and not as ruler of the Prussian state. He indicated that he had discussed the matter with Bismarck, who had advised him not in his official capacity but as a private citizen. He maintained that he was in touch with Leopold and his father and that he would await news of their plans before formulating his own. In reply, Benedetti pointed out the difficulty of admitting the distinction the king had drawn in respect to his role and declared that French public opinion would not accept it. Agreeing with William, that the selection of a king was essentially an internal matter, he nonetheless reminded the monarch that he was in a position to terminate a project which might lead to disaster. The ambassador was referring to the fact that Leopold was a member of the Prussian army and that the king could simply forbid him to leave Prussia and accept the crown. William indicated that he would not oppose Leopold's withdrawal but that he would not intervene in the prince's plans.[1]

The interview clearly showed to Benedetti the policy which the Prussian government expected to follow in the candidacy controversy. The ambassador drew from it the following points: the king rejected any contention that the Prussian government was responsible for the affair; he regarded the candidacy as a matter concerning only the Hohenzollern family and the Spanish government; he did not see any threat to the peace, since neither Prussia nor France would suffer or

---

not, retreat in the face of French threats (Werther to Bismarck, Paris, 4 July 1870, 7:50, LORD, p. 122, T.; Abeken to foreign office, Ems, 5 July 1870, *ibid.*, p. 124; Thile to Bucher, Berlin, 5 July 1870, *ibid.*, p. 215; Werther to William, Paris, 5 July 1870, *ibid.*, pp. 125–127; Werther to foreign office, Paris, 5 July 1870, *ibid.*, p. 127; Bucher to Thile, Varzin, 5 July 1870, *ibid.*, p. 128; Bismarck to Abeken, Varzin, 5 July 1870, *ibid.*, pp. 129–132; Abeken to Bismarck, Ems, 6 July 1870, *ibid.*, p. 134).

[1] Benedetti to Gramont, Ems, 9 July 1870, FAE CP, Prusse/379, no. 1. Although the king refused to comply with Benedetti's suggestion that he persuade Leopold to withdraw, William did express his regret in a letter to Charles Anton that no prior assurances had been obtained relative to French acceptance of the candidacy (William to Charles Anton, Ems, 6 July 1870, DITTRICH, pp. 406–407; Abeken to Charles Anton, Ems, 6 July 1870, *ibid.*, pp. 404–406; Charles Anton to Abeken, Sigmaringen, 8 July 1870, BONNIN, pp. 229–231; Charles Anton to William, Sigmaringen, 8 July 1870, *ibid.*, pp. 231–233). For the Prussian impressions about Benedetti's remarks, see Abeken to Bismarck, Ems, 9 July 1870, T., LORD, pp. 165–166; Bismarck to foreign office, Varzin, 10 July 1870, T., *ibid.*, p. 174).

benefit from the election of Leopold; he could advise Leopold only in his capacity as head of the family; he actually preferred to await the outcome of the Cortes vote. As for the future course the king would follow, Benedetti noted two possibilities. Either William would leave the decision up to Leopold, in order to save himself from embarrassment and national disapproval, or else he would play for time in order to complete military preparations for war against France. Benedetti did not venture any definite opinion but simply concluded his report with the hope that the foreign minister would approve of his conduct in the interview with the king.[1]

The differences in the views of William and Benedetti did not disturb the cordial atmosphere in which the ambassador had been received in Ems. As a matter of fact, King William, in conversation with Aristarchi Bey, had expressed his solicitude for the ailing ambassador and thought that he should console him.[2] Not only did Benedetti dine with the king, but he also accompanied him, along with Werther, to a comedy presentation that same evening at the Ems theater. Mention of the Hohenzollern candidacy was carefully avoided during these social functions, and Ambassador Benedetti could not bring up the issue himself without violating all rules of protocol and convention.[3]

The king's determination to leave a decision to Leopold, before considering any action on his own part, was of course a major obstacle to Benedetti's efforts.[4] Moreover, the situation became somewhat more complicated when it was learned in Ems that Leopold was on an Alpine tour and out of touch with his father at Sigmaringen.[5] The ambassador's position was indeed a difficult one; condemned to inaction he was repeatedly requested on Sunday, 10 July, by Gramont to hasten the quick elimination of the Hohenzollern project. The foreign minister desired a communication, suitable for reading to the chambers or for publication, which was to show that the king had known and

[1] Benedetti to Gramont, Ems, 9 July 1870, FAE CP, Prusse/379, no. 1.
[2] Nothomb to Anethan, Berlin, 24 July 1870, BAE CP, Prusse/25, no. 80; H. DELBRÜCK, "Die Emser Depesche," *Forschungen und Fortschritte*, V (1929), p. 196.
[3] CHAPPUIS, pp. 72–73; FESTER, *Die Genesis*, p. 79.
[4] During the evening hours of 9 July, King William received word from Charles Anton, who evidently was concerned about the reaction in Paris, that a voluntary renunciation was out of the question. However, he clearly indicated that Leopold's candidacy would be withdrawn if the king, in the interests of Prussia, requested it (Charles Anton to William, Sigmaringen, 9 July 1870, BONNIN, pp. 231–233; Abeken to Bismarck, Ems, 10 July 1870, T., LORD, p. 171; KARL I., *Aus dem Leben*, II, 101).
[5] Already as early as 6 July Charles Anton had been out of touch with Leopold who, after a visit with the queen mother of Bavaria in Berchtesgaden, had left Reichenhall for a foot tour in the Alps (ZINGELER, "Briefe," *Deutsche Revue*, XXIX, Heft 3 [1914], p. 118).

authorized Leopold's acceptance and that he had asked for time to confer with the prince before making his own resolutions known. The fear that Prussia might outdistance France in the preparations for war was emphasized in Gramont's communications to Benedetti, and he indicated that, short of an appropriate communication, the imperial government would begin to arm.[1] Benedetti was no doubt anxious to carry on with the negotiations and during a conversation with Werther on Sunday afternoon he called his attention to the urgent communications he had received from Paris. Werther had come to tell him that he could expect to be summoned shortly to the king's residence. Benedetti, hopeful now of a peaceful solution, cautioned Gramont against premature military preparations which could make war inevitable.[2] Werther's prediction was fullfilled when later in the evening Benedetti encountered the king at the promenade. William stopped to tell him that he was as yet without news from Sigmaringen, and the ambassador seized the occasion to stress the inability of the imperial government to delay much longer the explanation it wished to make to the chambers and the nation. He asked for an opportunity to explain the situation which his government faced, and William agreed to receive him on the following morning, Monday, 11 July.[3]

The task which Benedetti faced must have appeared even more frustrating when he learned of the attacks against him in the Paris press. In the *Constitutionnel* of 8 and 9 July, Benedetti, along with Mercier de Lostende, had been excoriated for having failed to appreciate the consequences of the Hohenzollern candidacy. "Our two ambassadors in Berlin and Madrid will be to a large degree responsible for the events which are developing. If their diplomacy had not at all been faulty we would not be reduced today to apprehensions about an armed conflict which... would be fatal to all interests." [4] Benedetti resented these attacks which he considered rather absurd.[5] He asked Gramont, should he have occasion to discuss the Hohenzollern project

---

[1] Gramont to Benedetti, Paris, 10 July 1870, FAE CP, Prusse/379, T.; same to same, Paris, 10 July 1870, *ibid.*, P. Rumors about military preparations filled the air and were reflected in official and semi-official correspondence (Solms to foreign office, Paris, 9 July 1870, T., LORD, pp. 162, 164; Ducrot to his wife, Camp de Châlons, 9 July 1870, DUCROT, II, 332; same to same, Camp de Châlons, 10 July 1870 ,*ibid.*, p. 333; Bernstorff to foreign office, London, 10 July 1870, LORD, p. 176; Bismarck to foreign office, Varzin, 10 July 1870, *ibid.*, pp. 173–174).

[2] Benedetti to Gramont, Ems, 10 July 1870, 8:00 PM, FAE CP, Prusse/379, T.

[3] Same to same, Ems, 10 July 1870, 11:30 PM, *ibid.*

[4] *Le Constitutionnel*, 8 July 1870, no. 189; *ibid.*, 9 July 1870, no. 190.

[5] Benedetti to Gramont, Ems, 9 July 1870, FAE CP, Prusse/379, P.

again in the chambers, to mention his reports about efforts to place the Hohenzollern prince upon the Spanish throne.[1]

Before the morning audience with the king, Ambassador Benedetti received a telegram from Gramont requesting that he obtain a definite statement from the king:

You cannot imagine to what point public opinion is excited. It bursts over us from all sides, and we count the hours. It is absolutely necessary to insist on receiving an answer from the king, negative or affirmative. We must have it by tomorrow, the day after tomorrow would be too late.[2]

The picture of the situation existing in Paris, as painted by Gramont, contrasted sharply with the serious but calm atmosphere still prevailing in Ems.[3] Benedetti had spent much of his time with Hermann von Chappuis and Count Lehnsdorff, both members of the king's staff. To Chappuis, who had been a frequent guest at the Benedetti residence in Berlin, the ambassador had not hidden his apprehensions over the demands voiced in Paris. He spoke with annoyance about the tendency in Paris to make a mountain out of a molehill.[4] To convey to the king the full impact of the urgency which marked Gramont's communications was no easy matter for Benedetti who, like William, found it somewhat difficult to comprehend the incessant and determined demands formulated in Paris. Nevertheless, as soon as he was received in audience, he asked William if he might inform his superiors in Paris that the king would invite Leopold to renounce his candidacy. Since the prince could hardly reject such advice, the French government would be in a position to calm all apprehensions. Benedetti cited the irritation of French public opinion, the impatience of the legislature, and the obligation of the cabinet toward the nation.

---

[1] Benedetti to Gramont, Ems, 10 July 1870, 11:30 PM, *ibid.*, T.

[2] Gramont to Benedetti, Paris, 11 July 1870, 1 AM, *ibid.*, T.

[3] "We have already seen then, that even before the Gramont declaration [of 6 July], the public was strongly incensed against Prussia. His statement was thus not out of line with opinion, but it also seemed to have greatly intensified warlike sentiment. Although the press was divided, it leaned to the side of Gramont. But observations by five diplomats, the *Times* correspondent, and the police reporters, based on the public as well as on the press, seemed unanimous in commenting on the increase of anti-Prussian and prowar sentiment in line with the spirit of Gramont's words. Then the special prefect reports came in with a 63 to 17 majority for war, if necessary, as a confirmation of provincial sentiment. Especially to be noted is the fact that the Paris and provincial publics both wanted satisfaction from Prussia rather than from Leopold. Therefore from a reexamination of the press, the diplomatic dispatches, and the prefect reports it seems as if the evidence swings back again in favor of Ollivier and of the view that opinion was moving the government toward a more belligerent policy and that the response to Gramont's declaration was strongly and predominantly favorable to the extent of accepting war if necessary" (CASE, p. 251).

[4] CHAPPUIS, p. 72; Radziwill to his wife, Ems, 11 July 1870, RADZIWILL, p. 159.

William rejected the request, observing once again that he was only concerned in the matter as head of the Hohenzollern family and not as the sovereign of Prussia. Benedetti replied that such a distinction could not be accepted. He maintained that by virtue of the fact that he was king William was also head of the family and that the two qualities were inseparable. Moreover, he pointed out that the Hohenzollern princes owed the king absolute obedience because in him the two qualities were united.[1] William refused to modify his views and demand that Leopold withdraw after he had given his permission earlier to accept a throne offer. Benedetti concluded that the king simply did not wish to accept the responsibility for a concession which might insult public opinion in Germany and that he therefore preferred to leave the final responsibility with Leopold and his father.[2] The king believed that a few days of waiting would not aggravate an issue in which there was no danger anyhow. Should France refuse to abide by the necessitated delay he, William, would have to conclude that France was deliberately seeking war. Yet, in order to allay French fears he asked Benedetti to telegraph to Gramont, in his own name, that news from Leopold was expected by evening or early morning which would be communicated at once to the ambassador.[3]

Yet, an ominous note was introduced in the conversation between William and Benedetti when the king alluded to reports from Paris which mentioned French military preparations.[4] He warned that the Prussian government could not tolerate such threatening measures without taking military precautions of its own.[5]

---

[1] Benedetti to Gramont, Ems, 11 July 1870, FAE CP, Prusse/379, no. 2. "The Prussian government has not at all participated, and I only as family-chief. Yet, one does not *want* to understand this in Paris and makes *Prussia* responsible for the *Spanish* candidacy" (William to Crown Prince Frederick, Ems, 11 July 1870, RIESS, *FbpG*, XXVI, Pt. 1 [1913], p. 189). Cf. *Hohenzollerisches Hausgesetz vom 24. Januar 1821, Titel IV, Artikel I*, ZINGELER, "Das fürstliche Haus Hohenzollern," *Deutsche Revue*, XXXVII [1912], no. 1, p. 61, which gives the king exclusive control over the entry of any member of his house into foreign civil or military service.

[2] Cf. Abeken to foreign office, Ems, 11 July 1870, 8:10 PM, LORD, p. 192, T., who reports that the king insisted Leopold should communicate his decision directly to Madrid and that subsequently one could tell Benedetti what had been done.

[3] Benedetti to Gramont, Ems, 11 July 1870, FAE CP, Prusse/379, no. 2; Abeken to foreign office, Ems, 11 July 1870, 2 PM, LORD, p. 189, T.

[4] Benedetti to Gramont, Ems, 11 July 1870, FAE CP, Prusse/379, no. 2.

[5] William was indeed greatly concerned about reports of French military preparations sent by Solms, whose impressions were also shared by Waldersee. The king even considered returning to Berlin and was anxious that Roon be informed of the reports on military measures taken in France. Moreover, William was evidently willing to have Werther take a personal letter from him to Emperor Napoleon, and he also considered the possibility of appealing to the great powers to use their good offices. Bismarck, on the other hand, was opposed to such precipitate steps (Waldersee report on Paris situation, Paris, 10 July 1870,

Although Benedetti had not been able to induce William to request Leopold to withdraw, he nevertheless could report to Gramont that as soon as news was received from Sigmaringen he would be informed. His ardent plea relative to the situation in which the French cabinet found itself had not failed to impress the king who, almost immediately after the audience, decided to send Werther to Paris in hopes of convincing the French government of his good faith in the matter.[1] Indeed, Benedetti was still optimistic on Monday and expected a peaceful solution in the very near future; like William and Werther he considered the incident almost closed.[2]

The king lets me guess and he gives me to understand through his entourage, as Werther will report to you, that the prince must spontaneously renounce the crown which has been offered to him and that the king will not hesitate to approve his resolution. He tells me furthermore that the communication from the prince will reach him shortly, that he should receive it tomorrow; but he absolutely refuses to give me authorization to let you know as of now, which would be tantamount to a guarantee or an engagement, that the prince will withdraw his candidacy.[3]

The king's opposition to the wishes of the French government was emphasized anew when Count Daru, son of the former foreign minister, arrived on Monday afternoon, 11 July, with a letter from Gramont, written the day before, in which the minister threatened military preparations in case King William should refuse to advise Leopold to withdraw. Although the letter was now outdated, it nevertheless served to show Benedetti that his government expected a speedy clarification of the issue at hand.[4] The ambassador decided not to act upon this

---

LORD, p. 184; Solms to foreign office, Paris, 11 July 1870, *ibid.*, p. 189; Roon to William, Berlin, 11 July 1870, *ibid.*, pp. 190–191; Abeken to Bismarck, Ems, 10 July 1870, *ibid.*, p. 173; Bismarck to Abeken, Varzin, 10 July 1870, *ibid.*, p. 175); STEEFEL, *Bismarck*, pp. 129–130.

[1] Benedetti to Gramont, Ems, 11 July 1870, 2:30, FAE CP, Prusse/379, T. On 10 July, King William sent Colonel Karl von Strantz to Sigmaringen to inform Charles Anton of the latest developments. He made it quite clear that he would not stand in the way of a renunciation on the part of Leopold (William to Charles Anton, Ems, 10 July 1870, FESTER, *Briefe*, II, no. 399; Strantz to Abeken, Sigmaringen, 12 July 1870, BONNIN, p. 248; cf. Crown Prince Frederick to Bismarck, Potsdam, 11 July 1870, *ibid.*, p. 247; Charles Anton to William, Sigmaringen, 12 July 1870, *ibid.*, pp. 250–251).

[2] FRANCE. ASSEMBLÉE NATIONALE, I, 88. Benedetti told Werther that he would remain in Ems, at his own risk, twenty-four hours longer, although an answer from the king was already expected that afternoon in Paris (Abeken to foreign office, Ems, 11 July 1870, LORD, p. 192, T.).

[3] Benedetti to Gramont, Ems, 11 July 1870, FAE CP, Prusse/ 379, P.

[4] Gramont to Benedetti ,Paris, 10 July 1870, *ibid.*, P. In his letter the foreign minister wrote that a refusal on the part of William to secure Leopold's renunciation would mean war. Gramont's bellicose attitude was partly influenced by his colleagues, who had come to the conclusion that war was the only alternative to Prussian intransigence. French military preparations had also been initiated, indicating the degree to which war was thought a

demand of the foreign minister; he had become convinced that a decision would soon be communicated from Sigmaringen and that it would be best not to strain the relations with the monarch at this time.

The agitation which had developed since the news of Leopold's acceptance had been revealed to the world had greatly disturbed Charles Anton. Fearful that a serious conflict might result if Leopold were to maintain his candidacy, Charles Anton decided, in his son's absence, to announce the withdrawal of the Hohenzollern candidacy.[1] Unknown to Ambassador Benedetti the news was released from Sigmaringen on Monday evening. It was not until the following afternoon, Tuesday, 12 July, that the king informed Benedetti of the new developments and then only to tell him that Leopold's reply would definitely be in Ems on Wednesday morning.[2] Relating the

likely outcome of the issue. At the time the council of ministers met on 11 July, no satisfaction had as yet been obtained in Ems. However, Benedetti had made it clear that he would be summoned to another audience with William. Thus, the possibility of a peaceful solution of the crisis existed. In the light of Benedetti's caution against premature military measures, the council ordered only limited measures put into effect. Gramont's statement to the chamber on the 11th also reflected a more cautious attitude. However, the reaction in the legislature was none too reassuring, for many deputies were only too eager to eradicate past frustrations through a humiliation of Prussia (OLLIVIER, XIV, pp. 198 ff.; GRAMONT, pp. 80–83; STEEFEL, *Bismarck*, pp. 134–135).

[1] The decision of Charles Anton to announce the withdrawal of Leopold was made on the 11th. The rather violent reaction in Paris to the Hohenzollern candidacy, as well as the growing threat of war, had created a great deal of anxiety in Sigmaringen. Of considerable impact upon the prince was the appearance of J. Strat, who arrived late in the evening of the 11th with a letter from the Spanish ambassador in Paris, Salustiano de Olózaga. Strat was the Rumanian envoy in Paris, and as such was greatly concerned over the effect the Spanish throne issue might have upon the reign of King Charles. Although Charles Anton showed himself at first opposed to Leopold's withdrawal, he did begin to appreciate Strat's careful analysis of the situation. The envoy stressed the view that, while the prospects for Leopold's rule in Spain were dimming, the danger of French-supported machinations against Charles in Rumania was mounting. Voluntary renunciation by the Hohenzollern prince was the course of action Strat recommended, and Charles Anton came to accept the recommendation. When Colonel Strantz arrived in Sigmaringen, the decision to withdraw Leopold's candidacy was made definite. The predicament in which Charles Anton found himself was made worse by the fact that Leopold was on an outing tour in the Alps and out of touch with his father (Solms to Bismarck, Paris, 10 July 1870, LORD, p. 183; Morlock to Lasser, Paris, 9 July 1870, DITTRICH, p. 410; OLLIVIER, XIV, 139–141, 206–210; LORD, p. 65, ft. 7; Strantz to Abeken, Sigmaringen, 12 July 1870, BONNIN, p. 289; Charles Anton to William, Sigmaringen, 12 July 1870, *ibid.*, pp. 250–251). In his later reflections, Charles Anton thought his decision well timed, in that it neutralized the French pretext for war, made later a "German" war popular, and gave Prussia the active support of South Germany (Charles Anton to Charles, Sigmaringen, 10 August 1870, KARL I., *Aus dem Leben*, II, 112). "Because of the new... inevitable outbreak of war between Prussia and France [I] decided to refrain from the throne candidacy in Spain and to telegraph this directly to Madrid as well as to the Spanish embassy in Paris" (*Aktennotiz Karl Antons*, ZINGELER, *Karl Anton*, p. 258).

[2] It appears that the first communication announcing the withdrawal of Leopold was a telegram dispatched at 11 PM on 11 July, by Strat to Ambassador Olózaga (P. MURET, "Émile Ollivier et le duc de Gramont le 12 et 13 Juillet 1870," *RHMC*, XIII, no. 3 [1910], p. 305). During the morning hours of 12 July, Charles Anton telegraphed the news of Leopold's withdrawal to Ambassador Olózaga and, subsequently, to Prim. The reason for the

king's message to Gramont, Benedetti suggested that he be authorized to leave Ems at once, should Leopold's decision conflict in any way with the expectations of the French government.[1] Only the fact that the king had indicated a definite time for communicating Leopold's reply had decided the ambassador to accept this last delay, a decision which the foreign minister also approved in a telegram that afternoon.[2] Benedetti was convinced that if the prince withdrew there would be no further difficulty in achieving a satisfactory settlement. When on Tuesday afternoon he accepted a dinner invitation from the king at the *Vier Türmen* he had, in his own opinion, every reason to believe that his mission would soon be successfully terminated.[3] He did not expect that Gramont's latest demand, that the renunciation of Leopold be "announced, communicated or transmitted to him by the king of Prussia or his government," [4] would create any new difficulties. The king had already stated that he would communicate to him whatever decision was to be made in Sigmaringen and the ambassador assumed of course that William would perform such an act as Prussian sovereign and not simply as head of the Hohenzollern family. If, therefore, the king were to communicate Leopold's renunciation to him his mission to Ems would be concluded, and concluded successfully.[5]

The ambassador's optimistic expectation was, however, shortlived. When he returned to his hotel after the dinner with the king, he found instructions which went far beyond the orginal demands the imperial

---

withdrawal had been developed in a formula supplied by Olózaga. Accordingly, Leopold withdrew because the circumstances which had arisen would make it impossible to learn the true wishes of the Spanish nation in an election (Charles Anton to Olózaga, Sigmaringen, 12 July 1870, BONNIN, p. 252; Charles Anton to Prim, Sigmaringen, 12 July 1870, LORD, p. 274).

Charles Anton also prepared a suitable release for the press, which was sent to the *Schwäbische Merkur* and the *Augsburger Allgemeine Zeitung* (for text see BONNIN, p. 252).

Copies of the communications sent by Charles Anton were forwarded by him to King William (*ibid.*, pp. 251–252). Apparently the first news of Leopold's withdrawal in Ems came in a telegram from Strantz (see William to Augusta, Ems, 12 July 1870, ONCKEN, *Rheinpolitik*, III, 188–199). In the afternoon of the 12th, a telegram announcing the decision was received in Ems, with the addition that Strantz would bring official word to the king (Abeken to Bismarck, Ems, 12 July 1870, 6:50 PM, LORD, p. 202, T.).

William's decision not to acquaint Benedetti at once with the "semi-official" news he had received from Sigmaringen was made in hopes that the ambassador would hear meanwhile of Leopold's withdrawal from another source. Thus, the king would be able to avoid an initial and direct communication to the ambassador, and would weaken the impression that he was closely associated with Leopold's candidacy (*ibid.*).

[1] Benedetti to Gramont, Ems, 12 July 1870, 6 PM, FAE CP, Prusse/379, T.
[2] Gramont to Benedetti, Paris, 12 July 1870, 2:15PM , *ibid.*
[3] CHAPPUIS, pp. 72–73.
[4] Gramont to Benedetti, Paris, 12 July 1870, 2 PM, FAE CP, Prusse/ 379, T.
[5] *MMP*, pp. 336–338.

government had made. Indeed, Gramont's new demands put an entirely different complexion on the negotiations and jeopardized all that had been achieved thus far.

We have received, as of now, from the ambassador of Spain the renunciation of Prince Anton, in the name of his son Leopold, of his candidacy to the throne of Spain. In order that this renunciation of Prince Anton have its full effect, it seems necessary that the king of Prussia associate himself with it, and give us the assurance that he shall not again authorize this candidacy. Will you please go immediately to the king to ask this declaration of him, which he could not refuse to give if he is really not animated by ulterior motives.[1]

---

[1] Gramont to Benedetti, Paris, 12 July 1870, 7 PM, FAE CP, Prusse/379, T. During the forenoon of 12 July, Napoleon was called out of a council of ministers to receive the Spanish ambassador who had received word from Strat that Charles Anton was about to inform Prim of the withdrawal of the Hohenzollern candidacy. At the request of Olózaga, the emperor did not tell his ministers of the very important development. However, during the afternoon hours copies of the telegrams of Charles Anton to Olózaga and to Prim, intercepted in Paris, were brought to the emperor and to Ollivier. Although the latter withheld the news from the deputies, the information became quickly known when Olózaga appeared at the chamber to bring official confirmation from Charles Anton (OLLIVIER, XIV, 227 ff.; Arnim to Bismarck, Paris, 14 January 1873, BONNIN, pp. 257–259).

Benedetti was not alone in believing that the Hohenzollern withdrawal, if communicated by William to the French government in some suitable mode, would end the crisis. Many diplomats were quite prepared to concede a moral victory to France (Nigra to Visconti-Venosta, Paris, 12 July 1870, S. W. HALPERIN, Diplomat under Stress. Visconti-Venosta and the Crisis of July, 1870 [Chicago, 1963], p. 130; Loftus to Granville, Berlin, 12 July 1870, 11:45 PM, PRO FO 64/688, T.; Lyons to Granville, Paris, 12 July, FESTER, Briefe, II, 109–110; Beust to Metternich, Vienna, 12 July 1870, 1:25 PM, ONCKEN, Rheinpolitik, III, 432, T.: same to same, Vienna, 13 July 1870, 4:30 PM, ibid., 433–434, T.).

The optimism of the diplomatic world was quite ill-founded. The reaction of the chamber did not augur well for the peace of Europe. From the left as well as the right demands were voiced that more than a mere association of Prussia with Leopold's withdrawal ought to be obtained. Duvernois' interpellation, calling for a guarantee by Prussia, set in motion a tragic sequence of events. All Ollivier could do was to delay debate on it. To be sure, the manner in which the news of Leopold's withdrawal reached the French government only served to increase suspicion and resentment in Paris. The fact that William had not ordered the withdrawal made it impossible for the French government to issue a statement to that effect. Thus, no claim of having humiliated Prussia and forced her to abandon the Spanish throne project could be established by France. Yet, it was precisely for such a victory that the French public clamored. Interestingly enough, there is every reason to believe that Napoleon was willing to accept Leopold's withdrawal as the final act (OLLIVIER, XIV, 230 ff.; Nigra to Visconti-Venosta, Paris, 13 July 1870, HALPERIN, p. 133; CASE, pp. 253 ff.).

Gramont, at the foreign office, spent the afternoon of the 12th drafting communications to Benedetti, in which he stressed the necessity of associating William with the withdrawal and also indicated that the French government was prepared to wait further for official news. Gramont was aware of the fact that news of Leopold's withdrawal had reached Paris. He was determined, however, to force Prussia into the role of having to acknowledge the abandonment of the project (GRAMONT, pp. 112 ff.; STEEFEL, Bismarck, pp. 151–152). In mid-afternoon, Gramont received Ambassador Werther with whom he discussed at length the implications of the crisis and the role of the Prussian king. He insisted that William had authorized the candidacy and that the monarch should therefore also take the responsibility for ending the crisis. Gramont, supported by Ollivier who had joined the discussion, even proposed a draft suitable for a communication from William to Napoleon. This draft, stronger in its language than one Gramont had prepared before the meeting with Werther, actually had little effect on the course of events. The draft, as well as Werther's report, reached William after he had already decided to reject the guarantee demand and to end

Benedetti of course realized that these demands opened a new phase in the negotiations. The hope of a peaceful solution appeared to fade away, and the ambassador began to fear that war might yet be the tragic outcome of all his endeavors in Ems. The tone of the instructions was far too determined to permit any remonstrance on his part. Perhaps he too felt that the guarantee demand was not altogether out of place. Diplomats remembered only too well the manner in which Leopold's brother had ascended the throne of Rumania. One can assume, however, that the ambassador would have been satisfied without such a guarantee.[1]

Worried about the new development, Benedetti went directly to the royal residence on Wednesday morning, 13 July, to request an audience in order to acquaint King William with the guarantee demand, although he expected to be called in any case to hear Leopold's decision. Finding that the king had already left on his morning promenade, the ambassador decided to return to his quarters. On the way

the talks with Benedetti in Ems (GRAMONT, pp. 107 ff.; OLLIVIER, XIV, pp. 244 ff.; Werther to William, Paris, 12 July 1870, LORD, pp. 206–209; STEEFEL, *Bismarck*, p. 154).

Steefel's very meticulous inquiry into the genesis of the guarantee instructions sent to Benedetti refutes some of Ollivier's assertions. It would appear then that Gramont dispatched the fateful message at 7 PM on the 12th. He had conferred at the Tuileries Palace with the emperor following the Werther interview, and, after Napoleon's departure for St.-Cloud, had returned to the foreign office to draft the instructions. Late in the evening, Ollivier called on Gramont and was shown a text of the message sent to Benedetti as well as a letter which Gramont had meanwhile received from the emperor in St.-Cloud. Ollivier fully realized that a new element was being introduced in the controversy, and that after the council of ministers had decided in its morning session to postpone any immediate steps. He could not, he felt, countermand a decision reached by the emperor and the foreign minister but did convince Gramont to send Benedetti additional instructions. These messages, dispatched at 12:15 AM and 1:45 AM on the 13th, tended to shift the emphasis from a general guarantee against a future recurrence of the candidacy to an immediate assurance. The moderation of these instructions was to no avail, because Benedetti had already acted upon the earlier dispatch and had presented the guarantee demand in its original form to William (P. SAINT MARC, *Émile Ollivier [1825–1913]* [Paris, 1950], pp. 292–293; OLLIVIER, XIV, 265–272; Gramont to Benedetti, Paris, 13 July 1870, 12:15 AM, FAE CP, Prusse/379, T.; same to same, Paris, 13 July 1870, 1:45 AM, *ibid.*; GRAMONT, pp. 137–138; STEEFEL, *Bismarck*, pp. 159–160; MURET, *RHMC*, XIII, no. 3 [1910], p. 325, ft. 2; FESTER, *Briefe*, II, 111; FRANCE. ASSEMBLÉE NATIONALE, I, 99–101; V. BENEDETTI, "Ma mission à Ems," *Revue de Paris*, II, t. 5 [1895], pp. 225–257).

[1] V. BENEDETTI, *Essais diplomatiques* (Paris, 1895), p. 385; FRANCE. ASSEMBLÉE NATIONALE, I, 88. During the meeting of the council of ministers in the morning of the 13th, Gramont's new instructions were criticized by some of the members. Moreover, it was decided by vote that the guarantee demand should not be interpreted as an ultimatum. Thus, if William should refuse to give the guarantee, the French government would consider the matter closed. During the afternoon, Gramont went before the chamber to state that the Spanish government had officially communicated to the French government the withdrawal of Leopold's candidacy. He went on to say that the negotiations, carried on to this effect with Prussia, were still in progress and that no complete account could be presented as yet. Gramont's inconclusive statement came under sharp attack and, after a heated debate, it was agreed that the government would make a statement on the matter on the 15th (OLLIVIER, XIV, 284 ff.; MURET, *RHMC*, XIV, no. 2 [1910], pp. 201 ff.).

he encountered the king's aide-de-camp, Radziwill, whom he asked to inform the king of his request for an audience. Radziwill probably told Benedetti that the king was at the promenade and that he could relay his request at once. The ambassador, expecting only a brief delay, did not return to his quarters to await William's reply but remained at the promenade. Radziwill rejoined him there a few moments later and told him that the king would receive him in audience during the afternoon. After Benedetti had been assured of an audience with William, he decided to remain a while longer at the *Brunnenpromenade*. Here he was met again, shortly later, by Radziwill who, at the king's request, brought him a *Kölnische Zeitung* supplement with the news of Leopold's withdrawal. Benedetti told the officer that the news was already known in Paris, and that he had received word to that effect. In returning the newspaper to Radziwill, Benedetti also apparently transmitted to him, for the king's perusal, a telegram from Paris announcing that Charles Anton had communicated officially to the Spanish government in Madrid the withdrawal of his son's candidacy. Radziwill did take the message to the king, who returned it with an expression of thanks. When the ambassador, after the flurry of meetings with Radziwill, entered one of the tree-lined walks, he suddenly encountered the king, walking with Prince Albrecht and his aides near the *Direktionsgebäude*. William, unaware as yet of the guarantee demand Benedetti planned to present in the forthcoming audience, stepped toward the ambassador to exchange a few civilities. He told Benedetti that he had not yet received the expected official communication from Sigmaringen. Believing that the reference to Leopold's withdrawal, as announced in the press, was a proper opening, the ambassador decided to introduce the new demand forwarded by Gramont. After stating that Charles Anton's announcement was of no value to the French government without royal approbation, Benedetti asked the king to authorize a communication to Paris stating that he, William, would use his authority to prevent a renewal of the candidacy in the future. William was visibly disturbed by this unexpected request, and he absolutely refused to consider such an engagement, unlimited in time, although the ambassador strongly pleaded for it. The public promenade was hardly the place for a prolonged discussion of the subject, particularly after a crowd of onlookers had begun to gather. Thus, William took leave of the ambassador and quickly walked toward his residence.[1] The ambassador returned to his hotel to draw up a

---

[1] Benedetti told Radziwill that he deemed it important to see King William before the

dispatch to Gramont, informing him of the king's initial reaction to the guarantee demand.[1] Although Benedetti had picked a most inappropriate place for the introduction of the guarantee demand, it is safe to assume that it would have met the same opposition if introduced in the afternoon audience. To be sure, the discussion in public did not give Benedetti the proper chance to develop his case, a fact which he apparently had not sufficiently considered, but the urgency of Gramont's telegram had brooked no delay. Indeed, almost as soon as he had dispatched this first account, he received the Gramont-Ollivier instructions to seek a guarantee from William.[2]

Benedetti was rather surprised when, after one o'clock, Radziwill called on him to transmit the official communication of Leopold's renunciation but without making any reference to the scheduled audience.[3] The ambassador reminded him that the king had agreed to give his approbation to the prince's decision. He also told Radziwill that he still expected to be received in audience to present the king with the new demand of his government, to which he had referred in his morning conversation with the monarch. He was anxious to expose at length the considerations he had been ordered to submit in reference to the guarantee demand.[4] The aide-de-camp agreed to inform the king of the ambassador's wishes, indicating that he would probably return at once with a reply. He did call on the ambassador within the hour and reported that the king authorized him, Benedetti, to declare to the imperial government that the king of Prussia had given his entire approbation to Leopold's renunciation. Thus, the original demand of the French government had been met, however long the delay.[2] In respect to the guarantee demand, Radziwill stated that

scheduled session of the chamber in Paris. Evidently, Benedetti hoped to obtain from William the official communication of Leopold's withdrawal and to telegraph the final *dénouement* to Gramont. It may well be that the ambassador was also anxious to resolve the issue with William before the arrival of Bismarck, whom Benedetti erroneously expected in Ems (Benedetti to Gramont, Ems, 13 July, FAE CP, Prusse/379, no. 4; Abeken to Bismarck, Ems, 13 July 1870, 10:15 AM, LORD, p. 218, T.; William to Augusta, Ems, 13 July 1870, FESTER, *Briefe*, II, 118–119; memorandum of William,, entitled *Der 13te Juli in Ems*, LORD, pp. 276–278; *MMP*, pp. 371–372; CHAPPUIS, pp. 72–73; FRANCE. ASSEMBLÉE NATIONALE, I, 86–87; LORD, pp. 84 ff.).

[1] Benedetti to Gramont, Ems, 13 July 1870, 10:30 AM, FAE CP, Prusse/379, T.

[2] See footnote 1, p. 253 above.

[3] Shortly after noon, Colonel Strantz had arrived in Ems with a letter from Charles Anton, officially confirming the withdrawal of Leopold (ZINGELER, *Karl Anton*, pp. 256–257).

[4] Although Benedetti made repeated efforts to secure an audience, the king's initial reaction to the guarantee demand caused him to despair of a favorable reply. "I have strong reasons for supposing that I will obtain no concession [in respect to the guarantee demand]" (Benedetti to Gramont, Ems, 13 July 1870, 3:45 PM, FAE CP, Prusse/ 379, T.)

[5] Same to same, Ems, 13 July 1870, 7 PM, *ibid.*

William, having nothing to add to his remarks of the morning meeting, thought it superfluous to resume the discussion. Ambassador Benedetti refused to abandon his efforts for an audience, and he asked the officer to again relay his request, adding that since the morning interview he had received further instructions from his government. Yet, these repeated efforts were to no avail. Shortly after five o'clock Radziwill returned to the ambassador's hotel with the reply that the king could not resume the discussion relative to the guarantee demand. Instead, the monarch referred the ambassador to his remarks at the promenade and declared that he would not go beyond giving his approbation to Leopold's decision.[1] Benedetti felt that any further attempt would be futile and resigned himself to waiting for Gramont's order recalling him to Paris. Although he did not refer to the future course of events in his

---

[1] Benedetti, in his book, attributes the decision of the king not to receive him in audience during the afternoon of the 13th to the adverse effect of Werther's report on the interview the previous afternoon with Gramont and Ollivier. Actually the account, with its references to the infamous *Entschuldigungsbrief* proposal, did not reach Ems until mid-afternoon on the 13th. Well before being informed of the Werther communication, the king had made his decision not to receive the French ambassador. In fact, the refusal to proceed with the promised audience must be attributed to Bismarck who did not approve of William's conciliatory attitude. Bismarck had offered to go to Ems from Varzin and had left his estate on the 12th, bound for Berlin, where he had arrived in the late afternoon. He had informed the king of his intention to proceed next day to Ems and urged that no statement be made to Benedetti meanwhile. At dinner that evening he was joined by Roon and Eulenburg who supported his recommendation that Benedetti should simply be told that Leopold would inform the Spanish government directly of his decision (LORD, p. 68; STEEFEL, *Bismarck*, pp. 165–166; *BGW*, VI, 305–306; Bismarck to Abeken, Berlin, 12 July 1870, 5:50 PM, LORD, p. 202, T.; Bismarck to Thile, Varzin, 11 July 1870, BONNIN, p. 245, T.; Bismarck to William, Berlin, 12 July 1870, 7:20 PM, LORD, p. 203).

Rather than continue on to Ems, Bismarck decided to remain in Berlin and to send Eulenburg instead. In the early evening hours, the chancellor was also informed of a telegram from Werther, announcing that Ambassador Olózaga had informed Gramont of Leopold's withdrawal. Anxious to prevent an embarrassing statement by William to Benedetti, Bismarck took immediate steps to have the news from Paris released to the Wolff news agency. On his way to call on Prince Gorchakov, passing through Berlin on his way to Wildbad, Bismarck met Count Launay, the Italian ambassador. In his remarks, Bismarck gave the appearance of a man who was embarrassed, exasperated and dejected by the effect Fench threats had had upon the Hohenzollern candidacy. Implying that he was running a grave medical risk in trying to join the king at Ems, he told Launay that Leopold's withdrawal had taken him by surprise and that he planned to return to Varzin. In his subsequent visit with the Russian statesman, Bismarck lamented the manner in which the prestige of the Hohenzollern house was weakened by the failure to take a much more vigorous stand against French accusations and insinuations (Bismarck to Abeken, Berlin, 12 July 1870, 7:23 PM, *ibid.*, p. 204, T.; Werther to foreign office, Paris, 12 July 1870, 4:45 PM, *ibid.*, pp. 201–202, T.; for marginal commentary by Bismarck, see *ibid.*, p. 202, ft. 1; Bismarck to William, 12 July 1870, 7:20 PM, *ibid.*, p. 203, T.; S. W. HALPERIN, "Bismarck and the Italian Envoy in Berlin on the Eve of the Franco-Prussian War," *Journal of Modern History*, XXXIII, no. 1 [1961], pp. 33 ff.; C. W. CLARK, "Bismarck, Russia, and the War of 1870," *ibid.*, XIV, no. 2 [1942], pp. 195 ff.; cf. H. WELSCHINGER, "Le rapport Werther et la dépêche du 12 juillet 1870," *Journal des débats*, 5 June 1909; A. DARIMON, *Histoire d'un jour; la journée du 12 juillet 1870* [Paris, 1888], pp. 92–93).

communications, one can assume that he expected the worst. The gravity of the situation was only too clear to one who had spent his life in diplomacy. The continued deterioration in the situation since the introduction of the guarantee demand was not likely to be redressed, in view of the determination of both parties to concede nothing. The optimism Benedetti had shown earlier had been quickly dispelled by the developments of the last twenty-four hours.

Despite his pessimism Benedetti did not fail to make still another effort when, after receiving during the night orders from Gramont, as yet unaware of William's refusal, to insist on the guarantee declaration.

Make a last effort upon the king, tell him that we limit ourselves to asking him to forbid the prince of Hohenzollern to retract his renunciation. Have him tell you, 'I will forbid him to do so,' and authorize you to communicate that to me, or that he charge his minister or ambassador to let me know. That will satisfy us. If in effect the king nourishes no ulterior motives, it is only a secondary question for him, but for us it is very important. The king's word alone can constitute a sufficient guarantee for the future. I have reason to believe that the other cabinets of Europe find us just and moderate. . . . In any case, leave Ems and come to Paris with the affirmative or negative answer. It is necessary for me to have seen you by Friday morning. . . . Perhaps, while receiving from the king the news of the renunciation of the prince of Hohenzollern you could tell him: Sir, Your Majesty is the guarantor of the word of the prince of Hohenzollern because you are aware of the fact that as a power we have no contact with the prince, and as a consequence thereof, before the nation, our official guarantee lies in the word of the king.[1]

Benedetti did not think it possible to take the issue up with the king and so he discussed it next morning, the 14th, with Count Eulenburg who had arrived in Ems from Berlin. He told the minister that the French government would be satisfied with almost any form of guarantee the king wished to give. He asked Eulenburg to inform William of this last request of Gramont. But once again the ambassador was disappointed, for the minister told him shortly later that King William had nothing to add to his statement, made the previous morning at the promenade.[2]

In view of the fact that Gramont had asked him to return to Paris, Benedetti notified Radziwill that he wished to bid farewell to King William. Since the king was planning to leave for Coblenz, Benedetti was asked to come to the railroad station where the king would meee him privately. This last interview, taking place at three o'clock in tht

---

[1] Gramont to Benedetti, Paris ,13 July 1870, 9 PM, FAE CP, Prusse/379, T.
[2] Benedetti to Gramont, Ems, 14 July 1870, 12:30 PM, *ibid.*

afternoon, was very brief. Although very friendly toward the ambassador, the monarch told Benedetti that he could add nothing to his expressed opinion and that the negotiations could, if feasible, be continued by his government. Taking leave of the ambassador, William said, *"Nous deux, nous resterons amis!"* [1]

Before Benedetti left the relatively calm resort of Ems, he had occasion to see the *Kölnische Zeitung* edition carrying the famous "Ems Dispatch."[2] His matter-of-fact reference to the account, destined to stimulate chauvinism in both France and Prussia, might

---

[1] Benedetti to Gramont, Ems, 14 July 1870, 3:45 PM, *ibid.*; O. AUBRY, *Le Second Empire* (Paris, 1939), p. 212; CHAPPUIS, p. 74. In contrast with the courteous attitude toward Benedetti in Ems, the French military attaché in Berlin, Baron Stoffel, found it necessary to ask Bismarck for protection against hostile crowds (Stoffel to Bismarck, Berlin, 19 July 1870, I.A.A.a63).

[2] The genesis of the Ems Dispatch may be traced back to the account of the events in Ems on the 13th, which William authorized Abeken to telegraph to Bismarck. The king also gave explicit permission to the chancellor to inform the press and the German legations abroad of the guarantee demand presented by Benedetti and rejected by the monarch. Abeken's summary, composed with a great deal of care, did not take into proper account all of the events which actually took place. Moreover, the wording itself lacked precision and tended to distort a few of the incidents. "On the whole, the events of the day were related with tolerable accuracy, but with a bluntness and acerbity which, while permissible enough in a confidential document, were out of place in one destined for publication" (LORD, p. 91). The course of events in Ems fitted Bismarck's hopes only too well. He wished to keep the controversy alive, depict France as the aggressor, and derive political advantage out of a situation which could be expected to rally Germans north and south of the Main. His instructions to Busch for a counter-attack against France in the press, his talk of resignation should war be avoided in a meeting with Crown Prince Frederick, as well as his remarks to Gorchakov and Loftus about preparations against French military measures, all would seem to indicate that Bismarck was not prepared to see the issue end with the withdrawal of Leopold (HAHN, *Fürst Bismarck* [Berlin, 1878–1891], V, 571; M. BUSCH, *Tagebuchblätter* [Leipzig, 1899], I, 40–42; FRIEDRICH III., *Das Kriegstagebuch von 1870/71*, ed. H. O. Meisner [Leipzig, 1926], pp. 1 ff.; Loftus to Granville, Berlin, 13 July 1870, 3 PM, PRO FO 64/688, T.; for Loftus' discussion with LeSourd about Bismarck's attitude and the impact of the latter's report on the 14 July imperial cabinet meeting, see OLLIVIER, XIV, 319).
In the course of dinner the evening of 13 July, Bismarck, Roon and Moltke telegraphed the king that they thought his return to Berlin both necessary and desirable. In the light of reports reaching Berlin, it was evident that the imperial government did not consider the crisis ended. Renewed French demands could well lead to war and Bismarck was anxious to call the *Reichstag* into session. His plan was to send France an ultimatum, demanding an explanation of the intentions of the French government (Bismarck to William, Berlin, 13 July 1870, 8:10 PM, LORD, pp. 228–229).
Very soon following the telegram urging the king to return to Berlin, Abeken's "Ems Dispatch" was handed to Bismarck. After studying its contents, as well as the authorization to publish them, Bismarck undertook his famous revision and ordered its publication in the press and communication to diplomatic missions abroad. By nine o'clock in the evening a special *Norddeutsche Allgemeine Zeitung* edition was on sale in the streets in Berlin (for a precise, critical edition of the various texts, see E. WALDER, *Die Emser Depesche*, "Quellen zur Neueren Geschichte," [Bern, 1959], pp. 16–24; O. VON BISMARCK, *Gedanken und Erinnerungen* [Stuttgart, 1898], II, pp. 87–93; cf. W. LANGER, "Bismarck as a Dramatist," *Studies in Diplomatic History and Historiography in Honor of G. P. Gooch, C. H.*, ed.A.O. Sarkissian, pp. 199 ff.; R. PAHNCKE, *Die Parallel-Erzählungen Bismarcks zu seinen Gedanken und Erinnerungen* [Halle, 1914], pp. 162–170; LORD, pp. 99 ff.; GEUSS, pp. 252 ff.; SAUREL, p. 212).

appear a bit surprising. However, one must keep in mind that William had treated Benedetti in the most courteous fashion and had parted from him on a friendly note. Benedetti arrived in Paris during the morning hours on 15 July,[1] and of course called at once on Gramont at the *Quai d'Orsay*, where he met also Ollivier.[2] Although the ambassador had little to add to his reports telegraphed from Ems, his final impressions were nevertheless of value. Despite the fact that this report contained important information, neither Gramont nor Ollivier considered it worthwhile to have Benedetti make an oral report to the council of ministers, where his remarks might perhaps have strengthened the pacific attitude of ministers like Plichon, Louvet and Segris, who opposed Gramont's uncompromising attitude.[2] On Friday afternoon, Benedetti witnessed the exciting debates in the chamber, where much of the discussions revolved around the version of the Ems negotiations as presented in the Ems Dispatch. Nobody thought of calling him or of listening to him; in the agitated assembly the presence of the imperial ambassador to Prussia was hardly noticed.[3] Indeed, Benedetti thought that his reports on the negotiations, of which Ollivier was reading excerpts to the deputies, caused hardly a ripple.[4] Clearly the hour of reason had passed and Benedetti, coming from tranquil Bad Ems, must have been surprised by the agitation and excitement about him.[5] Later in the evening he asked Gramont to solicit an audience for him with the emperor.[6] In accordance with protocol, the ambassador called to announce his return to Paris and to report on his mission to Ems. He met the emperor on Saturday afternoon,[7] at Saint Cloud, but no record exists of the conversation. Whatever Benedetti told Napoleon did not affect the events which were destined to crumble the Second Empire.

When Benedetti had returned to Berlin in the fall of 1869 his attention had been directed to a number of developments in Germany. No doubt the most important one concerned the prospect of German

---

[1] Jonas to Servais, Paris, [15] July 1870, LAE, H/18; SAINT MARC, p. 332.

[2] P. MURET, "Les articles de M. Welschinger et de M. Joseph Reinach sur la déclaration de guerre et sur les papiers de Cerçay," *RHMC*, XIV, no. 1 (1910), pp. 80–88.

[3] SAINT MARC, p. 332.

[4] FRANCE. ASSEMBLÉE NATIONALE, I, 88; MURET, "Les articles," *RHMC*, XIV, no. 1 (1910), p. 84.

[5] For the fateful meeting of the imperial cabinet on the 14th, and the subsequent events see CASE, pp. 256 ff.; LORD, pp. 107–117; LEHAUTCOURT, pp. 481 ff.; STEEFEL, *Bismarck*, pp. 195 ff.).

[6] Gramont to Napoleon III, Paris, 15 July 1870, ODG, XXVIII, 396, T.

[7] Napoleon III to Gramont, Saint Cloud, 16 July 1870, ODG, XXIX, 9, T.

unification. Recurrent rumors about the possible entry of Baden into the North German Confederation had pointed up the state of flux relative to German affairs. Contrary to the alarm shown by Lefèbvre de Béhaine, the ambassador had not expected a major development in Germany in the near future. The movement toward unification had lost considerable momentum, and the opponents of unification had begun to play a more effective role, especially in Bavaria. Yet, apart from internal political considerations Benedetti had felt that the prospect of war, should Bismarck try to upset the precarious balance of power, had become a major deterrent. French hostility to unification had crystallized rather sharply since the disappointing compensation talks of 1866 and 1867. Although Benedetti and Daru were fully agreed on the necessity of opposing efforts to unify Germany, the ambassador had appeared more adamant in his stand than the minister. While he believed that Bismarck would not advance unification at present by a series of positive actions, he had suspected the chancellor of contemplating various schemes to that end. Rumors such as those about the *Kaiserplan* were indicative of activity on Bismarck's part, and Benedetti had stressed the necessity that the imperial government take a stand which would discourage all contemplations envisaging the disappearance of the independent south German states. He had emphasized the certainty that Bismarck would try to implement his plans at the first opportunity.

It is not surprising, on the basis of his opinions, that Benedetti had been pessimistic about the prospects of disarmament. The constancy of Bismarck's hope to unify Germany, as well as the constancy of King William's opposition to reductions in Prussia's military power, had amply substantiated the ambassador's expectations. Daru's indirect approach to Bismarck in the disarmament question had been justified, but it is somewhat surprising that he had kept the ambassador in the dark. Had he consulted Benedetti as to the prospects for his proposal, he perhaps might have been able to change his approach or advance other alternatives.

The finality with which the Hohenzollern candidacy affected Franco-Prussian relations gives a very real importance to Benedetti's part in this event. During the phase preceding the Ems negotiations, Benedetti had shown a rather inconsistent interest in the candidacy. The very fact that he had initially drawn the attention of his government to the possibility of this candidacy makes it difficult to understand his prolonged failure later to relay bits of information to the imperial government. Although the negotiations proper remained secret for a long time, it does not excuse the ambassador's negligence to explore all channels of information open to him. For instance, in this light, his utter reserve toward the Spanish envoy in Berlin is inexcusable. It is likely that conversations with Rascón would have given Benedetti some clues about the state of negotiations between Prim and Bismarck. Had he paid greater attention to the rumors, his references would no doubt have been more numerous and perhaps would have awakened a far greater interest at the *Quai d'Orsay* in the Hohenzollern candidacy. The very fact that Benedetti was so concerned about the ways and means Bismarck sought to advance the unification and about the possibility of a war between France and Prussia should have aroused his suspicions. Yet, it did not, and he made only inquiries when directed to do so. Without attempting to lessen Benedetti's shortcomings, one must take into consideration that the French government also failed to gather corroborating information on Leopold's candidacy. No doubt the silence of the foreign office had the effect of minimizing the concern of its representatives abroad.

During the second phase of the candidacy, in his mission to Ems, Ambassador Benedetti had carried on vitally important negotiations. The serious implications of the candidacy had become fully clear to him, and already his interview with the queen, on the way to Ems, had pointed up this concern. He had thought it essential that the negotiations not be threatened by exaggerated demands; for this reason he had decided to ignore the instructions in Gramont's private letter and act upon the more restrained official communication. Benedetti had quickly discovered the king's reluctance to order Leopold's withdrawal, and he therefore had decided not to press too vigorously at first. He did obtain William's promise to give his approbation should Leopold decide to withdraw. This demand then of the French government was fulfilled. For a time Benedetti had withstood the pressure of Gramont and had indeed succeeded in restraining the latter until the fateful guarantee had been introduced. This demand had its profound effect upon the negotiations, and it is surprising that Benedetti should have chosen such an ill-opportune time to acquaint the king with it. The fact that this action contrasted so sharply with his cautious attitude earlier suggests that he was vitally concerned about the time element. The delays he had experienced in obtaining the official communication from the king of his approbation of Leopold's withdrawal, the rumors about military preparations as well as Gramont's clear-cut order to see the king "immediately" no doubt had influenced his decision to bring up the guarantee demand at the *Brunnenpromenade*. One must assume that it was not so much a lack of caution as the pressure of time which had led Benedetti to this step. It was the king's unwillingness to satisfy the demand from Gramont, rather than the time and place Benedetti had chosen to make the overture, which was decisive in the final analysis. The introduction of the guarantee demand at a formal audience would not have made it any less obnoxious to William.

The awkward way in which Benedetti handled the guarantee demand at Ems has obscured his achievement both in Ems and in Berlin. His share of the blame for the *dénouement* of the Hohenzollern candidacy is slight and centers primarily in the phase prior to the Ems negotiations. Even then his failure was largely the failure of the imperial diplomatic apparatus.

CHAPTER IX

DIPLOMACY OF DISTORTION

Although Benedetti's report to the emperor marked the conclusion of his ambassadorial duties, his connection with Franco-Prussian diplomacy did not cease with the outbreak of hostilities. Indeed, within the week following the official French declaration of war he was the subject of numerous diplomatic conversations and press reports. This notoriety was occasioned by Bismarck's decision to make public the alliance and compensation draft treaty which Benedetti had left with him in late August 1866. Anxious to influence favorably the attitude of the British government toward Prussia, the chancellor used this unique document to further his aims.[1] When Ambassador Bernstorff had tried on 19 July to persuade Gladstone and Granville to oppose an intended French blockade of the German coast, he had briefly alluded to the existence of the Benedetti draft. The small impression this reference had made upon the British statesmen did not satisfy the chancellor, and he decided upon a more persuasive course to win Britain's sympathies as well as those of the other powers.[2] Ambassador Bernstorff was instructed to arrange the publication of the Benedetti draft in the English press. The release was to be prefaced by a statement to the effect that Prussia had refused to avoid the war at the cost of betrayal of her south German allies and Belgium.[3] Furthermore, Bern-

---

[1] Cf. Thile to Balan, Berlin, 22 December 1866, SASS, *PJ*, CCXVII, Heft 3 (September 1929), 268: "Meanwhile the Luxemburg question remains for us a *noli me tangere*. It will be kept for eventual use for or against N[apoleon]."

[2] See explanatory note in *BGW*, VIb, 418–419; cf. Gladstone to Victoria, London, 25 July 1870, VICTORIA, *Letters*, 2nd series, ed. G. Buckle (London, 1926), II, 46.

[3] Efforts to publish the so-called Benedetti Memorandum in the English press were part of a general plan to gain support of public opinion in England for the Prussian and German cause. Oral intructions from the chancellor to Bernstorff were relayed on or before 19 July by legation counsellor Krause, who probably carried the copy of the draft treaty to London (Bernstorff to Bismarck, London, 19 July 1870, I.A.A.a. 14.; Bismarck to Bernstorff, Berlin, 23 July 1870, *BGW*, VIb, 419, T.). Arrangements were also made to send copies of the document to most of the European cabinets (BUSCH, *Tagebuchblätter*, I, 54).

storff was urged not to indicate too precisely the date of origin of the document.[1] Bismarck was anxious to convey the impression that the imperial government had never abandoned its hope, even after the London Treaty of 1867, to annex both Luxemburg and Belgium. Little time was lost in complying with the chancellor's order and on Sunday evening, 24 July, Krause called on Delane, the influential editor of *The Times*, at his rooms at Serjeant's Inn.[2] During the interview the counsellor avoided mention of the precise date of the document and gave Delane to understand that it had been drafted after the creation of the North German Confederation. In reply to the editor's repeated efforts to pinpoint the date, Krause intimated that the proposal had been made during the Belgian railway dispute of 1869. Delane finally accepted Krause's explanation and satisfied himself that the copy was authentic.[3] His publication of the document next day greatly aided Bismarck in his efforts to further Prussia's cause.[4]

However, the chancellor had not neglected other channels for bringing the French proposal to light. On 22 July he had summoned Nothomb, the Belgian envoy, to his office and had acquainted him with Benedetti's draft. Deeply shocked by the revelation, Nothomb had identified Benedetti's handwriting and had learned that the proposal had been offered as late as 1869. Within a few hours he had prepared and dispatched a full report by courier to Brussels.[5] On Sunday, the day Krause called on Delane, Bismarck also mentioned the document to Loftus during a reception in Potsdam. The ambassador called next day, examined the document and agreed that it was in Benedetti's handwriting.[6] In order to convince the British cabinet completely, Bismarck, on 26 July, gave Loftus a lithograph copy of the document for examination by the foreign office in London. The ambassador forwarded it to the British capital, adding the statement that the proposal had been offered to Prussia during the Belgian railroad crisis.[7]

---

[1] Bismarck to Bernstorff, Berlin, 23 July 1870, *BGW*, VIb, 420, T.

[2] Bernstorff to Delane, London, 24 July 1870, *The History of The Times* (London, 1935–1939), II, 424.

[3] For Krause's report on the interview with Delane see K. RHEINDORF, *England und der deutsch-französische Krieg 1870/71* (Bonn, 1923), p. 172; E. COOK, *Delane of "The Times"* (London, 1915), pp. 226–227.

[4] *The Times* (London), Monday, 25 July 1870, p. 9.

[5] Thile to Balan, Berlin, 24 July 1870, SASS, *PJ*, CCXVII, Heft 3 (September 1929), 272; cf. Nothomb to Juste, Berlin, 28 August 1870, BAE, Papiers Nothomb, film 117, dossier 245, section 21; Devaux to Beyens, Brussels, 24 July 1870, BEYENS, II, 457–458.

[6] Loftus to Granville, Berlin, 25 July 1870, PRO FO 64/689, no. 81; LOFTUS, I, 113–115.

[7] Loftus to Granville, Berlin, 26 July 1870, PRO FO 64/689, no. 83.

Although Bismarck had revealed the existence of the draft treaty to certain diplomats, its publication in *The Times* on 25 July had very considerable impact in England and abroad. In Paris the adverse effect of the revelation was fully appreciated. The imperial government was anxious to combat Bismarck's intentions, and next day Gramont declared to Lord Lyons, the British ambassador in Paris, that the Prussian chancellor was the originator of the compensation and alliance project.[1] He likewise instructed La Valette in London to inform the British government that the initiative for the treaty had come from Bismarck. The foreign minister gave an account of the many occasions on which the chancellor had suggested that France annex Belgium and stressed every detail which linked Bismarck to the authorship of the project. While Gramont's version contained elements of truth, he too failed to present a correct picture of the negotiations. In particular, he insisted that all suggestions in reference to Belgium had been made by Prussia and that the emperor had rejected them categorically. He urged La Valette to make it clear in London that Benedetti had drawn up the treaty under Bismarck's dictation.[2] On 28 July, the *Journal officiel* offered the French version of the negotiations. It did not deny the fact that talks had taken place in Berlin but maintained that the French government "never had knowledge of a written, formulated project" and that the emperor had rejected all propositions which might have been discussed during those talks.[3] The inaccuracies of the official French version need not be elaborated upon; the efforts which were made to blame the Prussian government attest to the importance the belligerent powers attached to Britain's attitude.

Gramont's efforts to dispel the suspicions which *The Times* publications had created received the full support of Benedetti. The nefarious scheme which had come to light implicated the ambassador as much as his government. It was not until 29 July, however, that he entered into the controversy. Benedetti's version of the episode appeared in the form of a letter which he addressed to Gramont. He asserted first of all that Bismarck, prior to the war with Austria, had repeatedly suggested that France annex Belgium. Benedetti then went on to deal specifically with the draft which he had made:

At the time of the conclusion of the Prague peace and in the presence of the emotion which the annexation of Hanover, Electoral Hesse and the city of

---

[1] Lyons to Granville, Paris, 26 July 1870, NEWTON, I, 303–304.
[2] Gramont to La Valette, Paris, 27 July 1870, *AD*, 1871–72, I, 282–283.
[3] "Note du *Journal officiel*," Paris, 28 July 1870, *ibid.*, 285–286; cf. de MAZADE, "Chronique de la quinzaine," *Revue des deux mondes*, LXXXVIII (1 August 1870), pp. 747–748.

Frankfort to Prussia had created in France, Bismarck showed again the strongest desire to re-establish the equilibrium which these acquisitions had destroyed. Various combinations, regarding the integrity of the neighbor states of France and Germany, were put forth; they became the object of several talks during which Bismarck inclined to make his personal views prevail.

During one of these conversations, and in order to furnish myself with an exact account of these combinations, I agreed à les transcrire en quelque sorte sous sa dictée. The form, no less than the content, show clearly that I limited myself to reproducing a project conceived and developed by him. On my part, I gave an account in substance to the imperial government of the communications which had been made to me.

The emperor rejected them as soon as they came to his attention.

I must say that the king of Prussia himself did not seem to want to agree to the basis, and since that time, that is to say, during the last four years, I did not enter again into a new exchange of ideas on this subject with Bismarck. If the initiative for such a treaty had been taken by the government of the emperor the project would have been drawn up by the ministry and I would not have had to reproduce a copy in my handwriting; it would have been drafted differently and, moreover, it would have led to negotiations which would have been carried on simultaneously in Paris and Berlin.[1]

The thorough and deliberate falsification of the events by Benedetti is self-evident; that Gramont was sufficiently aware of that fact is likely. The foreign minister, however, was determined to erase the distrust which had arisen in London relative to the aims of French foreign policy. The very day he received Benedetti's letter, he dispatched a copy of it to La Valette for his use in clearing the air of suspicion: "I think it helpful to send you a letter which I received from Benedetti and in which he establishes, on the basis of the personal knowledge he has of the respective negotiations, the truth of the facts. ... You can communicate it to Lord Granville. I am convinced that after these frank explanations, the queen's government and public opinion in England will see that there is no cause to occupy oneself any longer with the contentious revelations of Bismarck." [2] At the time Gramont communicated Benedetti's letter to La Valette, Bismarck sent a dispatch to Bernstorff in which he maintained his previous assertions and claimed that if he had not made public the treaty project the French government would undoubtedly have proposed an end to hostilities and suggested French and Prussian annexations in Belgium and South Germany respectively.[3]

---

[1] Benedetti to Gramont, Paris, 29 July 1870, AD, 1871–72, I, 201–211. This letter was published in the Journal officiel on 30 July 1870 and was annexed to a circular of the foreign minister to French diplomatic representatives abroad (Gramont to diplomatic agents, Paris, 30 July 1870, FAE CP, Espagne/876). See also T. JUSTE, M. de Bismarck et Napoléon III; à propos des provinces belges et rhénanes (Brussels, 1871), p. 31.

[2] Gramont to La Valette, Paris, 29 July 1870, AD, 1871–72, I, 289.

[3] Bismarck to Bernstorff, Berlin, 28 July 1870, BGW, VIb, 428–429.

In the face of these conflicting accounts the uncertainty of the British government was apparent. During the discussion of *The Times* publication in parliament, Granville could do little more than acquaint his listeners with the conflicting versions presented to him by the Prussian and French ambassadors.[1] The mutual accusations of Prussia and France did not provoke in Britain a felicitous attitude toward either of the belligerents. The only certainty which the British did establish was that Belgium clearly had been the object of Franco-Prussian alliance and compensation talks. Whatever anxiety the revelations caused in Britain, the fact that Belgium's neutrality was respected helped to calm the apprehensions of the British statesmen, to whom the fate of Belgium would always be a vital concern.

The controversy over the draft treaty was not concluded in the summer of 1870.[2] In October 1871, a book appeared in Paris in which Benedetti presented an account of his diplomatic mission to the Prussian court. *Ma mission en Prusse* was written in a effort to absolve the author of all blame for the fiasco of imperial policy toward Prussia and clear him of all suspicion in regard to the draft treaty. Benedetti, who wanted to "rectify" existing distortions, succeeded admirably in adding a few of his own. His account, subjective and selective, offers a mass of inaccuracies. For instance, he failed to go into detail about the negotiations with Bismarck between 17 and 31 August 1866; he preferred not to include his correspondence with Rouher of this period which would have revealed the truth. Since Rouher had never deposited his papers in the foreign ministry archives, Benedetti did not expect that a correct version of the episode would ever be revealed. His illusions were shattered, however, in the very same month his account appeared in the bookstore of Henri Plon.

Unknown to Benedetti, Bismarck was in an excellent position to refute his interpretation of the 1866 negotiations. Benedetti had not learned that the Cerçay papers, comprising the papers of Rouher and Thouvenel, had passed into Prussian hands.[3] The fortunes of war had placed Mecklemburg troops in occupation of Rouher's home, Cerçay castle, near Bruney (Seine-et-Marne), where they had accidentally

---

[1] GREAT BRITAIN, 3 Hansard, CCIII (1870), 926; Granville to Ponsonby, London, 26 July 1870, VICTORIA, II, 52–53.

[2] Bismarck did not think it necessary to reply to Benedetti's version because he felt that the French government had not succeeded in repudiating the Prussian charges (Bismarck to diplomatic agents, Berlin, 10 August 1870, *Das Staatsarchiv* [Hamburg: 1861–1919], XIX, 161–162).

[3] *The Times* (London), Wednesday, 25 October 1871, p. 10.

discovered a cache holding this highly important collection.[1] Not
realizing the value of the discovery at once, the soldiers had burned part
of the papers before an officer had examined the find and had it
transported, about 12 October, to Bismarck's headquarters in Versailles. The papers were later transferred to Berlin,[2] and in October
1871 Bismarck made use of them to refute Benedetti's assertions.

Whether Bismarck's new revelations were designed to destroy
Benedetti's historical reliability – in order to weaken that part of his
book which portrays Bismarck as constantly seeking a *rapprochement*
with France for the purpose of promoting the preponderance of Prussia
in Germany – is impossible to say. It is true that Benedetti's account
did tend to blur the image of Bismarck as the German, and not merely
Prussian, patriot. On 21 October 1871, the *Reichsanzeiger* published
a lengthy article "to correct [Benedetti] on those points in which he
aims to throw doubt upon the accuracy of our publication of last
year." The exposé effectively convicted Benedetti of falsifications and
of trying to "jumble together" two different phases of the negotiations;
yet, in order to give the lie to Benedetti, it was necessary to expose
Bismarck's efforts of the previous year to post-date the proposal.
Apparently the chancellor believed that that point would be largely
ignored in view of the detailed evidence amassed against the former
ambassador. By citing conclusive selections from the French diplomatic
correspondence of late August 1866, not mentioned by Benedetti,
irrefutable evidence of the ambassador's fabrications was presented.
Particularly devastating was the inclusion of Rouher's instructions to
Benedetti of 16 August and the latter's reply of the 23rd, as well as
the subsequent reports on the meetings with Bismarck. To be sure,
the letters were not reproduced in full, but they did establish the fact
that the convention had been drawn up by Benedetti on instructions
from Paris.[3] The evidence silenced the former diplomat, and he made
no attempt to answer the *Reichsanzeiger* article. Benedetti had hoped
to free himself of all blame but instead found himself judged by his own
fabrications.

---

[1] J. REINACH, "Un chantage historique. La fondation de l'empire allemand et les papiers
de Cerçay," *Récits et portraits contemporains* (Paris, 1915), pp. 225–257, offers an account of
the discovery of the papers as well as of the use to which they were put by Bismarck. An
inventory of the Cerçay Papers has been included as an appendix in *ODG*, XII.

[2] ROTHAN, *La politique française en 1866*, p. 8, ft. 1, indicates that the documents were
transferred to Berlin on 8 November 1870. They were returned to France in accordance
with Article 245 of the Versailles Treaty.

[3] See *The Times* (London), Wednesday, 25 October 1871, p. 8.

CHAPTER X

AMBASSADOR IN RETROSPECT

The mission of Ambassador Benedetti covers a vital segment of the history of the Second Empire. Appointed to the Berlin post at the conclusion of the Danish war in 1864, he became a witness to the decisive struggle which ensued between Austria and Prussia soon after the peace treaty with Denmark had been signed in Vienna. Prussia's victory at Sadowa and her subsequent rise to supremacy in Germany had far-reaching implications for the future of Europe and the Second Empire and thus gave added significance to Benedetti's role. A study of his mission to Berlin would not be complete without an evaluation of his performance.

Benedetti's appointment was the outgrowth of French preoccupation with a revival of the Holy Alliance. In order to forestall such an adverse development, it was deemed necessary that a close *entente* between Prussia and Austria be prevented. The evident fact of Prussian aspirations toward political pre-eminence in Germany made it desirable that the French envoy in Berlin be sympathetic to Prussia and, at the same time, hostile to Austria and the 1815 system she represented. Benedetti, previously the first French envoy to the Italian kingdom, was well qualified for this post. His long service in the diplomatic corps and his aversion to Austria and the 1815 treaties, logical consequence of his strong sympathy for the cause of Italian unification, recommended him for the task. His association with the Italian faction in French political circles contributed decisively to the nomination. Benedetti's appointment was considered a boon to Franco-Prussian relations.

The fact that Drouyn de Lhuys, a supporter of Austria an thed *status quo*, remained foreign minister for about two more year sndicated that the emperor was not completely prepared as yet to support one German power to the detriment of the other. Benedetti's instructions did not call for negotiations for a close political *entente* with Prussia. His primary task was to observe developments in Germany and to instill in the Prussian government the belief that France was sympathetic toward its aspirations. The political situation in Germany at the time of Benedetti's appointment was too uncertain to permit a different course. It was necessary to gain a better indication of the course of future Austro-Prussian relations before the imperial government could consider a close alignment with either power.

In accord with his rather general instructions, Ambassador Benedetti's initial conversations with Bismarck displayed a marked reserve, an attitude dictated partly by a desire to become acquainted with the views and policies of the Prussian government on matters of interest to French diplomacy. Yet the ambassador had no difficulty in establishing a *rapport* with the Prussian statesman, and his dispatches reflect the precise knowledge he gained of Prussian policies. He soon was able to conclude that Prussia aspired to the ultimate annexation of Schleswig-Holstein, that Austrian opposition was the greatest check to this hope, but that no break between the two powers could be expected in the near future. His accurate prediction relative to the withdrawal of the Saxon and Hanoverian troops serves to illustrate his swift familiarization with German affairs. Although Benedetti characterized the Schleswig-Holstein question as a means to promote Prussian hopes of hegemony, he repeatedly warned of the fluctuations in Austro-Prussian negotiations and did not rule out a compromise settlement. As early as mid-February 1865, he mentioned the possibility that Bismarck might forego outright annexation in favor of concessions of almost equal value – a prediction fulfilled by the Gastein convention. During the entire phase preceding the Gastein compromise, Ambassador Benedetti urged that the imperial government retain its freedom of action and refrain from alliance propositions. He felt that on the basic issue between Prussia and Austria – supremacy in Germany – there could be no compromise. Benedetti's reports and recommendations did not occasion any change in instructions until early May 1865, when he was ordered, against his own judgment, to make an overture to Bismarck. Nothing more than continued benevolent neutrality – the course Benedetti advocated – was asked by Bismarck and the attempt was unproductive. Benedetti criticized the move as a superfluous gesture because he was convinced that Prussia needed no encouragement in her quest. Indeed, a successful French overture could at best only postpone a decision, since

its conditions might arouse the opposition of the Prussian conservatives. One may assume that the ambassador's observations did have
some effect, for no further overture was made prior to Gastein.

Upon his return to Berlin in the late fall of 1865, Benedetti was
decidedly handicapped in that he had not participated in the Biarritz
talks. Although he probably had learned something in Paris about the
conversations, he could not have been fully informed of the emperor's
intentions. He returned to Berlin convinced that his government had
retained its freedom of action – a correct assumption – and resumed his
reserved but observant attitude. While his dispatches do not reveal
his ideas about the Gastein convention and its implications for Germany, one can assume that he shared the adverse reaction of the French
government. As a result, Benedetti's attitude toward Prussia seemed
more cautious. The Austro-Prussian accord, an event he had believed
likely, might even have induced a degree of distrust. Perhaps the almost
ridiculous disputes over matters of protocol had a more deep-seated
cause than mere preoccupation with status. The ambassador may well
have exaggerated them to emphasize the fact that Prussia would do
well not to ignore France. Bismarck's quick amends suggest as much
and reveal his concern about the attitude of France. Although Gastein represented a setback for Benedetti's mission, he continued to
believe that the duchies question would again become a source of
contention between the two German powers. Thus, he had little reason
to recommend a change of course. He reiterated the belief that assurances of French benevolent neutrality would suffice to bring along
the expected break between Austria and Prussia. His reflections also
point up his realistic consideration of French foreign policy problems.
His hostility toward Austria did not blind him to the fact that Austria
could play a significant role in French hopes of containing Prussia.
His observations clearly indicate that Benedetti was not prepared to
let Prussian expansion keep the European equilibrium permanently
disturbed.

The difficulties of representing the imperial government were
brought home to the ambassador when he found that he had been
temporarily by-passed during the Prussian overture in Paris in
February and March 1866. Although he knew of Prussian intentions to
open talks for an *entente* in Paris, his own government did not inform
him at once of the Prussian proposition. Instead, he had to wait until
the imperial government made its formal reply to learn the details.
He not only felt neglected but feared that his inability to discuss

French policy might prompt Bismarck to discontinue the candor with which he had discussed his plans. While Benedetti could approve of his government's decision not to pursue the Prussian overture, he resented the devious conduct of French foreign affairs. Perhaps he failed to realize that the distrust between emperor and foreign minister was partly responsible for this glaring defect. The lack of coordination was particularly intolerable during the Prusso-Italian alliance negotiations: the emperor advised the Italian government to abandon the alliance while Benedetti worked for the completion of the treaty. Whatever the intent of imperial action, the incident illustrates the circumstances under which Benedetti had to carry out his duties. Not only did he have to rely on instructions of a general nature, but his efforts to act upon the formulated principles of policy were likely to be disavowed and frustrated by the emperor.

After the Austro-Prussian dispute became intensified through the introduction of the federal reform plan and mobilization orders, Benedetti was careful to relate the developments in Germany in great detail. He expected the relations between the two powers to deteriorate continuously; yet, he did not think it advisable to change the course followed thus far. A change was nevertheless proposed by the emperor when he suggested the convocation of an international congress. He had neither asked the ambassador for his opinion nor had he found it expedient to inform him of the proposal before making an announcement to the Prussian ambassador. Benedetti learned of it from Bismarck, a procedure which could only undermine the ambassador's self-confidence and effectiveness. In addition, the congress proposal implied a reversal of French policy: whereas the object had been to further the break between Austria and Prussia, the emperor's proposal sought to prevent a rupture. This incident illustrates anew the lack of co-ordination in the conduct of imperial foreign policy. Although Benedetti did not predict failure of the congress proposal, he did make it clear that the convocation of a congress would not remove the danger of war. He continued to believe that a compromise on the basic issue would not evolve: Prussian hegemony plans could not be realized without a military defeat of Austria. War was of course imminent but Benedetti continued to recommend a course of neutrality. Interestingly enough, the emperor's decision – to remain neutral – came to Benedetti's attention through a circular forwarded by the foreign ministry.

The ambassador's attitude toward the war of 1866 was primarily conditioned by his support of the Italian cause and by his desire to see France freed from the 1815 treaties. However, he was not ready to sacrifice the interests and the security of France and undoubtedly expected his government to redress the balance of power should war upset it. His scheme of using Austria after the war as a counterweight to Prussia – presumably along with the south German states – indicates that he would welcome neither unchecked Prussian expansion nor total defeat of Austria. His outlook toward Germany, conditioned no doubt by traditions of French foreign policy established since Richelieu's time, shows that Benedetti's idealism was thus decidedly tempered by realism. His unreserved adherence to French mediation at Nikolsburg, and his impatience with exaggerated Italian claims, indicate that he was well aware of the implications of Sadowa.

French mediation at Nikolsburg showed Ambassador Benedetti at his best. Provided with general instructions for a speedy termination of hostilities, he entered upon the task with remarkable swiftness and determination. Despite the fatigue of the long trek to the Prussian headquarters, he entered without delay upon his mediation efforts. To promote restraint on the part of the Prussian government after the spectacular victory at Sadowa required tact and perseverance. Benedetti's efforts did result in more restricted claims in the instructions sent to Goltz. The dangerous voyage to Vienna, his advice to the negotiators, his intervention on behalf of Pfordten, in short, his continuous efforts to bring about a cessation of hostilities attest to Benedetti's courage, skill and endurance as a mediator. The delays in regard to communications to and from the foreign ministry forced the ambassador to use his own judgment, a necessity which was particularly hazardous in view of the unpredictable course of French foreign policy. His realistic outlook during the mediation effort showed itself again when his conversation with Bismarck turned to the badly disturbed power equilibrium.

Initial compensation conversations opened with Bismarck at Nikolsburg found the French ambassador determined not to see Prussia expand alone. He emphasized that French neutrality had made partly possible the extent of Prussia's victory and that France had a right to commensurate compensation. His recommendations to Drouyn de Lhuys showed Benedetti optimistic but fully aware of the need for firm and resolute language. He did not minimize the opposition to French claims in Berlin but felt certain that it could be overcome. However, his cautious behavior when the compensation talks definitely opened in Berlin suggests that he was uneasy about the extent of the claim. Since his request for a consultation in Paris had been curtly dismissed, he had no choice but to present the first compensation project. The decision to send Bismarck the demands prior to a conference did not affect the outcome, although Benedetti's cautious approach may actually have strengthened the minister-president's opposition. Yet Benedetti's defense of the Mainz project was vigorous and, despite the adverse result, he recommended that the demand for compensations be continued. The inflexible stand of Bismarck, and the lack of authorization to modify the project, finally forced Benedetti to acknowledge defeat of the Mainz project.

The substitution of the Luxemburg compensation demand signified the renewed ascendancy of the Italian faction in matters affecting foreign affairs. Benedetti welcomed the development and expected that the resignation of Drouyn de Lhuys would end the dichotomy of views which had hampered the conduct of French foreign affairs. The differences between Benedetti and Drouyn de Lhuys had made close collaboration an impossibility. During Rouher's direction of the compensation negotiations, Benedetti was kept far better informed. The second compensation proposal, while encompassing much of the Mainz project, was far more flexible and, therefore, more likely to overcome Prussian objections. The fact that the core of the French demands would not center on purely German territory was expected to make them readily acceptable in Berlin. Although Rouher formulated the demands, there is good reason to assume that Benedetti exerted considerable influence. He must have been fully initiated into the matter, since it was left to him to give final form to the demands. The treaty project was drawn up by the ambassador himself, but it cannot be denied that Bismarck played an integral role through his recommendations and suggestions. Though the draft is in Benedetti's handwriting, the minister-president was unequivocally associated with the formulation of it. Leaving a copy of the project with Bismarck, as Benedetti did, was an imprudent act. When he failed to retrieve it in 1867, his carelessness grew into a diplomatic blunder.

The offer of the foreign ministry to Benedetti indicated not only imperial respect for Benedetti's talents but also French concern with developments in Germany. His decision to refuse the offer was evidently based on personal reasons, since the re-emergence of the Italian faction would have made unity in the conduct of French foreign affairs a less difficult problem. Instead, Benedetti returned to Berlin

determined to help redress the balance of power through the conclusion of the alliance and compensation treaty with Prussia. Negotiations on the Luxemburg project were slow getting under way and,
upon returning to Berlin in mid-November, Benedetti discovered
that the Prussian government was not at all anxious to settle the
matter. His belief that King William was the major obstacle was only
partly correct, for Bismarck too was most reluctant to enter into
negotiations. His complaints that Benedetti's impatience jeopardized
the success of French aspirations and his request that the ambassador
be restrained were part of a process of procrastination designed to
delay, if not prevent, a French annexation of Luxemburg. The minister-president knew that Benedetti would never relax his efforts to
obtain compensation, unless so instructed. Well aware of Moustier's
aversion to complicated and protracted negotiations, Bismarck did
not wish to see the minister's inertia ended by Benedetti's consistent
prodding. Yet, he never requested the recall of the ambassador; he
knew him well and preferred to deal with him, hoping of course that
Moustier's indolence would frustrate Benedetti's hopes. Bismarck's
expectations were largely fulfilled, for the French foreign minister
readily agreed to restrain the ambassador. Benedetti discovered that
his efforts to keep French claims alive in Berlin were rewarded with
admonitions from Moustier. Much time was lost when demands were
made upon the ambassador to seek Prussian collaboration on the
Roman question. He opposed this deviation while Bismarck used it to
delay action on the compensation issue. The constant frustrations
finally decided Benedetti to suggest that the imperial government adopt
a very reserved attitude and see if Bismarck would, without prompting,
offer to carry the negotiations to a close. By the end of the year the
ambassador came to the bitter realization that the Prussian government had no intention of accepting the treaty project.

The reserve which Benedetti had recommended proved abortive
and his sympathy for Prussian aims began to undergo a decided
change. He no longer believed that Bismarck was prepared to grant
France her claims and embark upon a policy of collaboration with the
imperial government in international diplomacy. Up until now he had
entertained the belief that Prussia would, in recognition for French
neutrality during the war, ultimately agree to French expansion.
Benedetti's dispatches began to sound a note of warning. He drew
the attention of the foreign minister to the potential danger arising
from German unification and stressed the need to redress the balance

of power. He told Moustier that Prussia would only heed the powerful – alluding to the need for French military preparations to back up her demands. His correspondence conveys the feeling that war might well become the consequence of abortive negotiations with Prussia. His observations were well founded; yet they were greeted with silence, for he received only *one* official communication from the foreign minister between mid-January and mid-February 1867. Perhaps his repeated warnings did have a delayed effect, because in early spring the French government began efforts for a settlement of the compensation issue. However, Bismarck's speech in the North German parliament only served to strengthen Benedetti's suspicions. In his view the important question was whether it was expedient for France to go to war for the Luxemburg area. The imperial government did not believe so, and the London conference temporarily assured the peace of Europe.

The London Treaty symbolized for Benedetti the legal incarnation of the disturbed balance of power. His disappointment over the failure to re-establish the equilibrium was profound, and one senses a desire for revenge. He was convinced that the imperial government had been deliberately misled and his antipathy toward Bismarck was not concealed. Despite the diplomatic defeat Ambassador Benedetti returned to his post. Did his own vanity bring him back to Berlin and did he hope to witness the ultimate downfall of the Prussian minister-president? Their friendly and intimate association turned into a relationship which was official and distant to the point of hostility. Moreover, Bismarck saw in Benedetti a constant reminder of unfulfilled promises to France; had he been able to select the successor, he undoubtedly would have requested the recall of Benedetti. The ambassador, on the other hand, saw in the minister-president the perpetrator of designs hostile and dangerous to the security of France, designs whose defeat Benedetti thought imperative. The growing estrangement between Prussia and France, culminating in the war of 1870, prompted Benedetti to cultivate the friendship of Count Wimpffen. No doubt the ouster of Austria from Italy facilitated the change in attitude. Benedetti expected that his government, realizing the threat of a unified Germany, would attempt to contain Prussia. He was convinced that France had to make a choice between accepting or opposing the unification trend. He did not neglect to emphasize his conviction that Bismarck was determined to effect the ultimate unity of Germany, and he warned against the means Bismarck would use to further his aims. Hence the constant flow of information from the

Berlin embassy on the creation and the deliberations of the *Zollparla-ment*, the petitions and agitation in Baden, Hesse and elsewhere, the pressure of press and public opinion, the agreements and conventions for military collaboration and integration, the *Kaiserplan*, and a multitude of other events. He cautioned against the minister-president's use of the Roman and North Schleswig questions as tactical diversions, designed to hide the real intentions of Prussia. Benedetti hoped to bring about a realistic appreciation of the ferment in Germany and timely decisions as to the course the imperial government should pursue. But the ambassador saw no tangible evidence that decisions were being made in Paris. To be sure, he knew of the reorganization in the military field, yet the communications from the foreign ministry reflected indecision. Moustier, La Valette, La Tour d'Auvergne and Daru seemed to accept the transformation in Germany, stressed their desire for harmonious relations with Prussia, and remained silent as to the intentions of the emperor in the face of Prussian unification efforts.

In view of its devastating consequences, the Hohenzollern candidacy was an issue of capital importance for French diplomacy. Benedetti's comportment during the genesis of the candidacy was not beyond reproach. During the phase preceding the official announcement of Leopold's candidacy the behavior of Ambassador Benedetti was rather startling. The commendable initial attention to indications of a possible Hohenzollern candidacy gave way to regrettable disinterest. He made little effort to check recurring rumors and to ascertain the real status of Leopold's candidacy. He limited his inquiries to official requests for information from the Prussian foreign office and made only general remarks on Prussian denials. Yet, he can hardly be blamed for the unhappy surprise the announcement caused in Paris. The foreign ministry had known of rumors linking Leopold with the Spanish throne but, like the ambassador, had made little effort to verify them in Spain and Germany. During the second phase of the candidacy, centered around the negotiations at Ems, Benedetti showed remarkable foresight when, at the outset, he decided to disregard Gramont's private letter and refrain from making demands which would have spelled the end of the talks. The negotiations with William show that Benedetti realized the implications of the issue; he took note of the king's position and of his reluctance to force a decision on Leopold for reasons of state. Benedetti did not share the sense of urgency of Gramont, and he was anxious to keep the talks free from pressure. This attitude might have encouraged the long delay in the king's official announcement of Leopold's withdrawal to Benedetti but, in all fairness, it must be noted that he did obtain satisfaction of the first French demand. Only when he was ordered to insist on a guarantee against a future recurrence of the candidacy, with explicit instructions to do so at once, did Benedetti give way to the pressure upon him. His overture at the *Brunnenpromenade* was made with the necessary tact and consideration for the king's person. While time and place for the communication were badly chosen, they were the cause neither for the break-up of the negotiations nor for war. The reasons for the fatal *dénouement* must be sought elsewhere, in Berlin and Paris. Benedetti's influence upon the course of events – once France had decided on a guarantee demand – was nil.

Bismarck's publication of the draft treaty revealed the full magnitude of Benedetti's blunder of 1866/67, and, unfortunately, set the stage for another one. Anxious to refute the charges against himself and the imperial government, Benedetti deliberately falsified the account of the compensation negotiations. The letter to Gramont might have been urged upon Benedetti, for reasons of state, in order to counter the effect of Bismarck's revelations in England. The fact that Bismarck had not replied to the French refutations of July 1870 had evidently convinced the ambassador that he could present his version of Franco-Prussian diplomatic relations without fear of contradiction. His deliberate falsifications, exposed so swiftly and devastatingly, did much to tarnish his reputation as a man and as a diplomat.

The study of Ambassador Benedetti's mission must of necessity include an appreciation of his general effectiveness as a diplomatic representative. His correspondence reveals him as an outstanding political observer. He possessed a very keen and analytical mind, permitting him to indicate and evaluate the true significance of political developments. Accuracy of style and language gave his dispatches added clarity, and even Ollivier had to concede that no one could have reported the events more ably. Contrary to Ollivier's criticism, Benedetti did not simply limit himself to mere reportage; he repeatedly made recommendations, offered suggestions and made predictions as to the course of events. He maintained a very regular correspondence and endeavored to discuss political as well as other factors of public life in Prussia. His observations were based primarily upon factual information; there is a definite inclination in his reports not to discuss rumors, an exclusion not always advisable as Benedetti discovered. He made little or no reference to the opinions of colleagues, although there is ample evidence that he maintained fairly regular contact with them. His close association with Bismarck up to the London conference benefited him very much in the quest for information, and he was considered far better informed than his colleagues. Just as he excluded rumors and opinions of his colleagues from his dispatches, so he avoided social and political gossip, a forte with some of his colleagues. A slight tendency to exaggerate his own importance does not detract noticeably from the quality of his reports and may be partly ascribed to his preoccupation and increasing concern over the relations between France and Prussia. Compared to Napier, Loftus, Zuylen, Bylandt, Nothomb, Chotek and Wimpffen, Benedetti was the best informed and one of the ablest diplomats in Berlin. He was perhaps less outstanding as a negotiator than as an observer. To be sure, like most diplomats of the period, he suffers from comparison with Bismarck whose political sagacity, technical finesse and constancy of purpose he was unable to match. Benedetti was always handicapped in his negotiations with Bismarck by the simple fact that he acted as an agent, and one who was not always informed of his emperor's policies and objectives. He tended at times to be unduly optimistic at the opening of negotiations, as shown during the compensation and the Hohenzollern candidacy issues. This trait caused him vexations during the lengthy negotiations on the Luxemburg question, while at Ems he initially under-estimated the gravity of the issue. He apparently also had an implicit faith in the integrity of others, prompting the grievous error of leaving in Bismarck's hands the copy of the alliance treaty.

The pursuit of information as well as the negotiations on problems affecting the relations between powers demand considerable and varied efforts on the part of an ambassador. It forces him to maintain a multitude of sources of information, to verify rumors, to separate fact from fiction, and to show good-will – social and political – through appropriate gestures. Benedetti was fully cognizant of these aspects of ambassadorial duties and did not neglect them. He maintained contact with officials of the Prussian government, ranging from members of the royal family to officers on the king's staff. He consulted with his colleagues, particularly Wimpffen, Bylandt and Nothomb on Prussian politics. He entertained on a scale which made the French embassy a focal point during the social season in the Prussian capital. Benedetti was in a sense an *ambassadeur par excel-*

lence, although his prolonged absences did detract at times from his effectiveness.

The degree of success which an ambassador achieves depends of course to some extent upon matters actually beyond his control. In reference to Benedetti, the personal conduct of imperial foreign affairs added considerably to the difficulties with which he had to cope. Repeated interventions by the emperor, independently of foreign minister and representatives abroad, lent a damaging degree of uncertainty to the course of French foreign policy. It occasioned some amazingly uncoordinated evolutions in French policy and spread confusion through the ranks of the French diplomats abroad. In judging the performance of Ambassador Benedetti note must be taken of this phenomenon in imperial diplomacy. It need not serve as an excuse in this case, for Vincent Benedetti represented the interests of France in Berlin in a conscientious manner.

APPENDICES

In view of the textual differences in published texts, here appended, of the Benedetti draft treaty, a brief commentary is deemed useful. It will be remembered that when Benedetti obtained his instructions on 17 August 1866, sent from Paris by courier, he did not receive a preliminary draft but simply explicit guide-lines for a treaty yet to be formulated. The first meeting between Benedetti and Bismarck took place during the evening of the 17th, at which time the ambassador outlined the demands of his government. There is no positive indication as to the time of the second meeting, although it would appear that Benedetti was received by Bismarck on the 22nd. It was before or during the negotiations on the 23rd, that Benedetti committed the proposed treaty terms to paper and left a copy of the draft treaty with the minister-president. His report of that day makes it apparent that another copy was sent to Paris for imperial review. Emperor Napoleon did examine the draft, made marginal comments upon the document and forwarded it to Rouher. The fact that Benedetti referred specifically to the marginal comments – to the point of *verbatim* quotes – in his reports of the 30th and 31st of August would suggest that Chauvy had actually returned the draft copy to the ambassador. It is also possible that a letter from Rouher to Benedetti of 27 August, not now extant,[1] may have spelled out the modifications favored by the French government. Benedetti met Bismarck again on the 29th, and learned that King William had already been acquainted with the French alliance and compensation proposal on or before the 27th. This fact is established by the remark of Bismarck that William, after hearing of the proposal, had requested that Goltz return to Berlin for consultation. A message to that effect had been sent on the 27th. During a meeting of the 31st, the draft in Bismarck's possession was revised according to the recommendations of the emperor and left with the minister-president. The other copy was again returned to Paris by Chauvy. Evidence to this effect may be derived from a statement by Goltz, that Rouher had read the French proposals to him from a document containing marginal commentary.[2] It may be assumed also that this is the same document which is now contained in the Cerçay or Rouher Papers at the *Quai d'Orsay*.

The copy left with Bismarck was shown to Ambassador Loftus and others in July 1870; lithographs of it were distributed, among others, to the British foreign office.[3] The text published in *The Times* on 25 July 1870 was of course

[1] See *ODG*, XII, p. 225, ft. 2.

[2] Goltz to Bismarck, Paris, 11 September 1866, *ibid.*, pp. 101–109.

[3] Loftus to Granville, Berlin, 26 July 1870, PRO FO 64/689, no 83. It may well be that the version in the *Archives diplomatiques* was based on such a lithograph.

also based on that copy.[1] The very slight textual differences appear to be nothing more than errors of transcription. The present location of Bismarck's copy has not been established.

Mention is made by the editors of the *ODG* of the possibility that a third draft may exist.[2] However, this assumption rests solely upon Rothan's translation of the *Reichsanzeiger* revelations.[3] This writer's examination of the same material does *not* convey the impression, contrary to Rothan's account, that Bismarck alluded to marginal commentary other than that made by Emperor Napoleon upon the Cerçay copy.[4]

On the basis of available evidence, it may be assumed that only two draft treaty copies ever existed: (1) the copy left by Benedetti with Bismarck, and (2) the text returned finally on 31 August 1866 to Rouher and ultimately deposited in the Cerçay Papers.

(1) COPY OF DRAFT SENT TO PARIS

with indications to, and text of, the emperor's comments (Papiers de Cerçay)

S.M. l'Empereur des Français et S. M. le Roi de Prusse, jugeant utile de se concerter en vue de resserrer les liens d'amitié qui les unissent et de consolider les rapports de bon voisinage heureusement existant entre les deux pays, convaincus d'autre part que, pour atteindre ce double résultat, propre d'ailleurs à assurer le maintien de la paix générale, il leur importe de s'entendre sur des questions qui intéressent leurs relations futures, ont résolu de conclure un traité à cet effet, et nommé en conséquence pour leurs Plénipotentiaires, savoir :
>   S.M.......
>   S.M......

Lesquels, après avoir échangé leurs pleins pouvoirs trouvés en bonne et due forme, sont convenus des articles suivants :

Article premier. S. M. l'Empereur des Français admet et reconnait les ac-quisitions que la Prusse a faites à la suite de la dernière guerre qu'elle a soutenue contre l'Autriche et ses alliés, ainsi que les arrangements pris ou à prendre(1) pour la constitution d'une Confédération dans l'Allemagne du Nord, s'engageant en même temps à prêter tout son appui à la conservation de cette oeuvre.

Art. II. S. M. le Roi de Prusse promet de faciliter à la France l'acquisition du Luxembourg. A cet effet, ladite Majesté entrera en négociations avec S. M. le Roi des Pays-Bas pour le déterminer à faire à l'Empereur des Français la cession de ses droits souverains sur ce Duché, moyennant telle compensation qui sera jugée suffisante ou autrement. De son côté, S. M. l'Empereur des Français s'engage à assumer les charges pécuniaires que cette transaction peut comporter(2).

Art. III. S. M. l'Empereur des Français ne s'opposera pas à une union fédérale de la Confédération du Nord avec les Etats du Midi de l'Allemagne, à l'exception de l'Autriche, laquelle union pourra être basée sur un Parlement commun, tout en respectant, dans une juste mesure, la souveraineté desdits Etats.

---

[1] *The Times*, Monday, 25 July 1870, p. 9.
[2] *ODG*, XII, 173, ft. 1.
[3] Rothan, *Les origines*, pp. 471–480.
[4] *The Times*, Wednesday, 25 October 1871, p. 8.

Art. IV. De son côté, S. M. le Roi de Prusse, dans le cas où S. M. l'Empereur des Français serait amené par les circonstances à faire entrer ses troupes en Belgique ou à la conquérir, accordera le concours de ses armées à la France, et la soutiendra, avec toutes ses forces de terre et de mer, envers et contre toute Puissance qui, dans cette éventualité, lui déclarerait la guerre.

Art. V. Pour assurer l'entière exécution des dispositions qui précèdent, S. M. l'Empereur des Français et S. M. le Roi de Prusse contractent, par le présent traité, une alliance offensive et défensive, qu'ils s'engagent solennellement à maintenir(3). Leurs Majestés s'obligent, en outre et notamment, à l'observer dans tous les cas où leurs Etats respectifs, dont Elles se garantissent mutuellement l'intégrité, seraient menacés d'une agression. se tenant pour liées, en pareille conjoncture, de prendre sans retard et de ne décliner sous aucun prétexte les arrangements militaires qui seraient commandés par leur intérêt commun, conformément aux clauses et aux prévisions ci-dessus énoncées.

Marginal comments of Napoleon:
1. *"Ou à prendre* me parait un peu vague."
2. "Pourvu qu'il soit bien entendu que la compensation sera donnée par la Prusse."
3. "Pour combien de temps? Généralement un traité offensif et défensif ne se fait que pour un but à atteindre, et, lorsque le but est atteint, le traité cesse. Il faut trouver un terme."

(2) COPY OF DRAFT GIVEN TO BISMARCK

(shown to Ambassador Loftus in July 1870; sent to foreign office in London)

S. M. le Roi de Prusse et S. M. l'Empereur des Français, jugeant utile de resserrer les liens d'amitié qui les unissent et de consolider les rapports de bon voisinage heureusement existant entre les deux pays, convaincus d'autre part que pour atteindre ce résultat, propre d'ailleurs à assurer le maintien de la paix générale, il leur importe de s'entendre des questions qui intéressent leurs relations futures, ont résolu de conclure un traité à cet effet, et nommé en conséquence pour leurs plénipotentiaires, savoir:
  S. M. . . . . .
  S. M. . . . . .
Lesquels, après avoir échangé leurs pleins pouvoirs trouvés en bonne et due forme, sont convenus des articles suivants:

Art. I. S. M. l'Empereur des Français admet et reconnait les acquisitions que la Prusse a faites à la suite de la dernière guerre qu'elle a soutenue contre l'Autriche et contre ses alliés, ainsi que les arrangements pris ou à prendre pour la constitution d'une confédération dans l'Allemagne du Nord, s'engageant en même temps à prêter son appui à la conservation de cette oeuvre(1).

Art. II. S. M. le Roi de Prusse promet de faciliter à la France l'acquisition du Luxembourg. A cet effet, ladite Majesté entrera en négociations avec S. M. le Roi des Pays-Bas pour le déterminer à faire à l'Empereur des Français la cession de ses droits souverains sur ce Duché, moyennant telle compensation qui sera jugée suffisante ou autrement. De son côté, S. M. l'Empereur des Français s'engage à assumer les charges pécuniaires que cette transaction peut comporter(2).

Art. III. S. M. l'Empereur des Français ne s'opposera pas à une union fédérale de la Confédération du Nord avec les Etats du Midi de l'Allemagne, à l'exception de l'Autriche, laquelle union pourra être basée sur un Parlement commun, tout en respectant, dans une juste mesure, la souveraineté desdits Etats.

Art. IV. De son côté, S. M. le Roi de Prusse, au cas où S. M. l'Empereur des Français serait amené par les circonstances à faire entrer ses troupes en Belgique ou à la conquérir, accordera le concours de ses armées à la France, et il la soutiendra, avec toutes ses forces de terre et de mer, envers et contre toute Puissance qui, dans cette éventualité, lui déclarerait la guerre.

Art. V. Pour assurer l'entière exécution des dispositions qui précèdent, S. M. le Roi de Prusse et S. M. l'Empereur des Français contractent, par le présent traité, une alliance offensive et défensive, qu'ils s'engagent solennellement à maintenir. L. L. M. M. s'obligent, en outre et notamment, à l'observer dans tous les cas où leurs Etats respectifs, dont Elles se garantissent mutuellement l'intégrité, seraient menacés d'une agression, se tenant pour liées, en pareille conjoncture, de prendre sans retard et de ne décliner sous aucun prétexte les arrangements militaires qui seraient commandés par leur intérêt commun, conformément aux clauses et prévisions ci-dessus énoncées.

Corrections made by Benedetti:
1. The clause beginning with the word *ainsi* and ending with *oeuvre* was enclosed in brackets.
2. The last sentence in Article II was struck out and replaced with the following:
   "Pour faciliter cette transaction, l'Empereur des Français, de son côté, s'engage à assurer accessoirement les charges pécuniaires qu'elle pourrait comporter."

(2a) COPY OF DRAFT PUBLISHED IN *THE TIMES*

S. M. le Roi de Prusse et S. M. l'Empereur des Français, jugeant utile de resserrer les liens d'amitié qui les unissent et de consolider les rapports de bon voisinage heureusement existant entre les deux pays, convaincus d'autre part que pour atteindre ce résultat, propre d'ailleurs à assurer le maintien de la paix générale, il leur importe de s'entendre des questions qui intéressent leurs relations futures, ont résolu de conclure un traité à cet effet, et nommé en conséquence pour leurs plénipotentiaires, savoir:
   S. M......
   S. M......
Lesquels, après avoir échangé leurs pleins pouvoirs trouvés en bonne et due forme, sont convenus des articles suivants:

Art. I. S. M. l'Empereur des Français admet et reconnait les acquisitions que la Prusse a faites à la suite de la dernière guerre qu'elle a soutenue contre l'Autriche et contre ses alliés.

Art. II. S. M. le Roi de Prusse promet de faciliter à la France l'acquisition du Luxembourg; à cet effet, ladite Majesté entrera en négociations avec S. M. le Roi des Pays-Bas pour le déterminer à faire, à l'Empereur des Français, la cession de ses droits souverains sur ce Duché, moyennant telle compensation qui sera jugée suffisante ou autrement. De son côté l'Empereur des Français s'engage à assumer les charges pécuniaires que cette transaction peut comporter.

Art. III. S. M. l'Empereur des Français ne s'opposera pas à une union fédérale de la Confédération du Nord avec les Etats du Midi de l'Allemagne, à l'exception de l'Autriche, laquelle union pourra être basée sur un Parlement commun, tout en respectant, dans une juste mesure, la souveraineté desdits Etats.

Art. IV. De son côté, S. M. le Roi de Prusse, au cas où S. M. l'Empereur des Français serait amené par les circonstances à faire entrer ses troupes en Belgique ou à la conquérir, accordera le secours de ses armées à la France, et it la soutiendra, avec toutes ses forces de terre et de mer, envers et contre toute Puissance qui, dans cette éventualité, lui déclarerait la guerre.

Art. V. Pour assurer l'entière exécution des dispositions qui précèdent, S. M. le Roi de Prusse et S. M. l'Empereur contractent, par le présent traité, une alliance offensive et défensive, qu'ils s'engagent solennellement à maintenir. L. L. M. M. s' obligent, en outre et notamment, à l'observer dans tous les cas où leurs Etats respectifs, dont Elles se garantissent mutuellement l'intégrité, seraient menacés d'une agression, se tenant pour liées, en pareille conjoncture, de prendre sans retard et de ne décliner sous aucun prétexte les arrangements militaires qui seraient commandés par leur intérêt commun, conformément aux clauses et prévisions ci-dessus énoncées.

SELECTED BIBLIOGRAPHY

I ARCHIVAL SOURCES

AUSTRIA, *Haus- Hof- und Staats-Archiv.* Politisches Archiv. Preussen/89, 91, 92, 95, 96, 98, 99, 100, 101.

BELGIUM, *Ministère des Affaires Étrangères. Archives.* Série générale. Correspondance politique. Légations: Autriche-Hongrie/33; France/23; Italie/2 (1863-1865); Prusse/22, 23 (Part I, II), 24, 25; Dossiers: Incident Franco-Belge/2, 3 (1869–1870); Question du Grand-Duché de Luxembourg/1 (Part II); Papiers privés: Papiers Nothomb, film 117, dossier 245, section 21.

FRANCE, *Ministère des Affaires Étrangères. Archives.* Correspondance consulaire. Fonds: Francfort/5; Pays-Bas, Eich-Luxembourg/6; Correspondance politique. Fonds: Angleterre/737, 738, 739, 740; Autriche/491, 492, 498; Bavière/241; Belgique/247; Confédération Germanique/842; Danemark/ 248, 251, 253, 254; Espagne/874, 876; Hesse-Darmstadt/30; Hollande/665; Pays-Bas/666; Prusse/350, 351, 352, 353, 354, 355, 356, 357, 358, 359, 360, 361, 362, 363, 364, 365, 366, 367, 368, 369, 370, 371, 372, 373, 374, 375, 376, 377, 378, 379; Russie/237, 239; Württemberg/88; Mémoires et documents. Fonds: Allemagne/171; Autriche/67; France/ Circulaires politiques, 1863–1869; Hollande/149, 150; Papiers de Cerçay. Fonds: Rouher/Allemagne.

GERMANY, *Auswärtiges Amt. I. A. (Deutschland) 158 secreta.* Die Benutzung der politischen Akten des Auswärtigen Amtes zu publicistischen Zwecken. Bde. 1–5, 1890–1920. Microfilm copy; *I.A.A.a.14.* Acta betreffend die Einwirkung auf die Presse im Interesse Preussens. Bde. 7–8. Microfilm copy; *I.A.A.A.a.27.* Acta betreffend Auszüge aus den Protokollen der Conseil- und Staats-Ministerial Berathungen welche die auswärtigen Angelegenheiten berühren. Band 1. Microfilm copy; *I.A.A.a.63.* Acta betreffend ganz vertrauliche Correspondenz Seiner Durchlaucht des Reichskanzlers Fürsten von Bismarck aus den Jahren 1866 bis 1873. Bd. 2. Microfilm copy; *I.A.A.b.84.* Acta betreffend die kriegerischen und politischen Folgen der Abstimmung am Bunde vom 14. Juni 1866 über den österreichischen Mobilisierungsantrag gegen Preussen vom 11. ejd. Bd. 10. Microfilm copy; *I.A.B.o. (Spanien) 32 secreta.* Acta secreta betreffend die Berufung eines Prinzen von Hohenzollern auf den Spanischen Thron. Microfilm copy.

GREAT BRITAIN, *Public Record Office. Foreign Office. Archives.* Dispatches: Prussia 64/574, 597, 599, 601A, 601B, 602, 617, 168, 619, 620, 624, 625, 639, 640, 645, 661, 663, 687, 688, 689.

THE NETHERLANDS, *Rijksarchief. Ministerie van Buitenlandse Zaken. Archief.* Correspondentie. Legatie: Frankrijk/1867; Pruisen/1865, 1866, 1867, 1868, 1870.

LUXEMBURG, *Archives de l'Etat.* H. Régime constitutionnel. 1857–1880; Papiers concernant la gestion de M. Foehr à Berlin. 1867-1875. Papiers concernant la gestion de M. Jonas à Paris. 1867–1884. L. Secrétariat du Roi Grand-Duc à la Haye. 1848-1890. Maison souveraine. Relations étrangères. Constitutions. Déclaration de neutralité. Démantèlement de la forteresse.

II PRINTED WORKS

ABEKEN, Heinrich. *Ein schlichtes Leben in bewegter Zeit. Aus Briefen zusammengestellt.* Edited by Hedwig Abeken. Berlin, 1898.
ACTON, John E., First Baron. *Historical Essays and Studies.* Edited by John N. Figgis and Reginald Laurence. London, 1908.
ALBEDYLL-ALTEN, Julie von. *Aus Hannover und Preussen. Lebenserinnerungen aus einem halben Jahrhundert.* Edited by Richard Boschan. Potsdam, 1914.
ALNOR, Karl. "Der Artikel V des Prager Friedens; eine negative Kritik," *Zeitschrift der Gesellschaft für schleswig-holsteinische Geschichte, LV* (1926), pp. 532-568.
Archives diplomatiques: recueil mensuel de diplomatie, d'histoire et de droit international. Paris, 1866, Volume II; 1871-1872, Volume I.
ASSER, Hendrik. *De Buitenlandsche Betrekkingen van Nederland, 1860–1889.* Haarlem, 1889.
AUBRY, Octave. *Le Second Empire.* "Les grandes études historiques." Paris, 1938.
[AUSTRIA.] GENERALSTABS-BUREAU FÜR KRIEGSGESCHICHTE. *Österreichs Kämpfe im Jahre 1866.* Vienna, 1867-1868. 5 vols.
[AUSTRIA.] MINISTERIUM DES ÄUSSERN. *Austrian Red Book: diplomatic correspondence of the imperial-royal ministry of foreign affairs, from November 1866 to 31st December 1867, no. 1.* London, 1868.
BALDICK, Robert (ed.). *Pages from the Goncourt Journal.* London, 1962.
BAPST, Germain. *Le maréchal Canrobert. Souvenirs d'un siècle.* Paris, 1898–1911. 5 vols.
BAUMGARTEN, Hermann. *Staatsminister Jolly.* Tübingen, 1897.
[BAVARIA.] KÖNIGLICHE AKADEMIE DER WISSENSCHAFTEN. HISTORISCHE KOMMISSION. *Im Ring der Gegner Bismarcks: Denkschriften und politischer Briefwechsel Franz von Roggenbachs mit Kaiserin Augusta und Albrecht von Stosch, 1865–1896.* Edited by Julius Heyderhoff. "Deutsche Geschichtsquellen des 19. Jahrhunderts," XXXV, 2d. ed. Leipzig, 1943.
BECKER, Otto. *Bismarcks Ringen um Deutschlands Gestaltung.* Edited and supplemented by Alexander Scharff. Heidelberg, 1958.
BEICHE, Friedrich. *Bismarck und Italien. Ein Beitrag zur Vorgeschichte des Krieges 1866.* "Historische Studien," Vol. 208. Berlin, 1931.
BENEDETTI, Vincent. *Essais diplomatiques.* Paris, 1895.
— "Ma mission à Ems," *Revue de Paris,* V (September 15, 1895), pp. 225-257.
— *Ma mission en Prusse.* 2nd edition. Paris, 1871.
BENEDETTI, 2nd Count. "Du 9 au 14 juillet 1870 à Ems," *Revue de Paris,* XIII (July 1, 1909), pp. 49-60.
BERNHARDI, Theodor von. *Aus dem Leben Theodor von Bernhardis, Vol. VII, Der Krieg 1866 gegen Oesterreich und seine unmittelbaren Folgen. Tagebuchblätter aus den Jahren 1866 und 1867.* Edited by Friedrich von Bernhardi. Leipzig, 1867.
BERNSTEIN, Paul. "Biarritz." *Yearbook of the American Philosophical Society, 1960.* Philadelphia, 1961. Pp. 364–369.

— "The Rhine Policy of Napoleon III: A new Interpretation," *The Lock Haven Bulletin*, Series 1, Number 4 (1962), pp. 47–61.
BEUST, Friedrich Ferdinand, Graf von. *Aus drei Viertel-jahrhunderten. Erinnerungen und Aufzeichnungen, 1809–1885.* Stutgart, 1887. 2 vols.
— *Erinnerungen zu Erinnerungen.* Leipzig, 1881.
BEYENS, Napoléon. *Le Second Empire vu par un diplomate belge (Baron Eugène Beyens).* Bruges, 1924–1926. 2 vols.
BISMARCK-SCHÖNHAUSEN, Otto, Fürst von. *Die gesammelten Werke.* Edited by Friedrich Thimme. Berlin 1927-1931. 15 vols.
— *Gedanken und Erinnerungen.* Stuttgart, 1898. 2 vols.
BLANCHARD, Marcel. "D'une version de l'affaire des 'chemins de fer belges,'" *Revue historique* (Avril-Juin, 1940), pp. 218–233.
BLENNERHASSET, Rowland, Sir. "The Origin of the Franco-Prussian War of 1870," *The National Review*, XL (October 1902), pp. 216–230.
BLUMENTHAL, Leonhart, Graf von. *Tagebücher des Generalfeldmarschalls Graf von Blumenthals aus den Jahren 1866 und 1870/71.* Edited by Albrecht Graf von Blumenthal. Stuttgart, 1902.
BONNIN, Georges. See [Germany.] Auswärtiges Amt.
BOSBACH, Heinz. *Fürst Bismarck und die Kaiserin Augusta.* Cologne, 1936.
BOURGEOIS, Émile, and É. CLERMONT. *Rome et Napoléon III 1849–1870: étude sur les origines et la chute du Second Empire.* Paris, 1907.
BRANDENBURG, Erich. "Bismarck und die Reichsgründung," *Das Bismarck-Jahr: eine Würdigung Bismarcks und seiner Politik in Einzelschilderungen.* Edited by M. Lenz and E. Marcks. Hamburg, 1915. Pp. 171-184.
— "Die Verhandlungen über die Gründung des deutschen Reiches 1870," *Historische Vierteljahrschrift*, IX, Heft 4 (1912), pp. 493–546.
— *Untersuchungen und Aktenstücke zur Geschichte der Reichsgründung.* Leipzig, 1916.
BRAY-STEINBURG, Otto von. *Denkwürdigkeiten aus seinem Leben.* Leipzig, 1901.
BUCKLE, George. *The Life of Benjamin Disraeli, earl of Beaconsfield.* London, 1916–1920. Vols. 4–5.
BUSCH, Moritz. *Tagebuchblätter.* Leipzig, 1899. 3 vols.
BUSCH, Wilhelm. "Bismarck und die Entstehung des Norddeutschen Bundes," *Historische Zeitschrift*, CIII, Heft 1 (1909), pp. 52–78.
— "Der Kampf um den Frieden in dem preussischen Hauptquartier zu Nikolsburg im Juli 1866," *Historische Zeitschrift*, XCII, Heft 1 (1904), pp. 418–554.
CASE, Lynn M. *French Opinion on War and Diplomacy during the Second Empire.* Philadelphia, 1954.
CHAPPIUS, Hermann von. *Bei Hof und im Felde: Lebenserinnerungen.* Frankfurt, 1902.
[CHARLES I, King of Rumania.] *Chroniques, actes, documents.* Edited by D. Sturdza. Bucarest, 1899-1904. 2 vols.
CHIALA, Luigi. *Ancora un po' piu di luce sugli eventi politici e militari dell'anno 1866.* Florence, 1902.
CLARK, Chester W. "Bismarck, Russia, and the War of 1870," *Journal of Modern History*, XIV, no. 2 (1942), pp. 195–208.
— *Franz Joseph and Bismarck. The Diplomacy of Austria before the War of 1866.* "Harvard Historical Studies," XXXVI. Cambridge, 1934.
Constitutionnel, Le.
COOK, Edward, Sir. *Delane of "The Times."* London, 1915.
CRAIG, Gordon A. "Great Britain and the Belgian Railway Dispute of 1869," *American Historical Review*, L (July 1945), pp. 738–761.

CRUMMENERL, Lotte. *Zur Geschichte der Entstehung des Friedens von Nikolsburg 1866*. Emsdetten, 1936.

DALWIGK ZU LICHTENFELS, Reinhard, Freiherr von. *Die Tagebücher des Freiherrn Reinhard von Dalwigk zu Lichtenfels aus den Jahren 1860-71*. Edited by W. Schüssler. "Deutsche Geschichtsquellen des 19. Jahrhunderts," II. Stuttgart, 1920.

Das Staatsarchiv. See *Staatsarchiv*.

DARIMON, Alfred. *Histoire d'un jour: la journée du 12 juillet 1870*. Paris, 1888.

DELBRÜCK, Hans. "Die Emser Depesche," *Forschungen und Fortschritte. Nachrichtenblatt der deutschen Wissenschaft und Technik*, V (1929), pp. 196–197.

DIEST, Gustav von. *Meine Erinnerungen an Kaiser Wilhelm den Grossen*. Berlin, 1898.

DITTRICH, Jochen. *Bismarck, Frankreich und die spanische Thronkandidatur der Hohenzollern. Die "Kriegsschuldfrage" von 1870. Im Anhang Briefe und Aktenstücke aus dem Fürstlich Hohenzollernschen Hausarchiv*. Munich, 1962.

DOEBERL, Michael. *Bayern und Deutschland*. Vol. II, *Bayern und die Bismarkische Reichsgründung*. Munich, 1925.

DOVE, Alfred. *Grossherzog Friedrich von Baden als Landesherr und deutscher Fürst*. Heidelberg, 1902.

DRIAULT, Édouard. "Après Sadowa: la question d'Autriche et la question d'Orient, 1866-1867; d'après les Origines diplomatiques de la guerre 1870-1871," *Revue des études napoléoniennes*, XXXV(September 1932), pp. 126–140.

DUCROT, Auguste. *La vie militaire du général Ducrot, d'après sa correspondance, 1839-1871*. Edited by his childern. Paris, 1895. 2 vols.

DUNCKER, Max. *Politischer Briefwechsel aus seinem Nachlass*. Edited by J. Schultze. "Deutsche Geschichtsquellen des 19. Jahrhunderts," XII. Leipzig, 1923.

DURIEUX, Joseph. *Le ministre Pierre Magne, 1806-1879, d'après ses lettres et ses souvenirs*. Paris, 1929. 2 vols.

DURUY, Victor. *Notes et souvenirs (1811-1894)*. Paris, 1901. 2 vols.

ERNST II. [Duke of Saxe-Coburg and Gotha.] *Aus meinem Leben und aus meiner Zeit*. Berlin, 1892.

EYCK, Erich. *Bismarck. Leben und Werk*. Zurich, 1941-1944. 3 vols.

FARAT,H. *Persigny. Un ministre de Napoléon III 1808-1872. Paris*, n.d.

FESTER, Richard. "Biarritz, eine Bismarck-Studie," *Deutsche Rundschau*, CXIII, Heft 2 (November 1902), pp. 212–236.

— "Bismarck und die hohenzollernsche Thronkandidatur in Spanien," *Deutsche Rundschau*, CXL, Heft 10 (1909), pp. 24–59.

— *Briefe, Aktenstücke und Regesten zur Geschichte der hohenzollernschen Thronkandidatur in Spanien*. "Quellensammlung zur deutschen Geschichte." Leipzig, 1911. 2 vols.

— *Die Genesis der Emser Depesche*. Berlin, 1915.

— "Neue Beiträge zur Geschichte der hohenzollernschen Thronkandidatur in Spanien," *Historische Vierteljahrschrift*, XV, Heft 2 (1912), pp. 222–250.

FLETCHER, Willard Allen. "The Benedetti Memorandum: An Episode in Franco-Prussian Diplomatic Relations," *The Lock Haven Bulletin*, Series 1, Number 3 (1961), pp. 51-66.

FLEURY, Maurice. *Memoirs of the Empress Eugénie*. London, 1920. 2 vols.

FRAHM, Friedrich. "Biarritz," *Historische Vierteljahrschrift*, XV, Heft 3 (1912), pp. 337–361.

— "Frankreich und die Hohenzollernkandidatur bis zum Frühjahr 1869." *Historische Vierteljahrschrift*, XXIX, Heft 2 (1934), pp. 342–370.

[FRANCE.] ASSEMBLÉE NATIONALE. COMMISSION D'ENQUÊTE SUR LES ACTES DU

GOUVERNEMENT DE LA DÉFENSE NATIONALE. *Enquête parlementaire sur les actes du gouvernement de la défense nationale. Dépositions des témoins.* Versailles, 1872–1875. 6 vols.

[FRANCE.] COMMISSION DES PAPIERS SAISIES AUX TUILERIES. *Papiers et correspondance de la famille impériale.* Paris, 1870. 2 vols.

[FRANCE.] CORPS LÉGISLATIF. *Annales.* Paris, 1861–1870. 41 vols. in 47.

[FRANCE.] MINISTÈRE DES AFFAIRES ÉTRANGÈRES. *Les origines diplomatiques de la guerre de 1870–71. Recueil de documents.* Paris, 1910–1934. 29 vols.

FRANGULIS, A. (ed.). *Dictionnaire diplomatique.* Paris, 1933–1937. 5 vols.

FRENSDORFF, E. "Graf Benedetti," *Preussische Jahrbücher,* XXVI, Heft 2 (1870), pp. 192–204.

FRIEDRICH III. [Crown Prince of Prussia, German Emperor.] *Das Kriegstagebuch von 1870/71.* Edited by H. O. Meisner. Leipzig, 1926.

— *Tagebücher von 1848–1866: mit einer Einleitung und Ergänzung.* Edited by H. O. Meisner. Leipzig, 1929.

FRIESEN, Richard von. *Erinnerungen aus meinem Leben.* Dresden, 1880. 2 vols.

FRÖBEL, Julius. *Ein Lebenslauf. Aufzeichnungen, Erinnerungen und Bekenntnisse.* Stuttgart, 1890–1891. 2 vols.

[GERMANY.] AUSWÄRTIGES AMT. *Bismarck and the Hohenzollern Candidature for the Spanish Throne. The Documents in the German Diplomatic Archives.* Edited by G. Bonnin. Translated by I. Massey. London. 1957.

— *Bismarck und die nordschleswigsche Frage: 1864–1879: die diplomatischen Akten.* Edited by W. Platzhoff, K. Rheindorff, J. Tiedje. Berlin, 1925.

[GERMANY.] DEUTSCHER ZOLLVEREIN. ZOLLPARLAMENT. *Stenographische Berichte über die Verhandlungen des deutschen Zollparlaments, 1868.* Berlin, 1868.

[GERMANY.] HISTORISCHE REICHSKOMMISSION. *Die auswärtige Politik Preussens 1850–1871. Diplomatische Aktenstücke.* Edited by E. Brandenburg, O. Hoetzsch, H. Oncken. Oldenbourg, i.O., 1932–1939. 9 vols. in 10.

[GERMANY.] NORDDEUTSCHER BUND. *Bundesgesetzblatt des Norddeutschen Bundes.* Berlin, 1868–1871. 4 vols.

[GERMANY.] NORDDEUTSCHER BUND. BUNDESTAG. *Stenographische Berichte über die Verhandlungen des Reichstages des Norddeutschen Bundes.* Berlin, 1867–1870. 12 vols. in 9.

[GERMANY.] REICHSTAG. *Stenographische Berichte [und Anlagen] über die Verhandlungen des deutschen Reichstages.* Berlin, 1871. 3 vols.

GEUSS, Herbert. *Bismarck und Napoleon III. Ein Beitrag zur Geschichte der preussisch-französischen Beziehungen 1851–1871.* Cologne ,1959.

GORIAINOV, Sergiei. *Le Bosphore et les Dardanelles: étude historique sur la question des détroits, d'après la correspondance diplomatique déposée aux Archives centrales de Saint-Pétersbourg et à celle de l'Empire.* Paris, 1910.

GÖTZ, E. *Die Stellung Hessen-Darmstadts zur deutschen Einigungsfrage in den Jahren 1866–1871.* Darmstadt, 1914.

GOVONE, Guiseppe. *Mémoires, 1848–1870.* Edited by U. Govone. Translated by M. Weil. Paris, 1905.

GRABINSKI, Joseph. *Un ami de Napoléon III; le comte Arese et la politique italienne sous le Second Empire.* Paris, 1897.

GRAMONT, Antoine Agénor, duke of. *La France et la Prusse avant la guerre.* Paris, 1872.

[GREAT BRITAIN.] *Hansard's Parliamentary Debates* (3d series). Volumes CLXXXVI, CCIII.

GRUNWALD, Constantin de. *Le Duc de Gramont: gentilhomme et diplomate.* Paris, 1950.

HAHN, Ludwig. *Fürst Bismarck.* Berlin, 1878-1891. 5 vols.

— *Zwei Jahre preussisch-deutscher Politik, 1866–1867. Sammlung amtlicher Kundgebungen und halbamtlicher Aeusserungen von der schleswig-holsteinschen Krisis bis zur Gründung des Zoll-Parlaments.* Berlin, 1868.

HÄHNSEN, Fritz (ed.). *Ursprung und Geschichte des Artikel V des Prager Friedens: die deutschen Akten zur Frage der Teilung Schleswigs, 1863–1879.* "Veröffentlichungen der Schleswig-Holsteinischen Universitäts-Gesellschaft," XXI, no. 1–2; "Schriften der Baltischen Kommission zu Kiel," XV, no. 1–2. Breslau, 1929. 2 vols.

HALPERIN, S. William. "Bismarck and the Italian Envoy in Berlin on the Eve of the Franco-Prussian War," *Journal of Modern History,* XXXIII, no. 1 (1961), pp. 33–39.

— *Diplomat under Stress. Visconti-Venosta and the Crisis of July, 1870.* Chicago, 1963.

HALT, Robert (ed.). *Papiers sauvés des Tuileries, suite à la correspondance de la famille impériale.* Paris, 1871.

HAMSTRA, Johannes. *De Luxemburgsche Kwestie, 1867.* Groningen, 1927.

HANSEN, Jules. *Les coulisses de la diplomatie: quinze ans à l'étranger, 1864–1879.* Paris, 1880.

HARCOURT, Bernard d'. *Diplomatie et diplomates: les quatre ministères de M. Drouyn de Lhuys.* Paris, 1882.

HAUTERIVE, Ernest d'. *Napoléon III et le prince Napoléon; correspondance inédite.* Paris, 1925.

HOHENLOHE-SCHILLINGSFÜRST, Chlodwig, Fürst zu. *Denkwürdigkeiten.* Edited by F. Curtius. Stuttgart, 1902. 2 vols.

HOHENZOLLERN, Friedrich Karl von [Prince of Prussia.] *Memoires du Prince Frédéric-Charles de Prusse.* Edited by W. Foerster. Translated and summarized by Corteys. Paris, n.d. 2 vols.

HYMANS, Paul. *Frère-Orban.* Brussels, 1905. 2 vols.

IDEVILLE, Henri d'. *Journal d'un diplomate en Allemagne et Grèce: notes intimes pourrant servir à l'histoire du Second Empire.* Dresde-Athènes, 1867–1868. Paris, 1875.

JESSEN, Franz de. *L'intervention de la France dans la question du Sleswig du Nord; étude historique.* Paris, 1919.

Journal des débats.

JUSTE, Théodore. *M. de Bismarck et Napoléon III: à propos des provinces belges et rhénanes.* Brussels, 1871.

[KARL I., King of Rumania.] *Aus dem Leben König Karls von Rumänien. Aufzeichnungen eines Augenzeugen.* Stuttgart, 1894-1900. 4 vols. in 3.

KESSEL, Eberhard. "Gastein," *Historische Zeitschrift,* CLXXVI, Heft 3 (1953), pp. 521–544.

KEUDELL, Robert von. *Fürst und Fürstin Bismarck. Erinnerungen aus den Jahren 1846 bis 1872.* Berlin, 1902.

KOHL, Horst. *Fürst Bismarck: Regesten zu einer wissenschaftlichen Biographie des ersten deutschen Reichskanzlers.* Leipzig, 1891–1892. 2 vols.

KOLLER, Adolf. *Archiv des norddeutschen Bundes und des Zollvereins. Jahrbuch für Staats-Verwaltungs-Recht und Diplomatie des Norddeutschen Bundes und des Zollvereins. Mit Beilagen enthaltend: Verfassungen und Gesetze anderer Staaten.* Berlin, 1868–1870. 4 vols.

KULESSA, Adolf. *Die Kongressidee Napoleons III. im Mai 1866.* Leipzig, 1927.

LA GORCE, Pierre de. *Études d'histoire contemporaine: La Prusse avant Sadowa.* N.p., n.d.

— *Histoire du second empire.* Paris, 1894–1905. 7 vols.

LA MARMORA, Alfonso de. *Un peu plus de lumière sur les événements politiques et militaires de l'année 1866*. Translated by Niox and Descoubès. Paris, 1874.

LANGE, Karl. *Bismarcks Kampf um die Militär-Konvention mit Braunschweig 1867–68.* "Quellen und Studien zur Verfassungsgeschichte des deutschen Reiches in Mittelalter und Neuzeit," VII, Pt. 2. Weimar, 1934.

LANGER, William L. "Bismarck as a Dramatist," *Studies in Diplomatic History and Historiography in Honor of G. P. Gooch, C. H.* Edited by A. O. Sarkissian. New York, 1962. Pp. 199–216.

LECLÈRE, Léon. "Bismarck et la Belgique, 1866–1867," *Académie royale de la Belgique. Bulletin de la classe des lettres et des sciences morales et politiques,* Series V, XIII, no. 4 (1927), pp. 165–173.

LEHAUTCOURT, Pierre [pseud. of General B. Palat.] *La candidature Hohenzollern.* Paris, 1912.

LEONARDON, Henri. "Prim et la candidature Hohenzollern," *Revue historique,* LXXIV (Novembre-Décembre 1900), pp. 287–310.

LEYH, Max. *Die bayerische Heeresreform unter König Ludwig II. 1866–1870.* "Darstellungen aus der bayerischen Kriegs- und Heeresgeschichte," Vol. 23. Munich, 1923.

LIPGENS, Walter. "Bismarcks Österreich-Politik vor 1866. Die Urheberschaft des Schönbrunner Vertragsentwurf vom August 1864," *Die Welt als Geschichte,* X (1950), pp. 240–262.

LOË, Walther von. *Erinnerungen aus meinem Berufsleben, 1849 bis 1867.* 2nd edition. Stuttgart, 1906.

LOFTUS, Augustus, Lord. *The Diplomatic Reminiscences of Lord Augustus Loftus, 1862–1879.* Second Series. London, 1894. 2 vols.

LORD, Robert. *The Origins of the War of 1870; new documents from the German Archives.* "Harvard Historical Studies," XXVIII. Cambridge, 1924.

LORENZ, Ottokar. *Kaiser Wilhelm und die Begründung des Reichs, 1866–71, nach Schriften und Mitteilungen beteiligter Fürsten und Staatsmänner.* Jena, 1902.

MATSCHOSS, Alexander. *Die Kriegsgefahr von 1867: die Luxemburg Frage.* Bunzlau, 1908.

MATTER, Paul. *Bismarck et son temps.* "Bibliothèque d'histoire contemporaine." Paris, 1905–1908. 3 vols.

MAXWELL, Herbert, Sir. *The Life and Letters of George William Frederick, fourth earl of Clarendon.* London, 1913. 2 vols.

MAZADE, Charles de. "Chronique de la quinzaine," *Revue des deux mondes,* LXXXVIII, t. 5 (1 August 1870), pp. 747–748.

MEDING, Oscar. *De Sadowa à Sedan. Mémoires d'un ambassadeur secret aux Tuileries.* Edited by V. Tissot. Paris, 1885.

— *Memoiren zur Zeitgeschichte.* Vol. III, *Im Exil.* Leipzig, 1884.

MÉRIMÉE, Prosper. *Lettres à M. Panizzi, 1850–1870.* Paris, 1881. 2 vols.

MEYER, Arnold O. "Der preussische Kronrat vom 29. Mai 1865." *Gesamtdeutsche Vergangenheit. Festgabe für Heinrich Ritter von Srbik.* Munich, 1938.

— "Die Zielsetzung in Bismarcks schleswig-holsteinischer Politik von 1855 bis 1864," *Zeitschrift der Gesellschaft für Schleswig-Holsteinische Geschichte,* LIII (1923), pp. 103–134.

MEYER, Gustav. "Die Reichsgründung und das Grossherzogtum Baden," *Festgabe zur Feier des siebzigsten Geburtstages... des Grossherzogs Friedrich von Baden, dargebracht von den Mitgliedern der juristischen Fakultät der Universität Heidelberg.* Heidelberg, 1896.

MICHAEL, Horst. *Bismarck und Europa von 1866–1870. Eine Studie zur Geschichte Bismarcks und der Reichsgründung.* Munich, 1929.

MOHL, Robert von. *Lebenserinnerungen, 1799–1875.* Stuttgart, 1902. 2 vols.

Moniteur universel.

MORIER, Robert, Sir. *Memoirs and Letters, 1826–1876.* Edited by R. Wemyss. London, 1911. 2 vols.

MOSSE, W. E. *The European Powers and the German Question, 1848–1871* Cambridge, 1958.

MÜLLER, Karl A. *Bayern im Jahre 1866 und die Berufung des Fürsten Hohenlohe; eine Studie.* "Historische Bibliothek," XX. Munich, 1909.

— "Die Tauffkirchensche Mission nach Berlin und Wien: Bayern, Deutschland und Österreich im Frühjahr 1867," *Rietzler-Festschrift: Beiträge zur Geschichte.* Gotha, 1913.

MURET, Pierre. "Émile Ollivier et le duc de Gramont le 12 et 13 juillet 1870," *Revue d'histoire moderne et contemporaine,* XIII, no. 3 (1910), pp. 305–328; XIV, no. 2 (1910), pp. 178–213.

— "Les articles de M. Welschinger et de M. Joseph Reinach sur la déclaration de guerre et sur les papiers de Cerçay," *Revue d'histoire moderne et contemporaine,* XIV, no. 1 (1910), pp. 80–88.

NEWTON, Thomas. *Lord Lyons, a Record of British Diplomacy.* London, 1913. 2 vols.

OLLIVIER, Émile. *L'empire libéral: études, récits, souvenirs.* Paris, 1895–1918. 18 vols.

ONCKEN, Hermann. *Die Rheinpolitik Kaiser Napoleons III. von 1863 bis 1870 und der Ursprung des Krieges von 1870/71; nach den Staatsakten von Österreich, Preussen und den süddeutschen Mittelstaaten.* Stuttgart, 1926. 3 vols.

— *Rudolf von Bennigsen. Ein deutscher liberaler Politiker. Nach seinen Briefen und hinterlassenen Papieren.* Stuttgart, 1910. 2 vols.

PAGÈS, Georges. "L'affaire du Luxembourg," *Revue d'histoire moderne,* I, no. 1 (1926), pp. 5–23; I, no. 6 (1926), pp. 401–423.

PAHNCKE, Robert. *Die Parallel-Erzählungen Bismarcks zu seinen Gedanken und Erinnerungen.* Halle, 1914.

PERSIGNY, Jean de. *Mémoires, publiés avec les documents inédits.* Edited by H. d'Espagny. Paris, 1896.

PETRICH, J. "Die Friedensverhandlungen mit den Süddeutschen 1866; nach den Akten der beteiligten Staaten," *Forschungen zur brandenburgischen und preussischen Geschichte,* XXXXVI (1934), pp. 321–352.

PFLANZE, Otto. *Bismarck and the Development of Germany. Vol. I, The Period of Unification, 1851–1871.* Princeton, 1963.

PINGAUD, Albert. "La politique extérieure du Second Empire," *Revue historique,* CLVI (1927), pp. 41–68.

— "Un projet de désarmement en 1870," *Revue des deux mondes,* CII, t. 7 (15 February 1932), pp. 905-914.

PIRALA Y CRIADA, Antonio. *Historia contemporanea. Anales desde 1843 hasta el conclusion de la ultima guerra civil.* Madrid, 1875–1879. 6 vols.

PLATZHOFF, Walter. "England und der Kaiserplan vom Frühjahr 1870; mit Benutzung unveröffentlichten Materials," *Historische Zeitschrift,* CXXVII, Heft 3 (1923), pp. 454–475.

POSCHINGER, Heinrich von (ed.). *Aktenstücke zur Wirtschaftspolitik des Fürsten Bismarck.* Berlin, 1890–1891. 2 vols.

— *Bismarck und die Diplomaten, 1852–1890.* Hamburg, 1900.

— "Eigenhändige Aufzeichnungen des Präsidenten des badischen Ministeriums des Auswärtigen Rudolf von Freydorf über die militärischen Einigungsversuche der süddeutschen Staaten," *Annalen des deutschen Rechts für Gesetzgebung, Verwaltung und Volkswirtschaft,* XXXVIII, no. 1 (1905), pp. 1–30.

— *Fürst Bismarck und die Parlamentarier.* Breslau, 1894–1896. 3 vols.

PRADIER-FODÉRÉ, Paul. *Documents pour l'histoire contemporaine.* Paris. 1871.

[PRUSSIA.] KRIEGSGESCHICHTLICHE ABTEILUNG DES GROSSEN GENERALSTABES. *Der Feldzug von 1866 in Deutschland.* Berlin, 1876.

RADOWITZ, Joseph Maria von. *Aufzeichnungen und Erinnerungen aus dem Leben des Botschafters Joseph Maria von Radowitz.* Edited by H. Holborn. Stuttgart, 1925. 2 vols.

RADZIWILL, Antoine, Princesse de. *Souvenirs de la princesse Radziwill (née Castellane) 1840–1873.* Edited by E. and H. Potocka. Paris, 1931.

RANDON, Jacques. *Mémoires.* Paris, 1875–1877. 2 vols.

RAOUL–DUVAL, Maurice. "Projets de désarmement franco–prussien en 1870," *Revue de Paris,* XXI, no. 4 (15 February 1914), pp. 727–739.

RAPP, Adolf. *Die Württemberger und die nationale Frage 1863–1871.* "Darstellungen aus der württembergischen Geschichte," IV. Stuttgart, 1910.

REINACH, Joseph. "Un chantage historique. La fondation de l'empire allemand et les papiers de Cerçay," *Récits et portraits contemporains.* Paris, 1915.

REISET, Gustave de. *Mes souvenirs.* Vol. III, *L'unité de l'Italie et l'unité de l'Allemagne.* Paris, 1903.

RHEINDORF, Kurt. "Der belgische-französische Eisenbahnkonflikt und die grossen Mächte 1868/69; ein Beitrag zur Vorgeschichte des Krieges von 1870/71. Mit Benutzung unveröffentlichten Materials," *Deutsche Rundschau,* CXCV (May 1923), pp. 113–136.

— *Die Schwarze-Meer-(Pontus-) Frage vom Pariser Frieden von 1856 bis zum Abschluss der Londoner Konferenz von 1871. Ein Beitrag zu den orientalischen Fragen und zur Politik der Grossmächte im Zeitalter Bismarcks. Unter Benutzung bisher unveröffentlichten amtlichen Materials.* Berlin, 1925.

— *England und der deutsch-französische Krieg 1870/71. Ein Beitrag zur englischen Politik in der Zeit des Überganges vom Manchestertum zum Imperialismus mit Benutzung bisher unveröffentlichten Materials.* Bonn, 1923.

RIESS, Ludwig. "Eine noch unveröffentlichte Emser Depesche König Wilhelms I. vom 11. Juli 1870," *Forschungen zur brandenburgischen und preussischen Geschichte,* XXVI, Pt. 1 (1913), pp. 187–212.

RINGHOFFER, Karl (ed.). *Im Kampfe für Preussens Ehre: aus dem Nachlasse des Grafen Albrecht von Bernstorff, Staatsminister und kaiserlich deutschen ausserordentlichen und bevollmächtigten Botschafters in London und seiner Gemahlin Anna geb. Freiin v. Koenneritz.* Berlin, 1906.

ROLOFF, Gustav. "Abrüstung und Kaiserplan vor dem Kriege von 1870," *Preussische Jahrbücher,* CCXIV, Heft 2 (November 1828), pp. 183–198.

— "Bismarcks Friedensschlüsse mit den Süddeutschen im Jahre 1866," *Historische Zeitschrift,* CXXXVI, Heft 1 (1932), pp. 1–70.

— "Brünn und Nikolsburg: nicht Bismarck sondern der König isoliert," *Historische Zeitschrift,* CXXXVI, Heft 3 (1927), pp. 457–501.

— "Frankreich, Preussen und der Kirchenstaat im Jahre 1866; eine Episode aus dem Kampfe zwischen Bismarck und Napoleon," *Forschungen zur brandenburgischen und preussischen Geschichte,* LI, Pt. 1 (1939), pp. 103–133.

ROMANONES, Alvaro de Figueroa y Torres, Conde de. *Amadeo de Saboya. El rey efirmero. Espana y los origenes de la guerra franco-prusiano de 1870.* Madrid,1935.

[ROON, Albrecht, Graf von.] *Denkwürdigkeiten aus dem Leben des Generalfeldmarschalls Kriegsministers Grafen von Roon: Sammlung von Briefen, Schriftstücken und Erinnerungen.* Edited by W. von Roon. Breslau, 1892. 2 vols.

ROTHAN, Gustave. *Les origines de la guerre de 1870. La politique française en 1866.* Paris, 1879.

— *Souvenirs diplomatiques. L'affaire du Luxembourg. La prélude de la guerre de 1870.* Paris, 1882.

ROTHFRITZ, Herbert. *Die Politik des preussischen Botschafters Grafen Robert von der Goltz in Paris, 1863–69. Ein Beitrag zum Problem der deutsch-französischen Verständigung im Zeitalter der Reichsgründung.* "Abhandlungen zur mittleren und neueren Geschichte," LXXIV. Berlin, 1934.

SAINT MARC, Pierre. *Émile Ollivier (1825–1913).* Paris, 1950.

SALOMON, Henri. *L'incident Hohenzollern. L'événement; les hommes; les responsabilités.* 2nd edition. Paris, 1922.

SÄLTER, Wilhelm. *Theodor von Bernhardi als Politiker.* Hagen/Westfalen, n.d.

SASS, Johann. "Hermann von Thile und Bismarck," *Preussische Jahrbücher,* CCXVII, Heft 3 (September, 1929), pp. 257–279.

SAUREL, Charles. *Juillet 1870. Le drame de la dépêche d'Ems.* "Bibliothèque historique." Paris, 1930.

SCHARFF, Alexander. "Zur Problematik der Bismarckschen Nordschleswigpolitik," *Die Welt als Geschichte,* XVI, Heft 3–4 (1956), pp. 211–217.

SCHIERENBERG, Kurt. *Die deutsch-französische Auseinandersetzung und die Luxemburger Frage, dargestellt vor allem an der Luxemburger Angelegenheit des Jahres 1867.* "Publication de la Section Historique de l'Institut Grand-Ducal de Luxembourg," Vol. 65. Marburg, 1933.

SCHLÖZER, Kurt von. *Römische Briefe, 1864–1869.* 2nd edition. Stuttgart, 1913.

SCHNEIDER, Louis. *Aus dem Leben Wilhelms I., 1849–73.* Berlin, 1888. 3 vols.

SCHNERB, Robert. *Rouher et le Second Empire.* Paris, 1949.

SCHOEPS, Luise. *Graf Vincent Benedetti.* "Historische Studien," VII. Halle, 1915.

SCHÜBELIN, Walter. *Das Zollparlament und die Politik von Baden, Bayern und Württemberg 1866–1870.* Berlin, 1935.

SCHÜSSLER, Wilhelm. *Bismarcks Kampf um Süddeutschland 1867.* Berlin, 1929.

[SCHWEINITZ, Hans von.] *Denkwürdigkeiten des Botschafters General von Schweinitz.* Berlin, 1927. 2 vols.

SERVAIS, Émile. *Le Grand-Duché de Luxembourg et le traité de Londres de 11 mai 1867.* Paris, 1879.

SOREL, Albert. *Histoire diplomatique de la guerre franco-allemande.* Paris, 1875. 2 vols.

SRBIK, Heinrich, Ritter von. "Der Geheimvertrag Österreichs und Frankreichs vom 12. Juni 1866," *Historisches Jahrbuch,* Vol. 57 (1937), pp. 454–507.

— *Deutsche Einheit. Idee und Wirklichkeit vom Heiligen Reich bis Königgrätz.* Munich, 1935–1942. 4 vols.

— "Die Schönbrunner Konferenzen vom August 1864," *Historische Zeitschrift,* CLIII, Heft 1 (1935–1936), pp. 43–88.

— (ed.). *Quellen zur deutschen Politik Österreichs 1859–1866.* "Deutsche Geschichtsquellen des 19. Jahrhunderts," XXIX–XXXIII. Oldenburg, 1934–1938. 5 vols. in 6.

Das Staatsarchiv. Sammlung der offiziellen Aktenstücke zur Geschichte der Gegenwart. Edited by K. Aegidi and A. Klaushold. Hamburg, 1861-1919. Vol. XIX (1870).

STADELMANN, Rudolf. "Das Jahr 1865 und das Problem von Bismarcks deutscher Politik," *Historische Zeitschrift,* Beiheft 29. Munich, 1933.

STEEFEL, Lawrence D. "Bismarck and Bucher. The Letter of Instructions," *Studies in Diplomatic History and Historiography in Honor of G. P. Gooch, C. H.* Edited by A. O. Sarkissian. New York, 1962. Pp. 217–224.

— *Bismarck, the Hohenzollern Candidacy, and the Origins of the Franco-German War of 1870.* Cambridge, 1962.

— *The Schleswig-Holstein Question.* "Harvard Historical Studies," XXXII. Cambridge, 1932.

STOFFEL, Eugène. *Rapports militaires écrits de Berlin, 1866–1870.* Paris, 1871.

STOLBERG-WERNIGERODE, Albrecht, Graf zu. *Bismarck und die schleswig-holsteinische Frage.* Kiel, 1928.
— *Robert Heinrich Graf von der Goltz, Botschafter in Paris 1863–1869.* Oldenburg, 1943.
STOSCH, Albrecht von. *Denkwürdigkeiten des Generals Admirals Albrecht von Stosch, ersten Chefs der Admiralität: Briefe und Tagebuchblätter.* Edited by Ulrich von Stosch. 2nd edition. Stuttgart, 1904.
SYBEL, Heinrich von. *Die Begründung des deutschen Reiches durch Wilhelm I.* Munich, 1889–1895. 7 vols.
TEMPERLEY, Harold. "Lord Acton on the Origins of the War of 1870; with some unpublished letters from the British and Viennese archives," *The Cambridge Historical Journal*, II, no. 1 (1926), pp. 68–82.
The History of The Times. London, 1935–1939. 2 vols.
The Times (London).
THIMME, Friedrich. "Wilhelm I., Bismarck und der Ursprung des Annexionsgedanken 1866," *Historische Zeitschrift*, LXXXIX, Heft 3 (1902), pp. 401–456.
THOMPSON, James M. *Louis Napoleon and the Second Empire.* Oxford, 1954.
THOUVENEL, Louis. *Pages de l'histoire du Second Empire; d'après les papiers de M. Thouvenel, ancien ministre des affaires étrangères, 1854–1866.* Paris, 1903.
TSCHUDI, Clara. *Augusta, Empress of Germany.* Translated by E. M. Cope. London, 1900.
TÜMPLING, Wolf von. *Erinnerungen aus dem Leben des Generaladjutanten Kaiser Wilhelms I. Hermann von Boyen.* Berlin, 1898.
UNRUH, Hans-Viktor von. *Erinnerungen aus dem Leben von Hans Viktor von Unruh.* Edited by H. von Poschinger. Stuttgart, 1895.
VALENTIN, Veit. *Bismarcks Reichsgründung im Urteil englischer Diplomaten.* Amsterdam, 1938.
VALSECCHI, Franco. "Considerazioni sulla politica europea di Napoleone III," *Rivista storica italiana*, LXII, fasciolo I (1950), pp. 30–65.
VANDAM, A. *Undercurrents of the Second Empire.* New York, 1896.
VICTORIA [Queen of England.] *Letters.* Second Series. Edited by G. Buckle. London, 1926. 2 vols.
VILBORT, Joseph. *L'oeuvre de M. de Bismarck, 1863–1866; Sadowa et la campagne des sept jours.* Paris, 1889.
VITZTHUM VON ECKSTÄDT, Karl Friedrich, Graf. *London, Gastein und Sadowa. Denkwürdigkeiten 1864–1866.* Stuttgart, 1889.
WALDER, Ernst. *Die Emser Depesche.* "Quellen zur Neueren Geschichte," 27/27/29. Bern, 1959.
[WALDERSEE, Alfred, Graf von.] *Denkwürdigkeiten des General-Feldmarschalls Alfred Grafen von Waldersee.* Edited by H. O. Meisner. Stuttgart, 1922. 3 vols.
WARNHOLTZ, Herta. *Bismarcks Kampf um den Vorfrieden von Nikolsburg 1866.* Hamburg, 1939.
WELSCHINGER, Henri. "Le rapport Werther et la dépêche du 12 juillet 1870," *Journal des débats*, 5 June 1909.
WENTZCKE, Paul. "Zur Luxemburger Frage von 1867," *Deutsche Rundschau*, CICIII (December 1922), pp. 225–235.
WERTHEIMER, Eduard von. "Franz Joseph I. und Napoleon III. in Salzburg; nach ungedruckten Akten," *Österreichische Rundschau*, LXII (1920), pp. 164–174, 224–229.
— "Kronprinz Friedrich Wilhelm und die spanische Hohenzollern-Thronkandidatur [1868–1870]. Mit Benutzung ungedruckter Quellen," *Preussische Jahrbücher*, CCV, Heft 3 (1926), pp. 273–307.

WERTHERN, Georg von. *General von Versen. Ein militärisches Zeit- und Lebensbild. Aus hinterlassenen Briefen und Aufzeichnungen.* Berlin, 1898.

WILHELM I. [King of Prussia, German Emperor.] *Der alte Kaiser: Briefe und Aufzeichnungen Wilhelms I.* Edited by K. Pagel. Leipzig, 1924.

— *Kaiser- und Kanzler-Briefe. Briefwechsel zwischen Kaiser Wilhelm I. und Fürst Bismarck.* Edited by J. Penzler. Leipzig, 1900.

— *Kaiser Wilhelms des Grossen Briefe, Reden und Schriften.* Edited by E. Berner. Berlin, 1906. 2 vols.

— *Weimarer Briefe,* "Die Briefe Kaiser Wilhelm I." Edited by J. Schultze. Berlin, 1924. 2 vols.

WINCKLER, M. "Die Aufhebung des Artikels V des Prager Friedens und Bismarcks Weg zum Zweibund," *Historische Zeitschrift,* CLXXIX, Heft 3 (1955), pp. 471–509.

— "Die Zielsetzung in Bismarcks Nordschleswig–Politik und die Schleswigsche Grenzfrage," *Die Welt als Geschichte,* XVI, Heft 1 (1956), pp. 41–63.

– "Noch einmal: Zur Zielsetzung in Bismarcks Nordschleswig–Politik," *Die Welt als Geschichte,* XVII, Heft 3 (1957), pp. 203–210.

WINDELL, George G. *The Catholics and German Unity 1866–1871.* Minneapolis, 1954.

ZINGELER, Karl. "Briefe des Fürsten Karl Anton von Hohenzollern an seine Gemahlin Josephine, geborene Prinzessin von Baden," *Deutsche Revue,* XXXIX, Heft 2–3 (1914), pp. 338–348, 112–120.

— "Das fürstliche Haus Hohenzollern und die spanische Thronkandidatur. Unter Benutzung bisher ungedruckter Schriftstücke," *Deutsche Revue,* XXXVII, Heft 1 (1912), pp. 59–68.

— *Karl Anton Fürst von Hohenzollern, ein Lebensbild nach seinen hinterlassenen Papieren.* Stuttgart, 1911.

LIBRARY
NEW YORK, N. Y.